r501 r9co

' 5 / 96

Jackson

County

Library

System

HEADQUARTERS:

413 W. Main

Medford, Oregon 97501

3 99

GAYLORD M2G

ALAN JAY LERNER

ALAN JAY LERNER

A BIOGRAPHY

—⁂—

EDWARD JABLONSKI

Henry Holt and Company

New York

Henry Holt and Company, Inc.
Publishers since 1866
115 West 18th Street
New York, New York 10011

Henry Holt® is a registered
trademark of Henry Holt and Company, Inc.

Library of Congress Cataloging-in-Publication Data
Jablonski, Edward.
Alan Jay Lerner: a biography—1st ed.
p.   cm.
Includes bibliographical references and index.
1. Lerner, Alan Jay, 1918–1986.   2. Librettists—United States—
Biography.   3. Lyricists—United States—Biography.   I. Title.
ML423.L3J3   1996   95–37656
782.1´4´092—dc20   CIP
[B]   MN

ISBN 0-8050-4076-5

Henry Holt books are available for special
promotions and premiums. For details contact:
Director, Special Markets.

First Edition—1996

Book design by Kate Nichols

Printed in the United States of America
All first editions are printed on acid-free paper. ∞

1 3 5 7 9 10 8 6 4 2

Grateful acknowledgment is made to the following for excerpts herein: From *What's Up?* (music by
Frederick Loewe): "My Last Love" and "You Wash and I'll Dry" © 1943 Chappell & Co. From *Love
Life* (music by Kurt Weill): "Progress" and Economics"; © 1948 Chappell & Co. From *Royal Wedding*
(music by Burton Lane): "How Could You Believe Me When I Said I Love You When You Know I've
Been a Liar All My Life?" © 1950–51 Loews Inc. From *Paint Your Wagon* (music by Frederick Loewe):
"What's Goin' on Here?" and "I Talk to the Trees"; © 1951 Chappell & Co. From *Paint Your Wagon*
(film; music by André Previn): "A Million Miles Behind the Door," "The First Thing You Know," and
"Gospel of No Name City"; © 1969 Chappell & Co. From *Brigadoon* (music by Frederick Loewe):
"My Mother's Weddin' Day"; © 1947 United Artist Music Publishing Co., EMI Music Publishing Co.
From *Coco* (music by André Previn): "The World Belongs to the Young," "The Money Rings Out Like
Freedom," "A Woman Is How She Loves," and "Ohrbach's, Bloomingdales, Best, and Saks' "; © 1969
Chappell Music Co. From *Lolita, My Love* (music by John Barry): "Tell Me, Tell Me" and "All You Can
Do Is Tell Me You Love Me"; © 1971 by Alan Jay Lerner and John Barry; all rights controlled by the
Edwin H. Morris Co. From *The Little Prince* (music by Frederick Loewe): "A Snake in the Grass" and
"Why is the Desert?"; © 1974 Famous Music Corp. From *1600 Pennsylvania Avenue* (music by
Leonard Bernstein): "Sonatina," "American Dreaming," and "Duet for One"; © 1976 Amberson Pro-
ductions. From *Dance a Little Closer* (music by Charles Strouse): "What Are You Gonna Do About
It?" and "There's Never Been Anything Like Us"; © 1983 by Charles Strouse Publications; administered
by Musique Enterprises International, Inc. (ASCAP); reprinted by permission; all rights reserved.

CONTENTS

Contents

PREFACE

IN THE MONTHS following the sweeping success of *My Fair Lady*, lyricist-librettist Alan Jay Lerner was subjected to numerous interviews. He reveled in them. He and his collaborators, composer, director, choreographer—everyone, including an extraordinary cast—had created one of the most perfect (and profitable) musicals ever staged. Still, two bitter losses diminished the exhilaration of his triumph: his father (and his severest critic) had died before the show opened and would not savor his son's achievement, and his third wife, the actress Nancy Olson, to whom the libretto and lyrics were dedicated, was suing for divorce.

In one of these interviews, in a rare public revelation of angst, Lerner proposed as his own epitaph the simple line "Nobody Really Knew Him." It was partly true, for he was an elusive man, but if anyone wrote with his heart on his sleeve, it was Alan Jay Lerner—one of the last of the musical theater's true romantics.

Less than a month after this interview, he married a young, celebrated French attorney, Micheline Muselli Pozzo di Borgo (a name conspicuously and deliberately missing from Lerner's autobiography), who would bear him his only son. This initially storybook union would end seven years later in an acrid tabloid divorce. Soon after the hostilities were resolved (only temporarily, as it turned out), the vanquished Lerner married Mrs. Lerner number five, to be followed by numbers six, seven, and, finally, eight. Except for the joyous eighth, to the English singer Liz Robertson, all Lerner's marriages ended in well-publicized dissolutions—though none compared with that of number four.

Lerner's marital ventures generated Hollywood and Broadway japings and semi-witticisms, and Lerner himself was all too aware of the melancholy whimsy that thoughtlessly ignored the distressing effects of these upheavals on his professional and personal life. "All I can say," he admitted, "is that I had no flair for marriage," adding, "I also had no flair for bachelorhood."

The creator of so many happy endings found them disturbingly elusive in real life; the miracle of his career is that he could be creative at all under such irksome and exhausting circumstances. Add to these the inexorable backstage tribulations of fabricating a musical, even a hit, and Alan Jay Lerner takes the stage as an imposing personality and artist.

Multitalented, literate, erudite, a confessed romantic, he lived to fulfill a youthful dream of a life spent in the American musical theater—and at times saw that dream turn into a cruel nightmare. In a career extending over four decades, Lerner experienced some of Broadway's highest peaks and lowest hollows, as well as a few merely disappointing in-betweens. *My Fair Lady*, for example, ran for 2,717 performances in New York; *Dance a Little Closer*, his last completed musical, never made it past opening night. But whether a show was a success or a failure, he was always driven to get on to the next project. He knew elation and despair; happiness, for Lerner, was a sometime thing. His failed marriages, with inarguable female cooperation, comprised sufficient emotional stress and financial complexity for a dozen men. But he was resilient, sensitive, strong-willed, and determined—and he prevailed.

Alan Jay Lerner was driven by an autocratic, obdurate, opinionated father, Joseph, who goaded and chided him from boyhood on. While Lerner said he "adored" his father, there was minimal adoration between mother and son and, early in the marriage, between mother and father.

In his work Lerner strove for an often exasperating—to collaborators who *did* know him—"perfection." Translated from theaterese, that means he fretted, suffered, revised, consumed his fingernails to the bleeding point, and was tormented by stress-induced ailments. Collaborating with Burton Lane on a show score, Lerner took eight months, and went through more than ninety versions, to come up with a lyric that satisfied him for "On a Clear Day You Can See Forever." In the end it was worth the wait, and to a point, Lane was a patient and understanding composer.

Not so, however, Richard Rodgers. What might have been a historic collaboration was called off by Rodgers after months of discussion, some work, and even casting for a musical entitled *I Picked a Daisy*. Rodgers, one of the most businesslike men in the American theater, simply gave up, explaining that over those several months, Lerner had produced "only bits and pieces." Himself married to one woman his whole life, Rodgers was unaware of Lerner's marital strife at that time.

In his elegant, and personal, history, *The Musical Theatre*, Lerner was as kind to Rodgers as Rodgers had been to him in *Musical Stages*, though Lerner could not resist the temptation to quote Stephen Sondheim's characterization of his onetime collaborator as a "man of infinite talent but limited soul."

In the same book, Lerner described Cole Porter as a man born "with a platinum spoon encrusted with diamonds in his mouth, [who] grew up enjoying all the privileges of the rich that Scott Fitzgerald envied"—a description that applied equally well to Alan Jay Lerner himself.

Joseph Lerner, founder of the chain of shops carrying his name, was already possessed of great wealth by the time Alan was born. When it became clear that the son had no interest in the family trade, Joseph reached higher for him: It was his ambition that Alan should prepare for a career in government—say, with the State Department.

With this aim in view, Alan was enrolled in private schools at home and abroad. The Depression passed him by on Park Avenue, the other street where he lived, as did the Second World War, though not by his choice. This enabled him to concentrate on writing after graduating from Harvard, and then to move gracefully into the profession that had beguiled him from childhood. Joseph Lerner had been instrumental in nurturing this love, taking Alan to the theater with him from an early age—musicals especially. He also initiated his son into the arcane rituals of boxing in their regular visits to Madison Square Garden. Both initiations would profoundly affect Alan's future.

That future, in both theater and films, was one that the demanding father could admire, however stinting he was in praise. Following one of Lerner's successes, Joseph's comment was, "I don't see how you can make a career as a writer with an active vocabulary of 297 words." His pride in his son's work Lerner learned of only indirectly, from others.

Lerner's ascent began accidentally, and with an unlikely collaborator. Seventeen years Lerner's senior, Frederick Loewe was a Berlin-born musician of the Viennese operetta school. With Lerner he would evolve into a kind of musical chameleon, one of the most stylistically flexible and versatile composers of the American theater. Without suffering any impairment of his own musical voice, Loewe was to provide Lerner with songs ranging from Scots ballads and dances to cowboy songs (rowdy as well as poetically wistful), from turn-of-the-century English music-hall songs to melodies recalling a simpler Britain of mythical times.

When the pair achieved the zenith of *My Fair Lady*, their sixth collaboration over some fourteen years off and on, they were hailed in the same glowing terms that had been lavished on Rodgers and Hammerstein when they transformed the American musical in 1943 with *Oklahoma!* While neither innovators nor revolutionaries, Rodgers and Hammerstein, like Lerner and Loewe, endowed their musicals with a high degree of professionalism and polish, a full measure of song and dance—even ballet—a "book" that made sense (most of the time), and songs and dances that were related to the plot. Lerner and Loewe in a sense represent the end of the line stretching from Victor Herbert to Jerome Kern and Richard Rodgers—traditionalists all, with a gift for creating excellence. For a decade and a half, Lerner and Loewe were the heirs apparent to Rodgers and Hammerstein, the monarchs of Broadway. But a few failures and some personal frictions and illnesses truncated their charmed era of optimistic, romantic make-believe.

Lerner once told an interviewer, "Fritz and I don't believe in musical plays with a message—particularly if the message deals with teenage rumbles with switch-blade knives." The allusion to *West Side Story* is obvious; the Bernstein-Sondheim ballet-musical took a giant step away from the conventional musical of the Rodgers and Hammerstein period. "To us," Lerner continued, "the best message a musical can convey is: 'Come back and see us again, and often.'"

Loewe, for his part, was content to continue mining the lode of the sophisticated operetta until his retirement in the wake of the extended adversities of *Camelot*. Lerner, then in his early forties, could not stop; though he would go on to conceive some more "no message" musicals, in his final Broadway efforts he would stray from his traditional roots (with the exception of *Carmelina*). He realized that the Rodgers and Hammerstein—and, by extension, the Lerner and Loewe—epoch was over, that it had been invaded (now and then literally, from England) by a new kind of musical. He turned to harder-edged sources for inspiration.

Rather than float on the dreamy stream of the past, Lerner was determined to swim with the tide of the "liberated" present and the apocalyptic future. In this mood, he rewrote *Paint Your Wagon*, fashioning a screenplay that was more in the spirit of the times (the Swinging Sixties) if also uncharacter-istically meanspirited. The messages of his last musical plays did not encour-age audiences to come back again, despite their better-than-average scores.

Ira Gershwin praised seldom (because he did not want to injure anyone by omission) and criticized even more rarely. In his memoir *Lyrics on Several Occasions* he named a handful of lyricists he admired; among them was Alan Jay Lerner. Gershwin wisely noted that a "career of lyric-writing isn't one that anyone can easily muscle in on," that a good lyricist must be "at least literate and conscientious; that even when his words sound like something off the cuff, lots of hard work and experience have made them so." His sole criticism was addressed directly to his colleague: "Alan, you don't understand trick rhymes."

This was true. Tricky rhymes were most prevalent in the twenties songs of Rodgers and Hart, Cole Porter, and, of course, the Gershwins; it was a time when a song didn't need to have anything to do with the plot (if there was any). Lerner, in contrast, was a master of gentle intellectual humor (predom-inantly; there is some fine sarcastic wit in many songs). Intricate, clever rhymes, he felt, called attention to the words, to the detriment of the song and its function in the play. As a librettist, Lerner kept a wary eye on the lyricist.

"Lerner has never indulged in cuteness and tricks," composer-conduc-tor-author Lehman Engle wrote. "His best lyrics first of all sing. Then too they are literate to a very high degree. There is a sense of inevitability about the shape of the songs, and a clear organization of his thought processes."

Literacy and logic were but two of Alan Jay Lerner's attributes; his lyrics "sing" because he was one of the few great lyricists who were musically trained. At his best—and that was often, from the glamorous beginning to the pain-racked end—he wrote with a brilliance unequaled in American pop-ular song. And he lived an exhilarating life, with low moments; he was happy and he was distressed; he experienced professional and emotional turbulence, despite which he was extraordinarily productive. His life is a study of the price of privilege and the gift of unique artistry—and that artistry's tragic tri-umphs. He learned the meaning of author Paul Horgan's observation that "everybody applauded fame," and he loved both—applause and fame. But he also learned that there never was a Camelot.

ALAN JAY LERNER

1

—⚹—

"THE CHILD WHO
BECAME THE FATHER"

N O OEDIPAL ANXIETIES distressed the early, affluent, formative years of
Alan Jay Lerner. He loved, admired, and respected his father and
strongly believed that Joseph J. Lerner "created the child who became the father of the man." He was the middle of three sons born to Edith Adelson and
Joseph Lerner; the oldest was named Richard Martin, and the youngest
Robert Warren. The father made no effort to conceal his favoritism, which
made Alan's life among his siblings "very difficult." Nor did his father's bias
endear Alan to his mother.

Joseph Lerner ran his household as he did his business—autocratically,
uncompromisingly, with a decisive firm hand and closed mind. He was the
most important influence on Alan's life and career, but not on his character.
There were many issues on which father and son did not agree. Lerner senior
was politically conservative, a ruthless businessman, cultured, and caustic of
tongue. He was also a bon vivant, a wit, a misogynistic womanizer, a coura-
geous man (his last seventeen years were scourged by a particularly vicious
oral cancer), and very, very rich.

Joseph J. Lerner was born on January 23, 1887, to Sophia and Charles
Lerner of Philadelphia, a comfortably off, middle-class Republican couple. By
1903 the family had moved to Brooklyn, where Joseph attended the Boys'
High School for exceptional students. From there he enrolled, in 1906, in the

Pennsylvania Dental School; three years later he began practicing in Atlantic City, New Jersey, famous for its Boardwalk, its saltwater taffy, and the Miss America Pageant—and convenient to both New York and Philadelphia.

"While still in his twenties," Lerner later wrote, "[my father] had the good sense to realize that among his many talents, dentistry was not one of them, and before World War I he became the founder of a highly successful chain of stores that still bears his name." Joseph was actually only *one* of the founders: In 1917 he established the Lorraine Stores Corporation with his brothers Michael and Samuel. With success came expansion and a new name: Lerner Stores Corporation, specializing in quality clothing for women at reasonable prices. The chain grew and prospered during the profiteering twenties and even during the Depression thirties. The Lerner shops continue to do business today, but Joseph Lerner sold out his share in the early fifties, by which time the cancer that had been consuming him since 1937 was ending his life.

Lerner recalled his father as an "almost handsome man, firmly built, of medium height, [with] brownish-blonde hair . . . a ruddy complexion, and very large sky blue eyes."

Alan's mother, for her part, remains a somewhat shadowy figure. In his book Lerner wrote, "My Pappy was rich and my Ma was good lookin'"—the latter a slight exaggeration, to judge from an early photograph in which Edith Adelson Lerner appears rather more formidable than handsome. Lerner devoted little space to her in his book, and neither his father nor he thought to mention her in their *Who's Who* entries, a curious convergence of omission.

Joseph and Edith probably met in Philadelphia and were married around 1916. They soon had a son, Richard, but according to their second child, Alan, their marriage was in shambles by the time of his birth, in 1918. Even so, a third son, Robert, was born in 1921. Lerner recalled the constant bickering, the separations and reunions, and the final separation after Joseph Lerner was discovered in an infidelity one Friday night in the late 1920s when he was supposed to be attending a boxing match at Madison Square Garden.

When his wife asked him the next morning who had won the main bout, Lerner senior took a wild—and wrong—guess, as he soon learned from that morning's *New York Times*. Later, from his office, he called the maid and asked her to pack his clothes and send them to the Waldorf. Whether this upset his mother, Alan never said, but he and his brothers remained with her until they went off to school.

2

Even though he lived with his mother, Lerner was not close to her. She did all the right things, as was expected of a Park Avenue resident—the travels, the clothes, the schools (in whose choice Joseph Lerner's was the dominant voice)—but affection was not given, and she was intimidating. Even as an adult, Lerner was smaller than she.

The marriage that began so romantically soured quickly. Within a year of the founding of the Lorraine Corporation, the Lerners occupied a spacious (seventeen-room) apartment on Park Avenue, with a necessary staff of servants to please the madame and master. Alan Jay Lerner was born into this luxurious but unloving environment on Saturday, August 31, 1918. For weeks he was nameless.

That his parents could not agree on what to call the baby is hardly surprising; by this time, they agreed on very little. The sybaritic Joseph tended to avoid his home, instead spending much of his time at the theater and with theater people (an affection he would later pass on to his temporarily nameless son). One night, while ranging the better night spots, Lerner had a drink with the then powerful drama critic Alan Hale, characterized by a colleague, Brooks Atkinson, as the "insolent critic for the Hearst papers." Joseph Lerner liked the ring of the name Alan and felt it would go well with his surname. His son later dryly observed that "it was as if Napoleon had a son and named him after Wellington." Alan would eventually come to loathe critics, maintaining that they exercised by dancing on the graves of shows, especially musicals.

The origin of Alan Lerner's middle name is not known for certain; it may merely represent the spelling-out of his father's middle initial.

When Alan Jay was five, he began to study the piano, and around the same time, his father took him to see his first musical. This introduction would coincide with the flowering of the musical theater during the 1920s. Lerner never specified which shows he saw as a youngster; even at six, he would be unlikely to recall much about them. But his seventh year saw the production of the Gershwins' *Lady, Be Good!*, Kern's *Sitting Pretty*, and Berlin's *Music Box Revue*, among others. Lerner was enthralled by the fantasy of it all, by the songs and dances, the costumes, the magic, and the inevitable happy ending. "By the age of twelve," he wrote, "I had only one ambition and that was to be involved, someday, somehow, in the musical theatre." (Since his father took him to virtually every musical that played, that year he may also have seen Rodgers's *Simple Simon*, Kay Swift's *Fine and Dandy*, the

Gershwins' *Girl Crazy*, and Cole Porter's *The New Yorkers*; the following year his father invested in Harold Arlen's first musical, *You Said It*.)

Meanwhile, Alan was receiving another kind of education under his mother's supervision. Enrolled in the West Side's Columbia Grammar and Preparatory School, he arrived for classes in a chauffeur-driven limousine. When he was in the third grade, aged ten, he dutifully attended Sunday dancing classes, wearing the mandatory white gloves (to which he would return years later). His most vivid memory of dancing school involved his infatuation with the "prettiest girl in class."

The fact that she was also the most popular girl aggravated his natural shyness and rendered him speechless. Hoping to catch her alone, away from his more self-possessed classmates, he learned that she lived on Fifth Avenue, and for several Saturdays he kept vigil on a park bench adjacent to Central Park, across the street from her apartment house. His plan was, as soon as he spotted her, to bound across the avenue and confess his feelings. It was not to be; he had the wrong address.

Joseph Lerner, who spoke four languages, loved English and was determined that his sons should speak and write it properly. (He later constantly criticized his writer son's vocabulary and syntax, both of which he considered inadequate for a man of his profession.) To this end, young Alan was shipped off at twelve to have his English burnished at the Bedales School in the smallish town of Petersfield, in Hampshire, England. There the boy discovered another interest, in the occult, extrasensory perception, reincarnation, and other psychic phenomena.

This fascination had been unwittingly instigated by his father, when, two years earlier, Alan had asked him where people went when they died.

Joseph Lerner, though born into the Jewish faith, was an unbeliever, and he answered, "Nowhere. And if anyone ever tells you differently, he's lying to you."

"Stunned" by this revelation, Alan had stoically remained silent. When you die, his father concluded, "you go to sleep and never wake up." For several weeks after that, Alan had trouble sleeping and was afraid to close his eyes.

By the time he got to Bedales, the boy was preoccupied by the concept of life after death, unable to accept that death was the ultimate end. He wanted somehow to prove his father wrong.

One Sunday, while reading the London *Times* (a weekly school assignment), Alan learned that one of his favorite authors, Sir Arthur Conan Doyle, was scheduled to deliver a speech to the British Psychic Society entitled "The Nature and Existence of God." (A trained physician, Doyle had turned to spiritualism after the death of his son in the First World War.)

Excited and impatient, Lerner waited for subsequent issues of the *Times*, only to learn that within weeks after the announcement about the lecture, Doyle had died. The boy was certain that the creator of Sherlock Holmes had "solved the mystery, but [that] God did not want him to tell anyone"—a sentiment his father would find foolish.

Disappointed, Alan wrote to the society to inquire whether a copy of the speech existed. None did, but he was invited to become a member anyway, and regularly received issues of the organization's journal, the contents of which were rather arcane for a twelve-year-old. Nonetheless, a stray sentence or two, even a paragraph, made sense to him, convincing him at an early age that "all the answers were not in," and that his father was probably wrong on this point.

He never discussed this revelation with Joseph, wary as he was of the acerbic commentaries that skeptic was likely to offer on such surrealisms. Lerner senior was a nonromantic realist who could not abide belief in the occult or even in organized religions; his son, however, clung to his feelings and would one day draw on them for his work.

After a single semester at Bedales, Alan returned to Manhattan and attended Columbia Grammar from 1931 through 1935 (sixth through ninth grade). Even though the Lerners' marriage was practically nonexistent, they fulfilled certain expected responsibilities. Joseph paid the bills and saw to other matters; when school closed for the summer, Edith Lerner took her sons to Europe for cultural polishing in the museums, the cathedrals, the concert halls of England, France, Italy, Austria, and so on.

Edith's husband preferred less cultural pursuits, notably his business, his prizefights, the theater, and dabbling in stocks. When his sons were still in their teens, sometime during the Depression, Lerner senior made an investment in a poor investment era, buying shares in a gold mine in the boys' names, with the proviso that none could sell his shares before he reached the age of twenty-one. Gold-mine stock was a rare commodity in the thirties, but when Lerner recalled it, long after he turned twenty-one, it proved to be a godsend, financing a return trip to Britain that would have pleased his father.

In his teens, while still a student at Columbia Grammar, Alan began tinkering at the keyboard, with an occasional resultant song, revealing an interest in a curious, impractical occupation. His father did not mind this useless but entertaining activity, confident that his son would outgrow it and attend to the serious business of preparing himself for a real profession.

Lerner's next educational step was at the exclusive Choate School in Wallingford, Connecticut, in 1934. This was a most solid step in Joseph Lerner's plans for his son's education: After Choate, he would move on to the Sorbonne, in Paris, then to Spain, to Italy, and finally to Georgetown University, in Washington, D.C., where he would prepare for a career in the foreign service.

As it happened, it was at Choate that Alan Jay Lerner himself would take the first step—on the wrong foot, according to school regulations—toward a career in the theater. As he later frequently recounted, this came about because of three separate but related events: "a cigarette on a golf course, a left hook to the side of the head, and a wrong turn on the way to the men's room."

The first of these incidents occurred on Choate's golf course. Seventeen at the time—a male adult, he felt—Lerner was on the green with his sticks, out of sight of the school, when he lighted a cigarette (at Choate, smokers, if caught, were expelled). He was caught and, in the middle of his final term, placed on a train to face his father's wrath.

"This flagrant act of disobedience," he recalled, "so enraged my father that he cancelled my diplomatic career and sentenced me to four years of hard labor at an American university, which was a little like punishing a prisoner by kicking him out of jail."

He had been doing well at Choate and had attended his share of debutante parties in white tie and tails, "unaware of the unintentional cruelty of my presence as I passed men on street corners selling apples." Park Avenue and Choate were a world away from the Depression's sting. As the train approached New York, he looked back on the good times at Choate—the sports, the writing he so loved, and his stint as co-editor of the Choate yearbook with a student from Massachusetts, John F. Kennedy.

Saved from a European education, he considered the alternatives. Princeton (Scott Fitzgerald's alma mater) seemed attractive and was close to Broadway. He talked it over with one of his golfing companions from Westchester. John Paul Austin was then a junior at Harvard and spoke well of his school, its fine faculty, the clubs, the sports—and as Lerner well knew, practically every musical that eventually made it to Broadway first had to suffer its out-of-town tryout in Boston. Harvard was also known for its smart, annual Hasty Pudding musicals.

So Harvard it was.

"Thus it was," Lerner would later write, "that in September, 1936, instead of living *la vie de boheme* along the Boulevard St. Germain, I found myself more provincially ensconced at Harvard University, Cambridge, Massachusetts, twenty-eight hundred miles closer to Times Square."

2

—ᴟ—

TRANSITION:
"HASTY PUDDINGS" TO
LAMBS "GAMBOLS"

BESIDES BEING CLOSER to Times Square, Cambridge was but a short trolley ride across the Charles River from Boston, where Lerner could indulge his "passion for the theater" by going to every show, dramatic or musical, that came to town. During his Harvard years he would see musicals primarily by Cole Porter and Rodgers and Hart, shows especially notable for their brilliant lyrics. Even one of the exceptions, a revue called *The Show Is On* (1936, his first year), had a multiple score, with songs by the Gershwins, Cole Porter, Harold Arlen, and E. Y. Harburg and a single Rodgers and Hart entry. Another exception was *Hooray for What?*, which featured songs by Arlen and Harburg castigating diplomacy and warmongers. One of the directors of *The Show Is On* was the young and talented Vincente Minnelli. The choreographer for *Hooray for What?*, soon fired by the Shuberts, was an equally young and talented Agnes de Mille. While he did not meet any of these theater people, who seemed giants to him at the time, Lerner was deeply influenced by the work of Hart, Ira Gershwin, Porter, and Harburg.

He became an authority on show tunes, often playing them for his classmates (his suite in Lowell House had a piano). One night, as he walked along Mount Auburn Street, he was heard to exclaim, "I want to write songs!"

Another abiding passion was writing, though he took no courses in English or playwriting, on the advice of his faculty adviser. While his graduation

8

yearbook listed his field of concentration as sociology, he dabbled in the Romance languages (he was fluent in French), French and Italian Romanticism, Eastern religions and culture (which appealed to his mystical side), and psychology. Five years later, in a Harvard class report, his profession is given as Letters.

As a Harvard freshman, he had an opportunity to satisfy yet another father-induced interest. Boxing would be responsible for the second incident that was to affect his future.

Once enrolled in the college, Lerner was determined to become a member of Harvard's boxing team. He tried out in the lightweight class—at about five foot five, he was described by a fellow student as "thin, wiry, dynamic . . . with a large smile and a large pair of spectacles"—but was not fated to make the team. During a tryout session with a fellow aspirant, he recalled, "my mind wandered, my guard dropped, and a left hook to the side of the head removed all sense from my expression."

After two weeks of deteriorating vision, during which "New England's clear, winter days grew murkier and murkier," an examination revealed that Lerner was losing the retina in his left eye. Surgery was necessary to save his other eye, but following some weeks of recuperation, and wearing a blindfold, he was "back in school with all exercise forbidden and a stern warning that sneezing and bending over could make me a candidate for a cane and dog."

The accident also forced Lerner to cancel the flying lessons he had begun in preparation for service in the Air Corps, in anticipation of the war that he now sensed was inevitable. Lerner was remarkably prescient: just prior to his first semester, Hitler had reoccupied the Rhineland, and the Spanish Civil War had erupted. (With his compact, trim physique, Lerner might have made a superior fighter pilot. He was a striver, always reaching for excellence and, if possible, perfection—an essential quality for a pilot.)

Boxing and flying were out, but Lerner found another outlet. A contemporary Harvardian, Cleveland Amory (Class of '39), recalled Lerner as

> a mere Harvard sophomore, only a cut—crew, of course—above a freshman, and I was a junior. Besides this, I was president elect of the *Harvard Crimson*—a job so exalted that though you believed that life afterwards would probably go on from there, nothing else, on Earth at least, would really matter very much. . . .
>
> Nonetheless, there was a corner of Harvard's Yard far removed from the inner sancta of the *Crimson*, a strange place which was—

well, different. It was called the Hasty Pudding Club, and though
it was, in the Boston-Harvard vernacular, a "perfectly good" club—
it had been founded in 1770—still it insisted on putting on each
spring, for the edification of Boston debutantes and their beaux
(as well as a few errant New Yorkers), a musical comedy.

Founded as a social club, the Hasty Pudding was pledged "to cultivate
the social affections and cherish the feeling of friendship." The three-story
clubhouse was comfortable and endowed with a dining hall, a library, and a
small theater; it was intended to provide a setting for the sons of "proper
Bostonians to go to taste of pudding and tobacco." (The eponymous concoc-
tion was a mixture of cornmeal, ginger, nutmeg, milk, eggs, water, molasses,
and butter. It grew into the club's traditional snack, especially during a show's
rehearsal period.)

Originally, the Hasty Pudding productions were parodies of classic dramas, "altered to the robust specifications of a hairy-leg show [the cast was all
male, Harvard not yet having gone co-ed]. It is the world's oldest college dramatic club." It was not until December 1884, however, that undergraduates
Lemuel Hayward and Peter Augustus Porter established the tradition of presenting dramas that either had "plots" or were based on themes relating to
the Cambridge scene. With the first such offering, *Bombastes Furioso*, reported *Life* magazine, the "Pudding theatricals struck out on their own, a
path subsequently marked by pitfalls, profits, and notoriety."

As early as 1882, the raucous, often bawdy romps introduced a new turn,
metamorphosing into their present form. That year Owen Wister (who would
later write the popular Western novel *The Virginian*) adapted *The Aeneid*,
converting it into an extremely successful musical and setting the pattern to
be followed from then on.

The Hasty Pudding musicals became more popular and profitable until,
seven years after its production of *The Aeneid*, the club suffered its greatest financial failure up to that time under the business management of John Pier-
pont Morgan, Class of '89.

Alan Jay Lerner contributed to, and appeared in, the ninety-third Hasty
Pudding show, *So Proudly We Hail*. "This particular show," recalled Cleveland
Amory, was

a satirical salute to Hitler, Mussolini, et al. Remarkable as it was as
a show, it was even more remarkable for the fact that all three of its

coauthors were not only sons of distinguished men but also the sons of men who were extreme individualists. One was Nathaniel Benchley, son of humorist Robert Benchley, another was Benjamin Welles, son of Under-secretary Sumner Welles, and the third was Alan Jay Lerner, son of Joseph Lerner, founder of the Lerner Stores. The fact that all three such silver-spoon, "second generation" boys should go on from there to outstanding careers of their own would have seemed, at that time, an extraordinary defiance of the immutable laws of Harvard heredity.

(In fact, Lerner was not a coauthor but a lyricist; Amory omitted the book's other author, John Graham. Benchley went on to write a number of works, including a biography of his father. Welles, who brought Lerner into the club, would become a distinguished member of the staff of the *New York Times* and remained a lifelong friend of Lerner's.)

After its premiere in Cambridge, *So Proudly We Hail* was presented at New York's Waldorf in early April 1938. The *New York Times* reporter described it as a spoof of the "European scene in general and dictators Adolf Hitler and Benito Mussolini in particular." One skit featured the queen of England shooting dice.

The Waldorf opening was very social, with the audience getting as much attention as the show itself. Pauline Williams, in the *Times*, wrote that the production "was applauded by a big crowd," among which were Mrs. Angier Biddle Duke, Diana Barrymore, and Barrymore's "mother, Mrs. Harrison Tweed," a playwright-poet who wrote under the name Michael Strange and who had once been married to the actor John Barrymore.

In her comments on the show, Williams remarked that Vinton Freedley, Jr. (son of the producer Vinton Freedley), as Joan Peasley, the "feminine lead," along with Stanley Miller as Kenneth, "brought many a laugh with their singing and dancing." She added that "Alan Lerner ('Third Girl From the Left'), who wrote many of the lyrics, made a hit with his tap dancing" and as a "singing mannequin."

Williams continued, "Following the show the patrons went to the Astor Gallery to dance. Later some of Broadway's show people entertained. George M. Cohan came over with some of the cast from *I'd Rather Be Right*," the Rodgers and Hart musical then on Broadway. The Hasty Pudding shows often traveled after their Cambridge premieres, with the troupe sometimes touring as far south as Washington, D.C., with stops in New York and Philadelphia.

If Lerner was capable of amusing an audience with a song and dance at this time, obviously the danger to his eyesight was over, and he had been fitted with an artificial left eye. With the removal of physical restrictions on his activities, he joined the track team.

In 1939 Lerner was once again involved with the Hasty Pudding show, this one entitled *Fair Enough*, a satire on café society. The Pudding productions afforded him the opportunity to publish his first songs, both words and music; according to the *ASCAP Index*, "Chance to Dream" (1939, published by Chappell) and "From Me to You" (1939, Mills Music) were actually performed. Alan Jay Lerner, as he had wished on Mount Auburn Street, was now a bona fide songwriter.

He devoted his senior year, 1939–40, to study, with little extracurricular diversion. What free time he had (when he wasn't seeing the shows) he spent with a pretty young woman he had met on his most recent European excursion. In the summer of 1937, with his mother and his younger brother, Robert, Alan had visited England, France, Austria, Hungary, and Italy, where his mother "eventually settled down for the summer at the Lido in Venice." There Lerner met another American, Ruth O'Day Boyd, who was likewise between semesters and was the daughter of a New Jersey newspaper publisher, William Boyd. (Years later, *Time* would make it known that she was "Social Register" material.)

Lerner's graduation from Harvard, in June 1940, was not without incident. Owing to a disagreement with "one of the local shopkeepers around Harvard Square," he graduated with a "fleshy handshake" instead of a sheepskin. The merchant said Lerner owed him sixty dollars; Lerner insisted it was only forty and refused to pay anything at all "as a matter of principle—plus a dash of smart-Aleckness." It was the rule at Harvard that if a student owed money at the close of the school year and the debt was reported to the bursar's office, the student's diploma would be withheld.

There was a sequel. Later in that summer of 1940, Lerner and the "said Uriah Heep," as he put it, settled the disagreement, and some months later the bursar notified Lerner that, upon receipt of five dollars, he would finally have proof of his graduation from Harvard, Class of '40. "The five dollars seemed entirely reasonable and well within my means," Lerner reported, "but I forgot about it." Some years went by, and he received another notice of the certificate's availability; busy, he forgot again. Sixteen years after he graduated, and two months after the opening of *My Fair Lady*, he received the diploma, postage free, in the mail. (Still later, at the request of his alma mater, he deposited the *My Fair Lady* manuscripts, and others, "without tax deduction" at Harvard's Widener Library.

Lerner's graduation year was memorable for another reason as well: on June 26, 1940, he and Ruth Boyd were married in a Catholic ceremony in New York. Their daughter, Susan, was born three years later, in May 1943, by which time the marriage had already gone bad.

The couple at first settled in an East Side apartment, with Alan soon finding work writing copy for fifty dollars a week in the radio department of Lord and Thomas, an advertising agency. He often had lunch with two Harvard friends, Benjamin Welles, who had begun working at the *Times*, and Stanley Miller, who had portrayed Kenneth in *So Proudly We Hail* and was musically ambitious. Miller and Lerner teamed up to write some songs during this period, with no success.

Quickly bored with the advertising routine, Lerner struck out on his own soon after as a free-lance writer. In his book he recalled that "at one point I was writing five daytime shows a week, comedy for Victor Borge, twenty minutes of comedic material for a Tuesday night show called 'The Raleigh Room,' and a one hour program on Sunday called 'The Philco Hall of Fame.'" In an interview he also referred to the Chamber Music Society of Lower Basin Street, a quasi-jazz-popular-music half-hour show featuring such vocalists as Dinah Shore and Lena Horne. The quasi-jazz band was conducted by Paul Lavalle, moonlighting from the reed section of Toscanini's NBC Symphony. Lerner's tongue-in-cheek scripts parodied the commentaries that were then being read between selections during broadcasts of serious symphonic music; his satiric introductions to the jazzy numbers and songs were meant to be delivered in somber, exaggeratedly oleaginous tones.

During this time, Lerner also worked on a play destined for nonproduction. He was a very busy and ambitious writer, whose dedication to his career left little room for family life.

That something was awry was evident in a 1946 "report" on the Harvard Class of '40, in which Lerner and other members of his class brought their activities up to date. Lerner's entry acknowledges his marriage to Ruth Boyd and the birth of their daughter; as to his career, he notes, "Since 1940 I have written over 500 radio shows. I left radio writing in 1945. No ulcers—just got restless." Whereas the yearbook for the Class of '40 had given his home address as 470 Park Avenue (his mother's place), the class report cites the "Hotel Algonquin, W. 44th St.," an unlikely residence for a man with a wife and young daughter. Some time before, he had left their apartment in the East

Seventies and lived for a while at the Lambs Club, an all-male haven for actors, writers, comedians, and producers—theatrical types, his kind of people. The club became his true home, and some of its members his family. His college romance had by then deteriorated into a marriage via short-distance telephone.

From the Lambs, he moved into the nearby Royalton; after about a year and a half there, he moved again, this time across the street to the fabled Algonquin, with all its literary and theatrical associations. By the 1940s, the Algonquin's Round Table had been disbanded, but the legends lived on.

Lerner's report entry is brief compared to adjacent classmates'; both the entry before his and the two after it mention military service. This was a sore point with Lerner, and a source of patriotic guilt.

The Japanese attack on Pearl Harbor on December 7, 1941, did not affect Lerner as it did his contemporaries. Ruefully he wrote that his one good eye "saw my brothers and friends go off to war." His 4-F classification left him "anguished and ashamed"; he tried strenuously to enlist in one of the services (flying was definitely out) and even, according to one interviewer, "made a personal appeal to the Surgeon General of the U.S." Getting nowhere, he "complained, 'They won't take me unless the Nazis get to Rockefeller Plaza.'"

He was fated to spend the Second World War in New York, writing his radio scripts, working on his play, and going to the theater. The American wartime musicals produced between Lerner's graduation and his own Broadway debut were, with some critical exceptions, much the same mixture as before: There were operetta revivals, some shows that acknowledged the fact that there was a war on, and, after March 1943, a good deal of patriotic, nostalgic Americana. During this period, roughly from 1940 to 1943, Lerner also saw Broadway musicals that revolutionized the genre. Two of the most innovative were Rodgers and Hart's *Pal Joey* (1940) and Kurt Weill and Ira Gershwin's *Lady in the Dark* (1941), which opened within a month of each other. Lerner believed that these two shows "raise[ed] the level of the libretto" where other attempts had failed, and proved that "it was possible for a musical to be something more than an evening of light-hearted entertainment, [with] the introduction of ballet offer[ing] promise of unlimited horizons for the use of movement as an integral part of the play."

Pal Joey, though quite successful (and even more so in a later revival), was not appreciated by the critics, who objected to the "odious story" (Brooks Atkinson in the *Times*) by John O'Hara, and by extension to the unusual, literate book, with its rougish "hero" (played by Gene Kelly) and not-so-nice heroine, a rich woman (Vivienne Segal) who keeps and subsidizes the Kelly character only to be deceived by him. The sleazy nightclub setting, too, alienated the more genteel sensibilities of Atkinson and John Mason Brown of the *Post*, but Abel Green of *Variety*, "despite [spending] a quite unpleasant evening because of the complete lack of sympathy for our heel of a hero," praised the show. Wolcott Gibbs of *The New Yorker* suggested that with *Pal Joey*, "Musical comedy took a long step toward maturity," and Richard Watts, Jr., (of the *Tribune*) found the show "brilliant, sardonic and strikingly original." These sentiments were in agreement with Lerner's own, as he continued on-the-scene apprenticeship in the musical theater.

Lady in the Dark had another literate libretto, this time by Moss Hart, justifying Hart's costly investment in psychoanalysis. Drawing on the sessions with his analyst, Hart wrote a play about the editor of a slick magazine—the lady of the title—who cannot make up her mind about its next cover nor about her romance with her married boss. Her weekly visits to her analyst were set to music (once Hart realized he had written a musical and not a play) by Kurt Weill, with lyrics by Ira Gershwin. Lerner regarded *Lady in the Dark* as the most significant musical—with the most innovative book, music, and lyrics—of the period between the production of *Pal Joey* and 1943, the year that marked a "dramatic turning point in the history of the musical theatre." Stars Gertrude Lawrence, a veteran, and Danny Kaye, making his debut in a major Broadway production, contributed to the success of the show, which ran even longer than *Pal Joey* (467 performances versus 374).

Abetted by his warm reception in *Lady in the Dark*, Kaye went on to star in one of the first musicals inspired by the war—or, more precisely, by the American preparation for war. *Let's Face It* opened in October 1941, about two months before Pearl Harbor. The libretto, by Herbert and Dorothy Fields, centered on the tribulations of draftees and their kindly treatment by patriotic women from Long Island's elegant Southampton. (A couple of years later, the war having come home, Cole Porter, who had contributed the songs to *Let's Face It*, insisted on a more explicit title for the next topical musical: *Something for the Boys* starred Ethel Merman.)

These popular, racy musicals did not exhibit the same style and tone as the productions Lerner most admired. Porter's lyrics and melodies were commendable, but these shows added nothing to the development of the musical theater. Probably the most important of the service-inspired musicals, though hardly "innovative," was Irving Berlin's revue *This Is the Army*, which Lerner admitted was a "stunning army show . . . with an all-military cast except one: the great man himself."

Then, on the last day of March 1943, came Rodgers and Hammerstein's "turning point": the opening of *Oklahoma!* In appraising the influence of *Pal Joey* and *Lady in the Dark*, Lerner later concluded that "all that was needed was the atmosphere in which the proper lyrical and romantic subject matter required to bring all these elements—'intelligent texts, well-wrought songs related to the texts, ballet'—together could bloom. The atmosphere was provided by war."

By March 1943 the war had begun to shift in favor of the United States and its Allies, after nearly two years of military setbacks. The Allies were beginning to drive the Japanese out of Papua, New Guinea; the battle for Guadalcanal was over; the Battle of Stalingrad still raged, but the Germans were losing; and Rommel was forced out of Africa, leaving General von Armin behind to face defeat. After almost two years of gloom, Americans could once again look to the future with the hope of victory.

As Lerner saw it,

> Political and social satire, which by their very nature are critical, no longer suited the mood of the country that was rallying together to preserve a way of life that suddenly was seen clearly and deeply as precious as existence itself. If anything, people wanted to be reminded of who they were and the roots from which they had sprung; not what was wrong but what was right. Looking back to earlier times may be an escape, but it can also be a reaffirmation.

He believed, too, that "writing of the past is intrinsically lyrical."

A key word in this statement is *escape*, which might as well be a synonym for *fantasy*, something to which Lerner was strongly drawn. Later he would draft his credo as a librettist and lyricist, asserting that it was up to the author to select from the "mass of mosaic pieces that form the pattern of each human being" those that would best create the character he wished to present to the audience. These pieces, or the "few predominant ones," made it "possible to tell the story."

In emphasizing a particular point, Lerner indicated that he indeed saw the theater as a place of make-believe. "No character in the theatre is actually 'true to life,'" he wrote. "In fact I do not believe there is such a thing as 'realism' in the theatre at all. If there were, there would never be a third act."

This dedication to romantic fantasy would permeate most of Lerner's work in the theater. In the beginning of his career, it was *Oklahoma!* that excited his aspirations, for he judged it to be the "most totally realized amalgamation of all the theatrical arts. The book was legitimate play writing, every song flowed from the dramatic action," and the choreography was some of the "most imaginative . . . yet seen in the theatre." With *Oklahoma!*, the "musical theatre began its belle époque," which Lerner fervently wished to take part in.

In the reflected glow of *Pal Joey* and *Lady in the Dark*, Lerner meanwhile earned his living grinding out scripts. More importantly, perhaps, he enjoyed a vicarious theater existence as a habitué of the Lambs Club, where he made friends, talked theater, and contributed songs to the annual *Gambols* of 1941–42. His way with words did not go unnoticed, and it was at the Lambs Club that the third incident—"a wrong turn on the way to the men's room"—occurred and changed his life completely.

One day late in August 1942, Lerner was having lunch in the grill at the Lambs Club when a "short, well-built, tightly strung man with a large head and hands and immensely dark circles under his eyes strode to a few feet from my table and stopped short."

Lerner recognized him as Frederick Loewe, a pianist and not quite successful composer. He was known to everyone else at the Lambs simply as "Fritz," but not yet to Alan Jay Lerner.

Loewe turned to get back on the right track to the men's room, saw Lerner, and "stared for a moment." Then he came over to the table, sat down, and asked, "You write lyrics, don't you?"

"I try," Lerner answered.

"Would you like to write with me?"

"Yes." He had no idea what Loewe had in mind and didn't care. Loewe was a professional musician-composer, and Lerner wanted "to write songs!"

3

—ɯ—

"FRITZ"

WHEN THIS ACCIDENTAL ENCOUNTER took place, Lerner was still a
week or so away from his twenty-fourth birthday; the tightly strung
man with the large head sitting opposite him was, he would learn, forty-one.

Of Viennese parentage, Loewe had been born in Berlin on June 10, 1901
(his ASCAP biography says 1904), the son of a famous operetta tenor, Edmund Loewe. His father's chief claim to fame was the creation of the role of
Prince Danilo in the 1906 Berlin production of Franz Lehar's *Die lustige
Witwe* (a success in America as *The Merry Widow*).

Musically gifted, Loewe began to study piano early in life and later
boasted that at "five I even wrote music." He continued in music with such
teachers as Eugene d'Albert and Emil von Reznicek; he may have studied,
too, with Ferruccio Busoni (the celebrated teacher of Kurt Weill). He was
proud to claim that at "thirteen I was awarded the Hollander Medal, which
was given to the most promising student in the Stearns Conservatory in
Berlin." He admitted to being a Wunderkind and, when still in his teens, to
touring as a "guest artist with a symphony orchestra all over Europe." Around
this time, he was also writing songs, some of which were performed by his father in his traveling music-hall act. Loewe's "Katarina," published when he
was fifteen, became an enormous hit across Europe.

Some years later, producer David Belasco invited Edmund Loewe to appear in one of his theatrical extravaganzas in New York. All three Loewes arrived there in 1924, but during rehearsals, Edmund suffered a heart attack and died. A chronic gambler, he left his wife and son, then aged about twenty-three, virtually penniless in a strange land. Young Frederick attempted to revive his concert career by playing at Town Hall, but nothing came of it. A brief run at the Rivoli Theatre showed his approach to music to be too Viennese for the then jazzy American taste.

Still stranded in America, Loewe drifted from nondescript job to job: busboy, riding instructor in New Hampshire, nightclub pianist, boxer in a Brooklyn athletic club. While his experience as a pugilist was less dramatic than his future partner's, he, too, suffered a setback that made him decide to forgo boxing as a career: in his ninth bout he took a tooth-shattering blow to the face and resolved to find work elsewhere (according to Lerner, Loewe's opponent was Tony Canzoneri, the future lightweight champion).

Job hunting again, Loewe headed west, where he learned to punch cows, prospected for gold (with no luck), and found work with the Post Office delivering mail on horseback. By the early thirties he had returned to New York and was playing piano in a restaurant in Yorkville, New York City's German enclave. In 1931 he married Ernestine Zwerleine, described as the daughter of a "well-known European architect" and an executive with Hattie Carnegie Fashion Enterprises. The marriage did not work out, and the couple was soon estranged (though they were not legally separated until 1957). The split may be attributed partly to Loewe's womanizing, which dated back to his youth.

Back in music, performing in Bierstubes during the early autumn of 1933, he worked as the rehearsal pianist for an English adaptation of Strauss's *Die Fledermaus*, called *Champagne Sec*, starring Peggy Wood and Kitty Carlisle (in the role of Prince Orlofsky). His marriage a mess and his musical career merely marginal, Loewe was inevitably drawn to the Lambs as a source of camaraderie, kindred theatrical-musical souls, and what have come to be known as "contacts."

One of these last was the English-born actor Dennis King, of *Rose-Marie*, *Vagabond King*, and *Show Boat* fame. King liked Loewe's "Love Tiptoed through My Heart" (lyric by Irene Alexander) enough to interpolate it into his nonmusical *Petticoat Fever*, which opened in March 1935. Loewe's Broadway debut earned him twenty-five dollars. His next effort was heard in a revue produced in 1936 by the Society of Illustrators, naturally enough entitled *The Illustrators' Show*; the song was "A Waltz Was Born in Vienna," with a lyric by a more experienced revue writer, Earle T. Crooker. Besides Loewe's contribution, the show also featured songs by a budding lyricist named Frank Loesser, whose work earned him a contract with Universal Pictures. The run lasted five performances.

Although Crooker and Loewe did not make it to Hollywood, their work got to St. Louis the following year in the Municipal Opera's successful *Salute to Spring*, which ran through the summer of 1937. Crooker wrote the book and lyrics, and Loewe composed his first full score for a musical, incorporating the earlier "A Waltz Was Born in Vienna."

Producer Dwight Deere Wiman, then just launching his series of Rodgers and Hart musicals, was impressed. He commissioned Crooker and Loewe to write an operetta score for what was to be an indulgence in nostalgia called *Great Lady*, starring, appropriately, three "great ladies" of the musical twenties, Norma Terris (*Show Boat*, 1927), Irene Bordoni (*Paris*, 1928), and Helen Ford (*Peggy-Ann*, 1926). Crooker also collaborated on the complex book (which effected numerous shifts in time and place) with Lowell Brentano. The show didn't work; it opened on December 1, 1938, and closed after only twenty performances. Loewe's first complete Broadway score included, of course, a song entitled "There Had to Be the Waltz."

Now in his mid-thirties, Loewe seemed to be going nowhere beyond the Lambs Club. He returned to playing piano in clubs and doing other small musical jobs, until that day, late in August 1942, when he took a wrong turn on his way to the men's room, spotted Alan Jay Lerner in the Lambs grill, and went over to speak with him.

A roving producer, Henry Duffy, had approached Loewe with a proposition. He had admired the *Salute to Spring* score and believed that parts of it could be salvaged for a musical he planned to produce in Detroit in early October, with rehearsals to begin two weeks hence. The production was to be based on a musical he had produced the year before in San Francisco, *Patricia*, which had in turn been adapted from a popular comedy by Barry Conners, a 1925 success called *The Patsy*. *Patricia* had starred Dorothy Stone (daughter of the vaudevillian Fred Stone) and her husband, Charles Collins. Duffy wanted to cast Stone again in a revised version of the musical, newly retitled *Life of the Party*. Would Loewe and Crooker join the project?

Loewe was willing, but Crooker had joined the navy and was unavailable. Spying Lerner and recalling some of his sketches and lyrics for the *Gambols*—and desperately in need of a librettist-lyricist—Loewe made his move.

According to Loewe, Lerner was initially a bit hesitant, knowing he would have to work over the *Patricia* book, updating some of the lyrics and writing new ones for any additional songs; he said something about being "busy." That was on a Friday. On Sunday Loewe called Lerner to tell him he had received an advance of five hundred dollars. "I'll be right over," Lerner told him, and they left at once by train for Detroit. They worked on the show all during the rehearsal period, and "finished the book," Lerner remembered, "the lyrics for fourteen song numbers and dances, in less than two weeks." *Life of the Party* was favorably reviewed and ran for nine weeks in Detroit— "which made it a hit there," Lerner observed. But Duffy did not bring it to New York.

The real importance of the show lay in the fact of Lerner and Loewe's union, and in the older man's belief that he and the kinetic, nervous, quick-thinking younger man would make ideal collaborators. Lerner agreed: Under pressure, they had worked well together. In itself *Life of the Party* did not amount to much; though two of the songs were published, both were appropriations from *Salute to Spring*, and neither Crooker and Loewe's "One Robin Doesn't Make a Spring" nor their "Somehow" rang any bells along Broadway, or cash registers at the publisher's.

Almost as soon as they returned from Detroit, the nascent collaborators resolved to tackle a real Broadway show. It being wartime, they would do a timely but lighthearted musical (the news from all fronts, especially the Pacific, was grim) set in Miss Langley's School for Girls.

There was a brief interruption in the work when, on May 19, 1943, Lerner's first child, Susan, was born. The break didn't last long: the excitement over, the new father returned his attention to the new show.

The plot of *What's Up?*, on which Lerner collaborated with aspiring playwright Arthur Pierson, reflected the mood of the moment. An Air Corps aircraft carrying an Eastern potentate, the "Rawa of Tangliana" (portrayed by comedian Jimmy Savo), makes a forced landing on the grounds of Miss Langley's school, where all aboard must remain confined because of a measles quarantine. The female lead, Gloria Warren (then all of seventeen), played a State Department interpreter to the "Rawa," who expresses himself either in pantomime or in incomprehensible "Tanglianian"; needless to say, the interpreter eventually teams up with the plane's pilot. Savo, who was quite short, spent most of his time in quarantine chasing a tall showgirl—the major joke of the book. All in all, it was an "ill-advised little effort," as Lerner remembered it, that "lasted about a week" (actually about eight weeks, for sixty-three performances).

What's Up?, a post-Oklahoma! production, featured the by now mandatory dream ballet sequence, here choreographed by George Balanchine, who also staged it. The critics paid more attention to the tap dancing of Don Weismuller than to the arty doings of the corps de ballet; for their part, audiences preferred Kurt Weill's One Touch of Venus, which had opened a couple of months before and was choreographed by Agnes de Mille, the dream ballet's originator.

Lerner later dismissed What's Up? as a "not even promising" work, admittedly "co-authored and with lyrics by your embarrassed scribe." The score has disappeared into oblivion, save for four songs, one of which, "My Last Love," gives scant evidence of Alan Jay Lerner's talent:

> My last love didn't touch my heart this way.
> My last love wasn't on my mind all day.
>   I felt no yearning
>   Deep inside me burning,
>   But this time I'm learning
>   What it is love can do.

Some of the lyricist's future sparkle can, however, be glimpsed in "You Wash and I'll Dry":

> All that glitters isn't gold,
> There's no guarantee romance will hold.
>   Ev'ry infant knows it,
>   Nevada clearly shows it,
> That heated love can easily grow cold.

Some reviewers had good words to say about the words for "A Girl Is Like a Book," hinting at the touch of suggestiveness that would at the time have precluded publication. It was Lerner's first flop, and another in Loewe's succession of nonhits. The collaborators returned to the Lambs Club to brood. Lerner took up writing for radio and Loewe picked up odd jobs while they considered their next effort. But even before What's Up? closed, a greater tragedy touched their lives.

When, in 1940, Lerner had begun frequenting the Lambs Club, he had been befriended by his hero, the "terrifyingly lonely" lyricist Lorenz Hart. Shortly thereafter, Hart's undependability, acute drinking problem, and an emotional "disarray" (Lerner's term) led to the dissolution of his twenty-year collaboration with Richard Rodgers. Their last Broadway show together was *By Jupiter* (1941), after which Rodgers realized he simply could not count on the erratic Hart any longer. With some hesitation, Rodgers formed yet another fertile partnership, this time with Oscar Hammerstein II; their sweeping success with *Oklahoma!* in 1943 deeply affected Hart.

When he wasn't drinking at Ralph's Bar in the theater district or, as Rodgers put it, "getting steamed out" at the Luxor Baths, Hart could usually be found at the Lambs Club, where he and Lerner played gin rummy for hours on end, at "any hour of the day or night." With the hit songs from *Oklahoma!* ringing almost constantly in his ears—songs from a show he had refused to do—his despair intensified. However, that same year, while Hammerstein was converting Bizet's *Carmen* into *Carmen Jones*, Rodgers managed to interest Hart in another effort, a revival of their successful *A Connecticut Yankee* (1927), with the most popular songs to be salvaged and half a dozen new ones added.

This project temporarily revived Hart, who worked with unusual diligence and, Rodgers believed, sobriety, composing one of his most brilliant lyrics ever—"To Keep My Love Alive"—for the revival. But by the time *A Connecticut Yankee* opened in Philadelphia in October 1943—on a course almost parallel to that of Lerner and Loewe's floundering *What's Up?*—Hart had nothing further to contribute and began drinking again. On opening night in Philadelphia, October 28, according to Rodgers, his longtime collaborator "went on a drinking binge from which he never recovered." When the show premiered in New York, on November 17, Hart drank at a nearby bar between acts, returned incoherently drunk, and disturbed the audience by singing along with the star, Vivienne Segal. Rodgers, ready for this, had him taken from the Alvin Theatre to the apartment of his sister-in-law, Dorothy (Mrs. Teddy) Hart, where he sobered up before leaving quietly the next morning.

Hart was suffering from a cold he had caught in Philadelphia (he had a habit of leaving hats and coats behind in bars), and it had been raining when he slipped out of the theater, bareheaded and coatless. The day after the opening, his cousin Billy Friedberg, a theatrical publicist, called Loewe to tell him that no one could find Hart and to ask him to join in the search.

Loewe found him around three in the morning in a drenching rain, "sitting in the gutter outside a bar on Eighth Avenue." He managed to get him into a cab and dropped him off at the Hotel Delmonico, where he was living at the time. When a friend visited Hart the next day, he was obviously very ill (he had been walking around with pneumonia for several days) and had to be taken to Doctors Hospital, where he died on November 22.

With Hart's death, Lerner lost an admired friend. Of Hart he wrote, "The word *genius*, like most superlatives these days, has grown feeble from overwork, but if lyric writing is worthy of a genius it had one in Larry. . . . Life had ended for him much earlier and death was but a formality." In his own work he hoped to combine Hart's wit with Oscar Hammerstein's poetry; instead, he evolved into Alan Jay Lerner.

Even before *What's Up?* expired, Lerner was restless. Bored with writing advertising copy for Lord and Thomas, he concentrated on crafting radio scripts as a form of apprenticeship. His entry in Harvard's 1946 *Sexennial Report* claims that in two years he had written more than five hundred radio scripts. Such a schedule could not do much for a working marriage, either; he rarely saw his wife and daughter.

Loewe, for his part, was just as anxious as Lerner to achieve something memorable before time overtook him. It had taken him fourteen years to get to Broadway, only to be associated with two failures once he got there. The younger Lerner did not share his partner's anxieties; he merely wanted to create a good musical, and he soon found his plot, close to the home he hardly saw.

The main action of the new libretto, entitled *The Day Before Spring*, occurs during a college reunion that brings together a couple who almost eloped ten years earlier. In the interim, the woman has married a businessman, and her former beau has become a celebrated, and best-selling, author. One of his most popular books is based on their college romance and what might have been had they run off together. When Katherine reads the novel, she is determined to see Alex again and drags her husband, Peter, along to the reunion.

When Katherine and Alex meet again after ten years, it is love at second sight, and Lerner's book, in song and ballet, is spun around her dilemma: writer or husband? Lerner's fondness for fantasy is evident near the close of the first act, when Katherine receives advice from Voltaire, Freud, and Plato. The first suggests, as might be expected, that she choose both; Freud counsels her to yield to her libido and run off with Alex. The sage Plato, meanwhile, disagrees, advising:

> *To keep your life symphonic,*
> *Go back to your husband and keep it platonic.*

New Yorker critic Wolcott Gibbs began his review by stating, *"The Day Before Spring* . . . is my kind of show," but then proceeded to catalogue its weaknesses. He noted that

> a good many stretches of dialogue . . . might have been scissored out of an old copy of *College Humor*; a first-act ballet, one of those numbers in which a couple of dancers interpret the love life of the principals, . . . just made me laugh rather nervously; and a comedy sketch, involving the shades of Plato, Voltaire and Freud . . . didn't make me laugh at all.

Each act was graced by a ballet choreographed by Englishman Antony Tudor, with the principals, Alex and Katherine, represented by dancers, à la de Mille's "Laurey Makes Up Her Mind" ballet from *Oklahoma!* Tudor's work was not well received, and the ballets tended to clutter the plot of an already rather heavy-handed libretto.

Choosing Freud over Plato and Voltaire, Katherine decides to "elope" again, but just as had happened a decade before, the car breaks down. She has second thoughts—expressed in act 2, scene 2, in a "discouraging moral" ballet, according to Gibbs—and goes home with her husband.

Meanwhile, husband Peter has had an almost-fling with the campus widow, but he cannot dally. She expresses her disappointment in one of the show's finer songs, "My Love Is a Married Man," with its Hartian verse:

> *My lonely bitter heart has needed him to make it sweeter;*
> *He came, he saw, he conquered and then* sic transit *Peter*
> *And now I shouldn't cry, I should be brave instead;*
> *But bravery is cold in bed.*

A secondary lead, the character named Christopher, had yet another praiseworthy song, the lively "A Jug of Wine," with its arresting (though Gershwinesque) opening line, "A jug of wine, a loaf of bread and thou—baby!"

Lerner did his best to compensate for the Plato-Voltaire-Freud sketch with dramatic ingenuity. For Gibbs,

> [The] most original touch in the show comes when the husband is disgustedly reading aloud from his rival's book while the lovers act

out the same passage behind him on the stage, freezing in their tracks when his voice stops and even obligingly repeating themselves when he loses his place. Tiresome as this may sound on paper, it works out very well in the theatre, and I'm surprised that nobody seems to have thought of it before.

Good songs presaged the promise of Lerner and Loewe. The literate Gibbs found Lerner's rhymes "neat and witty," as exemplified by a couplet from "My Love Is a Married Man":

> We could have such fun,
> Clean or maybe "un."

A number of the songs, both music and words, were distinctive—from the title song to the anthem of virtually every college reunion, "You Haven't Changed at All," from the Latin "God's Green World" to the ebullient "I Love You This Morning." "The trouble, as usual," Lerner admitted,

> was the book. Period. . . . But unlike *What's Up?*, I am not prickling with embarrassment as I write its name. I was determined to write musicals with original stories, that is, not based on other plays, novels or short stories, and in doing so doubled the pitfalls. . . . But it ran the season, MGM bought the film rights, and Fritz and I became solvent professionals.

(The film was never made, though the book was rewritten with songs by Johnny Green and Frank Loesser.)

Encouraged by their near-success, the "professionals" were now eager for a new project. While working on *The Day Before Spring*, Loewe was reminded that faith could move mountains. "That started me thinking," Lerner later recalled. "For a while, I had a play about faith moving a mountain. From there we went to all sorts of miracles occurring through faith, and, eventually, faith moved a town."

Lerner claimed to have found his inspiration in the works of the Scots playwright, author, and fantasist James M. Barrie, best known for *Peter Pan* and *The Little Minister*. Barrie's *Dear Brutus* (1917) was a more mature novel with a skilled fusion of realism and fantasy that would have caught Lerner's attention. To devote his time to the new work, he left radio behind—"No ulcers," as he informed his Harvard classmates, "just restless."

But unusual conceptions such as the idea for *Brigadoon* do not simply materialize out of thin air. In his *New Yorker* review, John Lardner pointed to "strong similarities" between Lerner's book and a German folk tale entitled "Germelshausen" (also treated as a story by the writer Friedrich Gerstaecker), which had been discovered by the magazine's indefatigable researchers. Having planted this seed of doubt, Lardner dismissed it as "very likely . . . just a coincidence." (Although the two are close, there is one important difference: The German version has an unhappy ending. The "coincidence" would nonetheless bedevil Lerner, despite the fact that all folklore is in the public domain and is everyman's resource.)

Brigadoon (the Doon is a river in southwest Scotland, celebrated in the poetry of Robert Burns; a *brig*, in Scots, is a bridge) is the name of an enchanted village that appears in the highlands every one hundred years; its townspeople live for a day, and then the village vanishes for another century. This was the folkloric germ upon which Lerner based his libretto about two Americans on a hunting trip who stumble into Brigadoon on the day of its (post–Second World War) centennial. They step into the eighteenth century (as is obvious from the costumes of the townsfolk) from the twentieth; it is market day in the square. It is also the wedding day of pretty Jean MacLaren and Charlie Dalrymple, to the smoldering dismay of Harry Beaton—a crucial plot element presaging tragedy, as well as the near extirpation of Brigadoon itself.

Jean's older, and unmarried, sister Fiona, while shopping for the wedding, is questioned by the town's hoyden, Meg, about her unmarried state, and answers that she is "Waitin' for My Dearie." This is the musical cue for the appearance of the Americans, serious and troubled Tommy (who has fled New York to meditate on his engagement to socialite Jane Ashton) and the wisecracking, cynical Jeff. Tommy and Fiona pair off, of course, as do, for mild comedy and mild sensual touches, Jeff and Meg.

If the strangers are baffled at stumbling onto a village that doesn't exist on the map, the townspeople are no less puzzled by the Americans' peculiar dress. And so, economically, Lerner set his plot in motion, weaving together the triangular Jean-Charlie-Harry wedding theme, the Fiona-Tommy primary love story, and the casual Meg-Jeff lark. The climactic first-act curtain falls on Harry's threat to leave Brigadoon, an action that would destroy the village, causing it to vanish utterly rather than merely fade into the mist, only to reappear in a hundred years.

The second act opens with a chase in which Harry is accidentally killed when Jeff trips him in the forest and he strikes his head on a rock. The death is kept secret until after the wedding, which is followed by a funeral dance (both the chase and the funeral were brilliantly choreographed by Agnes de Mille, as were the wedding and sword dances at the close of act 1). To end the show, Lerner had to resolve the serious love between Fiona and Tommy. Initially, the stranger wishes to stay on in the village, which is acceptable to the town elder, the wise former schoolmaster Mr. Lundie, who also explains to the Americans the story of Brigadoon and its miracle. But after revealing that he was responsible for Harry's death, Jeff insists that Brigadoon is only a dream—an especially bad one for him. Tommy finally decides to leave with him after a gentle good-bye scene with Fiona.

The penultimate, fourth scene of act 2 is set in a New York bar. A very drunk Jeff is talking to the bartender, delivering a succinct exposition that informs the audience that Tommy has seemingly left town and is being sought by his fiancée. After Tommy himself appears and confesses that he really does not want to marry Jane, Jane enters, and as she speaks, certain words and phrases (Tommy hears little of what she is saying) evoke reprises of the songs of Brigadoon in the voices of Fiona (who is seen as if through a mist behind the bar) and the villagers. Tommy at last tells Jane that the wedding is off, and within three days he and Jeff are back at the site of Brigadoon.

The musical closes with another miracle: as the Americans are about to leave the spot where the village once stood, the title song, with which the show had opened, is heard. A sleepy Mr. Lundie appears to welcome Tommy into the town as Jeff looks on in bewilderment. Curtain.

The show's score was its own minor miracle, particularly for the remarkable authenticity of its indigenous songs; there are no Viennese echoes here. Loewe afforded some insight into the show's cohesiveness when he described the partners' methods: "We always work together, never separately." Once the whole was more or less blocked out, and the musical sequences determined, they would discuss the songs as they related to the plot and to the characters who sang them. This procedure would frequently suggest a title, or an idea on which to build, or, as Lerner put it, a "thought and its mood."

> Fritz sets it to music, then writes out the music for me. (I read music.) I go away with it and sketch in the lyric. Next meeting I try out what I've done on Fritz.
>
> His taste is incredibly fine and sensitive. He may find I've gone off the track or gone too fancy, or I may feel his music needs

development here or calming there, or there may even be a time when we're both delighted—but in the early stages that's rare.

(It may be noted that the same approach was taken by other songwriting teams as well, among them the Gershwins, Rodgers and Hammerstein, and others of the music-first-words-later school. In contrast, when working with E. Y. Harburg, Harold Arlen was inundated by a "torrent of words," though he often worked up melodic "possibles" that he distributed among potential collaborators. The intimacy of the Lerner and Loewe working partnership, however, was probably unique.)

Once the title and function of the song were agreed upon, Lerner and Loewe would frequently sit together while Loewe let his imagination play over the keyboard in rhythms and melodic phrases. When something caught Lerner's attention, he would say, "Wait! That's it!"; if Loewe had already gone on to something else, Lerner would remind him of the theme that had appealed to him, Loewe would play it again, and they might have the beginning of a song. There were times, however, when Loewe would dismiss the idea with, "It's terrible!" and continue his search.

Unlike many more conventional musicals, *Brigadoon* begins quietly, in the manner of *Oklahoma!*, without the traditional, lively "icebreaker" carried over from the twenties. The stage is dark when the curtain rises, and the chorus sings a prologue ("Once in the Highlands") that introduces the "two weary travelers" and prepares the audience for the "strange thing" the travelers are about to experience. The title song, also softly sung, is heard as Brigadoon magically appears out of the mist.

As the village springs to life, *Brigadoon*'s delayed icebreaker colorfully enlivens the stage with vendors' street cries and townspeople singing "Down on MacConnachy Square." This folkish rhythm number sets the fair scene into which the Americans wander. The score alternates among the customary rhythm numbers, ballads, comic songs, and choral pieces; also of great importance were de Mille's dances. Two of the folkish ballads, the poetic "Heather on the Hill" and "Almost Like Being in Love," are outstanding, the latter especially piquant in its use of a quarter rest—a kind of musical sigh—at the beginning of bar six, between "it's" in measure five and "almost" in the next bar. Such a distinctive, gentle, and effective touch could only have been worked out in close collaboration. The show's other memorable folk-ballads include "I'll Go Home with Bonnie Jean," "Come to Me, Bend to Me," and "There but for You Go I." Going unmentioned in most of the reviews was the fact that Loewe himself did the vocal arrangements, while Ted Royal accomplished the equally affecting orchestrations.

Two rhythm numbers, unusual in that they are not in the form of popular song, are embedded in the story: "Jeannie's Packin' Up," in which Jean's friends help her prepare to marry and leave her parents' house, and "The Chase," in which the men pursue the distressed fugitive Harry in an attempt to prevent him from destroying Brigadoon. The slashing music is complemented by Lerner's short, choppy words; the contrasting longer stanzas keep the audience aware of the reason for, and progress of, the chase. The melancholy tune in which the men decide to conceal Harry's death until after the wedding is followed by a return to a major key on the words "Thanks to heaven!"

Their work done, Lerner and Loewe began to search for a producer. They approached "literally almost every musical producer in New York and [were] unanimously rejected," as Lerner remembered it. They began with the Theatre Guild, whose coffers were swollen with the take from *Oklahoma!* and *Carousel*. But having rediscovered Americana (the Guild had produced *Porgy and Bess*, at a loss, in 1935), the board evinced little interest unless the locale of the Scots village could be switched to America (*Carousel*'s setting had been changed from Budapest to a small New England town, after all). "Somehow we did not know how" to comply with that suggestion, Lerner recalled, and so they continued: John C. Wilson (who had produced the Arlen-Harburg hit *Bloomer Girl*), George Abbott (then involved in *High Button Shoes*), Herman Shumlin (not known for his musical productions, but any port . . .), and even Rodgers and Hammerstein, who had begun producing in 1944 with the non-musical *I Remember Mama* and truly scored with Irving Berlin's *Annie Get Your Gun* two years later. All said no.

Their next step was producer-lyricist Billy Rose, who, on hearing their demonstrations of the libretto and songs, "registered immediate enthusiasm and agreed to produce [the show]." Enthusiasm was soon enough interspersed with friction as Rose initiated demands, from time to time cautioning them, "Never argue with a man who has more money than you have."

Lerner's first reaction on seeing their contract was that it "negated Abraham Lincoln's Emancipation Proclamation," but this, too, was Rose's way. He would control the casting and retained the right to bring in another writer, composer, or lyricist if he deemed it necessary; he even rejected Loewe, in advance, as vocal arranger. When the partners objected to these terms, Rose's rejoinder was, "Sign or else."

Asking for time to confer, the collaborators left the meeting, took a long walk, discussed their predicament, and decided to risk no production at all rather than suffer Rose's thralldom. There was another immediate ukase in the form of a telegram advising Lerner and Loewe that if the show was produced and used any of Rose's ideas, he would take legal action.

In reply, Lerner "wrote him a very polite letter asking [him] please to send me a list of his ideas and we would certainly avoid infringing on his creative genius."

There was no answer, though there would eventually be an ironic sequel.

Having exhausted virtually every possibility in town, they considered one final effort. Lerner's attorney, Irving Cohen, also represented a producer of fine taste, Cheryl Crawford, who had made her mark on Broadway with a most successful revival of Gershwin's *Porgy and Bess*, followed by Weill's *One Touch of Venus*. Although she was currently on the road with a touring show, she occasionally returned to New York on weekends. Cohen arranged for a meeting, and after hearing the songs, Crawford agreed to produce *Brigadoon*.

But that was merely a new beginning. To raise the production money ($150,000), Lerner and Loewe had to perform the score at more than fifty backer's auditions, sometimes as many as three a day. In late January 1947, when the show was three days into rehearsals, they gave their last (fifty-eighth) rendering of the score.

Cheryl Crawford astutely asked Agnes de Mille, with whom she had worked on *One Touch of Venus*, to choreograph the ballets and stage the musical numbers. She chose as director Robert Lewis, a former colleague from the Group Theater who had directed the Group's *My Heart's in the Highlands*, by William Saroyan. Lewis had also been an actor on Broadway and in Hollywood; *Brigadoon* would be his first Broadway musical. Lerner believed that de Mille's and Lewis's contributions were vital to what came after the rehearsals and the tryout period began: "Agnes's work was as original and creative as anything she had done and Bobby directed the play with rare sensitivity. Being one of the best acting coaches in America, he guided the cast into performances that were all any author could hope for."

After a brief tryout in New Haven, *Brigadoon* went on to Boston for a two-week stay; the critical reception was, in Lerner's words, "decidedly unfavorable." As was his practice, he never sat through even one performance but spent his time pacing in the back of the house; "the only way I can keep my abdominal lining from disintegrating," he claimed, "is to know that I am near a door." Loewe, according to Lerner, was an "in-and-outer," generally ducking out of the theater for a smoke during dialogue and returning for the music.

Pacing was not Lerner's only profession-induced exercise: He was also an inveterate nailbiter. Bleeding and infection were a frequent—and serious—problem, so much so that he was often seen in public wearing white gloves.

If the critics were discouraging in Boston, the public reaction was anything but, and by the second week *Brigadoon* was a sellout. After another two weeks in Philadelphia, it was clear that *Brigadoon* was on its way. It was pretty much the same show that had opened in Boston—both Lewis and de Mille wanted it to remain as it was, and Lerner made only a slight one-page change—but the Philadelphia reviews were, as Lerner reported, "ecstatic." These prepared the way for the New York premiere, at the Ziegfeld Theatre on March 13, 1947. According to Lerner, it was the only house available at the time; ironically, their landlord was their almost-producer, Billy Rose.

As he nervously paced the back of the hall on opening night, Lerner felt that the audience was more "appreciative than enthusiastic" and noted that during the second act, "there were several departures. It may have been less than half a dozen, but to me it seemed like a thundering herd." Instead of going along to the opening-night party, he returned to his rooms in the Algonquin to wait for the critics' verdict.

At around one in the morning, Cheryl Crawford called and virtually ordered him to come to the party at once. Lerner complied and on arriving was greeted by a happy throng; the morning reviews were in, and they were enough to make everyone, from creators to cast to backers, "ecstatic."

The first paragraph of Brooks Atkinson's review in the *New York Times* brought a surge of joy: "To the growing list of major achievements on the musical stage add one—*Brigadoon.* . . . For once, the modest label 'musical play' has a precise meaning. For it is impossible to say where the music and dancing leave off and the story begins in this beautifully orchestrated Scottish idyll." He concluded, "This excursion into an imagined Scottish village is an orchestration of the theatre's myriad arts, like a singing storybook for an idealized country fair long ago." One by one, the other critics joined him in singing the praises of the season's new hit.

Atkinson followed up his morning-after review with a longer essay in his Sunday column, in which he agreed with Lerner's assessment of the contributions of Lewis and de Mille (though he had some reservations regarding the latter's work, remarking that "she has not yet purged it clean of its campus clichés, which are, in turn, shopworn reminders from the Isadora Duncan school"). He unequivocally noted that *Brigadoon* was proof that the "musical stage is the most creative branch of the American commercial theatre." While celebrating the show's artistic "weaving [of] music, dancing and story into a single fabric of brightness and enchantment," he uncharacteristically touched upon some of the economic facts of Broadway.

"To come right out with the bookkeeping facts," he wrote,

> "Brigadoon" cost about $160,000 to produce and costs $22,000 a week to operate. It dangles before the public none of the usual show-shop enticements: the cast includes no stars or comedians; the production dispenses with the Broadway chorus and the book contains only faint traces of humor. Yet "Brigadoon" had an advance sale of $400,000 before the critics magniloquently endorsed it—which, incidentally, dispenses with the latter-day superstition that the fate of Gotham productions hangs on the critics' reviews.

Whether a superstition or a hard-headed judgment based on experience, this "latter-day" assumption continues to be believed to this day; it would haunt Lerner throughout his career, to the very bitter end.

One of the musicals Atkinson referred to in his piece was *Finian's Rainbow*, which had opened only two months earlier. With an outstanding score by Burton Lane and E. Y. Harburg, it, like *Brigadoon*, was a fantasy peopled with foreign-born characters—in this case an Irish dreamer looking for a pot of gold, and his daughter—set in a mythical state, Missitucky, somewhere in the American South (close, obviously, to Fort Knox). It is one of the curiosities of Broadway that two shows so closely related thematically and yet so different should have appeared almost simultaneously and been so successful, with neither one depending for that success on big-name stars.

The best-known actor in *Brigadoon* was David Brooks, a Curtis Institute of Music (Philadelphia) graduate who had made his debut in the 1944 Harold Arlen musical *Bloomer Girl*. Playing opposite him was Marion Bell, who had appeared with the San Francisco Opera and sung Verdi with James Melton in the film version of *The Ziegfeld Follies* (released in 1946), directed mostly by Vincente Minnelli. (Robert Lewis also directed some of the sketches in the movie, and appeared as a "Chinese Gentleman" in the "Limehouse Blues" sequence.) According to Bell's biographical entry in the show's program, "Talent-hungry Broadway producers began to pursue her and ultimately she was grabbed by Alan Lerner and Frederick Loewe . . . who were able to persuade the studio to loan her out."

The "grabbing" of Marion Bell would profoundly affect Lerner's life, both professionally and personally. He left the Lambs to take an apartment in the Royalton Hotel, also on Forty-fourth Street, where one of his neighbors was the eminent, disdainful, difficult critic (a term he took seriously, to a fault) George Jean Nathan, of Mencken and Nathan fame from the heyday of the irreverent *American Mercury*. Nathan, a bachelor, lived in two cluttered, dingy, smoke-filled rooms in the Royalton that he refused to have redecorated or neatened. "This domestic squalor," Brooks Atkinson observed, "was part of the attitude he assiduously cultivated: it proved that a gentleman who dressed beautifully and dined in the finest restaurants and drank only the most select European wines could live frowsily without losing dignity." (This would all change when, in his seventies, Nathan married the fine dramatic actress Julie Haydon, best remembered for her portrayal of the daughter in Tennessee Williams's *The Glass Menagerie* in 1945.)

When *Brigadoon* opened, Nathan was still ensconced in his slovenly rooms, though Lerner had moved across the street to the storied setting of the Round Table, the Algonquin Hotel. Upon seeing and hearing Marion Bell (her voice a glorious soprano), Nathan forfeited his renowned indifference to other people and not a little of his celebrated hauteur. He developed, in Lerner's phrase, a "high-school crush" on the actress, courting her with inscribed copies of his books and inviting her to dine, all without luck. Calling on her one weekend, he learned that she had left for bucolic Rockland County, a bit north of Manhattan, with Alan Jay Lerner.

For some time, Lerner's marriage to Ruth Boyd had been deteriorating. "Our marriage was not a happy one," he ruefully admitted, much as he hoped, having had a Catholic wedding, that it would last and he would not follow in his father's marital footsteps. But it had not worked—and thus his lodgings in the Lambs Club, the Royalton, and the Algonquin instead of in the house on East Seventy-first Street. When his wife asked for a divorce, he did not contest it, and it was amicably granted, "under the friendliest of circumstances." When friends expressed concern about this, Lerner airily replied that it was all right, adding, "I was getting bored." So in the late spring of 1947 he, too, was free—free to contend with George Jean Nathan for the heart of Marion Bell.

But now it was Nathan's turn to inject a bit of vindictive agitation into Lerner's already troubled life. Using his column in the *Journal-American*, he accused Lerner of plagiarizing the plot for *Brigadoon* from "Germelshausen," and even went so far as to suggest that he had lifted the plot for *The Day*

Before Spring. His negative campaign continued for close to a month of columns before the *New York Times* offered Lerner space to answer the accusations. This he did, tracing the evolution of each plot and dismissing Nathan's fulminations as "rubbish." Nathan finally ran out of steam, but when the time came for the New York Drama Critics Circle to select the year's outstanding musical, he cast his vote for *Finian's Rainbow* over *Brigadoon.* When all the votes were in, Nathan's was the major dissenting voice, reported Brooks Atkinson.

Not only did Lerner win the award, he also won the girl: He and Marion Bell were married later that year. He was happy, too, to learn that his father, who never broached the topic of his work in the theater with him, had been pleased with his triumph.

When *Brigadoon* opened, Joseph Lerner was at his winter home in Golden Beach, Florida. He was sitting in the sun one day when an acquaintance (he had few real friends) approached and remarked on the exceptionally fine reviews the musical had been getting, concluding, "Your son is certainly a lucky boy."

Lerner took up the pencil and pad that he carried with him at all times; he was unable to speak. For the past decade, since 1937, at the age of fifty, he had been suffering from cancer of the jaw. In the seventeen years he lived with the cancer, Joseph Lerner would undergo more than fifty major operations, one of which had already resulted in the removal of his tongue. Even without it, however, he was as caustic as ever.

On the pad he wrote, "Yes, it's a funny thing about Alan. The harder he works the luckier he gets."

4

—ᵐ—

LOVE LIFE

Soon after *Brigadoon*'s premiere, Kurt Weill, composer of *The Three Penny Opera* and a refugee from Nazi Germany, attended an evening performance with his wife, Lotte Lenya, as the guest of producer Cheryl Crawford. Four years before, Crawford had produced Weill and Ogden Nash's *One Touch of Venus*, and she believed that her friend and Lerner might prove to be ideal collaborators.

After the show, about which Weill was most enthusiastic, Crawford arranged for the two men to meet. "We had a drink together afterwards," Lerner recalled.

> A couple of weeks later I went up to his house in the country. We talked of working together. He was going off to Israel to see his family (this was in April, 1947). He said he'd be back in June. Somewhere along the line, while he was gone, I'd gotten the idea of doing a cavalcade of American marriage; of taking one family, beginning with the start of the Industrial Revolution and showing what happened to them in a satirical way.
>
> I called up Kurt and told him about it. He said it sounded interesting, that it needed a vehicle—a way of telling it. A week or so later, I thought of doing it as a vaudeville! I called him again and told him my idea. He was fascinated!

Along with his future bride, Marion Bell, Lerner headed north from Manhattan to New City, in rural Rockland County, the heart of the storied Hudson River Valley. Convenient to but removed from New York, New City had become an artists' colony, a unique community with an "all-star cast" that included playwright Maxwell Anderson, around whom an intellectual circle had formed: painter Henry Varnum Poor, and his wife, writer Bessie Breur; cartoonists Bill Mauldin and Milton Caniff; actor Burgess Meredith and his then wife, Paulette Goddard; and, most important, composer Kurt Weill and Lotte Lenya. The latter duo had lived since 1941 in an eighteenth-century farmhouse on South Mountain Road, next to the Andersons. Lerner felt both comfortable and stimulated in this company, and he soon became a member of the Anderson-Weill circle.

Lenya found Lerner "well-bred and charming" and thought he "looked like a college kid—alert and clever." She sensed that he was "very much in love with Marion Bell." He was also "deep in psychoanalysis" with Dr. Béla Mittelmann; obviously the idea for a musical about a troubled marriage did not materialize out of thin air. For his part, Weill, Lenya recalled, "liked Alan because he was very flexible . . . excited by ideas . . . a wonderful listener."

He was also anxious to get to work. Loewe, now experiencing his first solid Broadway success, chose to revel in that fulfillment, spending his time at gaming tables in France and elsewhere, enjoying the company of very young women ("nymphets," one writer called them), and, from time to time, relaxing. Then in his late forties, he believed he had earned this holiday. For Lerner, who was not yet thirty, relaxation was virtually intolerable.

Although he admired Weill's operatic *Street Scene* (which, though critically acclaimed, closed prematurely after a mere 148 performances), Lerner suspected that the subject—jealous, neglectful husband kills love-starved, unfaithful wife in a New York Depression setting—was "too uncompromising for popular Broadway taste."

Weill, too, was anxious to work. After *Street Scene* closed, in May 1947, three months after *Brigadoon* began its extended stay at the Ziegfeld, he and Anderson spoke of collaborating on a less operatic musical, along the lines of his earlier major successes, *Lady in the Dark* and *One Touch of Venus*. Nothing came of it. Weill was also approached by the whimsical playwright-novelist William Saroyan, but a little whimsy went a long way, and Weill begged off. He worked briefly with Herman Wouk on the score for a musical version of *Aurora Dawn*, a satirical novel about radio, but Wouk gave up to write a second novel, so that project, too, came to nothing. (With his third book, *The Caine Mutiny*, a few years later, Wouk left the music business for good.)

Lerner's April call and his innovative idea for a musical about marriage sounded good to Weill, whose substantial European stature was based largely on unconventional musicals that got him into trouble with the authorities. Having fled Hitler's Germany in 1933, he and Lenya had arrived in the United States in September 1935. He was reputed to be a cerebral composer whose theater works leaned leftward, especially in such cases as *Die Dreigroschenoper* (*The Three Penny Opera*, 1928) and *Aufstieg und Fall der Stadt Mahagonny* (*Rise and Fall of the City of Mahagonny*, 1927–29), a collaboration with the brilliant, and leftist, playwright Bertolt Brecht.

The latter play and another, *Der Silbersee, Ein Wintermarchen* (*The Silverlake: A Winter's Tale*, 1932), written with Georg Kaiser in 1933, enraged the Nazis and led to Weill's flight to France and later to America.

An exceptionally well trained musician who had studied under Engelbert Humperdinck and the more advanced Ferruccio Busoni, Weill had played and taught piano and been a choral and opera conductor for a time before turning his concentration to composition. His rather Schoenbergian instrumental works—symphonies, string quartets, a violin concerto, some choral pieces—were virtually unknown in the United States at the time of his arrival in 1935. (A 1933 production of *The Three Penny Opera* in New York had lasted only twelve performances; a revival at the Theatre de Lys in Greenwich Village after his death ran for more than twenty-six hundred.)

In America as in Germany, Weill was drawn to literate, intellectual plays with a message. Musical Americanisms also fascinated him, and he borrowed from jazz and popular recordings for his European plays with music. Soon after their arrival, the Weills were invited to a party at the East Seventy-second Street duplex of George Gershwin, whom they had met in Berlin during the 1928 European trip that resulted in Gershwin's "An American in Paris." During the party, Ira Gershwin was rather surprised by Weill's suggestion that they collaborate on a musical. Gershwin approached new projects warily and new collaborators reluctantly, so he gently dismissed the invitation, offering instead to take Weill to a rehearsal of his brother's recently completed opera *Porgy and Bess*.

Weill took him up on the offer and was impressed as he and Gershwin stood in the back of the theater. Turning to the lyricist, he said, "It's a great country where music like that can be written—and played." His admiration for Gershwin's opera is evident in the score for *Street Scene*.

Anxious to assimilate musically as well as personally, Weill sought out established American authors for his first attempts at American musicals. His first partner was dramatist-folklorist Paul Green, with whom he collaborated on the antiwar musical *Johnny Johnson* in 1936, followed two years later by *Knickerbocker Holiday*. This marked the beginning of his friendship with Maxwell Anderson, who provided the book (which condemned dictatorship) as well as the lyrics. Neither musical flourished at the box office, but both were graced with fine scores for which Weill, in a most un-Broadwaylike move, did his own orchestrations. *Knickerbocker Holiday* was the source of the classic "September Song."

Weill finally got his chance to work with Ira Gershwin in 1939, two years after George Gershwin died. Ira Gershwin's first musical since his brother's death was based on Moss Hart's psychological play, *Lady in the Dark*. Starring a dazzling Gertrude Lawrence, it was an enormous success, giving Weill an American hit.

With *Lady in the Dark* solidly established at the Alvin Theatre, Lenya and Weill could attend more fully to their Americanization. They acquired Brook House (so named because a stream ran through its fourteen-acre grounds) in New City. Lerner liked the setting—the greenery, country roads, white picket fences—and decided to join the Weills and the Andersons. He leased the equally quaint Henry Poort house, adjacent to Brook House, in August 1947 and began work on the new score. There was, however, "one slight obstacle," Lerner recalled. "We were walking along the road one day, early in our work, and I was showing [Kurt] what a vaudeville clog dance is. I was doing it for him on the road. I came to the kick—my legs locked and I collapsed!"

Work stopped for two weeks while Lerner recovered from the clogging. Their working title for the show was initially *A Dish for the Gods*; early in the collaboration, both men began considering casting as their female lead, in the pivotal role of Susan Cooper, Gertrude Lawrence, who would be free once *Lady in the Dark* closed after an extended Broadway run and a brief tour.

Lawrence had given Weill and Gershwin headaches, but as Brooks Atkinson once put it, "She's a goddess, that's all." Weill was willing to risk a migraine or two to court her devoted following: Though she was a curious choice for so American a play, there was the box office to consider. However, when producer Crawford met with the star's agent and the subject turned to money, it became clear that Weill and Lerner would not be needing aspirin to cure any Lawrence-induced headaches. (The year that *A Dish for the Gods*—

now retitled *Love Life*—was produced, Gertrude Lawrence was appearing in a revival of Noël Coward's *Tonight at 8:30*.)

In November, with work coming along but Susan still uncast, Lerner and Weill met with Mary Martin, then touring with Irving Berlin's *Annie Get Your Gun*, in Chicago. Of the completed songs, her favorite was the bluesy "Susan's Dream," definitely not a Mary Martin number, and in fact intended for a black singer. In any case, she was committed to *Annie* well into 1949, and Crawford hoped to present *Love Life* by the autumn of 1948. Lerner would encounter Mary Martin again, with devastating results.

"Working with Weill was quite different from working with Loewe," Lerner once wrote.

> With Kurt we would first discuss the song, and then I would go home and write the whole lyric—and he would set it. Every now and then he'd write a melody first, but this was very rare.
>
> I remember when he wrote "Here I'll Stay." Kurt, because he was European, in setting the lyric accented some of the words in the wrong places. I loved the melody so much that I didn't want to tell him. So instead, I told him the music was so beautiful that I didn't think the lyrics were adequate. I then went home and rewrote them entirely. Incidentally, Kurt never knew the real story.

As work slowly progressed in New City, Cheryl Crawford continued the search for their Susan, an essential role in Lerner's book, with its early pro-feminist theme. Sometime in February 1948, someone suggested Ginger Rogers for the part. She had been featured in a 1944 screen version of *Lady in the Dark*, which had unfortunately jettisoned most of the Weill-Gershwin score. Still, she was a "name," though she had not appeared on Broadway since 1930, in the Gershwins' *Girl Crazy*. A script was mailed to her in California, but she turned the role down because her mother objected to the "anti-capitalistic views" expressed in Lerner's book.

Still hoping to open the show by fall, Crawford kept hunting for other major people. She wanted to sign Robert Lewis, her old Group Theatre colleague and the honored director of *Brigadoon*, but Lewis and Weill did not agree (they had a "conflict of personalities"), and he withdrew. Crawford then considered another Group Theatre veteran, former actor turned screen and stage director Elia Kazan. In April 1948 Kazan was already known for such films as *A Tree Grows in Brooklyn* and the Academy Award–winning *Gentle-*

man's Agreement. Over the previous several months, he had made his directorial mark on Broadway with Arthur Miller's *All My Sons* and Tennessee Williams's *A Streetcar Named Desire*. But he had never done a musical.

As summer approached, and with rehearsals impending, casting became critical. The Susan problem was solved with the selection of Nanette Fabray, who had achieved stardom with her acclaimed and sparkling performance in the previous season's *High Button Shoes*. Ray Middleton was cast as her husband, Samuel Cooper; at the time, he was appearing in the long-running *Annie Get Your Gun*, which he left in August, when *Love Life* rehearsals were scheduled to begin. He had known Weill since 1938, having acted the role of Washington Irving in *Knickerbocker Holiday*.

Lenya later remembered that as rehearsals began, Lerner and Weill were still working on the score; the plan was to go to Boston to, as she put it, "unify style." In September, after seeing the production in New Haven, show-wise Moss Hart informed Lerner that the problem with *Love Life* was that it was really two plays, juxtaposing a satirical first act that ranged through time with a quasi-realistic second act set in the present. If the show were to open today, it would be called a "concept" musical and experimental, but in 1948 it was ahead of its time, a precursor of such later works as *Cabaret*, *A Chorus Line*, and *Follies*. *Love Life* dared to break with the traditional Broadway-musical format, in which, after some conflict or misunderstanding, the leads get together for all time in the final scene; instead, Lerner's book was about the effects of social and economic change on marriage.

The show's subtitle billed it as "A Vaudeville," and besides the traditional musical and dancing numbers, Lerner worked in a magic act, a trapeze artist, a Punch and Judy sketch, and a minstrel-show finale. These touches did not go over well with some of the critics, nor even with producer Crawford, who later held Lerner's libretto and lyrics responsible for *Love Life*'s failure (though 252 performances could hardly be considered a failure) and thought they had a damaging effect on the music. "Because Kurt's score served the style of writing," she believed "it didn't have the warmth of his best ballads." Weill's biographer Ronald Sanders agreed, finding the libretto "marred . . . by an unwarranted intellectual pretentiousness." One reviewer claimed to have overheard someone—a young woman—"brightly" say, "Oh, I'm not bored! I'm just puzzled."

In his offbeat, even revolutionary musical, Lerner synthesized the traditional with the unconventional, intermixing olios—the Punch and Judy show, the trapeze act, and so on—with his plot. Even the plot itself is innovative, tracing as it does the marriage of a couple over a period of 150 years. In keeping with his "vaudeville" concept, Lerner labeled the scenes "acts" and, in place of the usual acts, divided the show into two parts. Part 1, following an introduction by a cynical magician who levitates the man and saws the woman in half (to symbolize the state of their marriage), begins in a rural setting in 1791 and ends in the 1920s. Part 2 is set in the present (thus Moss Hart's two plays; one critic suggested that the audience would have been happier had it left the theater at the end of part 1).

The vaudeville acts serve as commentaries on the plot, with songs such as "Progress" and "Economics" preparing the audience for the scenes to follow. The more traditional musical-theater songs, such as "I Remember It Well" and "Green-Up Time," are plot-related. In song, and through dances and skits, the deterioration of the marriage of Susan and Samuel Cooper is tracked over a century and a half of American history, and the marriage, in turn, shows the effect of that history. The Coopers are already married, with two children, a girl and a boy, when the curtain opens on a pastoral setting (not unlike South Mountain Road): the Cooper homestead, in "Mayville, 1791." Sam has set up shop as a carpenter and is producing handcrafted furniture; Susan is a good wife and mother. They are warmly and tunefully welcomed by their neighbors. Life is simple, idyllic, promising, as expressed by Sam in "Here I'll Stay."

The second vaudeville turn features an octet, "The Go-Getters," who, to a soft-shoe tune, describe the destructive effect of "Progress" on the good life and on love. The group is a kind of Greek chorus commenting on what is to follow in the next scene, in which the love, warmth, and bucolic simplicity of the previous act are impinged upon by money-grubbing and competitiveness. Lerner has moved the time ahead three decades, during which period the Union has expanded from fourteen to twenty-four states, and the population has almost tripled as industry and financial manipulation have brought change to Mayville. Between George Washington's presidency and James Monroe's, love, once the "greatest force," has suffered.

> They discovered something better than affection,
> Far more rugged than a hug-ud ever be,

and that was:

> Progress!

The next scene, billed as "Act 4," once again opens on the farm, but now factories and mills spoil the once rustic landscape. Moving with the times, Sam decides to close his little shop and go to work in a factory. He and Susan reminisce with "I Remember It Well," a song whose idea Lerner would reuse ten years later, in the film *Gigi*. A joyful celebration of the vanishing good life, "Green-Up Time" closes the scene with the show's outstanding ballet number, choreographed by Michael Kidd.

The next vaudeville act employs a black quartet to carry the theme of "Progress" to "Economics":

> Man and woman you got to admire.
> They conquered cold and they conquered fire.
> They stuck together through thick and thin;
> Through lots of good and lots of sin.
>
> But there's one thing that beats them;
> That they just can't subdue;
> And splits 'em up in two.

To illustrate this thesis, Lerner came up with some examples that must have pleased his father, in which women take advantage of the new economics:

> Now Cora had a husband makin' seven a day,
> She left him for a guy who made eleven a day.
> Now that's good economics,
> That's good economics,
> But awful bad for love!

Between two of the stanzas, Lerner produced a pair of cynical, choppy couplets:

> Money go!
> Honey go!

and

> Dough come back!
> Flo come back!

In the early version of the libretto, "Economics" was followed by "Susan's Dream." Originally, the quartet consisted of three men and one woman, who, after the final "But awful bad for love!" steps out of the group upstage and sings of Susan's life as a wife and mother. The melody is one of Weill's finest creations, based on the blues but sounding more like an aria, and Lerner's lyric is ingenious in its working-out of the "plot" of the song. Miserable because "her man went drinkin'/ And the kids got sick and cried till morn," Susan "Plumb got tired of home and livin'/ And began to wish she'd not been born." One night, with her husband out and her kids having "worn her ragged," she falls to her knees in prayer, asking God to let the children sleep so she, too, can sleep and dream "of the way life should be." In her sleep, she hears a voice telling her to dream; in the dream she sees a husband whom she loves but who drinks too much, and children who wear her out—in short, she dreams "exactly what she had." The bittersweet song was eliminated before the show reached Broadway.

By scene 8, the time is the "early 1890s," and Lerner introduces a feminist theme (he was on solid historical footing here, for 1890 was the year in which the National American Woman Suffrage Association was founded). A contented Sam, now a successful businessman, is seen rocking on his porch and singing "My Kind of Evening," while in the living room (the set is split, revealing both porch and interior) Susan urges about a dozen of her women neighbors to join her in the fight for woman suffrage. When Sam finishes his self-satisfied song (another of Weill's best, to a pleasant rocking rhythm), Susan exhorts her group with "Women's Club Blues."

Lerner's lyric here deftly demolishes sexist stereotyping. Susan's "mouth as red as roses" will shout at public meetings; she longs to be squeezed, but only in a line at the polls; her "satin shoulders" she intends to "put to the wheel"; and she is sick of her domestic jail. She feels women have every right to be doctors, judges, or even traveling salesmen (here Lerner could not resist throwing in a reference to the farmer's son). "Women's Club Blues" is one of the earliest pro-feminist songs of the American theater, albeit anticipated by Harold Arlen and E. Y. Harburg's "It Was Good Enough for Grandma" (*Bloomer Girl*, 1944) and Arthur Schwartz and Ira Gershwin's "Don't Be a Woman If You Can" (*Park Avenue*, 1946). Those earlier treatments, however, were lighter, wittier; Lerner's darker, angrier lyric must rank with his most brilliant work.

In an early script, this scene is followed by a nonmusical sequence featuring a ventriloquist and his dummy. What is fascinating is that the ventriloquist's role might almost have been modeled on Joseph Lerner. The dialogue is a denigration of women, a catalogue of their congenital faults and the problems they bring to the superior male. The dummy is an unsuccessful philanderer, and the ventriloquist is his adviser on how to treat women—in a word, badly.

This scene was cut and replaced by a different vaudeville routine—a hobo singing a "Love Song"—to introduce the final act of part 1, set in the 1920s and staged in the style of the musicals of the period. The opening section of "Love Song," an extended verse, makes references to Wall Street, Prohibition, and money making before going on to extol the beauties of real love in a haunting Weill melody. When love dies, the hobo sings, "the world turns to gray/But nobody hears me what I say."

The twenties scene takes place on an ocean liner; a new year is about to dawn, and the passengers are awaiting the moment when the ship crosses out of U.S. waters so the drinking can begin. The Cooper marriage is obviously shaky: Sam seems interested only in business, and Susan is the neglected wife. Both have flirtations with others, and as the new year is rung in, the curtain descends on two unhappy Coopers.

Part 2 (the second act) is set in a New York apartment, in the present. Lerner had some problems making this work; in an early version of the script, the curtain opened on a madrigal group singing a mock-folksong entitled "Ho, Billy O!," a comment on contemporary neuroticism, alcoholism, and infidelity. In the final libretto, he began with a scene of the unhappy Cooper family, including the children, bickering in their apartment. Susan is now a source of the problem, as she has a job and spends little time with her family. Sam is caught in a probable lie when his daughter finds—and shows Susan— a ticket to a boxing match he was supposed to have attended the night before. (The scene, of course, has autobiographical overtones: a similar situation had led to Joseph Lerner's moving out of the family apartment and separating from his wife.)

One quatrain in the madrigal is particularly revealing:

> My father used to stay away,
> With home he'd never bother.
> And mother hit me twice a day
> Because I looked like father.

(*Time* later reported in an article on Lerner and Loewe that Edith Lerner had once slapped her son because he looked too much like his father.)

Trying to find a sequence that satisfied him, Lerner switched the "acts" around, beginning with the apartment scene entitled "Radio Night" (originally "A Ticket to the Fight"), moving on to the "Madrigal Singers," and ending up with "Act 3," "Farewell Again," in which Sam walks out and the Coopers decide to divorce. Yet another act was eliminated before the show came to Broadway; the first "Act 3," "The Locker Room Boys," had men being boys and singing of the joys of being themselves, away from their wives. Here Sam was to discuss his plans for a divorce with a sharp lawyer, but with this act cut, Lerner moved directly from the farewell scene to "Act 4," "Punch and Judy Get a Divorce" (originally "The All-American Ballet"). In this extended dance number, Weill combined music already heard with new music added to unify the variations on the themes (e.g., the lively "Green-Up Time" is heard here in a slowed-down half-tempo). Wolcott Gibbs, of *The New Yorker*, had a decidedly negative reaction:

> Incidentally, ballet, which has been responsible for a good share of the suffering in my life, comes up with its crowning lunacy in something I take to be a sociological study of divorce. Earlier in the evening, I thought we had hit bottom when the ladies of the chorus went prancing around in long woolen underwear [at the conclusion of act 8 of part 1, "Women's Club Blues"], but I was mistaken. "Punch and Judy Get a Divorce" made that look like high art.

After the divorce, the fifth vaudeville act, Sam sits alone in his room, declaiming in "This Is the Life" that he is free—but miserable.

The final "act" is "The Minstrel Show," which opens with "We're Selling Sunshine, Sweetness and Light," heavy on illusion and cynicism and light on love. An Interlocutor brings out various characters to enlighten the Coopers on love and marriage, with only negative effect. A Mr. Cynic sums up the point of the act with "Taking No Chances," and Susan and a Miss Ideal Man join in singing the satirical and cynical "Mr. Right." Nanette Fabray won high praise from several reviewers for her rendition of the latter, wherein she describes life with the perfect husband, who would father her, mother her, sister her, and brother her and not "mind if I spend all his earnings."

Despite the discouragement of the minstrels and the duplicitous Interlocutor, the Coopers continue to be wretched apart and decide to try marriage again. The final act concludes with Susan and Sam on opposite sides of the stage, as each mounts a platform and starts toward the other on a tightrope. The ending is hopeful but ambiguous; the curtain falls before the two touch.

BEFORE THE NEW YORK OPENING Lerner and Weill purportedly submitted a short "play" published in the *Times* in which they appeared in front of Boston's Shubert Theatre and discussed *Love Life* with a "Man." "Pardon me," the man says, "Do either of you know anything about this show?" "Yes," Lerner tells him. "We saw it in New Haven." The Man is confused, for the show is billed as a "vaudeville." Weill assures him it is that, with "lots of vaudeville acts." Relieved, the Man says, "Then I don't have to worry about the plot." Lerner cautions him, "No. There's a plot." Further confusion results, so Weill explains, "Well, the sketches and the vaudeville acts have a continuity and supplement each other."

> MAN: [scratching his head] Did you understand it?
> WEILL: I did.
> LERNER: So did I.

The Man comments that "it must be a very simple story. Weill informs him that on the contrary, "It not only tells the saga of 150 years of American home life but also the life of two people and the gradual changing of their personalities as life becomes more complex." To which Lerner adds, "Not to mention the disintegration of their home until divorce separates them." Weill: "You see, it's very simple."

And so on, as Weill and Lerner explain the structure and plot of their musical. For example, Lerner says, they use song and dances "which change with the mood of the play, from the simplicity of 150 years ago, through the frenzy of the prohibition era and on into the frenetic and zany torchiness of today."

The Man is more baffled than ever and, "looking around wildly for a road to escape," says he supposes it is easy to understand. "But, anyway," he adds, "there are no comics and no crooners but there *is* vaudeville."

> LERNER: That's right.
> MAN: For instance?

LERNER: There's a magician.
WEILL: And a trapeze artist.
LERNER: And a male quartet.
WEILL: And a female trio.
MAN: And all this has a plot?
WEILL: That's right.
MAN: And it is easy to follow?
WEILL: It was for us.
MAN: This I've got to see! [He walks to the window to buy a seat.
    Lerner and Weill shake hands and walk down the street.]

Lerner prepared this miniature drama to forestall some of the audience reaction that had been all too evident in New Haven and Boston. The piece was wittier than the traditional preopening puffery that appeared in print, and it had a real purpose: With this playlet, Lerner hoped to clarify his and Weill's intent and to inform potential attendees (and maybe the critics as well) that they would not be seeing a traditional musical comedy. It was inarguably a musical ahead of its time.

Not all the reviews of *Love Life* were bad, and some even provided neat, short quotes for postopening advertising, hailing it as "a musical play of excitement, distinction and style" (Richard Watts, Jr., of the *New York Post*); "a superior musical, being smart and handsome, too" (John Chapman, the *News*); and "a festive hit . . . an exhilarating and distinctive musical show" (Ward Morehouse, the *Sun*). But the three major critics—Abel Green of the trade paper and business-wise *Variety*, Brooks Atkinson of the *Times*, and Wolcott Gibbs of *The New Yorker*— were decidedly against it. Green, predicting a short run, called the show "one of those regretful Broadway legit adventures which hurts the show-wise observer as much as the artificers responsible for this noble adventure." He had kind words for the cast and score but considered Lerner's vaudeville skits to be nothing more than "disjointed interruption[s]."

Atkinson, as "one discontented theatregoer," pronounced *Love Life* an "intellectual idea about showmanship gone wrong. Vaudeville has nothing to do with the bitter ideas Mr. Lerner has to express about marriage. Although he is trying to be a philosopher, unhappiness keeps creeping in. He looks jocose on the surface, but he is full of anguish." He thought the tightrope conclusion an "adolescent fantasy" and the show in general "cute, complex and joyless," a "gripe masquerading as entertainment." He did, however, praise

Weill's contribution, and, with every other critic, applauded Nanette Fabray and Ray Middleton.

Gibbs, for his part, found the libretto "oppressive" and the show's theme ("sempiternal bickering") a "singularly melancholy inspiration," though he deemed the lyrics "pleasantly adroit." Although not a flop, Love Life was hardly a hit, either.

During the run of the show, Lerner and Weill went to Bel Air, California, to rest and ponder future musical ideas. While there, they discussed the possibility of doing an operatic Book of Ruth, with the working title My Name Is Love. A close friendship developed, and they continued to seek out new projects, though their biblical opera never came into being. Weill conceived a musical set in contemporary Israel, for which he and Lerner completed an outline, but that, too, was eventually abandoned. In January 1949, Weill was happy to learn that Brigadoon might be sold to MGM for $250,000. "I hope it works out," he wrote Lerner, "because that would ease your financial burden." Weill was by then collaborating with Maxwell Anderson on a musical based on Alan Paton's South African novel Cry, the Beloved Country, to be produced late in 1949 as Lost in the Stars; it was also Weill's last Broadway score.

During this period, Weill suggested still other ideas to Lerner. In one, a musical set in occupied Germany after the Second World War, an American soldier was to see a Lorelei in the Rhine and fall in love with her; another called for them to adapt Stephen Vincent Benét's short story "Too Early Spring." Lerner could not see much merit in either of these notions, and in any case he was preoccupied with other matters. A good friend and champion of his work, Lillie Messinger, had arranged for an introduction to Louis B. Mayer, then head of Metro-Goldwyn-Mayer. While working at MGM as a story editor, Messinger had recommended that the studio acquire rights to The Day Before Spring; though this was done, the film was never made. By the time Love Life opened, she had moved to Universal, but she retained her friendship with Mayer and, upon hearing that he was flying to New York to see Lerner's new show, headed East herself to bring the two men together. Mayer, impressed with both Brigadoon and Love Life (though mostly the former), immediately called Arthur Freed, the outstanding producer of musicals at MGM. Lerner flew out to California the next day.

In the spring of 1949, Weill was hard at work on Lost in the Stars, but he kept Lerner well informed about New York's musical and theater scene. That he trusted him is evidenced in a letter recording his impression of an honored colleague. He and Lenya, among others, had spent an evening at the home of Oscar Hammerstein, on New York's Upper East Side. "The evening at Oscar's was pleasant," he wrote, "until Dick [Rodgers] showed up—then everybody froze up into a sort of pompous silence and it was impossible to discuss anything except the cheapest kind of show talk." He was certain that Rodgers suffered from a "terrible case of inferiority complex which he tries desperately to hide behind arrogance." This became even more apparent when Weill was asked to play something from his work in progress. Rodgers's face clouded over when Weill sat at the piano and played,

> especially things like the great lament "Cry the beloved country," at the end of which he got so nervous that he couldn't sit in his chair anymore and started walking around so that I almost began feeling sorry for him, and that three days after the opening of *South Pacific*! It was all very strange and weird.

Three months later, returned to New City, Lerner had an ominous experience. He and Weill were playing tennis on his court when the composer collapsed, his face ashen and his breathing labored. Lerner managed to get him inside and was about to call for a doctor when Weill stopped him. Reluctantly he complied, but not before imploring his friend to get some medical attention; Weill agreed, provided that Lerner did not mention the incident to Lenya. Lerner kept his promise, but Weill did not; he continued work on the forthcoming musical and was soon immersed in preproduction stresses.

When *Lost in the Stars* finally premiered in New York, in October 1949, Lerner wrote a characteristic, warm note instead of the usual telegram:

> Dearest Kurt and Lenya—
> You know how I feel about the opening but I'll say it again anyhow.
> I couldn't be pulling for it any more if it was my own play.
> And that is not only because it is what it is but because I love you both so very much.
>
> Alan

Weill's death of a heart attack, in April 1950, just a month after his fiftieth birthday, put an end to any future Weill-Lerner collaboration.

5

———ᨠ———

A NEW YORKER
IN HOLLYWOOD

W HEN LERNER MET with Arthur Freed in November 1948, he had no
illusions about working on the Coast. Weill, he knew, had anguished
four years earlier over the "screen treatments" of *Knickerbocker Holiday* and
Lady in the Dark, and was to suffer through the experience again three weeks
after *Love Life* opened, when the screen version of *One Touch of Venus* was released. It was the same as before: Most of the score had been discarded, and
what remained had been relegated to the background.

Freed was mildly interested in *Love Life* but most drawn to *Brigadoon*.
Lerner was cautious; he may have had reservations about Hollywood's way
with Broadway musicals, but he had deep respect for Freed's touch with a film
musical. Freed had been associated with Metro-Goldwyn-Mayer ever since
1929, when, in collaboration with real-estate-salesman-turned-composer
Nacio Herb Brown, he had written the songs for one of the first musical films,
Broadway Melody. Over the decade that followed, the collaborators had produced some of the most popular songs to come out of Hollywood, including
"Singin' in the Rain," "You Were Meant for Me," "Pagan Love Song," "Temptation," "You Are My Lucky Star," "Should I (Reveal)?" "I've Got a Feelin'
You're Foolin'," and "Alone" (from *A Night at the Opera*). Their first complete
score was for *Broadway Melody of 1938*, after which they contributed a song or

two to various Metro films—a title song for Clark Gable's *China Seas*, something for Jeanette MacDonald to sing in *San Francisco*, "Would You?" and "Good Morning" from *Babes in Arms*, and so on. Brown retired in the late forties after working with several other lyricists, and around that same time, Freed decided that producing films was his true calling.

He had grown into the job by observing the technical advances being made in films, and especially in musicals, practically from their beginnings, from the advent of sound and the early, sometimes clumsy attempts to film Broadway shows to the second flowering with the pairing of Fred Astaire and Ginger Rogers. The third flowering, thanks to Arthur Freed, would belong to Metro. It began, auspiciously enough, with *The Wizard of Oz*; though his screen credit listed him as associate producer (Mervyn Le Roy was the nominal producer), Freed was actually the musical brain behind the film.

When he and Lerner met, the Freed Unit, as it was known at Metro, was an empire unto itself, already responsible for a number of tasteful and profitable musicals, among them *Babes in Arms*, *Strike Up the Band*, *For Me and My Gal*, *Cabin in the Sky*, *Best Foot Forward*, *Girl Crazy*, *Meet Me in St. Louis*, and *Ziegfeld Follies*. By 1948, however, the so-called Golden Age of the film musical had begun to turn leaden. Lavish productions were still contracted, but that year only a handful were worth noticing: the regrettable *One Touch of Venus* and two from the Freed Unit, Irving Berlin's *Easter Parade* and Cole Porter's *The Pirate*. Working in the Unit in 1949, Lerner was on hand for the release of the outstandingly successful *Jolson Sings Again* (not from Metro) and two productions from Freed and company, *The Barkleys of Broadway* (with songs by Ira Gershwin and Harry Warren, reuniting Fred Astaire with Ginger Rogers) and the not very faithful screen adaptation of *On the Town*, with songs added to an already adequate and sparkling score by Leonard Bernstein, Betty Comden, and Adolph Green. During this short period (ca. 1948–52), a sharp drop in movie attendance was attributed to the growing popularity of television. Musicals suffered badly; in 1948 alone, profits were off by 45 percent. Some film houses began booking television sports events, but by 1951 more than a thousand had simply closed down. That year would see the release of Alan Lerner's first film effort, among the biggest "blockbusters" ever produced by the Freed Unit.

Returning to New York after his first meeting with Freed, Lerner wrote to the producer:

I had a meeting a few days ago with my comrades in charge of the destiny of *Brigadoon* and I passed on to them the gist of our chats about it. I advised them in view of the not too savory conditions in Hollywood now not to be too unrealistic about selling our little golden goose.

As you know, we've never been in a great hurry because the show shows promise of still another two seasons of solid business. I did acquaint them, though, with the very plain fact that there are precious few men in Hollywood who have the setup, the taste and the stars to film it, and that after being out there for a few weeks I have more confidence in your unit at M-G-M than any other.

The result of the conclave was that if it were bought by you the price would be two hundred and fifty thousand. You can toss it around in your spare time and let me know what you think some time in the future while I'm out there.

As a personal favor, however, please don't bruit this figure around because in the talks there have been with other studios the asking price has been higher or a percentage arrangement was discussed. As a matter of fact, I'm looking forward to the whole venture with much more eagerness and anticipation than, frankly, I thought I would. Maybe that is because I feel at ease in the surroundings, for which I'm very grateful to you.

Hugh Fordin, historian of the Freed Unit, thought Freed's

emotional scale . . . limited and uncomplicated: admiration for some, respect for a few, rejection of mediocrity. Secure within himself, he has the courage, the daring to venture toward the unexplored. . . . His lack of social polish is deliberate. His anger is short-lived and never vindictive. He is nonverbal and conveys his thoughts by implication. . . . He is a romantic, a sentimental man, whose powers of imagination always lure him beyond the rainbow.

Freed also had an instinct for choosing the members of his Unit: William "Bill" Ryan to handle production details; Lela Simone, who understood music and sound; and particularly Roger Edens, composer, arranger, accompanist, and eventually Freed's associate producer. Other musical talents were brought in as needed, along with directors (with emphasis on the talented Vincente Minnelli), vocal arrangers (among them Kay Thompson), conductors (a favorite was Lennie Hayton), set and costume designers, and so on. For all his eccentricities, his taciturnity, his nonconversations, Freed was able to assemble extraordinary—and loyal—teams, and somehow to let them know what he wanted.

"Arthur was a strange and touching man," Lerner later wrote of him. He was "filled with contradictions, idiosyncracies, and surprises. By any standard, he was an original." Although seemingly preoccupied, abstruse, and circuitous, he could be powerfully persuasive. It was Freed who argued "Over the Rainbow" back into *The Wizard of Oz* after it was deleted from the film after a couple of previews; and Freed who talked Fred Astaire back into pictures after he retired on completing *Blue Skies* in 1946.

Even as he was tossing around the notion of a film version of *Brigadoon*, Freed suggested that Lerner come out for, say, ten weeks—"not to work on any specific film [but] to get the feel of the place." If no idea surfaced in that time, he could feel free to leave for other parts and works. While Freed often requested that the studio acquire rights to Broadway shows, he also had a great affinity for original musicals geared to a particular star or stars. Despite their titles, such films as *Strike Up the Band* and *Lady Be Good* were only remotely related to their Broadway predecessors.

After spending about three weeks with the Unit, Lerner met with Freed, who said he was looking for an original script for Fred Astaire. In the ensuing discussions, one of them mentioned Adele Astaire's career with her brother, which had ended prematurely with her marriage to a British lord and her subsequent retirement from the theater, leaving Astaire to go on alone on Broadway and to even greater successes in Hollywood. The marriage of Lord and Lady Cavendish brought up recollections of another lavish wedding, almost exactly two years earlier—that of Elizabeth, daughter of George VI of England, to Philip Mountbatten, Duke of Edinburgh. Thus: *Royal Wedding*. (For the film's happy ending, color footage of the real royal wedding was used, after permission was secured from the government and the British Board of Censors, at great cost.)

Once the general scheme had been decided upon, Lerner began work on the script. After completing a first draft, he wished to talk it over with Freed, only to find himself in unfamiliar waters, without a chart. "Although he knew perfectly well what he liked and did not like," Lerner wrote of this later, what he wanted and did not want, his method of conveying it was so circuitous that the mind grew vertiginous with *non sequiturs* and it took patience, respect, and maniacal determination to fer-ret out nuggets of information. . . .

Frequently he would begin a sentence on, let us say, Wednesday and complete it on Friday. Yet this same man could look at me and say: "Stop trying to be different. You don't have to be different to be good. To be good is different enough."

Thus began Alan Jay Lerner's true initiation into the fabled Freed Unit at Metro-Goldwyn-Mayer.

Lerner based his plot broadly on the Astaires' final years together. Like Fred and Adele, the film's Ellen and Tom Bowen are a brother-and-sister singing and dancing act; after the closing of their New York hit (in real life it would have been the Gershwins' *Funny Face*), they sail for London, where they repeat their New York success. During the Astaires' London run (in 1928), Adele had met Lord Charles Cavendish, whom she eventually married, retiring as Lady Cavendish after doing two final shows with her brother; in the film, Ellen meets a mildly philandering Lord John Brindale, and they marry, too. In a departure from strict biographical fact, her brother Tom also marries in the final scenes, along with Princess Elizabeth and Philip. Astaire's film ro-mance is pure fiction, meant to tie up loose ends; the romantic center of the screenplay is provided by the sister and the lord. The film is unusual in that Astaire dances with his (romantic) partner for less than a minute; his more elaborate duets are accomplished with his "sister." That they come off so well on film can be attributed largely to casting mishaps.

Initially, Freed had planned to star June Allyson in the sister role, which Lerner tailored especially for her. Charles Walters, a Broadway veteran and a choreographer, was assigned to direct, though Astaire's dances were a collab-oration between himself and Nick Castle. Shooting was scheduled to begin in early July; most of May was devoted to rehearsals, makeup tests, and wardrobe decisions. All went well until ten days into the preparations, when Allyson an-nounced that she was pregnant.

Lerner was about two thirds of the way through his script when he en-countered Freed in the corridor and was told that Judy Garland would appear opposite Astaire.

Garland had recently been hospitalized for emotional problems, but she had managed to complete *Summer Stock*, also directed by Walters, and was free to take over for Allyson. On hearing that Garland had joined the cast, Walters quit, declaring that after a year and a half of working with her, he himself "was ready for a mental institution." He in turn was replaced by Stanley Donen, in his first solo directorial job. By now it was early June. After three trouble-free weeks of rehearsals, and a celebration of her twenty-eighth birthday on the rehearsal stage, Garland began to object to the morning and afternoon rehearsals. Donen counterobjected, but Freed conceded: Rehearsals would be called for afternoons only. Then, on the day they were scheduled to prerecord the songs, Garland called in to say she could not make it. Three days later, on June 19, 1950, she was suspended by the studio; she would never work for Metro-Goldwyn-Mayer again.

The very same day, Freed asked Fred Astaire if he would like to work with Jane Powell. Astaire's instant reaction was, "Grab her—please!"

Just turned twenty-one, Jane Powell had been with Metro since 1946, invariably appearing as the pert, petite, teenaged troubleshooter who lyrically solves the problems of all the adults in the film. She was regarded as dependable, professional, and, in the words of one of her colleagues, conductor and music director André Previn, "always prepared." But could she dance? Astaire's comment after the film was released was something of a non sequitur: "She surprised everyone by her handling of the dances." Lerner, for his part, was unhappy to lose Judy Garland.

Astaire scholar John Mueller summed Powell up as an "excellent choice as a counterfeit Adele," who, as the film progressed, proved "to be a gifted dancer of considerable range. Not only can she handle the comedy and variety dance routines with flair and ease, but she also shows the requisite fluidity and sympathetic magnetism to be an excellent partner for Astaire in the film's brief ballroom number." While *Royal Wedding* was not intended to be biographically factual, Jane Powell's portrait of Adele Astaire was true to life, capturing her fondness for beaux, her racy charm, her wit, and her casual attitude toward work, taken so seriously by her never-satisfied brother. Playing opposite her as the titled Englishman was the urbane and bland Peter Lawford.

Early on in the writing, the question was, who would Astaire marry at fadeout? Powell had not yet come on the scene, and a known dancer was needed in any case. Freed suggested English ballerina Moira Shearer, who had scored an enormous success in the arty *Red Shoes* (1948), her first film. Astaire's reply was a quizzical, "I know she's wonderful, but what the hell could I do with her?"

Freed soon had another idea. He attended a theatrical revival of *The Philadelphia Story* in Los Angeles and was impressed by the leading lady with the radiant name: Sarah Churchill, acting-dancing daughter of England's prime minister. She was not a film novice; her first appearance had occurred ten years before, in a British production entitled *He Found a Star*. She passed her screen test, but then the studio ran into a snag: There was to be no exploitation of the Churchill name in the film's advertising. Because such promotion could readily be done by word of mouth and leaks, however, the restriction posed no serious problem.

Churchill was cast as an aspiring dancer-actress, the daughter of a saloon-keeper who was estranged from his wife. Her father was played by Albert Sharpe, who had portrayed Finian in the Broadway production of *Finian's Rainbow*. (In the 1967 film version of the Burton Lane–E. Y. Harburg musical, Astaire himself would appear as Finian.)

The major casting was complete with the signing of Keenan Wynn to play twin brothers, one a brassy American agent, the other a very English agent in London.

Having created the story and then the screenplay, Lerner now had to provide the lyrics for the musical numbers. It was no coincidence when Freed brought him together with composer Burton Lane: They had each worked on one of the two great fantasy musicals of 1947, *Brigadoon* and *Finian's Rainbow*. But whereas Lerner was just acquiring his initial musical-film experience, Lane was a veteran of the genre, having made his debut in 1933 with Joan Crawford's *Dancing Lady* (featuring "Everything I Have Is Yours"). His most recent movie musical was 1944's undistinguished *Rainbow Island*; in the interim he had slipped away from Hollywood to do two Broadway shows, *Laffing Room Only* (out of which had come the popular "Feudin' and Fightin'") and the classic *Finian*.

A musical prodigy from a young age, Lane had been born in 1912 into a wealthy real estate family whose patriarch, like Lerner's father, could see no future in music. The boy began to study piano at seven but stopped when he entered public school, as his parents felt a duple education was not for him; they relented again when he was eleven, allowing him to study privately until one of his teachers suggested that he be sent abroad to complete his musical education. His father did not agree to the plan but instead insisted that he continue with a more conventional academic life.

Like his hero, George Gershwin, Lane was a hapless student at the New York High School of Commerce; unlike Gershwin, he managed to graduate, only to begin failing courses at the Dwight Academy. Already by this time an exceptional pianist, he was heard one day by Harold Stern, musical director for the Shuberts, specialists in musical production. Stern arranged an audition for Lane with Jacob, better known as J.J. Although Lane was only fifteen, his playing and some of his original compositions won him a commission for an annual revue entitled *Greenwich Village Follies.* He completed about twenty songs before the illness of the star, James Barton, canceled that year's production. Disappointed, Lane found work as a pianist with the Remick Music Company, becoming a staff writer by the time he was sixteen. There he met such talented newcomers as Howard Dietz and Harold Adamson, with whom he collaborated on his first songs.

Before the Depression caught up with them in the early 1930s, they contributed songs to revues; Lane then worked as an accompanist and arranger until he and Adamson were hired by Metro to furnish the music for *Dancing Lady.* Although Lane would continue to write movie songs, mostly with Adamson, for the next two decades, he would never be given a real opportunity to demonstrate his full capabilities; the numbers that he and Adamson composed were either interpolated into films with songs by others or used as title songs. His first important "hit," again written with Adamson, was for *Dancing Lady,* in which Fred Astaire made his film debut in 1933. Lane-Adamson's "Everything I Have Is Yours" was used because producer David Selznick was unhappy with "That's the Rhythm of the Day," the song submitted by Rodgers and Hart, who were to have written the entire score; others were called in to finish the job, among them twenty-one-year-old Burton Lane. The song was introduced not by Astaire, nor by star Joan Crawford, but by popular singer Art Jarrett; after the film's release, it became one of the most popular songs of 1934, and remains a standard today.

After *Dancing Lady,* it was a matter of a song here, a song there for Lane, with a successful one occasionally emerging from a mixed bag: out of *Kid Millions,* for instance, starring Eddie Cantor, with the bulk of the score by Gus Kahn and Walter Donaldson, came "Your Head on My Shoulder." A switch to Paramount teamed him with Ralph Freed (Arthur's brother) and Frank Loesser. With Freed he wrote "Smarty" (for *Double or Nothing,* 1937) and, later, back at Metro, "How About You?" (for *Babes on Broadway,* 1941); with Loesser he collaborated on the poetic "I Wish I Was the Willow" (for *Spawn of the North,* 1938) and "The Lady's in Love with You" (for *Some Like It Hot,* 1939), among other songs. His assigned collaboration with E. Y. "Yip" Harburg on *Ship Ahoy,* in 1942, bore fruit five years later with *Finian's Rainbow,* after which Burton Lane was taken more seriously in Hollywood. *Royal Wedding* was his first full film score.

Most of the score was complete before June Allyson bowed out, in May 1950. Because the fictional Tom and Ellen were performers, Lerner was not obliged to fret over "integrations"; the musical numbers could be introduced as stage performances or rehearsals. Only for one ballad—Ellen's "Too Late Now," not yet written when rehearsals began—did he resort to Hollywood make-believe; another, "The Happiest Day of My Life," was written for Sarah Churchill, who declined to sing.

Seven songs were finished when Lerner, contemplating the score while driving to Culver City with Lane, said, "You know, this picture is so damn charming it's going to delicate itself to death. What it needs is a real corny vaudeville number." He thought awhile.

"How's this for a title?" he asked, and proposed, "How Could You Believe Me When I Said I Love You When You Know I've Been a Liar All My Life?" It suggested an idea to Lane, who began humming.

"I thought it very, very funny," Lane recalled. "By the time we got to the studio I had the tune. We played it for Astaire"—and the song was in the picture. One of the film's comic highlights, it is also one of Lerner's most ingenious lyrics. Astaire's costume for the sequence is definitely out of character for him: loud, loose-fitting jacket, baggy pants, cheap two-tone shoes, and straw hat. Jane Powell is encased in a tight skirt (complementing Astaire's slacks for taste), wearing ankle-strap shoes, with a black wig over her blond hair. They are a couple of toughs, their between-chorus dialogue right off the street:

> POWELL: *Dincha mudder never teach ya no manners?*
> ASTAIRE: *I never had no mudder. We was too poor.*
> POWELL: *Say, whatsa matter witcha lately? Ya used ta tell me ya loved me. Ya used ta treat me like a high-class dame. Well, usen'tcha?*
> ASTAIRE: *So I used.*

Lerner spotted four Astaire-Powell dances, in addition to which Astaire had two solo dances and Powell three vocal solos. In between, the hardly complex plot unfolded with Ellen and Lord Brindale's romance heading for matrimony, and Tom and Anne's (Sarah Churchill) complicated by her love for an American whom she hasn't seen in years (a problem solved when Tom has him checked out and finds that he is married). The Astaire character is depicted as the perpetual bachelor, some of whose lines reveal an attitude toward marriage that might have come straight out of *Love Life*. In a new twist on an old W. C. Fields line, when Tom is asked if he has ever been married, he replies yes, "almost," but his fiancée ran out on him and he has been "indebted to her ever since." He cynically admits that married men live longer, but claims it is "only so they can be bachelors again."

Lerner also introduced a tertiary plot line involving Anne's parents, the irascible pubkeeper and the wife who has left him; even *they* appear to be getting ready to rewed as the film ends. Except for the musical sequences and some of Keenan Wynn's dual role, *Royal Wedding* is not an especially exhilarating musical; the reviews ranged from favorable ("engaging") to tepid ("lightweight"). Bosley Crowther of the *Times*, for one, was not impressed. "It has one swell number built on the world's longest-titled song ["How Could You Believe Me . . ."; in fact, there is a Hoagy Carmichael song with a longer title], three or four that are good, a laugh here, a laugh there, colored newsreels of the British royal wedding, and so long, pal."

To some degree, Lerner himself agreed with this harsh judgment. "Although Burton Lane wrote some spiffy songs and Fred danced in a way that made all superlatives inadequate," he wrote, "my contribution left me in such a state of cringe that I could barely straighten up."

He was selling himself short. The film rejects the traditional boy-meets-girl, Astaire-Rogers type of plot; while Astaire and Powell are the central characters, their romances are with others, and Astaire's is almost peripheral. Lerner did not depend on their meeting, quarreling over some silly misunderstanding, and then resolving it all at the end. As John Mueller observed in *Astaire Dancing* (a point that few, if any, others have noted),

> the central characters are Astaire and Jane Powell, who play a successful brother-sister musical-comedy team, and the dramatic tension in the film (such as it is) derives from the circumstances that lead finally to their breakup as a performing unit: She falls in love and decides to retire from show business to marry. Though this central dilemma could have been developed with more depth and poignancy in the film, the characterizations of the brother and sister are quite rich; one believes in this attractive, talented pair from the beginning and delights in their wry banter, in which warm mutual dependency is cloaked in genial needling.

Mueller underscores, too, how Lerner spots Powell's three ballads subtly to reveal her feelings toward the Lawford character, deftly delineating them in three melodic phases. Thus, "Open Your Eyes," the ballroom sequence on the pitching ocean liner, is sung in a crowded room, though a couple of lines are obviously addressed to Lawford; "The Happiest Day of My Life," with Astaire at the piano in an informal rehearsal, is a bit more intimate; and the beautiful ballad "Too Late Now," her final admission of her feelings, is sung for Lawford alone, on a deserted London street. The film is especially notable for including two of Astaire's most imaginative dances. The first was suggested to him by a longtime colleague (since *Flying Down to Rio*, in 1933), choreographer Hermes Pan, who proposed his dancing with an inanimate object. Lerner worked it into the script by having the Astaire character be stood up by his sister for a rehearsal in the ship's gymnasium. After a little bit of business with a metronome, he realizes she is late (having found better things to do with Lord Brindale), and goes to the door to check on her. As he does, he places one hand on a clothes tree near the door; when he turns, it somehow remains in his hand. Since his partner has not shown up, he decides to rehearse with the clothes tree. *Time* called what followed a "little masterpiece of grace, timing and inventiveness." Lerner's lyric to the music, "Sunday Jumps," alludes to Astaire's drive for perfection and constant work (he was notorious for calling rehearsals even on Sundays during the making of a film):

> *All week I'm happier than a daisy,*
> *Then comes the day to relax and I go crazy.*
> *They tell me get some rest,*
> *But all that I get is depressed.*

These lines might also be considered autobiographical, in light of Lerner's confession that he was never able to sit down at a performance of any play he had written (a bit of an exaggeration, but not far from the truth). Mostly he paced—and when he wasn't working, he looked for work. In any case, his efforts on the lyric for "Sunday Jumps" were in vain: Only Burton Lane's riffy music can be heard in *Royal Wedding*.

The second Astaire solo dance was the spectacular "You're All the World to Me," in which he is seen dancing literally all over the place—on floor, walls, and ceiling. Lerner provided the cue for this scene in Sarah Churchill's admission to Astaire that she loves dancing, that it makes her so happy she feels she could dance on the ceiling. Astaire's wish to do such a dance dated back at least to 1945, when he confided in an interview published in Metro's house organ, *Lion's Roar*, that he had always wanted to choreograph something like that and hoped one day to find a screenwriter who could come up with a "reason for it."

(In fact, the idea had been attempted before, in a 1930 London production of Rodgers and Hart's *Ever Green*, which featured a couple dancing on a stage furnished with an inverted chandelier; if neither Lerner nor Astaire was aware of this precedent, they were both familiar with its song, "Dancing on the Ceiling.")

According to Astaire, the notion of how to work the number into the film came to him "at four in the morning." Lerner remembered it otherwise: "One night I dreamed that Fred was dancing up the wall, all across the ceiling and down the other wall. I mentioned it to Arthur at lunch the following day and lo, in the film Fred danced up one wall, across the ceiling and down the other wall." It was, he claimed, the "one creative moment" in the film that he liked, though it "had nothing to do with me consciously." Whatever its origin, it was one of Astaire's most memorable dances, coming after he has sung the praises of his Anne in terms of such places as Paris, New York, "a Swiss Alp," Loch Lomond, Cape Cod, Capri, and so on (but not, as Stanley Green noted in *Starring Fred Astaire*, London).

Notably, Lerner anticipated "You're All the World to Me" in "Open Your Eyes," sung earlier in the film by Jane Powell, who invites the Peter Lawford character "On a tour of this/Great new/Fabulous world/We own."

Since the film was to open regally (literally) with an onstage scene from the show within the show, *Every Night at Seven* (a crowned Fred Astaire, seated on a throne, sings the song of the same title to Powell's chambermaid character before chasing her around the throne and then dancing with her), it must close with a spectacular finale. This turned out to be the peculiar "I Left My Hat in Haiti," a typical MGM production number. Lane infused it with a hypnotic Latin beat, and Castle and Astaire created a dance of vast dimension. Astaire begins by singing about leaving his fedora in "some forgotten flat in Haiti"—alone, as Stanley Green so aptly put it, "against a simple backdrop which suddenly dissolves into a gaudy set approximating the size of the entire island." Neither the dance nor the song makes much sense, but they serve to place Astaire in a lush, colorful setting populated with dancers in vivid costumes, in what could pass for a finale. Astaire's search for his hat ends with his finding it on a monkey; here even Mueller, who analyzes virtually every dance number in *Royal Wedding*, is at a loss:

The "Haiti" number betrays no thought processes whatever. If Astaire is searching for the hat and the woman he left it with, why do several (but not all) of the women wear hats? And if he is going to do a duet with one of the women (Jane Powell), why does he choose one of the hatless ones? And if he is searching for his hat, why does he do a duet anyway? Perhaps the monkey knows.

The dance itself originated with choreographer Nick Castle, with Astaire's approval and cooperation. Lerner and Lane provided something Castle and Astaire could work with, but it was much ado about very little, and one of the aspects of the film that caused the librettist-lyricist to cringe.

Despite Lerner and Crowther's negative assessments, *Royal Wedding* was a box-office success; likewise at the cash register.

As Lerner struggled with the twists and turns of film work, his personal life took its own turn: Unhappy with his marriage to Marion Bell, he commuted between California and Nevada, establishing a quasi-residence in Las Vegas. By late 1949 he and Marion Bell were divorced, and he was free for his next matrimonial venture. His new love, Nancy Olson, then about twenty-one and a graduate of the University of Southern California, had appeared in small dramatic roles in such epics as *Canadian Pacific* and *Union Station*; in 1950 she would be favorably noticed in a supporting role opposite Gloria Swanson and William Holden in *Sunset Boulevard*.

As Lerner's new romance was blossoming, even before *Royal Wedding* was completed, Arthur Freed proposed another project that he believed would be ideal for the lyricist. It had developed during one of Freed's regular evenings at Leonore and Ira Gershwin's, spent either at cards or playing pool in the basement of their home on North Roxbury Drive in Beverly Hills (for the record, Gershwin was better with words than at pool). While they played, Freed said he had an idea for a new musical and asked Gershwin to grant him permission to use the title of his brother's tone poem "An American in Paris"; he felt it would work wonderfully in a musical Gene Kelly had suggested to him—something about an American soldier who, after the close of the Second World War, remains in Paris to study painting. Freed visualized an outstanding finale with a ballet utilizing all of George Gershwin's "An American in Paris."

Ira Gershwin liked the idea and respected Freed—but why not, he suggested, use Gershwin songs as the score, making it an all-Gershwin musical? Freed liked that, and as they talked, he enlarged the project to include his protégé and longtime Gershwin friend Vincente Minnelli, an exceptional director of musicals (*Cabin in the Sky, Meet Me in St. Louis, The Pirate*, etc.) with a scenic artist's eye for design. With Lerner set to do the screenplay, production number 1501 was under way.

Once he and Lane were finished with the *Royal Wedding* songs, Lerner turned to his new script; within two weeks he could show Freed the first forty pages, accomplished in the quiet of Palm Springs, away from the busy social life of Beverly Hills. (Frederick Loewe joined him there for some relaxation.) Lerner had a problem, though: forty pages of beginning, and no ending. Two months went by, and as he prepared for his next marriage, he was no further along on the script.

Besides the Gershwin score (which, with its elaborate ballet, solved some of his ending problem), Lerner could turn for inspiration to the *Life* article that had originally captured Gene Kelly's interest, about ex-GIs studying in Paris on the GI Bill. Kelly would play an American painter who falls in love with a pretty French girl. She eventually reciprocates, but first Lerner introduced a complication: She is indebted to an older man who saved her life during the war, and feels she must marry him. The painter meanwhile encounters a wealthy American woman who, among other things, wants to advance his career.

Where to go from here?

Lerner's dramatic ingenuity took its cue from the music. Oscar Levant, then the definitive Gershwin interpreter, better known for his mordant wit than for his acting ability, was cast as Kelly's friend. A veteran of films since 1940 (though his first film appearance had come in *The Dance of Life*, of 1929), he invariably played himself, a wisecracking, neurotic pianist. In Lerner's film he refers to himself, in his own apt phrase, as the "world's oldest child prodigy."

After some searching, and the rejection of both Cyd Charisse and Vera-Ellen (because Freed insisted on casting a bona fide French citizen), an eighteen-year-old, gamine-like ballet dancer named Leslie Caron was selected to appear opposite Kelly. Although some in the Freed Unit found her less than glamorous—she was shy, unfashionably dressed, and accompanied by her mother—Lerner noted that she was "equipped with one of those adorable French accents that everyone is always so mad about."

Lerner also contributed to the casting: For Caron's guardian and husband-to-be, he had his heart set on a performer who "had been an idol of mine ever since every little breeze started whispering Louise" (i.e., Maurice

Chevalier, who had sung "Louise" in the 1929 film *Innocents in Paris*). Then in his early sixties, Chevalier, Lerner soon learned, was persona non grata in the United States because of (unfounded) reports that he had entertained German troops during the war. Disappointed, Lerner found a possible alternative in New York when he saw the musical *Arms and the Girl*. Set in Revolutionary times, the show starred Nanette Fabray, formerly of *Love Life*, and French cabaret singer Georges Guetary in the unlikely role of a Hessian. Guetary was only in his thirties, so the age gap between guardian and gamine would not be as great as it would have been with Chevalier (Guetary was, in fact, two years younger than Kelly). The elegant Nina Foch rounded out the romantic quartet as the wealthy art lover.

Progressing slowly as he endured another divorce and contemplated another wedding, Lerner willingly accepted script ideas from others. Freed, at the time also engaged in the production of *Show Boat*, suggested a mild comic touch. What if Kelly, sauntering down a Paris street carrying canvases to his exhibition space, were to come upon a portly man in white, wearing a Panama hat and seated at a stool before a canvas? The man could be smoking a sizable cigar. As he passed him, Kelly would do a double take: The man, of course, would be a dead ringer for Winston Churchill, a notable Sunday painter.

A second contribution came from Oscar Levant, having grown out of his own anxieties. Levant brooded between scenes, smoking constantly and drinking coffee, unhappy because early in the talking stages Freed had decreed that except for the title piece, there would be no other Gershwin instrumental music in the film—only songs. That left little for Levant to do, other than accompany Kelly and Guetary or perform intricate song variations (which he did, though several were deleted from the final print of the film). Finally, he had an idea about fattening his part.

Rather than approach Freed directly, he brought the notion to Minnelli, who thought it good and took it to Freed, who agreed; Lerner had several more minutes of his film filled in. Levant called it the Ego Fantasy; it has him performing the finale of Gershwin's Concerto in F, not only playing the solo piano part but also conducting (except for a brief shot in which lyricist Adolph Green, seen from the back, doubles for him) and taking the parts of all the first violinists and the percussionist—virtually the entire orchestra. At the conclusion, conductor Levant and pianist Levant stand to acknowledge the applause, slightly annoyed by a clamorous fan in a box—also Levant. The scene dissolves to Levant, alone, daydreaming on his cot. Shot in one day, the Ego Fantasy is one of the comic highlights of *An American in Paris*.

Levant also made other contributions to the script; his stint in the late thirties and early forties as a resident wit and musical authority on the popular radio show *Information Please* had turned him into a master ad-libber. So it was that he added an improvisational quip on occasion, such as the "oldest child prodigy" comment. In one scene where Kelly and Guetary are discussing the women they love—neither one knowing that both are speaking of the same woman—Levant, who does know, goes through a nervous routine as they talk with increasing excitement. He spills his coffee, refills his cup, lights a cigarette, and attempts to drink with it in his mouth. Retrieving the damp butt, Levant stops the conversation with the line, "Did I ever tell you about my command performance in front of Hitler?" The ad-lib remained in the film.

All in all, given the length of the song-and-dance numbers, Guetary's elaborate production sequence around "I'll Build a Stairway to Paradise," and the extended ballet, with some added bars from other sources, Lerner's script was rather slight; it was almost as if the Gershwins—and the unhappy Levant—were his collaborators. If the plot was a bit slender, however, it was nonetheless literate, and Lerner moved gracefully into the musical sequences.

Among the several Lernerisms scattered throughout the script, one of the best is Kelly's snappish comment about a philistine fellow art student (obviously American) who discusses a painting of Kelly's character in art critic jargon. He dismisses him with, "They are always making profound observations they've overheard."

After rehearsals and prerecording, the filming of *An American in Paris* began on August 1, 1950. Once it was under way, there was little for Lerner to do; by December he and his new bride had moved to Manhattan. Once there, though barely settled in, he got a call from Minnelli for a rewrite. The scene leading into the big ballet finale was set at an artists' masked ball, with Gershwin music playing in the background. The visual concept was unusual in that all participants were dressed in black and white—Minnelli's idea. This, he believed, would prepare the audience for the lush, color-drenched ballet. But while the ball was happening in "real life," the ballet was to occur in the mind of Kelly's character. How to switch from the real to the fantasy?

Lerner solved the dilemma by having Kelly leave the ballroom to stand on a terrace overlooking a sparkling panorama of Paris. He is joined there by Caron, and their conversation is overheard by Guetary, who has slipped out of the ballroom for a cigarette (in another good Lerner touch, the audience is made aware of his presence by a cloud of smoke wafting out from behind a pillar).

When Minnelli called, he told Lerner—"falteringly and often vaguely but in some manner that had nothing to do with logic"—that some dialogue might better prepare the audience to connect the plot with the art and artists to be featured in the ballet.

When Lerner asked when the additional dialogue would be needed, Minnelli told him, "Not right away. . . . We're shooting tomorrow." Lerner could phone it in to him, he said; he planned to be at home that night.

Lerner, perplexed, went to work and came up with some dialogue between Caron and Kelly, revealing their deepest feelings for each other, to the enlightenment of the innocently eavesdropping Guetary. Caron assures the distraught Kelly that he will get over her, that "Paris has ways of making people forget," but he doubted that, saying that the city is "too real, too beautiful; Paris never lets you forget anything." He then launches into a speech about why he came to Paris, his wish to study in the city of Toulouse-Lautrec, Utrillo, and others—exactly what Minnelli wanted. "I love what they created," he tells her, "but what do I have left? Paris." It is not enough, he tells her, for "the more beautiful everything is, the more it will hurt without you."

Later that evening, Lerner phoned Minnelli, who assured him that the new dialogue was "perfect!" (Even after seeing the finished film several times, Lerner had to confess that he was not certain what the speech really meant; nor had anyone ever asked him.)

After Caron leaves the terrace, Kelly sadly turns back to the vista. Below him he sees Caron and Guetary enter a car, bound for a ship, America, and marriage. Caron looks up unhappily, and Guetary is obviously deep in thought; thus did Lerner establish the prelude to his happy ending. As Kelly moodily studies Paris's nightscape, the fantasy opens with the Gershwin "walking theme," and the ballet begins. (Each sequence or movement of the ballet is executed against a backdrop in the style of Dufy, Manet, Utrillo, Rousseau, van Gogh, or Toulouse-Lautrec, an effect suggested by one of the art directors, Irene Sharaff, who also provided the costume designs. The choreography was done by Kelly, assisted by a pre-Broadway Carol Haney.)

Lerner's happy ending puzzled at least one other Broadway expatriate, Irving Berlin. Lunching with Freed and Minnelli in the MGM commissary one day, he was shown, with much fanfare, Sharaff's designs for the sets and costumes. On hearing that the film would conclude with a ballet sans dialogue, without even a final song, the show-wise Berlin made a depressing comment: "I hope you boys know what you're doing."

But Lerner solved that problem simply. When the ballet ends, the camera returns to Kelly, standing on the terrace in his black-and-white costume. He watches as an auto drives up to the curb and stops next to the long flight of stairs. Caron climbs out of the cab, and the two run toward each other; after their embrace, the film closes with a shot of Paris at night. No words are necessary.

Close to a year later, in November 1951, after travails that included objections from the front office about excessive costs (especially for the highbrow ballet) and unfortunate previews—none of these involving Lerner, who was already at work on other projects—the film was released, to nearly ecstatic reviews and lovely grosses. At Oscar time, it was nominated for several awards, in categories ranging from Color Costume Design to Story and Screenplay.

Lerner was not present at the ceremony, produced by coincidence that year by Arthur Freed and held on March 20, 1952, at the RKO Pantages Theatre. Instead, he was in New York; Joseph Lerner was scheduled for yet another cancer operation that same day. Somehow being with his father seemed more important to Lerner than participating in the Oscars charade, and besides, he believed—wrongly—that a musical had never won the Oscar. (While it was true that there was no category for musicals, in 1929, the second year of the awards, the Oscar for Best Picture had been bestowed on *The Broadway Melody*, the first of the backstage musicals; *The Great Ziegfeld*, as much a biography-drama as a musical, had won in 1936, as had Bing Crosby's priestly drama *Going My Way*, with music, in 1944.) Still, after his father entered the operating theater and was isolated in the recovery room, Lerner left to listen to the awards broadcast, to be aired beginning at 11:00 P.M. He had a stake in it, for his and Burton Lane's "Too Late Now" from *Royal Wedding* was nominated for Best Song, a category initiated in 1934. But that prize in 1951 went to "In the Cool, Cool, Cool of the Evening," by Hoagy Carmichael and Johnny Mercer.

Disappointed, Lerner was astonished to hear his name called as the recipient of the coveted statue for the year's best picture. It was a triumph he wished to share with his father, though he knew he was still heavily sedated. On his way home, he stopped at the hospital to ask the nurse to inform Joseph of the Oscar when he awakened.

"He knows," she told him.

"How?"

Five minutes before the broadcast began, Lerner's father had come out of the anesthesia and switched on the radio. After hearing his son win the Academy Award, he had turned the radio off again and slipped into a heavy sleep.

Happy at this news, Lerner recalled a typical Joseph Lerner antic. Before being wheeled into the operating room, he had been given the standard release form to sign. Noting that it indicated this was to be his forty-ninth operation, he signed the form and added, "When it gets to fifty, sell."

6

---—〰—---

ROCKY REUNIONS

BY DECEMBER 1950, Lerner had settled with Nancy Olson in their new Manhattan home. Happy in the glow of his recent marriage, he was especially elated at signing a Metro contract for three screenplays, one of them an adaptation of *Brigadoon*. Another was to be a musical written with Burton Lane, based on incidents from Mark Twain's *Adventures of Huckleberry Finn*; the nature of the third project was yet to be determined. With all that still in the future, however, Lerner decided to revisit an idea he had set aside in favor of his first Hollywood venture—which, despite his qualms over *Royal Wedding*, had turned out well.

Even the ongoing success of *Brigadoon* did not slow Lerner; he was anxious to return to Broadway. Frederick Loewe, in contrast, eager to savor that success, had acquired a farm near Pound Ridge, New York, where he reveled a bit and then brooded. Producer Cheryl Crawford believed that he was in fact depressed by his unexpected, though not at all sudden, good fortune: After all his previous failures in the theater, *Brigadoon*, Crawford thought, may have seemed his one and perhaps last big moment. Perhaps, but even so, Loewe, by then in his late forties, was content to reap the benefits of a long-running show, a movie sale, and a song ("Almost Like Being in Love") on the Hit Parade—he wanted to live well, drink the best, and enjoy the company of very pretty, very young women.

As much as Lerner's nervous drive and youthful enthusiasm—he was not yet thirty when *Brigadoon* opened—tried Loewe's patience, he found himself unable to work with anyone else in the four years of Lerner's collaboration with Weill, Lane, and Freed.

The then Mrs. Lerner, Nancy Olson, recalled that "after *An American in Paris* Alan wanted to go back to the theater," but "he had no one to work with" and "wanted Fritz." She indicated that while her husband could work with others, for Loewe, any other partnership was impossible. The two, for all their differences, somehow understood each other; their individual personalities meshed when they worked, and they "forgave each other their idiosyncracies"—Lerner's cool manipulation, for example, might even complement Loewe's temperamental outbursts. When the Lerners returned to the East, Olson felt, "in a way, Fritz was sitting and waiting for Alan." And Alan continued searching.

Several years earlier, while rereading Bret Harte's stories of the old West—he referred to them as yarns—Lerner had realized that he could not recall

> anything fresh and exciting having been written about the Gold Rush (theatrically, that is) since Chaplin's magnificent movie. So that was it. I would fashion a new musical about the Gold Rush.
>
> Like all ideas born overnight, it became an immediate and exciting project. I dropped everything and concentrated on hundreds of musty volumes [dealing] with that colorful era of American history.

Even by 1947–48, the Americana vein had been pretty well mined by Rodgers and Hammerstein, Jule Styne (*High Button Shoes*), Irving Berlin, and others, but Lerner was aiming more for realism than for folkiness.

He went on, "The more I read the more excited I became. The more excited I became the more I read. And the less I wrote. And pretty soon I was tired of reading and too tired to write and I dropped the project and went off to Hollywood to write *An American in Paris.*" And, too, there was another problem with the idea: Frederick Loewe was not interested.

But still, the notion "stuck," Lerner recalled.

> One day, I promised myself . . . one day I would get back on the Gold Rush train. Now, usually, this sort of thing becomes a writer's

bête-noire, a notion that haunts you and haunts you through the years but never becomes more than a "future project." In this case something quite wonderful happened. I was not aware that I was thinking about it, at all. But one day, about eighteen months ago [ca. July 1950], I literally woke up with a fully developed project. There it was, full blown, ready, a story outline that made sense, one that cried for completion. A musical story about the Gold Rush that avoided the usual clichés and that gave me room. There was only one thing to do. I did it. I reached for my typewriter.

And as he would say later, "the title was born with the idea": *Paint Your Wagon*.

Lerner, once he began, found that the Gold Rush idea

wasn't as easy as I thought it would be. I now realized that I had a great deal of respect for the ghosts that the mere mention of 1849 evoked. They were not musical comedy characters. They were full-blooded men and women. They had created a legend. They had cleaved a world. A minuscule world, it is true, a world that grew and developed and boomed and died. . . .

At which point, I realized quite clearly something that I had only felt casually previously[—]that there was a world-wide mis-conception about these people. They were not rough and tough villains; they were not greedy and lascivious; they were not drunk-ards. They were men and women.

This is a rather curious statement for Lerner to have made, for while the characters he created for *Paint Your Wagon* are indeed men and women, the prospectors are, as they were in real life, gold-hungry, and much of the first act focuses on the absence of women in the little town in which the musical is set. Then, too, the main character is a drinker who, with Lerner's blessing, holds the stage in an extended drunk routine (which was to lead to one of Loewe's temper eruptions).

With his gift for romanticism, Lerner visualized history his way. He wished to reclaim the typical forty-niner from the "tough hombre type" made famous by B-movies; the influence of Bret Harte is more evident than that of objective history. But as Lerner put it, "It was my job (albeit self-imposed) to

impale some of the life and breath of all this onto two hours of stage entertainment."

Historian W. E. Woodward called the Gold Rush of 1849

> pure madness. It was the flight from reality of an army of men; a
> feverish flight of men who were tired of their monotonous lives, of
> their petty shops and trades, of their wives and families. They
> could not run away without an objective that appeared to be wor-
> thy, or without an explanation that would be satisfactory to them-
> selves. In California there were both the objective and the
> explanation. It was a desperate adventure, of course; they made
> that clear to wives and friends, so that waves of sympathy would
> flow after them on their long trail. It could be justified, they ad-
> mitted, only on the ground of necessity. Wouldn't it be wonderful
> to return in a year or two, laden with gold, to live happy ever after?

That was the dream that attracted Lerner to this project, a dream that
had in fact come true for very few of the hordes of prospectors who descended
on San Francisco after gold was discovered at John Sutter's mill in Coloma,
east of San Francisco, in the Sacramento Valley. That year, 1848, what would
become the state of California had been wrested from Mexico in the Mexican
War. The Gold Rush, which began the next year, led to a population explosion, from about fifteen thousand in 1849 to almost three hundred thousand
seven years later, when the strike began to peter out.

It was a colorful time of rough-and-tumble lawlessness, vigilantism,
shattered dreams, misplaced values, inflation, and stories to beguile a Bret
Harte, a Mark Twain, or an Alan Jay Lerner. In 1850, for example (though statistics are not terribly precise), something like eighty thousand hopefuls arrived in California; of these, only about twenty-four thousand were women.
Many of these latter began earning fortunes as "clothing refreshers"—that is,
washerwomen—charging fees so exorbitant that some San Franciscans found
it more economical to send their laundry to Hawaii, despite the three-month
wait for the return of their shirts. Lerner would use the laundry motif in the
play, where the woman shortage would also comprise an important theme.

Closely related to this shortage was the arrival of great numbers of prostitutes (but never enough), literally from all over the world, in 1851. Lerner's
name for them was "fandangos," after the Spanish dance; in the Southwest of

the period, the word was used to designate a dance or a ball. In the play, the fandangos are euphemistically presented as dancing girls; by the time Lerner came to write the screenplay, they were "bawds."

When he began work on *Paint Your Wagon*, about a month after *Brigadoon* settled into the Shubert, in March 1947, Lerner visualized the first scene: two covered wagons pass onstage. One is rushing "hopefully" to the gold country, the other limping in the opposite direction, in "despair." The symbolism, he believed, "more or less represented the reaching for and achieving of personal success. I wanted to tell the story of these two wagons and what lay between their coming and going. Actually, as things developed, I finally decided to write the life and death of a ghost town and to do it in a serious tone."

Once Loewe was persuaded to go back to work in the fall of 1950, after three years of professional inactivity, the partners began their customary preliminary discussions. Lerner's serious intentions coincided with his approach once the musical tone of the show was set. According to the lyricist's new young protégé, Stone "Bud" Widney, a former classmate of Nancy Olson's who had come in from California, Lerner simply advised his collaborator to study a little Stephen Foster and to think of a "banjo score." As Loewe put it, "We don't write musical comedies but musical plays. . . . We're not interested in writing 'musical numbers.'" And he made another point as well: "The music of *Paint Your Wagon* is a complement of the words. . . . We tried to write real Americana, with all the roughness that went with the lives of the men of the Gold Rush. These men risked their lives every minute for gold."

Once the work was well under way, they had no problem getting Cheryl Crawford interested; the success of *Brigadoon* eased the burden of backing. Besides the faithful supporters with the deeper pockets, she solicited financial aid from such stellar Broadway backers as Mary Martin, Joshua Logan, Theresa Helburn, Lawrence Langner, Burton Lane, and Billy Rose, who would contribute a special piece of mischief to a troubled production.

That trouble was presaged early in the enterprise. In assembling her production staff, Crawford turned to her old friend from the Group Theater, director Robert Lewis, who had done so well with *Brigadoon* and had since directed Marc Blitzstein's near-opera, *Regina*. Agnes de Mille, who had worked reasonably smoothly with Lewis, was selected to choreograph and to stage the musical ensemble numbers.

Then, as work proceeded, Crawford became aware of what she termed "mysterious things. . . . Production meetings were being called without me.

Bobby Lewis was called . . . but I wasn't. I protested. In fact, I raised hell—then suddenly they abandoned Bobby, whose suggestions on book changes they disagreed with, and told me to find another director." She found Daniel Mann.

Mann saw the script for the first time in May 1951; it proved to be merely an "enlarged outline" for which about half the songs had been written. Rehearsals were not scheduled to begin until August, so there was still some time. Lerner had become bogged down in assiduous research—"too much for the play's good," he subsequently admitted.

> I think that I became so impassioned with realistic values that I forgot that musical theater is not really that kind of truth. I realize that I was trying to write what the British call a *gutsy* musical; a lusty, bawdy reproduction of an era. I even tried to write realistic, non-theatrical lyrics.

Some of this nontheatrical attention to detail would come home to roost in Philadelphia just a few months later.

Before rehearsals began, after one postponement, Lerner and Loewe had another run-in with Cheryl Crawford. By the end of June, Lerner had completed the book, and Crawford immediately saw Walter Huston as "ideal for the lead," in the role of the prospector Ben Rumson. But she was treated to another Lerner and Loewe (mostly Lerner) jolt—"more shenanigans," as she termed this latest escapade.

On one of their periodic trips to the West Coast, the duo surreptitiously took over the office of casting, choosing "two performers whose work I had never seen," Crawford wrote in *One Naked Individual*. This did not sit well with her; it was her firm belief that "a producer should be involved in casting."

Lerner had his heart set on starring not Huston but another veteran of the theater, vaudeville, and films. James Barton was then best known for his portrayal of Jeeter Lester in the long-running *Tobacco Road* (1933), in which he replaced Henry Hull for two thousand performances. In vaudeville he had toured with a group known as the Garter Girls; as a headliner in "straight" vaudeville (i.e., not burlesque), he was celebrated for his drunk routine, which, it would later be revealed, Lerner recalled with enthusiasm. Barton's experience in musicals was not especially laudable: between 1919 (*The Passing Show*) and 1930 (*Sweet and Low*), he had been featured in some less-than-memorable shows. When *Paint Your Wagon* was being assembled, he had recently completed his part as Kit Carson in the film version of William Saroyan's *The Time of Your Life*, starring James Cagney. Kit Carson was a flamboyant, tall-tale-telling, hard-drinking cowboy; to Lerner, he *was* Ben Rumson. Crawford must have been familiar with some of Barton's work, even though he had not been on Broadway in twenty years.

The other Lerner-Loewe casting "coup" was suggested by Nancy Lerner, who remembered that at a typical Hollywood party they attended, she and her husband had been delighted by a young—in her early twenties—singer-dancer named Olga San Juan (who would indeed have been unknown to the nettled Cheryl Crawford). During the evening's entertainment she had followed no less than actor-turned-screenwriter Sid Silvers, Groucho Marx, and Danny Kaye, and had done an especially hilarious impersonation of Ethel Merman. She was hardly a newcomer to the entertainment business; Brooklyn-born, she had begun in show business at the age of eleven, dancing in night-clubs in Spanish Harlem. By thirteen she was leader of her own rumba band, which filled in for the big bands (led by Harry James and Jimmy Dorsey) at the Astor Room. A year later, singing and dancing at the Copacabana, she was spotted by a Hollywood scout and flown out to the Coast. Initially she appeared in musical film shorts (usually as a Latin); in her first feature film, *Rainbow Island* (1944), she was cast as a pretty islander. She did a "specialty number" in a spoof on the Frank Sinatra bobby-socks cult, but her first important musical was the Bing Crosby–Irving Berlin extravaganza *Blue Skies*, in which she sang, among other songs, "You'd Be Surprised" and "Heat Wave." She was married to actor Edmond O'Brien and was the mother of two young daughters.

When Olga San Juan arrived in New York in December 1950 (Crawford had conceded on Barton the month before), the producer greeted a slightly edgy Lerner with a wager: She bet him five dollars that *she* would not want the young woman to be their Jennifer. A few songs later, she handed Lerner five dollars.

Another "unknown," Tony Bavaar, was chosen to play opposite San Juan as her Mexican true love, Julio. Bavaar had made his mark early in band and radio appearances and nightclubs, and had been a winner on the popular "Arthur Godfrey Talent Scout" show. When "discovered" by Lerner and Loewe, he was hosting his own television show, "Club 7"; his voice and Latin good looks made him an ideal Julio, a choice to which Cheryl Crawford did not object.

The delayed rehearsals finally began in mid-August 1951, by which time there were a libretto and no less than twenty-nine songs. On September 11, the company left for Philadelphia for six days of rehearsals and a projected three-week run. It was not to be. "The script we used in Philadelphia was a great dramatic story," Bavaar recalled. "We rehearsed it that way, but it was too heavy for a musical comedy. So the author and composer tried to lighten it, make it more humorous."

Later, Lerner would admit that there were even more serious problems beyond the paucity of laughs; like Loewe, he was trying to create not a musical comedy, but a musical play. Having abandoned the idea of opening with the symbolic converging wagons, he instead began act 1, scene 1, with a burial on a hilltop in "Northern California. A Spring evening, 1853." Three people—Jennifer and Ben Rumson and another prospector—are seeing off a friend who, in Rumson's words, "was a good man, Lord. Never drank too much—'cept this time when he was so fallin'-down drunk he didn't even know the town was on fire." Lerner used the eulogy to establish three facts having nothing whatsoever to do with the deceased—that Jennifer is a mere sixteen, that Ben wishes her to get the education he has never had, and that he is a born wanderer. Then the point of the grave is made evident: in its excavation they find gold. The town of Rumson springs up on the spot, populated by hundreds of men and one very young woman.

By the time rehearsals began in Philadelphia, eight songs had been eliminated. Lerner then began adjusting the book. He found that when the scenes were rehearsed individually,

> the show was fine. But when we put all the scenes together, the show fell apart. . . .
>
> One of the problems was a confusion of style. The scenery [by Oliver Smith] and the dancing [by de Mille] matched; they were done impressionistically. The music and the book also matched, but they were done realistically. . . . Looking back, [he observed upon rewriting the show for a tour,] I realize that the play got watered down by compromise after compromise.

The collaborators wrote four new songs in Philadelphia, including a comedy number for Jennifer entitled "What's Goin' On Here?"—her reaction to the peculiar antics of the female-starved residents of Rumson—and "Wand'rin' Star," which Loewe considered the "theme song" of *Paint Your*

Wagon. A romantic ballad for the character of Julio, "Another Autumn," doubled as a dance number. "All for Him," also written for Jennifer, was replaced after the New York opening by what Loewe called "The Wagon Song" in the second act. "What's Goin' On Here?" added a touch of humor, but not enough. One song, "I Talk to the Trees," though among the show's most enduring, proved a headache for Lerner—"it drove me up the wall!"

The team began in its customary fashion. "We go through very precise steps, very slowly," Lerner told an interviewer.

> First, we decide where a song is needed in a play. Second, what is it going to be about? Third, we discuss the mood of the song. Fourth, I give [Loewe] a title. Then he writes the music to the title and the general feeling of the song is established. After he's written the melody, then I write the lyrics. Only twice have I written the lyrics in advance: "There but for You Go I" and "They Call the Wind Maria."

In the second scene of act 1, in which the settlement of Rumson is seen and celebrated in song, Jennifer appears to ponder the attitude of the male population:

> *I sit down to tie my shoe*
> *And ev'ry single time I do,*
> *I'm circled by a hundred men or more.*
> *What's goin' on here? What's goin' on?*
> *Ain't no one ever seen a shoe before?*

This seemed an ideal moment to introduce Jennifer's love interest, Julio. Unlike the men of Rumson, he is clean-shaven, darkly handsome, and, as a Mexican, something of an outsider—though clearly not to Jennifer. He evidently lives somewhere else but comes to Rumson to send out his laundry with the weekly pickup, which he has just missed (it takes a month for the laundry to come back). The two young people meet, and Julio tells Jennifer a little about himself. Lerner reasoned that if the young man lived alone in the hills, he would have no one to talk to—only the trees. His admission would contrast with Jennifer's mildly suggestive but puzzled questioning, a melodic, romantic song—in other words, a ballad (to be followed by the more rhythmic, boisterous "They Call the Wind Maria"). Lerner's point, once he solved his problem with the song, was that though Julio does talk to the trees, the stars, the wind, he has not been heard until now:

> *But suddenly my words*
> *Reach someone else's ears;*
> *Touch someone else's heartstrings too.*
>
> *I tell you my dreams,*
> *And while you're list'ning to me,*
> *I suddenly see them come true.*

Given the placement of the song, and its subject, mood, and title, in "I Talk to the Trees" Loewe created a beautiful, flowing melody, with a light undercurrent of Latin rhythms. The release, called "Interlude" by Loewe, is strongly accented, as Julio sings of his dreams come true:

> *I can see us on an April night*
> *Sipping brandy underneath the stars.*
> *Reading poems in the candlelight.*
> *To the strumming of guitars.*

Loewe's refrain—flowing, asymmetrical—did not lend itself to facile rhyming. The lyricist fretted over the effective and affecting melody but was ready to admit defeat; he may not literally have climbed the walls, but his nails and fingers suffered. He came up with a possible solution to the problem, a device that had served Ira Gershwin well in a quite different song, "I Got Rhythm," but whereas Gershwin had had to contend with short, staccato musical phrases, Lerner was faced with long, legato sections of melody. His fretting ended when he realized that he could write an almost conversational lyric by eliminating, as had Gershwin before him, the rhymes in the refrain (those in the Interlude remain).

Paint Your Wagon began its out-of-town tryout at the Shubert Theatre in Philadelphia on September 17, 1951, in anticipation of a three-week run. The reception, though not exactly cool, confirmed everyone's earlier assessment: "needs further work on the book." On the twenty-fourth, the *New York Times* reported that the Philadelphia run had been extended another two weeks to allow that further work. The Philadelphia reviewers found good words for the cast, songs, choreography, sets, and costumes but had trouble with Lerner's story. He and Loewe settled in for the hectic process of revision.

During this same period, the production suffered yet another affliction when two Philadelphia papers, the *Bulletin* and the *Inquirer*, carried
an announcement that an anonymous backer of *Paint Your Wagon* had
put his shares up for sale. Upsetting news for a company already on shaky
ground, this was an obvious attempt to scuttle the show; though the announcement did not denigrate the production, it damned it with faint
praise. There was, however, no rush to buy, nor did the other investors
panic. The anonymous backer, it was soon learned, was none other than
Cheryl Crawford's rival Billy Rose. His "unprofessional" conduct, as she
termed it, had little lasting effect on the still-troubled *Paint Your Wagon*;
as the company prepared for the Boston tryout, Lerner continued to reshape
his book.

During the previews, Sam Zolotow of the *New York Times* received a
telegram from one of his reporters in Boston, who had a "definite conviction
that Alan Jay Lerner is still fumbling around with the plot—that he practically loses it in the second act." The reporter also indicated that to his mind,
there was too much of James Barton. Frederick Loewe agreed with the assessment; after some thought, he acted.

Lerner had decided to write Barton's venerable drunk routine into the
show. The spot he chose for it came in act 1, scene 6, following Ben's purchase
of a bride from a passing Mormon who happens to have a bothersome extra
and determines—she being eager to get out of the marriage and the association with the other wife—to auction her off to the miners. Lerner gave Jennifer a good line here: "Auctioning you off?" she asks. "You mean like you was
pigfeed?"

So Ben (Barton) brings her home and gets inebriated. As time went by
(there would be an extra week in Boston, too, after Lerner introduced some
major revisions), to Crawford's distress, Barton's nine-minute scene "was
stretching to twenty, making it a disaster." Loewe, whose habit was to look in
on the show's progress only during the musical portions, was also disturbed.
As Barton extended his act, the wait between musical numbers was likewise
elongated, to the degree that the already tenuous plot got lost. Crawford and
a friend were sitting in a bar near the theater when Loewe, his face pink, ordered two large water glasses filled "to the top" with liquor.

"I'm going to talk to Barton right after the curtain," he informed them,
with what Crawford interpreted as an "ominous glare."

When the curtain came down on the first act, with an ensemble dance
by the fandangos and the miners to "There's a Coach Comin' In," Loewe en-

tered Barton's dressing room, handed him the drinks, and snapped, "Drink this down, Barton, you're going to need it!"

He went on, "I mean what I'm telling you—if your drunk scene routine gets beyond nine minutes again I am going to get a gun and I'm going to kill you. I'm a fine shot and you'd better believe what I say. That's all. Good night."

Barton complied.

That was a small improvement. Barton gleaned generally good reactions to the scene in the New York reviews, perhaps because the Manhattan reviewers (like Lerner) were more attuned to old-time vaudeville than was Frederick Loewe. The premiere of *Paint Your Wagon* in Boston brought out the best in the critics. Elliot Norton was in complete disagreement with the undercover critic from the *Times*, finding it to be a "masterful musical play, big, bright, swift and turbulent. Alan Jay Lerner is writing at the top of his form here." Lerner could now feel, at least to judge by the respected Norton's appraisal, that the "stresses and strains" observed by Olga San Juan in the final turbulent days before New York had been worth it. It was with some elation and sense of accomplishment that Lerner told the *New York Post*'s Vernon Rice, "We really tried integrating music, dialogue, dance and song. All of them became a musical item. This show has been staged in a real choreographic pattern."

Paint Your Wagon opened the following evening, November 12, 1951, at the Sam S. Shubert Theatre. By morning the votes were in. *Variety*'s "Hobe," being clinically professional, doubted that the show would earn back its $247,000 investment; he liked the songs and dances but concluded that the "pervading fault of the offering is the attenuated book," though he believed that the musical was a "bet for film adaptation." His review also reported something that had disturbed Lerner, too, on opening night. "Granted," Hobe wrote, "that a premiere audience can be abnormally unresponsive and that the theatre was oppressively over-heated, the opening night performance brought an uncomfortable amount of coughing, which is an unconscious and deadly form of customer criticism."

Two of the most musical of the critics, Richard Watts, Jr., of the *Post* and Walter Kerr of the *Herald Tribune*, found the evening short on humor. Watts brought up the "book trouble," and suggested that Lerner's attempts at comedy were "of very little help." Although he found much to admire in the lyrics and music, in the end he was "mildly disappointed." He, like the other reviewers, particularly applauded Barton's drunk routine—in its nine-minute version.

Kerr, the most analytical of the critics, devoted about a third of his review to the deficiency of fun in the show.

> Writing an "integrated" musical comedy—where the people are believable and the songs are logically introduced—is no excuse for not being funny. "South Pacific" is funny. But the librettist of "Paint Your Wagon" seems more interested in the authenticity of his background than in the joy of his audience. When he does try to be funny, the humor is half-hearted or, what is worse, labored. Someone in the dance-hall shouts that he is destitute. One of the girls on the second floor appears instantly, asking who called her. . . . The "musical play" that isn't funny had better be moving.

The de Mille dances provided more genuine emotion than Lerner's book, Kerr believed.

He missed, somehow, the quality of Lerner's lyrics, which he found to be "like the book—direct statements without much embellishment in the way of sentiment. They keep sounding like the cues which introduced them, plausible and matter-of-fact." It is curious that Kerr should have overlooked the "sentiment" of "I Still See Elisa" and "Another Autumn," both of which he mentioned favorably in his critique. He makes no reference to "I Talk to the Trees."

The New Yorker's Wolcott Gibbs was the most negative, praising Loewe—who, he stated, had been most "responsible for the success of *Brigadoon*"—at Lerner's expense. "The lyrics," he wrote, "are the work of Alan Jay Lerner, who is also credited with the book, though it is hard to believe everybody around the premises didn't just make that up as they went along." The lyrics, he indicated, lacked Oscar Hammerstein's "honest sentiment" and the "wonderful ingenuity" of Cole Porter and Lorenz Hart, though admittedly they were "cheerful and . . . eminently suitable to the period and locale." The critic, or "grave dancer," Lerner asserted, could never resist an opportunity to prove himself a wit as well as a writer, and accordingly, Gibbs's piece both gave some and took some. He bestowed a uniqueness on the show, parenthetically: "(*Paint Your Wagon* is the only musical I can recall in which the ladies of the chorus do not put in their appearance until the final scene of the first act.)"

The nine scenes before this one dwelled on the female shortage, the boisterousness and loneliness of the hirsute miners, the purchase of a bride, and the arrival of the coachful of fandangos; scene 10 itself consisted of an energetic ensemble dance. The critics' consensus was that the first act, despite its preoccupation with the miners' frustrations, was good, lively musical entertainment, and all mentioned several favored songs. It was the second act, introducing the young lovers (Walter Kerr called it a "rather tenuous and deflated romance") and tracing the death of the town of Rumson after its lode runs out, that raised critical hackles. Hobe referred to it as the "shorter though long-seeming second act."

Just as the first act concluded with a dance sequence, the second began with one. In "Hand Me Down That Can o' Beans," a couple of miners announce their intention to throw the can out the window and go out on the town for a real dinner with one or another of the fandangos. A kind of hoedown endowed with an authentic essence, it leads into the dancing in "Jake's Palace," plus a rope dance and a cancan. While the critics praised the dancing, Lerner felt that the sequence "was so long it was difficult to remember the plot when it reappeared."

He was cheered by the "excellent" review in the *Times* by the town's most powerful critic, Brooks Atkinson. From its first sentence it was warming:

> By mixing Western gold dust with show vitality, the authors of *Paint Your Wagon* have produced a bountiful and exultant musical jubilee. . . . Mr. Lerner and Mr. Loewe have latched on to a yarn about the gold rush in 1853. In the simplest terms, *Paint Your Wagon* is concerned with the fact that there are too many men and not enough women in the mining camps. On the spur of the moment it is a little hard to explain how this situation results in some lusty ballads, some scorching ballets, James Barton's illustrious drunk routine and Olga San Juan's cameo loveliness and sprite-like singing.

But there was more: Atkinson expanded on his rather brief daily review in a Sunday column devoted to a comparison of *Top Banana* (which had opened eleven days before and starred Phil Silvers) and *Paint Your Wagon*, to the disadvantage of the former. Johnny Mercer, admired for his lyrics, had produced both words and music for *Top Banana*, but Atkinson dismissed the score as "negligible—hardly more than a reflex action to the necessity of having something that passes for music in a musical show." In contrast, Frederick Loewe—"a gifted composer"—had written the "most accomplished music

Broadway had fallen heir to since *The King and I* and *Guys and Dolls*." As for Lerner, Atkinson reported, the

> author of *Brigadoon* has written a more literate book. He is trying to recapture some of the comic naïveté of life in an old mining town. In the second act he runs into some mass resistance that impedes the movement of the production [too much ballet, Atkinson supposed], but the first act is freely sketched, spontaneous and convivial. As a whole *Paint Your Wagon* is heartily enjoyable [, though] a job of loosening and shortening the second act might still be worth attempting.

In the end it was the show's advance ticket sales that kept it going, not Atkinson's enthusiasm or John Chapman's unqualified rave in the *News*, which could not make up for the negativism of the other reviewers. By May 1952 James Barton, claiming illness, had left the show; his replacement was Eddie Dowling, a veteran of musicals and dramas who had starred in William Saroyan's *The Time of Your Life* in 1939. By June the box office was showing some strain, and *Paint Your Wagon* closed, ostensibly for a three-week "vacation." It closed officially on July 19, with a loss of $95,000. A tour was arranged in an effort to wipe out the debt, but that failed, too.

Lerner tried; to some degree, he took Atkinson's friendly criticism to heart. "I talked to a lot of people about the show," he said about the tour version,

> and I listened to their criticisms. Finally, I sat down and rewrote it. The really important thing is that my original intentions for the show [were] still valid and worthwhile. I believe in an honest reproduction of life on the musical stage. I believe in the gutsy musical I tried to do. I believe that musical theatre has to welcome that kind of treatment of earthy people.

The tour began in August, with folksinger-actor Burl Ives in the role of Ben Rumson. It did reasonably well until it got to Chicago, where it opened at the Blackstone Theatre on Friday, January 30, 1953, and, "after two reviewers jumped all over the production," closed on Saturday. When it premiered in London the next month, the critic for *Punch* was particularly hostile, musing that "Congreve's comments on this adolescent and witless ferment would have been worth hearing." The same reviewer then extrapolated a more general thesis: "During the last few years," he wrote, "the makers of American musicals have exploited every imaginable contemporary situation in which uninhibited young morons can find themselves sinking for want of female company."

But the saga was not over.

As has been predicted in *Variety*, *Paint Your Wagon* was "slow" to pay off its backers, but as was also predicted, it proved highly suitable for film adaptation. This process would take a number of years, but the story is worth telling here in its entirety as an illustration of Alan Lerner's working methods over time.

Thanks to a curious series of events, the screen credits for the film version, when it was finally released, included the line "An Alan Jay Lerner Production"; in this, his third attempt, he was determined to do the play his way. But in 1953 that was still a long way off.

Despite the mostly lukewarm reviews, Metro-Goldwyn-Mayer was interested in *Paint Your Wagon*. The studio's experience with Lerner had been good that year, from *Royal Wedding* in March to *An American in Paris*, which opened on November 9, 1951, three days before *Paint Your Wagon*. The evolution of the filmed *Paint Your Wagon* had actually begun earlier in the year, with the resignation of Louis B. Mayer from the company he had helped to found in 1924. As chief of production, he had fallen into severe disfavor with the New York office—the financial headquarters of MGM, run by Nicholas M. Schenck—over the disastrous and much-mutilated (for budgetary reasons) *Red Badge of Courage*. John Huston's adaptation of Stephen Crane's Civil War classic became a box-office failure of great magnitude on its 1951 release; a furious Schenck wanted Mayer's hide, but Mayer beat him to it by resigning on June 22.

Mayer got his revenge by founding Louis B. Mayer Enterprises with Jack Cummings, a producer with several well-received MGM musicals to his credit, among them *Three Little Words*, *Lovely to Look At*, *Kiss Me Kate*, and *Seven Brides for Seven Brothers*. In June 1957 it was announced that Mayer's company had acquired the screen rights to *Paint Your Wagon* for $200,000. The project was peculiar from the start, in that the rights were bought with Gary Cooper in mind for the Ben Rumson part. Barton, the original Ben, had not been much of a singer, but his whispered rendition of "I Still See Elisa" had been one of the touching high points of the show. It was obvious that Cooper was being considered for his name, not his vocal abilities (if any). And there was more: the screenplay was to be entrusted to John Lee Mahin (whose credits included *Captains Courageous* and *Quo Vadis*, among others) and William Ludwig (the Andy Hardy series, *The Great Caruso*, etc.), not to Alan Jay Lerner. Filming was scheduled to start in September, with Lerner and Loewe, so stated the press release, providing the additional songs that would be required for the "opened-up" Cinerama musical.

Loewe, in London at the time, was not terribly interested in participating, so other plans were implemented. Lerner was infuriated by a second press release naming Arthur Schwartz as the composer of the new songs and giving the impression (Lerner thought) that Schwartz would be writing an entirely new score for the film. The lyricist immediately approached *Variety* to put matters straight, and the paper reported that "Lerner stresses that Louis B. Mayer merely wanted a new tunesmith who was 'more familiar with film scores.'"

"The facts were distorted in such a way that a very important composer, and one of my closest friends," Lerner told *Variety*,

was [the] victim of an unfortunate news item. The facts are that the entire score of *Paint Your Wagon* is not being scrapped at all. The additional songs Arthur Schwartz is supplying result purely and simply from the plot changes that are necessary in converting the stage property to the new medium. In other words, in order to take advantage of the scope of Cinerama, new dramatic situations are being created and these new situations will require appropriate music. Wherever incidents of the stage play are retained so will be the stage music. The article makes it appear that Loewe's score is for some reason inadequate which is far from the case. The score not only received better notices than my book and lyrics but won *Variety*'s critical poll. . . . Loewe is too respected as a creative artist and too wonderful a man to be hurt by a needless error in facts.

He did not mention that Loewe, quite graciously, had turned down his request to work on the film.

Lerner was in California at the time for conferences in connection with another film; Schwartz was also there, for talks with Mayer. Their short-lived collaboration ended that same year with the death of Mayer. Unable to let go of the project, Lerner decided to do it himself, and to make it an "Alan Jay Lerner Production." It would be his third and final rewrite.

By the time he got to that point, seventeen years after *Paint Your Wagon*'s Broadway debut, he was *the* Alan Jay Lerner, with the success of *My Fair Lady*, among others, behind him. He had scripted several important films and felt that he could now produce his "gutsy" musical.

His choice for director was Joshua Logan, known on Broadway for his work on such musicals as *Annie Get Your Gun, South Pacific* (whose film version he had also directed), and *Wish You Were Here*, a show he almost single-handedly converted from a flop into a hit. This plus some film experience made him a natural in Lerner's estimation, but Logan himself was not so sure. "Frankly," he later admitted, "I was hesitant about doing [it] when Alan Lerner offered it to me. I thought the original show was weak, although it had great songs. Alan said that he never liked the story and suggested that Paddy Chayevsky adapt his book for the screen." This was accomplished through a series of long conferences—some, according to Logan, lasting "two weeks"—during which the three decided how the play would be translated onto film.

Chayevsky was, in some ways, a curious choice. He had begun in television, making a deep impression with his teleplay *Marty*, a touching story about two lonely, shy people, a butcher and a schoolteacher; his screen adaptation had won him an Academy Award in 1955. Another of his finest works was the adaptation of William Bradford Huie's cynical look at war, *The Americanization of Emily* (1964). On Broadway he had made a small ripple in the mainstream with *Middle of the Night*, a 1956 play about a middle-aged "Manufacturer" (as he is identified in the cast list) in love with a very young "Girl"; his screenplay was filmed three years later. By coincidence, Joshua Logan had been the producer-director of the original Broadway play.

When *Paint Your Wagon* was released, by Paramount, in 1969, the screen credits read "Lyrics and Screenplay by Alan Jay Lerner, Adaptation by Paddy Chayevsky." Much of Loewe's original score remained, though there were additional songs with music by André Previn. In comparing the Broadway show to the film, historian-biographer Stanley Green noted that the latter, "with Clint Eastwood, Lee Marvin and Jean Seberg[,] told another story."

Indeed it did.

Lerner opened the film with a funeral, as before, to allow the gold to be discovered. Since all the action was shot in the great outdoors (an area near East Eagle Creek, Oregon, stood in for•northern California), the funeral is predicated by the wagon's plunging down a steep hill, killing a young prospector and seriously injuring his brother. Witness to this is the film's Ben Rumson (played by Lee Marvin), himself a prospector with a mule. It is

Rumson who leads the burial group, stakes the claim, and takes on the surviving brother, a naive Michigan farmer (Eastwood) whom he dubs simply "Pardner."

In the film variant of his play, Lerner made a number of drastic and, as some have suggested, damaging changes. Writing in the free-wheeling sixties, he could make use of more sophisticated, "adult" situations and characters; he could be even more realistic than he had intended in 1951. The dedicated romantic in fact tampered with his own original conception, retaining the Mormon theme but eliminating the gentle father-daughter motif. There is no Jennifer in the film, only a Mormon woman, Elizabeth (Jean Seberg), of strong mind and beautiful face and arresting body. Lerner's ingenious twist on the theme was to endow *her*, before the film is over, with two spouses.

With the pragmatic Elizabeth herself encouraging the auction and proposing the ménage à trois, some of the sweetness of the original *Paint Your Wagon* is eliminated. The tone of the plot is hard: It is a man's world, but as the only woman in town until Ben kidnaps a stagecoachful of tarts, Elizabeth, too, is resilient and uncompromising, running her peculiar household with an iron hand. She is no stock character, not the compliant and admiring "little woman" of the more or less classic Westerns. The male protagonists, in contrast, are standard Western characters, and the Marvin-Eastwood bond between opposites renders *Paint Your Wagon* a conventional buddy movie. The Marvin character is scruffy, hard-drinking, and admittedly shifty (though he would never cheat a partner)—the quintessential roving mountain man of the period. Eastwood, fresh from a series of very successful gunfighter films made in Italy (the infamous but profitable "spaghetti Westerns"), plays an honest, clean-cut farmer (he is virtually the only member of the cast, excepting of course the handful of women, without a beard) who is seeking his fortune in order to return to farming. This latter sentiment is shared by Elizabeth, who wants—and gets—her own cabin; but the other half of her complement of husbands was born, in Lerner's phrase, "under a wandrin' star."

Instead of being the town's leading citizen, as in the two preceding versions of the story, Ben Rumson is here just another drunken miner, though apparently a wealthy one. The boomtown of Rumson is now called No Name City—"Population: Male."

The setting, a spectacular Oregon forest with a stream running through an authentic reproduction of a forty-niner mining camp, was in keeping with Lerner's passionate research. A city consisting predominantly of tents, a crude general store doubling as a saloon, flumes (overhead sluices of wood to carry water), a flutter wheel to lift the water from the stream to the sluices, mud and more mud—all these provided Logan with the means to compose his frames. There were long-shot vistas for the kidnapping of the Frenchwomen on the stagecoach as it rushes through the countryside against a background of hills, a lake, and distant snow-covered mountains; one medium shot—almost a still—for the "They Call the Wind Maria" sequence, is strikingly like a period photograph. And as Eastwood, alone on the screen, sings "I Talk to the Trees," the camera affectingly, though perhaps rather obviously, mixes close-ups with long shots, so that the audience sees the trees he talks to. Visually, the filmed *Paint Your Wagon* is compelling, but something is missing.

The contribution of Agnes de Mille, which so excited the original's reviewers, was eliminated for this version. The film's one dance sequence—a rowdy, athletic lurching of men in a muddy street—is decidedly unchoreographed. There is no show-stopping dance scene in the casino-brothel—merely a teeming assemblage of drinkers and gamblers. In short, Logan wanted none of de Mille's dazzling high stepping; the ultimate *Paint Your Wagon*, save for the strong, uncompromising Elizabeth, is at heart a man's picture.

The "adaptation" and direction also affected the score. Of Loewe's original eighteen songs, only eight were retained; six new tunes were written by Previn. What remained of Loewe's contribution worked well in the plot, but "I Still See Elisa" was thrown away, its point and its poignancy lost in the translation. Likewise pared away were the fine ballad "Another Autumn" and, because there was no longer a Mexican leading man, the haunting "Carino Mio."

Still, the film version features an outstanding ballad by Previn and Lerner, "A Million Miles Away behind the Door," the Elizabeth character's one song (dubbed by Anita Gordon). It is one of the lyricist's most poetic expressions, about the gentle goodness of sheltered roots. Lerner begins with:

> *Send back the world*
> *There's too much night for me.*
> *The sky is much too high*
> *To shelter me when darkness falls.*

His rhyme scheme is unusual: There are two refrains of ten lines each (no verse) and a concluding five-line statement, a kind of philosophical summation ending with the restatement of the title line. The first line in each major section has no rhyme, nor does the third; then, unexpectedly, lines four and five form a couplet. Only then does the second line rhyme (an internal rhyme, at that) with line six—so that in the first chorus, line two,

> *There's too much night for me,*

goes with line six,

> *Would be just right for me.*

Likewise, in the second chorus,

> *There's too much view for me*

is paired with

> *One room will do for me.*

The last four lines consist of two couplets.

The song is so effective that its unusual rhyming pattern seems perfectly logical; whatever damage Lerner may have done to his plot, his lyrical touch was as deft as ever.

The remaining Previn tunes are linked to character and plot, as with Ben Rumson's cynical "The First Thing You Know":

> *God made the mountains,*
> *God made the sky,*
> *God made the people,*
> *God knows why.*

This misanthropy is what feeds Ben's wanderlust; he trusts no one except his partner and their wives (though he has a special disdain for farmers, characteristic of mountain men of the period, for farmers inevitably brought civilization and its impediments: fences, churches, law). When Ben and a few of his friends begin undermining the town, retrieving the gold dust that has wafted through the rough-hewn floors of the gambling halls and saloons, they sing the praises of gold and declare that "The Best Things in Life Are Dirty." This digging will usher in the film's apocalyptic finale, as predicted by the fire-and-brimstone parson in his "Gospel of No Name City" (whose sign now states "No Name City/Population: Drunk"). Neither the character of the preacher (of no designated denomination) nor the destruction of the town had figured in either of Lerner's earlier versions of his play.

In the gospel, the parson exhorts:

Will you go to heav'n, will you go to hell?
Miners: Go to hell!
Either repent or fare thee well.
Miners: Fare thee well!
God will take care of No Name City.
Comes the end, it won't be pretty.

Three times he prophesies the end of the wicked town:

Here's what He's gonna do:
Gobble up this town
And swallow it down
And good-bye to you!

When, in 1952, the first revision of *Paint Your Wagon* was staged, Frederick Loewe had confidently stated that he and Lerner were "not interested" in writing musical comedies. The slapstick in the film, at times on a Three Stooges level (literally: characters slap faces, dodge long boards carried by co-workers, etc.), could only have distressed him—to say nothing of what was done to his score.

Marvin's performance, despite some subtle touches here and there, is quite broad; for much of the early part of the film, he merely continues in the role of the drunk cowboy he portrayed in *Cat Ballou*. Instead of letting the town simply die when the gold runs out, as it does in the play version, Lerner, with Chayevsky and Logan, opted for a smashing conclusion that was almost impossible to stage, in which virtually the entire town sinks into the earth or falls into the street. The scene was played for laughs. When a steer, imported for a Sunday bull-and-bear fight, falls into Ben's underground labyrinth, along with the parson, there is a good deal of scurrying around the diggings as Ben and Parson try to keep out of harm's way. Walls collapse around people, beds occupied by tarts and their clients catapult into the street, and so on—in color and Vistavision.

The implausible miracle of this shambles is that there appear to be no casualties. Once the manmade tremors have stopped, the wagons are loaded up (a roll call would reveal that all who were there at the beginning are there at the end), and everyone leaves No Name City, even Ben—or especially Ben, who must move on to the next gold find. The story ends happily, and without rancor, as Ben and Pardner bid manly farewells and Pardner turns away to enter their cabin, where he and Elizabeth will remain to farm. Ben joins the exodus to the strains of "Wand'rin Star," sung by the men's chorus.

"*Paint Your Wagon* was resoundingly booed at home, with occasional exception, and resoundingly cheered abroad," Lerner noted in *The Street Where I Live*, pointing out with undisguised satisfaction that in the end, the film "grossed a startlingly large sum of money."

In his translation of the musical play to film (with a time gap of nearly two decades, during which the social climate of the United States seethed with protest, and the arts, including film, turned raw), Lerner exploited the new freedoms and turned his quasi–folk tale from racy to raunchy. An aura of meanness afflicts the screenplay, as manifested by the corpse that flies out of its grave when gold is found, the arrant greed, Marvin's overdone inebriation, the kidnapping of the French prostitutes, and the lack of sufficient romance—Lerner's forte—to carry the score. The sprawling, brawling rough-and-tumble (which was perhaps not too far from the truth) may have impressed and entertained European audiences who loved Westerns, but it did not play well with home audiences or critics. Pauline Kael, in *The New Yorker*, put her critical finger on one of the film's most obvious features. It was, she noted, one of the most expensive musicals ever filmed, and she suggested *Paint Your Wagon* may have "finally broken the back of the American film industry." Vincent Canby of the *Times* was disturbed by the "rather peculiar psychological implications in the plot"—the Pardner–Ben Rumson relationship. Joshua Logan's direction of the crowd scenes, Canby wrote, "rocked with the sort of rousing, somewhat artificial, hearty masculinity that marked Logan's biggest hits, *South Pacific* and *Mr. Roberts*" and that the "Sodom and Gomorrah parallels are neither profound nor funny." One reviewer simply concluded that the film sank "inexorably like a dead tree in quicksand."

Lerner had better luck, though with some qualification, with his first adaptation of one of his works from stage to screen. In the early spring of 1952, with the stage *Paint Your Wagon* getting along reasonably well at the Shubert, Nancy and Alan Lerner, with their daughter Liza, who had been born the past November, settled into a bungalow in the Bel Air Hotel in Beverly Hills. Although pregnant (a second daughter, Jennifer, would be born in the summer), Nancy Olson planned to work in films while her husband attended to the screenplay for *Brigadoon*, slated to be filmed by the Freed Unit at Metro. His devoted agent Lillie Messinger (once a trusted aide and adviser to Louis B. Mayer) arranged for a recent UCLA graduate named Doris Warshaw to serve as his secretary for a couple of weeks while he crafted the script. Pretty, in her early twenties, Warshaw was delighted when anyone remarked on her resemblance to screen star Ava Gardner; though by then a confirmed Californian, she had spent the first sixteen years of her life in New York, where she had attended the prestigious High School of Music and Art.

She and Messinger had met while working for what both regarded as a corrupt, pimpish talent agency. After Mayer's death, MGM had no further use for Lillie Messinger's considerable talents; out of school, Doris Warshaw set out in the world. They slipped the bonds of the agency as soon as possible but remained good friends. Messinger had an uncanny gift for bringing the right people together, and she believed her young friend might prove valuable to her beloved Alan.

Warshaw, who had moved in a circle of artists (her brother was the renowned painter Howard Warshaw), writers, and serious musicians, nurtured, as she put it, an "ignorant indifference to Broadway musicals." She was aware of Lerner and Loewe, for she had heard Messinger speak glowingly of them (especially Lerner), but she had never seen any of their shows, nor did she know which of them wrote the words and which the music.

She associated the name Lerner with an earlier time, when, at eighteen, fresh out of high school, she had helped "put him through Harvard" (never mind the anachronism), for eighteen dollars a week, "selling $3.98 blouses and sweaters" in one of his father's shops—a shop, she recalled, that was "operated on the principles of terror and slavery." Having experienced the distant reach of the father's firm hand, she imagined it would be an adventure to know the son whom Lillie Messinger regarded as a genius. Would she like working for this gifted child of privilege? Would she even like *him?*

Arriving at his bungalow, she knocked and was summoned in. The still-boyish Lerner did not rise but sat barefoot, with pad in his lap. He was resplendent in cream slacks and a yellow turtleneck, with his daugher Liza at his knees. In another room, Nancy Lerner and a maid were unpacking.

"You're about to save my life," Lerner told her with the "sweetest smile that ever came to rest on a martyr's lips." Domesticity, she sensed, was not conducive to concentrated work, and, as he informed her in the next breath, he was on a deadline. To her, as to so many other women, he was a "charmer": as the object of his affection and attention, you were special—and as she would realize years later, "Alan was genuinely sincere for the full length of each encounter."

He asked her to take the chair opposite him, and they began work on

Brigadoon; the two-week assignment would stretch into an exciting, some-times troubled, even frantic fourteen years.

Lerner, she noted, "wrote out loud." As he refashioned his book for the screen, he would talk the story and dialogue, and she would take it all down in shorthand, often aware that he was studying her for any reaction to what he had conceived. Once Lerner felt comfortable with the work, Warshaw would type up the script. She was captivated by this compact, dynamic man, who took the opportunity to educate her in the songs of the American musical. As he played and sang at the small, white upright in the workroom, she began to appreciate the genius of the other half of the team, Frederick Loewe, particu-larly when Lerner ran through "Another Autumn."

His screenplay followed the musical's book closely, with minor excep-tions allowing for the use of film (intercutting, for example, eliminated the necessity for the stage scene changes). The film opens with the lost hunters, whose dialogue, taken virtually word-for-word from the stage musical, estab-lishes their characters—one a romantic (Gene Kelly) who is unsure about his approaching marriage, the other a cynic (Van Johnson) who only believes in things he "can touch, taste, hear, see, smell, and [taking out a flask] swallow."

The scene shifts to the village of Brigadoon coming to life, following the original book with the "MacConnachy Square" number, paralleling the Broadway version scene for scene.

The most significant change was a matter of emphasis. Whereas the original *Brigadoon* had been primarily a singing show enhanced by de Mille's choreography, with Kelly heading the cast of the film version (he had a small though pleasant voice), dancing tended to dominate. Casting Cyd Charisse in the female lead reinforced this, as would have been the case, too, with Freed's first choice, the British ballerina Moira Shearer, who was unavailable.

One obstacle Lerner encountered was the Breen Office. Enforcing the Production Code of the motion-picture industry, the censors practically elim-inated the musical's hoydenish comic character, the man-hunting Meg. Her two mildly wicked songs were early casualties: the first about how she willingly lets herself be exploited by men, "The Love of My Life"; the second, her big number in act 2 of the play, a description of "My Mother's Weddin' Day," a celebration of alcohol:

> The people were lyin' all over the room,
> A-lookin' as if they were dead.
> But Mother uncovered the minister quick,

An' she told 'im: Go ahead.
So Pa kneeled down on Bill MacRae,
An' Mother kneeled down on Jock MacKay;
The preacher stood on John MacVay;
An' that's how my ma was wed.
It was a sight beyond compare.
I ought to know, for I was there.

The last line especially bothered Joseph Breen, and the song was cut. Meg herself thus virtually disappeared from the screenplay, and with her went some of the fun. No new songs were written to fill the two empty spots, which were instead covered by extended dances, choreographed by Gene Kelly, not Agnes de Mille.

Lerner made another plot change as well. A rejected lover, bitter over a wedding he believes should be his, decides to escape from Brigadoon. He knows that should anyone leave the village, its magic spell will be broken and Brigadoon will disappear forever. A wild balletic chase ensues. In the show, the unhappy Harry Beaton is tripped while running through the forest, falls, and is killed when his head strikes a rock; the tripper is the cynical American. In the film, Harry Beaton is shot by the hero's friend, who thinks he has spotted a bird in a tree; thus Brigadoon is saved by the one man who does not believe in its magic. Like the musical play, the film ends happily, but not before some twists and turns. The two men leave Brigadoon after Tommy (Kelly) decides not to remain, as planned, and spend eternity with Fiona. Back home but still haunted by thoughts of Fiona and Brigadoon, he changes his mind again in a nightclub scene with his fiancée. Soon he and Jeff (Johnson) are back at the site of the magical village. There is one final miracle as the mists dissolve and Brigadoon reappears for long enough to allow Tommy and Fiona to reunite to the strains of the title song.

Brigadoon was not one of Vincente Minnelli's more vivacious efforts, even with all its CinemaScope possibilities. Despite its heathery vistas, the film was shot on a 600-by-60-foot set on Metro's Stage 15. Some of the Minnelli flair is evident in the opening MacConnachy Square sequence, with its lively but not especially original number "I'll Go Home with Bonnie Jean." Kelly's solo to "Almost Like Being in Love" seems strained and longish. Only the wedding scene and the chase that follows truly reveal the Minnelli touch; evidently his heart was not in this film, even though Arthur Freed had informed Lerner, before shooting began, that "Vincente is bubbling over with enthusiasm about *Brigadoon*." Part of the problem was that he and Kelly, as Kelly put it, were "never in synch." Also according to Kelly, Minnelli once confessed that he "hadn't liked the Broadway show at all." Freed had one Minnelli opinion, and Kelly another.

Although Kelly and Minnelli may not have been entirely "in synch," they nonetheless entered into a connivance when filming began in December of 1953: They improvised around the Lerner script as they went along, changing the dialogue, "touching it up." When Lerner heard about this via the studio grapevine, he stormed into Freed's office and then, fuming, stalked onto Stage 15. Confronting the offenders, he said, "I know I can write better than anybody on this set. So, if you want anything changed, ask me." There were no further changes.

The finished *Brigadoon*, released early in September 1954, has little of the spark of the stage version; the pacing is often turgid, and the obviously painted backdrops are distracting, though the painted sumac doubles effectively for the hillside heather. Although it was reasonably well received (and slightly profitable: cost, $2,352,625; gross, $3,385,000), *Brigadoon* proved a disappointment to Lerner, who considered it "one of those ventures that occur so often where we all knew we were going down the wrong road but no one could stop." His own major criticisms had to do with the use of a soundstage rather than location shooting in Scotland (where the weather might have been a serious problem); the fact that "it was a singing show that tried to become a dancing show"; and, curiously, his conviction that the cast should have been ethnically proper (conveniently ignoring the fact that the cast of the stage show had been all-American).

"After *Brigadoon* it was all downhill," Lerner wrote in *The Street Where I Live*. Not quite, for then he goes into the fate of *Huckleberry Finn*, ignoring the film that followed.

Huckleberry Finn was in fact written in the happy wake of *Royal Wedding*, not of the unhappy film *Brigadoon*. Freed, who regarded the Mark Twain classic as the "best book written in America," had been planning a musical film version since 1944. Sally Benson, whose *New Yorker* stories had provided the plot for one of Freed's—and Minnelli's—finest screen musicals, *Meet Me in St. Louis*, was signed to write the screenplay. Songwriters Hugh Martin and Ralph Blane, likewise veterans of that film, were assigned to do the score. By early 1946 the production was ready to go, with Claude Jarman, Jr., who had achieved star status as the boy in *The Yearling*, set to portray Huck. Then, with three musicals already in production and one on temporary hold because of the death of his friend Jerome Kern, an overworked Freed decided to post-pone the filming of *Huckleberry Finn*.

Four years later he would turn to it again, this time with an entirely dif-ferent cast of characters. Donald Ogden Stewart, much admired for his screen adaptations of the successful Broadway plays *Life with Father* and *The Philadelphia Story*, was called in to write the script, and Burton Lane and lyri-cist E. Y. Harburg (creators of *Finian's Rainbow*) were hired to compose a new score. Stewart had just completed the first draft when, in May 1950, Joseph McCarthy, the zealous Wisconsin Red-hunter, turned his baleful eye on Hol-lywood left-wingers, who were worth more newspaper space than either State Department or U.S. Army officials. Both Stewart and Harburg had been ac-tive in what was called "progressive" political thinking, and both had been publicly pro–Soviet Union during a period (the Second World War) when most Americans were likewise kindly disposed toward a wartime ally. Stewart and Harburg fell victim to the witch-hunt; the former fled to a then more tol-erant Britain, while the latter would not work in Hollywood for another dozen years, until finally teaming up with composer Harold Arlen to write the songs for the Judy Garland cartoon film *Gay Purr-ee*.

Lane and Harburg had finished three songs when Freed realized that Harburg had to go. Lane was not especially distressed by the news, for he did not much care for what they had done up to that point, and had already told Freed about it. Happy with the results of *Royal Wedding*, which Lerner and Lane had only recently completed, Freed gave them the job.

Lerner and Freed met in New York in early January 1951 to consider how to handle the sprawling tale of a wily orphan and a runaway slave drifting from one adventure to another on the Mississippi. Rather than attempting to tra-verse the total plot of the novel, Lerner suggested that it might make more sense to concentrate first on Huck and Jim and then on the misadventures of the two riverboat frauds who call themselves the Duke and the Dauphin. Danny Kaye, with his gift for pantomime, was immediately envisioned as the Dauphin, who poses as a deaf man; Gene Kelly, meanwhile, would make a fine Duke, a kind of Mississippi River Pal Joey. As the idea took shape, Dean Stockwell was selected as Huck, and William Warfield as Jim. Although he was also then engaged in the creation of *Paint Your Wagon*, Lerner began work on the film.

"When Arthur put Alan on the project," Burton Lane told Hugh Fordin, "everything started to happen. I became very excited and the songs came fast." By July 12, with rehearsals for *Paint Your Wagon* impending, Lane and

Lerner had finished more than half a dozen songs. The pressure had taken its toll, Lerner informed Freed: "I now weigh twenty-two pounds and have the color of the pages of the first edition of Dante's *Inferno*." But he assured the producer,

> Yes, I'm really enclosing a lyric. And there isn't one line missing! I hope the shock won't be too great.
> "I'm from Missouri" is in the works and I'll have it in a few days at the least. "I'll Wait for You by the River" has two lines missing. Gene's number ["The World's Full o' Suckers"] I'll get to next week-end.

He signed off with "Love, love, love" and gave himself a special position at Metro: "Fourth Assistant/To the Second Secretary/Of the First Ass-Kisser/Of the Head of the Music/Department."

As it turned out, however, "Gene's number" would never be filmed. Rehearsals for the musical film of Mark Twain's classic began at the end of August 1951, while Kelly was still shooting *Singin' in the Rain*. But suddenly, four days after the distressed *Paint Your Wagon* premiered in Philadelphia, Freed asked Minnelli to come to his office; on September 21, *Huckleberry Finn* was canceled. Kelly had decided to take advantage of a newly contrived tax loophole that enabled American citizens to live abroad tax-free for eighteen months or more. When his studio contract came up for renewal, he instructed his agent to renegotiate for what Lerner caustically called "tax-free loot." No attempt was made to force Kelly to make the film, nor to find another Duke; *Huckleberry Finn* simply closed down. Lerner had no time to fret over this, even though he considered the screenplay and songs "some of the best stuff I've ever written"; his energy was by now consumed with *Paint Your Wagon* repairs.

Kelly went off to Paris, had an appendectomy in Switzerland, and then proceeded to Munich and finally to England, to make a film that Freed said publicly he did not want to do. The result, a hodgepodge entitled *Invitation to the Dance*, was an all-dancing-plus-ballet extravaganza that would prove to be Kelly's least successful effort. This was little consolation for Lerner, who never forgot the star's defection.

Almost immediately after finishing *Brigadoon* in 1954, Lerner began a project that he neglected to mention in his autobiography, an adaptation of W. H. Hudson's fantasy *Green Mansions*. Set in a South American jungle, the novel tells the tragic story of the bird-girl Rima and a young outsider's ill-fated love for her. For Lerner it was a time of troubles: His father's health was deteriorating rapidly, his own was somewhat precarious, and he was overwhelmed by self-pity, believing that he was finished in the musical theater. Despite all of this, he drafted a scene with which director Vincente Minnelli could test the first candidate for the part of Rima, Pier Angeli, whose sensitive features and delicate body made her look right for the part (Italian-born, she had been appearing in American films since 1951, though would not have much of a career in Hollywood). Sending the scene along to Freed, Lerner referred to the script as "my lover"; it was his idea that Rima might speak like a bird. Minnelli, concurring, hoped for long stretches of bird sounds rather than dialogue. If the concept had worked, the film would have been highly original, but when Freed saw the finished test, he decided that no one, not even the ethereal Pier Angeli, could make Rima believable. He abandoned the project in October 1954. (A film version was later made starring Audrey Hepburn; Lerner's script was jettisoned because, in the opinion of producer Pandro S. Berman, the movie needed a "little more *Tarzan* and *King Solomon's Mines*." Released in 1959, *Green Mansions* was a major failure at the box office.)

The rejection of a screenplay he loved—with a romantic, fantastic, exotic, beautiful setting—depressed Lerner, but he was embarked on an uphill journey, not a downhill one. While that journey would not be without its obstacles, he would achieve pinnacles on Broadway and in Hollywood that he had not dared dream of. Besides, he owed Freed one more screenplay.

7

—𝔪—

CROSSROAD

WHEN THE LERNERS returned to Manhattan in the summer of 1954, Alan Lerner's spirits were "at a low ebb." He was, Nancy Lerner sensed, "truly at a crossroad."

In tears, he told her, "Nothing is working." He was dismayed by the "mediocrity" of the film version of *Brigadoon*, which was scheduled to be released in September; *Green Mansions* was a dead issue, and the project he and Arthur Schwartz had begun the previous year had fizzled out because he simply could not get a handle on it. This latter project—"a sort of Good Soldier Schweik"—was to have been a musical based on Al Capp's comic strip, *Li'l Abner*. With Schwartz out, Lerner turned to the reliable Burton Lane, who waited and fretted while he continued to flounder. That summer afternoon the lyricist lamented, "I may never work again. I should be working with Fritz and he won't have me."

Nancy Lerner did not agree. To console her husband, she suggested that it might be a good idea to invite Loewe to lunch at their country home in New City—a simple reunion. Loewe had his own place nearby, a forty-five-acre farm near Katonah, New York.

"He won't come," Lerner predicted.

But she phoned anyway, and Loewe accepted her invitation.

During lunch, Lerner brought up a work they had abandoned as hopeless two years before. "I have an idea for an opening," Lerner told Loewe, whose interest and eyes sparked. Both men seemed to forget Nancy Lerner as, she noted, "Alan began to spin his powerful web of storytelling. They never finished dessert." Caught in his own web, Lerner, accompanied by the spellbound Loewe, crossed the road to a small studio that served as his work quarters. For the next two years, Nancy Olson Lerner was destined to see little of her now driven husband. (And, too, it solved the *Li'l Abner* writer's block: With a score by Gene de Paul and Johnny Mercer, it would become a fairly successful musical in 1956, by which time Lerner and Loewe had evolved into Broadway titans.)

The web that reenergized Lerner and Loewe had begun as a steel net at the start of Lerner's work on *Brigadoon* in the spring of 1952. The weaver then had been a flamboyant film producer named Gabriel Pascal, described by publicist Richard Maney as a "part-time gypsy from the foothills of Transylvania." For his part, actor Rex Harrison, who appeared in the Pascal-directed film version of George Bernard Shaw's *Major Barbara* (1940), saw Pascal as a "marvelous gypsy rogue, with incredible panache and no guile, as open as a baby and as ruthless as a tiger. He really caught one's imagination."

Pascal claimed Hungarian birth, but Lerner asserted that he was actually a "Rumanian . . . who looked like a Himalayan." Short and "circular" in stature, he was celebrated in the film world as the man who had acquired screen rights to several of Shaw's plays, with the crotchety permission of the playwright himself. By the time he and Lerner met for lunch at a popular restaurant, Pascal had produced *Pygmalion* (1938) and produced and directed both *Major Barbara* and *Caesar and Cleopatra* (1945); he was in Hollywood to attend to the production of *Androcles and the Lion*. Just that April, Shaw, then in his ninety-fourth year, had granted him the musical rights to *Pygmalion*.

This was a unique concession in view of Shaw's prickly attitude toward *Arms and the Man*'s musical version, *The Chocolate Soldier*, a successful operetta scored by Oscar Straus. When that show opened in New York in 1909, Shaw had insisted that the program carry the following note: "With apologies to Mr. Bernard Shaw for an unauthorized parody of one of his comedies." Only Pascal's faithful film production of his plays could persuade Shaw to consider the possibility of a Shaw musical comedy.

During their lunch at Lucy's, Lerner was as much impressed by Pascal's coarseness as by his genius for manipulating the intractable Shaw. His highly accented speech, his comments about the sex lives of Shaw (none) and

Gandhi (much), his eating habits, his flair for mendacity—all of these surprised Lerner. Nor was the producer well informed, for when he announced that he wanted to make a musical of *Pygmalion*, he added, "I want you to write music"—apparently having never heard of the entity called Lerner and Loewe. After being apprised of the division of labor, Pascal ordered Lerner to summon his partner to California. Since Loewe was already planning a trip west, that request was easily fulfilled.

As they were leaving Lucy's, Lerner was exposed—so to speak—to another Pascalism. While they waited for an attendant to deliver their cars, still continuing to talk, the rotund "part-time gypsy" nonchalantly unzipped his fly and emptied his bladder onto the concrete, to the stupefaction of the others in line. As his car appeared, he rezipped and, without saying another word, drove off. After this demonstration, an astonished Lerner confided, "I have not been able to be embarrassed again."

Lerner was particularly drawn to the concept of a musical *Pygmalion* because he believed it would enable his favorite collaborator and himself to return to work with characters who would demand songs of wit and tenderness, which would "dramatize, musically and lyrically, legitimate situations." He hoped to revert to the early mode of *The Day before Spring* and to break away from the Rodgers and Hammerstein style of *Brigadoon* and *Paint Your Wagon*.

He and Loewe soon met with Pascal at the latter's house in Westwood, a suburb of Los Angeles. Once the home of silent-film star Milton Sills, it was an "enormous, neo-Spanish" hacienda "that had successfully extracted from Spanish architecture all that was ugly and depressing." And being rented, it was naturally neglected, the grounds a riot of untended California flora, weeds, and trees. "From time to time during our conversation," Lerner recalled, "overripe oranges would plop onto the terrace like decaying hot-water bottles." Pascal, indifferent to the pulpy sound effects, proceeded to tell the skeptical Lerner and Loewe that they were the only songwriting team on earth that could properly realize his dream of a musical *Pygmalion*. He was unaware, obviously, that word had already got around the insular world of Broadway that he had earlier (even before procuring the rights) approached Richard Rodgers and Oscar Hammerstein with the same proposition. They had had a go at it but eventually had given up, with Hammerstein explaining that Shaw's insistence that the play was not a love story posed a real obstacle, since he could not bring himself to contravene the playwright's intent.

Both Lerner and Loewe were intrigued by the idea; they told Pascal they would return to New York and, per their usual method, discuss the treatment, since at that moment they had no conception of how to handle Shaw's "non–love story." It was all very well that Pascal had the option for the musical, Lerner said, but he was not a theatrical producer, and Lerner and Loewe's "interest depended upon [his] aligning himself with a proper New York manager." Perhaps they could meet a few weeks hence, in New York.

During the summer, with the Lerners settled into their house in New City and Loewe in the Algonquin Hotel (he was separated from his wife by then, though the separation would not be official until 1957, when Ernestine Zwerleine Loewe would be awarded no less than $135,000 outright and $10,000 a year for life—"her life," as Loewe saw it, "not mine"), the collaborators considered the problem: how to convert a talky drawing-room comedy with sociological overtones—British sociology, at that—into an American musical comedy (though Lerner preferred the term "musical play").

By the summer of 1952, the traditional American musical had acquired a definite form, primarily because of the success and influence of Rodgers and Hammerstein. The invariable elements consisted of a major plot involving the stars, a subplot—perhaps comic, perhaps tragic (as in *South Pacific*)—a singing and dancing chorus, and, especially since *Oklahoma!*, at least one ballet. Then running on Broadway was a fine revival of 1940's *Pal Joey*, whose nightclub-singer antihero gave the musical a bitter tone that had put off the original audience. Other shows playing while Lerner and Loewe discussed *Pygmalion* included the more conventional revue *New Faces of 1952*, both *South Pacific* and *The King and I*, *Top Banana*, featuring Phil Silvers doing an impersonation of Milton Berle, and Harold Rome's folkish Valentine to the Catskills in the summer, *Wish You Were Here*.

The form, conventions, and traditions of these musicals, they began to sense, would not work with the plot and characters created by Bernard Shaw; what had been innovative in the forties was old hat by the early fifties. But what haunted Lerner most of all was the question, How does one write a non–love song?

They were still puzzling over this when Gabriel Pascal arrived and, after a display of spell-binding, talked the Theatre Guild into signing a coproduction contract for a musical version of *Pygmalion*, with songs by Lerner and Loewe.

There were as yet no songs, of course, and in any event, at around this same time, late in the summer of 1952, Lerner's attentions were diverted to another sort of stage: politics. Although born into a Republican household, he, like so many in the arts, was a democrat, and a Democrat, at heart.

Rockland County, New York, with a few rare exceptions such as the artists' colony grouped around New City, was, as the *Herald Tribune* tagged it, a "Traditional Republican Stronghold." Revolted by the turn that American politics had taken, with Senator Joseph McCarthy running wild and the Republican press advocating a Republican administration, Lerner threw himself into the presidential campaign of Adlai Stevenson, the nettlesome opponent of Republican candidate former general Dwight D. Eisenhower. Those were the days when a Stevenson campaign button could be worn in the "hallowed halls of NBC and CBS" only "at the risk of inviting unemployment."

Accompanied by another indignant political neophyte, his young neighbor the ex-GI cartoonist Bill Mauldin, Lerner flew out to Stevenson's campaign headquarters in Springfield, Illinois, to volunteer his services. Over the next two months he had little time to spare for *Pygmalion* as he and Mauldin organized Stevenson rallies in and around New York. At a final grand rally held at Madison Square Garden, however, he encountered another Stevensonite, lyricist-librettist Oscar Hammerstein, who asked how *Pygmalion* was coming along.

"Slowly," Lerner admitted.

"It can't be done," Hammerstein told him. "Dick and I worked on it for over a year and gave up." The problems he and Rodgers had faced in attempting to adapt such a seamlessly crafted play—not to mention the difficulty of dealing with the nonromantic characters and the plot, in which a common flower girl is transformed into a lady by learning to speak proper English—were, he said, just too daunting. The obstacles outlined by Hammerstein, Lerner later recalled, "coincided exactly with the difficulties Fritz and I had been having."

The next day, he and Loewe discussed their work; not long after, following a few more unproductive attempts, they, too, joined Rodgers and Hammerstein. Undaunted, Pascal continued on his quest, only to be rejected by Noël Coward, Cole Porter, Arthur Schwartz and Howard Dietz, and *Finian's Rainbow*'s librettists, Fred Saidy and E. Y. Harburg. Harburg, also that show's lyricist, probably spoke for most of the others when he said he was refusing because he regarded *Pygmalion* as a "perfect work of art" that should not be touched by others.

After giving up on *Pygmalion* in September 1952, Lerner and Loewe once again went their separate ways. Loewe attempted collaborations with Harold Rome and Leo Robin, to no avail; Lerner went off to Hollywood to work on *Brigadoon*, the *Green Mansions* debacle, and an abortive treatment of

Kismet in collaboration with Arthur Schwartz, soon abandoned because of Schwartz's "conduct," as Freed put it. Schwartz was constantly raising the question of proper credits and other issues. "I certainly resented his ultimatums," Freed wrote to Lerner, "and, it seems to me, pettiness in the whole affair. Frankly, I've lost my desire and enthusiasm for working with him. . . . I just don't like one-sided love affairs." So *Kismet* followed *Green Mansions* onto the shelf, though Freed eventually did produce the former, returning to the original Broadway score as adapted by Robert Wright and George Forrest, utilizing the music of Alexander Borodin.

The Lerner-Schwartz collaboration began with promise in the fall of 1953, when the two men took an office—with Schwartz's name coming first on the door—on West Forty-fifth Street. They closed the office after their intention to base a musical on *Li'l Abner* came to nothing (primarily because Lerner simply could not produce the book), and the *Kismet* troubles put a final end to the collaboration. It was then that Lerner turned to Burton Lane; but though the working conditions were more pleasant, he continued to feel himself "sinking into a stagnant sea of self-doubt." Despite his Drama Critics Circle Award (for *Brigadoon*) and his Academy Award (for *An American in Paris*), he looked back on his work and "felt dissatisfied with the best of it."

Nerve-racking inertia set in; he could not work, he brooded, his nerves were frayed—a condition that he believed led to encephalitis and then worsened into spinal meningitis. After several weeks in the hospital, during which he suffered an attack of delirium, he emerged with a paralyzed left leg (a symptom that eventually resolved itself) and a determination to return to work—for now, on the dispiriting *Li'l Abner*. There was a break in this unproductive tediousness when he and his little family went to California for the *Brigadoon* screenplay. That in control, Lerner returned to New York, bringing along his new employee, Doris Warshaw. He now had a staff of two, Warshaw and Bud Widney, with not much to do. Depressed after his Hollywood misadventures, he tried to get to work, establishing an office at 645 Madison Avenue thanks to the largesse of prospective *Li'l Abner* producer Herman Levin. A musical veteran of such successes as *Call Me Mister* (1946) and *Gentlemen Prefer Blondes* (1949), Levin was spending the summer of 1954 cruising on the Mediterranean.

One midsummer day, Lerner suffered a shock when he turned to the obituary page of the *Times* and read that Gabriel Pascal had died on July 6, at the age of sixty. In the two years since Lerner and Loewe had given up on

Pygmalion, he had been unable to find anyone else willing to take on the project. He left a wife, a mistress, and a tangled estate.

Pascal's death took Lerner's mind off *Li'l Abner* and got him thinking about *Pygmalion* again, though this resulted in little more than further doubts and depression until Nancy Lerner arranged the lunch with Loewe. Carried away by his own enthusiasm, he took Loewe with him; by the time they headed off to his studio, "blazing with excitement," they were once more Lerner and Loewe.

The celebration was dimmed within two weeks, however, when Joseph Lerner, after some fifty major cancer operations, finally succumbed, on July 18, 1954. His death, while inevitable, deeply affected his son. The senior Lerner's estate was valued at more than $3.5 million, based on holdings in New York and Florida, where he owned property worth more than $200,000. His will left $60,000 a year, according to an agreement reached in 1944, to the now remarried mother of his children, Edith A. Lloyd of 470 Park Avenue. He bequeathed $20,000 to the Museum of Natural History (with which his sportsman and philanthropist brother Michael was associated); another $20,000 to the Federated Jewish Philanthropies; and $10,000 to "my good friend" Cardinal (Francis J.) Spellman, archbishop of the diocese of New York, whom he had met at Memorial Hospital on one of the cardinal's visits to journalist and short-story writer Damon Runyon before the latter's death of cancer in 1946. (When Alan Lerner had inquired about his father's peculiar friendship with the cardinal—Lerner senior totally rejected all organized religion—the reply was, for he was then still capable of speaking, "We have a great deal in common. We're both in the chain-store business.") What remained of Joseph Lerner's estate was to be shared equally among his three sons, Richard, of Newport Beach, California; Alan; and Robert, of Encino, California.

In later years, Alan Lerner would most regret that his father had not lived to see the results of the work that his son and Loewe began a month after his death.

The project came as a complete surprise to Doris Warshaw, who had heard nothing about a musical *Pygmalion* and, on being told about it, was convinced that it could only be a desecration. She and Bud Widney were in the office one day when Lerner and Loewe burst in to announce, "We've solved *Pygmalion*!"

While Widney's response was all enthusiasm, hers was an attitude of skeptical perplexity. She added her congratulations but remembered "having the thought that turning *Pygmalion* into a musical would ruin it," thus unconsciously aligning herself with the likes of Noël Coward, Cole Porter, Rodgers and Hammerstein, et al. "How dare they touch Shaw?" she privately wondered.

Her own interest was nonetheless sparked when Loewe, his hand on Lerner's shoulder, said, "My boy, shall we make the call?"

Lerner gave her a slip of paper with a phone number on it. "Put in a call to Rex Harrison in London," he said with firm humor, "will you, dear?" They went into Lerner's office and closed the door, and according to Warshaw, "from that day on whatever doubts or fears they might have had were invisible in the gaiety and camaraderie between them. For the entire adventure I never saw a moment of pique or impatience or even stress. They were two gallants when they were together."

How had they reached such a point of exhilaration?

First had come the realization that the musical theater had been subtly changing. Even Rodgers and Hammerstein had revealed a slightly untraditional, even offbeat streak in such benignly experimental efforts as *Allegro* (1947) and *Me and Juliet* (1953), though they managed in between to turn out traditional "blockbusters" such as *South Pacific* and *The King and I*. Lerner sensed that it would be possible to work within the conventions of the musical—toying with the placement of songs, balancing the rhythm "number" and the ballad, the solos and choral pieces, and the dances—and yet produce something quite new. "What is exciting is to be aware of these conventions and use them for fresh expression," he indicated in *The Street Where I Live*. "It is not enough that there be a fast song after a slow song. Legitimate, dramatic ways must be found so that the character or characters arrive at the emotional moment that demands the right kind of music to balance the score."

Lerner and Loewe solved the problem when they decided that they "could do *Pygmalion* simply by doing *Pygmalion*": no secondary characters, no subplot need be added. Shaw's own creations provided the opportunity for a variety of musical expressions. The screenplay of Pascal's 1938 production, starring Leslie Howard and Wendy Hiller, had been written by Shaw himself, with, according to the screen credits, a "scenario" (i.e., adaptation) by Ian Dalrymple, Cecil Lewis, and W. P. Lipscomb; all four writers had received Academy Awards for their contributions. Determined to be true to Shaw, Lerner elected to retain as much of the dialogue as he could, though this meant the show would have "more dialogue than . . . any other musical to date." He explained further:

for the first time Fritz and I had to come to grips with somebody else's characters, Shaw's. They were too strong, too alive to let us push them around. They compelled us to see things their way so that when we moved them into scenes outside the story framework that had hitherto contained them, they were able to meet their new situations with their emotions, motivations, quirks intact.

When we felt we really knew them, then we began to work on the score. If we were right, the songs came out of what they are, out of the only way they could express themselves.

It goes virtually without saying that to Lerner, Rex Harrison *was* Henry Higgins, and that each of his songs was carefully tailored, both words and music, not only to his non-singer's voice but also, and equally importantly, to his character. Higgins is obsessively dedicated to the English language—"the language of Shakespeare and Milton and the Bible"—and, as Shaw visualized him, a devoted misogynist; among the first songs written was Higgins's "Please Don't Marry Me." Although they had no definite Eliza in mind, Lerner and Loewe planned a song in which she expresses her wrath over Higgins's heartless bullying, and soon they had "Just You Wait ('enry 'iggins)."

In plotting out the form of the musical *Pygmalion*, Lerner followed Shaw's model closely but took some imaginative liberties. While the original play had been conceived in five acts, with no discrete scenes, the traditional musical consisted of two acts, each divided into several scenes. Shaw's play is by definition a drawing-room drama, and most of the action occurs either in Higgins's "laboratory" or in his mother's drawing room; the exception is act 1, set in Covent Garden's vegetable market, in the shadow of a church and near the opera house. In this act, Shaw presents some minor characters: a daughter, a mother, and one Freddy—the Eynsford-Hills, whose Freddy becomes infatuated with Eliza, the flower seller. In Lerner's adaptation, the daughter is eliminated, and not missed.

Next, Shaw brings on the principals: Eliza Doolittle, the ill-spoken flower girl; Colonel Pickering, a student of languages; and Henry Higgins, imperious master of the "science of speech." Ingeniously, Lerner goes even further. In his act 1, comprising eleven scenes, he introduces another major character, Eliza's heavy-drinking, ne'er-do-well philosopher father, Alfred Doolittle, sooner than Shaw had chosen to do in the play or the film. After the curtain rises, the musical's audience is shown several aspects of pre–First

Marion Bell, star of *Brigadoon*, Lerner and Loewe's first major Broadway musical. She later became Lerner's second wife after the show opened in 1947. (*Photofest*)

Frederick Loewe around the time he met Lerner and initiated their collaboration (*AP/Wide World Photos*)

New City, New York: Kurt Weill at home in Brook House, where he and Lerner, a neighbor, wrote *Love Life*, the musical that followed *Brigadoon* (*Courtesy of ASCAP*)

Lerner and Lotte Lenya, Weill's widow, in 1978, at a celebration for her eightieth birthday (*Courtesy of the Weill-Lenya Research Center, Kurt Weill Foundation for Music, New York*)

Tony Bavaar serenades Olga San Juan
("I Talk to the Trees"), *Paint Your
Wagon*, 1951. (*Photofest*)

Director Joshua Logan and Lerner,
in costume, for a scene in the film
version of *Paint Your Wagon* (1968)
(*Photofest*)

Lerner in conference with Clint Eastwood, "Pardner" in Lerner's much revised filming of *Paint Your Wagon*. The setting is No Name City's Grizzly Bear Saloon. (*Photofest*)

At the party celebrating the end of the shooting of *Paint Your Wagon* in June 1968. *From left:* Harve Presnell (Rotten Luck Willie), Lee Marvin (Ben Rumson), Jean Seberg (Elizabeth), and producer-writer-lyricist Lerner. (*Photofest*)

Hollywood, summer 1951:
In the foreground, Lerner's third
wife, Nancy Olson, studies a
script while he works on a script
for the unproduced MGM film
musical *Huck Finn.* (*Photofest*)

Lerner was more fortunate
with his script for MGM's *An
American in Paris*, which featured
Gershwin songs. Here, Ira
Gershwin (*left*) visits the set to
meet with star Gene Kelly.
Lerner was awarded an Oscar for
the screenplay. (*Gershwin Archive
Photo*)

Fred Astaire and Jane Powell in their "How Could You Believe Me When I Said I Love You When You Know I've Been a Liar All My Life" number from the film *Royal Wedding*, released in 1951. (*Photofest*)

Loewe and Lerner, the creators of *My Fair Lady*, 1956 (*Courtesy Warner-Chappell Music*)

As director and adviser, Moss Hart (*right*) was greatly responsible for the sheen and rhythm—and the success—of *My Fair Lady* and undoubtedly salvaged the troubled *Camelot* four years later. He is seen with his sometime collaborator, George S. Kaufman, and his wife, Kitty Carlisle Hart. (*AP/Wide World Photos*)

"The Rain in Spain" number from *My Fair Lady*: Rex Harrison and Julie Andrews (*Zodiac Photo/Photofest*)

With Loewe at the piano, Leslie Caron rehearses "The Parisians" from *Gigi*. When the film was finally shot, her singing was dubbed by vocalist Betty Wand. The title song won Lerner and Loewe an Academy Award in 1958. (*Photofest*)

Lerner and Loewe around the time they became embroiled in the making of *Camelot*, 1960 (*Rothschild Photo, Courtesy of ASCAP*)

World War London, with an emphasis on the various strata of society as manifested in their manner of speaking. Lerner quickly establishes Professor Higgins's prickly temperament, drawing generously and word for word upon Shaw's dialogue, with "Why Can't the English (teach their children how to speak)?" The Professor and Pickering, finding they have much in common—the language and its variant dialects—depart for Higgins's home, whose address Higgins announces loudly enough for Eliza to overhear.

As he leaves, Higgins tosses some coins into the flower seller's basket, much more than she could earn even in a full night's work. The stage direction "she skips to the fire (around which a group of costermongers have gathered) to display her wealth" serves as the cue for a song in which she reveals her simple wants: warmth, chocolates, a little leisure time. The costermongers, the British equivalent of American pushcart sellers of fruits and vegetables, tease her with, "Shouldn't you stand up, gentlemen? We've got a bloomin' heiress in our midst!" Eliza then sings "Wouldn't It Be Loverly?" This is Lerner, not Shaw; in the play, she picks up the money just as Freddy arrives with a taxi, only to find that his mother and sister have already left. Grandly, Eliza commandeers the cab for a ride to her hovel.

In the musical, the scene shifts briefly to introduce Doolittle. He and two companions are ejected from a pub, to the bartender's reminder, "Drinks is to be paid for or not drunk." When Eliza wanders by, her father tries to talk her out of a little drinking money: "You wouldn't have the heart to send me home to your stepmother without a bit of liquid protection, now, would you?"

Eliza, announcing that she has "had a bit of luck," gives him half a crown. After one of his companions calls out for "three glorious beers," Doolittle breaks into "With a Little Bit of Luck," in which—true to his character—he delineates his notion of the good life: avoiding work and marriage, pursuing drink and philandering. This scene is another Lerner innovation.

After the show was finally produced, he would explain how he and Loewe had managed to tamper creatively with Shavian themes without upsetting Shavians. Early in their discussions, before a note of music had been set down, a question had arisen regarding the Covent Garden of Shaw's act 1: "What was Eliza doing between Higgins' departure from Covent Garden and her arrival at Higgins' house the following morning?" (the beginning of Shaw's act 2). She obviously goes home, or somewhere else. Lerner then expanded on the imagined entr'acte: She would celebrate her bit of luck and share it with her father, allowing Lerner and Loewe to contrast her wistful song about the good life with her father's rowdier take on the subject.

Because he was not limited by the constraints of stagecraft faced by Shaw in 1912, Lerner could elaborate on what occurred offstage in scenes that flowed smoothly from one to another or even merged (Shaw himself had taken advantage of such techniques in reworking his play for the screen in 1938).

Having agreed on the approach they would use, Lerner and Loewe began working on the songs. By November they had six possibles: Eliza's "Just You Wait" and "Say a Prayer for Me Tonight"; Doolittle's "With a Little Bit of Luck"; "The Ascot Gavotte" (another Lerner fabrication; a scene set at the Ascot racetrack had fine prospects for the set designer and costumer); and Higgins's "Please Don't Marry Me" and coaxing "Lady Liza" (his attempt to convince her that she can pass as a lady after her gaffe at Ascot). It was at about this time that word got around, as it will in that provincial region called Broadway, that Lerner and Loewe were converting Bernard Shaw's *Pygmalion* into a musical.

One day the phone rang, and Lerner picked it up to find Richard Halliday on the other end; Mary Martin was *Mrs.* Richard Halliday. The couple had read about the new enterprise and "would love to hear what [Lerner and Loewe] had written." Taken aback, Lerner remembered the dictum of his mentor Lorenz Hart: "If a star seems interested, do not say no for at least twenty-four hours." And a star Mary Martin was—she and Ethel Merman were then the two brightest female lights in the theater. Following her long run in *South Pacific* (in both New York and London), she had returned to Broadway only the month before (October 1954) in *Peter Pan*, which was being produced by her husband and Edwin Lester. Disinclined to say no to Martin, Lerner arranged for an afternoon audition for Halliday, who was, Lerner thought, "*most* enthusiastic." Halliday then asked the writers if they would repeat the six songs for his wife after one of her evening performances. Since Lerner and Loewe were both still living in Rockland County, Lerner arranged for the use of his mother's Park Avenue apartment a few nights later.

The Hallidays arrived after the theater, close to midnight, accompanied by their friend the designer Mainbocher (né Main Bocher, from the American Midwest), whose intelligent interest in the theater impressed Lerner. The trio sat and listened as Loewe played and Lerner sang the songs they had written to date. Practically with the final note, the Hallidays left without a comment; only Mainbocher managed to say he liked the songs very much before he was whisked away. Lerner and Loewe were mystified.

A week passed without a word. Finaly, Lerner couldn't take the silence anymore; he called Halliday and asked what Martin had thought. Halliday's voice seemed to take on a solemn tone when he suggested they meet two days later for lunch at the Hampshire House in town.

Once their orders had been taken, Halliday said, "Alan, you don't know what a *sad* night that was for Mary and me."

"Why?" the surprised lyricist managed to reply.

Halliday told him how Martin had paced the floor "half the night," asking over and over (as Lerner remembered it later), "How could it have happened?" He then repeated the words that Lerner said were "forever engraved on the walls of my duodenal lining": "'Richard, those dear boys have lost their talent.'"

Lerner listened, speechless, as Halliday informed him that "The Ascot Gavotte" was not at all funny (the song was to be sung by a bored, expressionless crowd at the racetrack; while the words express excitement, the upper-class English must not reveal emotion—a point evidently lost on Martin and Halliday). Even worse, he suggested that "Just You Wait" had been stolen from Cole Porter's "I Hate Men," a number featured in *Kiss Me Kate* (another misreading, for Porter's song was aimed at men in general, while Lerner's was directed at a specific member of the sex; it was a natural expression of the character, generated by the plot). Lerner could not later recall whether Halliday ever got to the other songs; benumbed, "shaken to the core" by this initial reaction to their work, he changed the subject and bolted. As he was leaving, Halliday took his hand and said, "I'm *so* sorry. *Really*, Alan. We're *so* sorry" (italics Lerner's).

Lerner drove back to the country and met with Loewe to tell him the whole appalling story. The imperturbable Loewe, after a little thought, merely said, "I guess they didn't like it." (When the musical opened, it may be noted, the two songs that the Hallidays particularly disliked were included in the score; three of the others had been discarded.) For Loewe the matter was closed; for Lerner there would come an aftershock.

For the time being, however, he, too, dismissed the incident; there were other, more important concerns, most notably the acquisition of the rights. When Herman Levin returned from his Mediterranean cruise, he expected to find Lerner and Burton Lane at work on *Li'l Abner*, and he asked Lerner how things were progressing.

The work was going well, he was assured.

"Have you found a way to do it?"

"I think so," Lerner replied.

"How does Burt like it?"

"I haven't the slightest idea," Lerner told him. "Fritz is doing it."
"Fritz!"
Then Lerner added, "But now the problem is to get the rights."
"But we have the rights."
Lerner informed Levin that it was unclear whether the estate had them or whether they had reverted back. He neglected to tell him exactly *whose* estate he was referring to.
Estate? A bewildered Levin asked, "Who died?"
It was then that Lerner realized he had failed to provide some essential details. "Oh, Herman," he said. "I forgot to tell you. You're not producing *Li'l Abner*. You're producing *Pygmalion*."
While Levin explored the disposition of the rights, Lerner and Loewe turned to the casting of their Eliza. It was more than clear that Mary Martin was not interested, and in any case, though Shaw had written the part for his friend Mrs. Patrick Campbell when she was about forty-nine, in his script Eliza is described as being "perhaps eighteen, perhaps twenty, hardly older." Mary Martin might successfully pass for a boy who refused to grow up, winging over the stage of the Winter Garden with Wendy and Tinker Bell, but she herself was then forty. Lerner and Loewe wanted a more credible Eliza, and they found her a few streets south of the Winter Garden, at the Royale, in an imported spoof of twenties musicals that had opened a month before *Peter Pan* and would remain long after the Barrie tale wafted away.
Making her American debut as the lead in Sandy Wilson's *The Boy Friend* was an exceptionally poised nineteen-year-old named Julie Andrews. Lerner, Loewe, and Levin attended a performance of the parody and found her voice, diction, presence, and beauty winning; she was in fact a veteran, having begun as a child performer in her native Britain. Lerner arranged to meet with her later for an informal audition (they still had neither the rights nor a director) and then worked alone with her long enough to be impressed by her "composure and ease beyond her years." After one spirited outburst from her, he told "Fritz and Herman that there was a lot more to Julie Andrews than met the eye and ear." Confessing that the rights problem remained, they asked if she would stay on call—that is, accept no future contracts until their legal situation was cleared up. Graciously, she agreed (and luckily, the extended run of *The Boy Friend* simplified that aspect of her career).
They had their Eliza all but signed, but were not certain of their Professor Higgins; all they needed at that point, in the winter of 1954, was the

rights. Assembling the various elements of a musical, or of any theatrical or film production—human, legal, technical, and financial, not to mention artistic—can be a complex, frustrating, infuriating, time-consuming (and time-wasting) process, but the key words are *legal* and *financial*, especially at the beginning of a project.

Although they had not yet acquired the rights to the play—no simple matter, they would learn—Loewe, with unusual optimism, suggested that they work on the score; that way, he believed, once the rights were released, they would be so far ahead of any other contenders that they would be granted the option. The Pascal estate operated out of New York, and Shaw's out of London, via the British Society of Authors; both claimed an interest in the musical rights to *Pygmalion,* and both would have to be dealt with. In New York, Pascal's legacy was in the grip of a bank, according to Lerner a perfect "model of catatonic timidity."

Lerner and company had just begun their importunities to that bastion of conservatism when a call came in from a man identifying himself as Charles Moscowitz, an executive in Metro-Goldwyn-Mayer's New York office. Like the Hallidays before him, he had picked up word about Lerner and Loewe and *Pygmalion.* Lerner accepted his invitation to meet with him at Metro's office, hoping that the film company might be interested in investing in the show, and perhaps later filming it. Not so: Within minutes Lerner was informed that Metro was considering acquiring the rights to the play for its own use (whether as a musical or not was not made clear). Since Metro kept its funds in the same bank that handled the Pascal estate, Moscowitz was certain the matter was closed. It was, quite simply, Lerner and Loewe versus Metro-Goldwyn-Mayer, and the bankers would never dream of jeopardizing the huge MGM account. When Lerner inquired as to the purpose of Moscowitz's call, he got a curt good-bye for an answer.

An inquiry at the bank gleaned only the information that the rights would be placed with that party which would best serve the interests of the Pascal estate, which Lerner already knew: that was what banks were *supposed* to do. Since, as Lerner phrased it, bankers "knew even less about the theatre than [they] did about forecasting economic trends," a decision was made to appoint a respected literary agent, Harold Freedman, to be the arbiter in the matter. On learning this—he had good sources at the bank, as his father's estate was nestled in the same vaults—Lerner moved quickly and approached Freedman to be the agent for Lerner and Loewe.

Ethically, this was something of a quandary. When Lerner and Loewe met with Freedman prior to the decision making, he told them he would have to think about it "carefully"; then, as Lerner reported it, "before he left the room he agreed." Upon hearing this, Lerner's personal attorney, Irving Cohen, insisted that the court be informed about the agreement. He had already been apprised of Freedman's vote, but he demanded that the agent make it plain that he was also representing the men he believed should be granted Pascal's interest in the rights to *Pygmalion*. In what can only be termed a peculiar but, in light of history, provident determination in November 1954, Lerner and Loewe were halfway in the *Pygmalion* business: Pascal's rights were now theirs. As Lerner noted, "The next battlefield would be London"— seat of the Shaw holdings and current venue of Rex Harrison, their Professor Higgins-to-be.

At that moment, they had half the rights, the promise of Julie Andrews, and a producer who had not yet begun to assemble the backing for an enterprise that was still more dream than solid fact. Infiltrating the next battleground, Lerner realized, would require funds for transportation and a few weeks' lodging for "our little brigade." He was, on paper, the sole millionaire in the enterprise, but his father's will was still moving slowly through probate, and there was as yet no cash on hand. Lerner recalled that some twenty years earlier, when he was still a teenager (he was now thirty-six), his father had acquired an interest in a gold mine and turned it over to his sons, to dispose of as they wished upon reaching the age of twenty-one. Neither he nor his brothers, all well past that age by now, had ever thought to ask Joseph Lerner for his shares; now was the time to see if this unknown quantity could "bankroll the expedition to London." Indeed it could: Lerner sold his interest for $150,000. Early in January 1955, not quite three years after his first encounter with Gabriel Pascal, the aircraft carrying Lerner's "little brigade" touched down at Heathrow, London's major airport. The brigade consisted of Lerner, Loewe, Levin, Irving Cohen, and Nancy Lerner.

It was almost two decades since Lerner had last been in Britain, with his brother Robert on one of their mother's cultural tours, and the drive to London through the usual bone-chilling winter mists stirred his imagination. Once settled into Claridge's, he and Loewe called and arranged to meet with Rex Harrison after the curtain came down on that night's performance of his current West End success, *Bell, Book, and Candle*, in which he was appearing with his estranged wife, Lilli Palmer.

Volatile, moody, irascible, Harrison was, Lerner would later say, "one of the few enduring friends I have made in the theatre." Although he was possessed of extraordinary range as an actor, it was his personal qualities that made him an ideal Professor Higgins (the one characteristic they did not share was misogyny). After the show and a late supper, he, Lerner, and Loewe found a piano so the collaborators could play him "Lady Liza" and "Please Don't Marry Me," the two completed Higgins songs. When they were finished, Harrison came straight to the point.

"I hate them," he said.

Unlike the Martin-Halliday calamity, however, Harrison's reaction did not distress Lerner (that still remained in the future). He assured the actor that the songs were merely early attempts, somewhat obvious and "slick," superficial "clever word games," rather than "acting pieces." Harrison listened but was not convinced; he had no doubts about the skills of Lerner and Loewe, but there were other obstacles to overcome. The most serious, and the one that concerned him most, was the fact that he was not a vocalist. Then, too, he was haunted by the film performance of Leslie Howard. Lerner had to persuade him that Howard's was not the definitive Higgins, that he and Harrison were decidedly different types, both physically and in style, and would create different characters. After viewing the film and rereading the play, both men agreed that Howard was perhaps a touch too romantic, and that too early in the film his expressions revealed un-Shavian feelings toward Eliza. (That may be so, but Howard's is still a fine portrayal, and if there is anything un-Shavian about it, Shaw himself did not notice.) That approach worked with Harrison.

Another problem was more personal. *Bell, Book and Candle* was doing very well, despite the strain—never evident on stage—between leading man and leading lady, caused by Harrison's romance with the beautiful and stylish Kay Kendall. Kendall was then busy in films and set for more, and Harrison was not anxious to go off without her, once his play closed (actually, it would run for the rest of the year), to begin work on *Pygmalion*. Lerner let that difficulty go for the time being.

They returned to the major impediment. In Loewe's suite at Claridge's, with Loewe at the piano, they asked Harrison to sing, and he did—the first chorus to "Molly Malone." As he was about to go into the second chorus, Loewe stopped him and said, "Fine. That's all you need." As for Lerner, he found Harrison "instinctively musical."

But still they did not quite have their Professor Higgins, as Harrison continued to hold off on making a final decision. While they waited, Lerner was reunited with a colleague from his Hasty Pudding days, Benjamin Welles, then stationed in the London bureau of the *New York Times*. Lerner's London trip now took on a more social color, with visits to Ben and Cynthia Welles's home in Wilton Place. Irving Cohen was meanwhile negotiating with the British Society of Authors over the rights, part of its stake in the Shaw estate.

Shaw's will was a peculiar document. His wife, who predeceased him, had left her money (she was already wealthy when they married) to a fund dedicated to teaching the Irish manners—which surely says something about their strange, asexual marriage. Shaw, not one to be outdone in the realm of eccentricity, wanted his royalties to be used to add twenty-three letters to the English alphabet, a gesture that would have excited his autobiographical creation Professor Higgins. In the five years since his death, however, no one had come forward with a plan for how this might be accomplished—or, for that matter, an explanation of *why* it should be done. After an undelineated "reasonable time," the monies were to be divided between the national galleries of Shaw's birthplace, Dublin, and London. Recognizing the promise of American dollars in a time of Conservative austerity, the Crown now more or less rewrote the will, and Cohen was ready to head home with the English rights to *Pygmalion* in hand.

Harrison, for his part, was still thinking things over.

One day Lerner encountered an old friend from Hollywood, director Lewis Milestone (*All Quiet on the Western Front, Of Mice and Men*), who, on hearing of their project, suggested an early—say 4:00 A.M.—excursion to Covent Garden to see the costermongers, flower sellers, and other small merchants begin their day. On an arctic English morning, with Milestone as their guide, Lerner—"a large dash of blue" from the neck down—and an uncomfortable Loewe spent a few miserable but valuable hours wandering around Covent Garden, listening to cockney talk and observing the activity. Seeing a group gathered around a warming smudge-pot gave Lerner a way to establish the chill of early-morning London in the first scene; within a couple of days he had the theme of Eliza's first song, "Wouldn't It Be Loverly?," on the subject of "creature comforts." Loewe took the title and in less than a day completed the melody.

The Sunday of their fifth week in London, Rex Harrison phoned and suggested a walk in Hyde Park. For about three hours, talking all the while, the actor led the trek, like a Great Dane trailed by two poodles. Then, stopping abruptly, he turned to the panting duo and said, "All right. I'll do it." So it was that in early February 1955, Lerner and Loewe (and Irving Cohen), having acquired all necessary rights to *Pygmalion*, and having found their Eliza, at last secured, amid typical Harrisonian unpredictability, their Professor Higgins.

While Loewe left the park and returned to the hotel for a "little" before-dinner nap (according to Lerner, he "woke up two days later"), Lerner remained with Harrison and continued their walk. There wasn't much more to say; the exultant lyricist was virtually breathless. When Lerner at last reached his destination and they were about to part, Harrison turned, silently studied his companion for a moment, and then said, "I don't know why, but I have faith in you."

Harrison was not Lerner and Loewe's only theatrical quarry in London. They also approached Stanley Holloway, a veteran of films, music halls, and the Old Vic who had also appeared in a series of successful revues, *The Co-Optimists*, in the early twenties. As a comic monologuist, he had created the character of the cockney Sam Small, which made him a natural for the role of Eliza's father. He had not been on the English stage since 1942, but he had been active on screen and would be no stranger to American audiences, having had parts in two of Pascal's Shaw films, *Major Barbara* (in which Harrison was one of the stars) and *Caesar and Cleopatra*, as well as in *Brief Encounter*, *Nicholas Nickleby*, *Hamlet* (as the gravedigger), *The Beggar's Opera*, and *The Lavender Hill Mob*, among others. Over lunch at Claridge's with Levin and Lerner, the casting of Doolittle was set.

Lerner and Loewe knew, too, who they wanted to design the costumes: Cecil Beaton, known primarily as a set designer for stage, film, and ballet. This might have created a problem, since they had already signed Oliver Smith (who had done well by them in *Brigadoon* and *Paint Your Wagon*) to do the sets, but Beaton's regard for Smith's work, and his eagerness to design in the style of the Edwardian era, led to a speedy agreement. Beaton had long been fascinated by "that world of floating chiffons, high waistlines, panniered skirts, and shepherdess hats" that was London before the Great War.

Lerner's happy little brigade could now return to New York with the rights and major casting of their *Pygmalion* assured. Two songs had been lost to Rex Harrison's objections, but they had the tune to another and as Lerner put it, "a year's work ahead of us." Almost immediately upon their arrival, Lerner and Loewe headed off to their homes in Rockland County. Although the Lerners' spacious, white-and-blue eighteenth-century farmhouse had room enough for Loewe, he refused to stay there, insisting that the house was haunted; according to Hudson Valley legend, it had been built by the father of Revolutionary War general "Mad" Anthony Wayne (a nickname referring to impetuousness in battle, not his mental condition).

In the seven years that he had lived in the house, Lerner, despite his fascination with extrasensory perception, had never encountered the heavy-footed ghost that, according to Loewe, regularly turned his and his girlfriend's bedroom into a freezer. After two of these incidents, both corroborated by "Virginia," Loewe had left the Lerners' and rented the nearby hillside home of actor Burgess Meredith. While the Lerners continued in their home undisturbed, most of the collaborators' working time was spent in Lerner's studio across the road, unvisited by Mad Anthony.

Before embarking on any new songs—or revising the survivors—they outlined their story, in accordance with their procedure on previous musicals. In the case of *Pygmalion*, Shaw had already provided the essentials of a book—except that his film version would be more useful to them than the play. Additional scenes, either suggested by Shaw or logically conceivable as entr'actes, gave them more musical space, as with "The Ascot Gavotte." They remained determined to use as much of Shaw's own dialogue as possible.

Once the outline had been sketched out and the musical sequences spotted, Lerner and Loewe could begin work on the songs. After they discussed each musical segment, identifying its function in the work and what form it would take, Lerner would come up with a title based on what the song was intended to contribute to the plot or character. They already had both title and tune for "Wouldn't It Be Loverly?," so why not begin there?

Lerner was an early-morning worker, beginning at around six-thirty, with an active coffeepot nearby. He settled into his studio, pencil in hand and recollections of that freezing morning in Covent Garden fresh in his mind. And he sat and sat. Six o'clock in the evening struck, and still not a word had come to him. He attributed this to his having been away from writing for too long; all that was required, he thought, was a little "limbering" of his "lyrical muscles."

At six-thirty the next morning, he was in his chair again, pad before him and the aroma of coffee suffusing the room; again nothing. This continued for a week. By the second week he was panicky, and the third was no better. What especially alarmed him was the fact that he knew what he wanted to say but could not find the words to say it. By the fourth week he had lost eight pounds and "become a basket case." Distraught, almost frantic, he realized he needed help and sought out the analyst who had helped him through his first divorce, Dr. Béla Mittelmann, "the only psychiatrist I had ever encountered who had a sense of humor and did not have modern furniture in his waiting room."

Encouched, Lerner tried to describe his anxieties, with scant enlightenment as to the cause of his mental inertia. The doctor observed, "You write as if your life depended on every line."

"It does."

Mittelmann began by asking him about his recent activities. He reviewed his productive London trip and then, letting his mind wander further back, recounted the Mary Martin–Richard Halliday incident: the audition and its aftermath. He heard an understanding chuckle and realized what a devastating effect, though suppressed for a time, this had had on him. That was it: "Those dear boys have *lost their talent.*"

Dr. Mittelmann had led him to the cause of his lyrical paralysis: In view of his accomplishments, he had taken Halliday too seriously. By the end of the hour, Lerner had got his life back in perspective, though for certainty's sake he asked if he might come by again in a week. Dr. Mittelmann agreed but suggested that he call in a day or so to let him know how his work was going. As it turned out, a second visit would not be necessary.

The next morning Lerner was in his studio at six-thirty; he gulped some coffee, and the day began. He was back in form, with Eliza among her friends in Covent Garden contemplating creature comforts. Half the lyric was completed by that afternoon, and "Wouldn't It Be Loverly?" was finished the next day.

(When *My Fair Lady* began its fourth year on Broadway, a special celebratory supplement was included in the Sunday *Times*. One of the contributors, Lerner's old Harvard friend Cleveland Amory, reported that the song had taken six weeks to write, with two of those spent on the last line alone—a curious assertion, given that the last *two* lines consist of nothing other than the word *loverly*, repeated twice per line. Amory revealed, too, that as often as Lerner saw the musical, he never felt the lyric was right. When Lerner appeared at the 92nd Street Y's "Lyrics and Lyricists" program in December 1971, he, too, recalled the song's having taken six weeks, but he maintained that the difficulty had lain in setting a lyric to a tune that was, he considered, among the "best examples of what a good dramatic composer can do." Inspired by the cheerful cockneys warming themselves around the smudge-pot in Covent Garden, Loewe had written an upbeat melody of a people in a miserable environment with no time for self-pity. Lerner wished to match the tune with a lyric expressing Eliza's desire for "creature comforts," but without "any mention of another person, or someone's head upon my knee, and all that;" he would thus remain true to Shaw's abhorrence of romance. His session with Dr. Mittelmann having cleared the way, he did just fine until the final eight bars after the release, where he had to resort to the cockneyisms, "absobloominlutely" and "loverly" because he could not find a climax for this crucial part of the song. "Finally I had to give up," he told the audience at the Y. Suggesting that he thought they would find the first sixteen bars in keeping with what he and Loewe had had in mind, he sang those, plus the release, and then came to his ultimate solution: "Someone's head restin' on my knee." Here he stopped singing. It was good for a laugh, though he was uncomfortable with the un-Shavian, if perfectly Lernerish, touch.

At the time the song was completed, both lyricist and composer were pleased with it, and Loewe proposed that they traverse the neighborhood looking for what he called "customers." This was a long-standing practice: On finding anyone home, they would demonstrate their new song and gauge the reaction. Although it was unlikely that any of their good friends would be anything but appreciative, they could instinctively sense whether the compliments were based on friendship or on the actual merit of the song; if too many plaudits seemed due to the former, they would revise the number. In the instance of "Wouldn't It Be Loverly?," their tour was most successful.

Heartened by this neighborly ramble, they turned their energies to Higgins. That Harrison was not a trained singer in fact simplified the songwriters' task, as they could write what Ira Gershwin termed "rhymed conversation"; melody as well as lyric would reflect his speech, and he could comfortably speak the lines or sing them, as he liked. The first song written for Harrison's character, after a couple of discarded attempts, exemplifies the Lerner-Loewe handling of his special songs; the idea was taken from Shaw's preface and transposed by Lerner to the musical's first scene.

Shaw acidly observed, "The English have no respect for their language, and will not teach their children to speak it." Using that cue, Lerner quotes the playwright word for word in Higgins's first-scene lines, beginning with "A woman who utters such depressing and disgusting sounds has no right to be anywhere." The professor reminds Eliza that hers is the "language of Shakespeare and Milton and the Bible," and orders her not to just "sit there crooning like a bilious pigeon."

Shaw's Higgins then pronounces, "You see this creature with her kerbstone English: the English that will keep her in the gutter to the end of her days." This becomes Lerner's lyric "Look at her—a pris'ner of the gutter;

Condemned by ev'ry syllable she utters," which would serve, were this a conventional Broadway song, as the verse of "Why Can't the English?" There follow three stanzas of varying length (from couplet to octave), the last of which succinctly states the theme of Shaw's play:

> *Why can't the English teach their children how to speak?*
> *This verbal class distinction by now should be antique.*

Satisfied with their establishment of Higgins's authoritarian professional attitude, Lerner and Loewe turned to characterization of a more personal sort. When Eliza arrives at his house to take, and pay for, elocution lessons, Higgins rejects her; he has made all the notes he needs on her speech and has no further use for this "squashed cabbage leaf" whom he has boasted he could teach to speak like a lady and pass off as a "duchess at an ambassador's garden party." (He makes this claim in the "kerbstone English" speech, which Lerner retained in its entirety, with one slight change: Where Shaw's Higgins wants only "three" months in which to convert a flower girl into a lady, Lerner substituted "six" for consistency with Shaw's act 2.) Both Mrs. Pearce, Higgins's capable and proper housekeeper, and Colonel Pickering, his new friend and fellow linguist, have their doubts about such a conversion, for obvious reasons. Mrs. Pearce worries about what is to become of Eliza *after* the experiment; what of the future? she asks. Man of the world Pickering, meanwhile, considers the present and asks (in play, film, and musical), "Are you a man of good character where women are concerned?"

Higgins retorts, "Have you ever met a man of good character where women are concerned?"

When Pickering replies that he has, Higgins launches into a misogynistic tirade. (Here Lerner adapted most of Shaw's speech as a lead-in to another song, in which another side of Higgins is revealed.) "Well, I haven't," he harrumphs. "I find that the moment I let a woman make friends with me she becomes jealous, exacting, suspicious, and a damned nuisance. I find that the moment I let myself become friends with a woman, I become selfish and tyrannical." At this point Lerner diverges from Shaw to have Higgins state that he is a "confirmed bachelor." Two sentences later, however, Shaw is back, providing a major theme of Lerner's musical declamation: "When you let them into your life, you find that the woman is driving at one thing and you're driving at another."

Higgins begins calmly and reasonably, declaring that he is but an "ordinary man" of simple desires—that is, master of all—but, he warns, "let a woman in your life/And your serenity is through!/She'll redecorate your home/From cellar to the dome,"

> *Then get on to the enthralling*
> *Fun of overhauling*
> *You.*

By turns genial (if self-servingly so), ingratiating, agitated, and violent—all extraordinarily expressed in Loewe's finely honed, contrasting melodies—Higgins concludes with the final exclamation, "I shall never let a woman in my life!" Lerner's words seem more in character than Shaw's bland and slightly ambiguous line, "So here I am, a confirmed old bachelor, and likely to remain so."

BY THE END OF SIX WEEKS, Lerner and Loewe had two replacement songs that they thought Harrison might not hate. There was other good news as well. Some weeks before, when the question of backing for the musical had come up, Lerner had called a childhood friend, someone he had known "since 'swingtime' in Central Park": Robert Sarnoff, now president of the National Broadcasting Company. Sarnoff had listened to Lerner's pitch and said—as the line went then and still goes today—"I'll get back to you." He never did.

Lerner then tried another friend, Goddard Lieberson, whom he and Loewe had known since their beginnings at the Lambs Club. Lieberson was then vice president of Columbia Records, a part of the Columbia Broadcasting System. A most astute and creative man—which also made him a rarity in his business—he had pioneered the recording of classic show scores of the twenties and thirties and was an outstanding advocate of recording worthwhile new musicals as well. It was Lieberson who got Columbia to produce recordings of composer-conducted works by Igor Stravinsky and Aaron Copland. A trained musician and onetime composer, he knew the field of music thoroughly, from concert hall to theater. In him Lerner was approaching a friend with imagination and a sympathetic ear; Goddard Lieberson got back to Alan Jay Lerner.

Lieberson's call came on a day when he was scheduled to have lunch with the president of CBS, William Paley. He had not forgotten the details of their earlier discussion, he said, but could not remember which of Shaw's plays Lerner and Loewe were working on. Lerner told him and reminded him that Rex Harrison had promised to play Professor Higgins.

"I'll get back to you," Lieberson assured him.

He meant what he said: "Some hours later he called to inform Lerner that Paley and CBS had agreed to put up the production money ($400,000); Lieberson would produce the cast album for Columbia Records. They were almost in business—but not quite.

At the moment of Lieberson's call, the musical had everything but a title and a director. In a meeting with producer Levin, Lerner and Loewe brought up the matter of finding a director who could handle Shaw/Lerner, the mercurial Rex Harrison, and—not the least important aspect of the show—song. Among the outstanding musical directors then working on Broadway were George Abbott, Joshua Logan, Jerome Robbins (a relative newcomer from the dance world), and the veteran writer-director Moss Hart. All had been hoping for Hart from the beginning, but he had left Broadway for Hollywood after the lukewarm reception of Irving Berlin's *Miss Liberty*, under his direction, in 1949. Hart had begun working with Berlin as early as 1932, with the revue *Face the Music*. His experience with musicals was impressive: He had worked with Rodgers and Hart, with Cole Porter, and with Kurt Weill and Ira Gershwin on his own *Lady in the Dark*. In Hollywood after the Second World War, he had provided the Academy Award–winning screenplay for *Gentleman's Agreement*, a film about anti-Semitism, and in the 1950s he scripted both Danny Kaye's *Hans Christian Andersen* (with songs by Frank Loesser) and Judy Garland's *A Star Is Born* (songs by Harold Arlen and Ira Gershwin). In the late fifties he would write a best-selling autobiography entitled *Act One*. At the time his name came up in Herman Levin's office, it was known that he was working on a new play, but Levin decided to call him anyway.

Hart was interested in hearing the half dozen or so songs that the writers were comfortable with, and within days he came around to Levin's office for a demonstration. Convinced, he set aside his own play to direct Lerner and Loewe's *Pygmalion*. Now they were ready to try out the new Higgins songs on their most cantankerous "customer."

8

—∭—

GOLD MINE

HAPPY WITH THE WORK they had done thus far, Lerner and Loewe flew back to London to present their latest efforts to Harrison, who, to their further pleasure, approved. Despite all his surface aplomb, however, their Higgins continued to suffer qualms about appearing in a singing role. Increasingly dubious ("frightened" might be a more apt description) about the prospect of getting on stage and possibly making a fool of himself, he had begun to study with a vocal coach who, Lerner discovered, had been recommended by none other than Mary Martin.

When they requested a demonstration of the fruits of this tutelage, Harrison, to their dismay, "belted out a few pear-shaped tones . . . with the large end of the pear coming out first." Much of the rest of their stay in England was devoted to reassuring the actor that his natural singing voice was sufficient for the part, and to finding him a less pretentious teacher—one with a taste for musical theater rather than opera.

There was another snag. When they left England in February, they assumed that by late spring *Bell, Book and Candle* would have run its course, freeing up Harrison for rehearsals in New York soon after. Ticket sales for the comedy, however, remained strong, a fiscal fact that would prove detrimental to their often frustrated plans and hard work. Only a theater landlord, not the star(s) or the happy producer, could close a play—and even then only if its attendance, and consequently its financial intake, fell below a set, specific figure. *Bell, Book and Candle* did not qualify on that count, nor did it promise to for some time to come.

The comedy's producer was the distinguished and powerful Hugh Beaumont, director of the production firm H. M. Tennent, Ltd., whose considerable influence in the British theatrical world made him an ideal intermediary. Theater owners and producers both needed each other, but a landlord with an empty theater was worse off than a producer with no venue. Lerner began plotting his approach to the man known in London and New York as Binkie Beaumont. It happened that his friend Irene Mayer Selznick—who had chosen Broadway over Hollywood, and production duties for plays such as Tennessee Williams's *A Streetcar Named Desire* over her father (the formidable Louis B.) and ex-husband (David O.)—was involved in the American production of *Bell, Book and Candle*.

Leaving Harrison with a Lerner-Loewe tape of "I'm an Ordinary Man" and "Why Can't the English?," plus a new coach, the collaborators flew back to New York, where Lerner arranged to meet with Irene Selznick over lunch. In his always-persuasive manner, articulately and with charm, he told his story. She was impressed and taken with the idea of a Shaw musical; if Herman Levin could be that persuasive with Beaumont, she would do all she could to help.

Armed with that assurance, Herman Levin flew off to London to meet with Beaumont, who recognized a good proposition when he heard one. For a consideration of what Lerner called a "cash settlement" (purportedly $50,000), Beaumont promised to close *Bell, Book and Candle* in November to free Harrison for rehearsals early in January 1956. One other concession was made: H. M. Tennent would mount the British production of *Pygmalion*—or whatever the musical version was to be called.

What *not* to call it was obvious: *Pygmalion*, especially starring a noted actor. With that title, it could readily be regarded as a revival, unlikely though that would be with the names of Lerner and Loewe associated with it. Initially both *Liza* and *Lady Liza* were considered; it amused Lerner to imagine a marquee emblazoned with the headline "Rex Harrison in 'Liza.'" (He did not contemplate, at least in his autobiography, what reaction Harrison himself might have to such a billing.) They even thought of *My Fair Lady* but rejected it as being too operetta-ish. By this time—late spring going into summer—they had completed a song for Harrison called "Come to the Ball," in which he urges Eliza to attend that most social of social functions despite her language gaffe at the Ascot races ("Move your bloomin' arse!" she bellows at a horse; in the play she uses the taboo adjective *bloody*, in the presence of ladies, gentlemen, and even [in the film] the vicar); *Come to the Ball* became a possible title for the show. Herman Levin suggested *The Talk of London*, which had some merit, but Loewe proposed the most bizarre name of all, *Fanfaroon*—a word of French-Spanish origin that in Britain applied to either a braggart or a fanfare. In the end, cooler heads prevailed, and as history knows, Alan Jay Lerner's musical adaptation of George Bernard Shaw's *Pygmalion* had become *My Fair Lady* by the summer of 1955, when Lerner and Loewe flew off to London with another two songs for Harrison.

The latter, happily, was "singing" better and felt easier about starring in a musical. Of the two earlier songs, he expressed some doubt about "Why Can't the English?," which reminded him of "inferior Coward": He did not wish, he said, to get onstage and do an impersonation of his witty, often arch countryman. Lerner agreed that the song's tricky, frequent rhymes came across as two "lyricky," and he reworked the rhyme scheme into its final, more conversational form. Harrison had no objections to either their latest cargo, "Come to the Ball" (of which Lerner was especially proud), or their second-act opener, "You Did It." Certain that he had now found Harrison's voice, Lerner continued to work well into the summer, as preparations proceeded under Levin's supervision for everything from sets, costumes, and lighting to the approaching auditions and impending rehearsals.

In September the Lerners and Loewe left Rockland County for Manhattan, the former taking an East Side duplex and the latter moving into rooms in his favorite retreat, the Algonquin Hotel. They had three months of concentrated work ahead of them—especially Lerner, who had not yet completed the libretto. One song seemed (to both) to come suspiciously easily. Taking a literal cue from the scene in the film where Eliza is suffering through a lesson with Higgins, Lerner suggested to Loewe that they compose a song for her based on Shaw's elocutionary phrase "The rain in Spain lies mainly in the plain"; her mastery of it would prove that she was making progress away from the world of the flower girl. The collaborators were in the street at the time and hurried up to Levin's offices, where they had their own work space. At the piano, Loewe set the phrase to an infectious Latin rhythm. Lerner then jotted down a couple of lines; Loewe set them; and so it went, until after about ten minutes, the song (unquestionably one of the highlights of the first act) was complete. Not surprisingly, perhaps, both felt it had come too easily—until they found a suitable "customer," Moss Hart, to bless it.

They were pleased with their efforts but continued to search for that "key song," as Lerner typed it, that would "reveal [Eliza's] unconscious feelings for Higgins"—a non-love love song. Then, too, Doolittle needed another song besides "With a Little Bit o' Luck"; and finally, to balance Eliza's, Higgins would require his own emotional—but not overly revelatory—key song. After six tries on Eliza's song, and six rejections, they had begun to experience some anxiety.

By mid-November, when vocalists and dancers were undergoing the ordeal of auditions, Lerner and Loewe, after some sixteen months of work, were still missing three crucial songs—and a completed book.

Although he knew what direction his final libretto would take (for he had both the play and the screenplay to go by, plus his own ideas), Lerner had not yet put it all down on paper. This worried director Moss Hart as he observed the various pieces of the show coming together and looked forward to the rehearsals that were scheduled to begin immediately after New Year's. Hart was delightfully amusing, informal, and easygoing—up to a point. He took suggestion gracefully, even invited it, but when he turned to a task, he was all business. He was not likely to flare up, but when he did, his word was definitive.

In their quest to fill the important position of choreographer, they first approached Gower Champion, who by then had a few—but significant—credits on Broadway; his agents, unfortunately, demanded an equally significant fee for his services. Next came Michael Kidd, whose promising work on *Finian's Rainbow* had been followed by, among others, *Guys and Dolls* and *Can-Can*; his one real non-hit was none other than *Love Life*. Lerner, Loewe, and Hart met with Kidd one evening to familiarize him with the score. Described by Lerner as a "rather unemotional fellow, not given to much facial expression," Kidd sat poker-faced and silent through all the music they had completed for the first act. As the second began, he spoke up to criticize "You Did It" because it recounted "offstage action."

"We are aware of that," Hart said icily, then, turning to Loewe, indicated, "Please go on."

Both Lerner and Loewe realized from that moment that they were merely going through the motions; Hart's mind was already made up. Before he left, Kidd offered a few comments on weaknesses in the second act.

Hart had one final comment: "No!" The way he said it rendered it a four-letter word.

The next candidate was German-born Hanya Holm, whose experience ranged from American opera (*The Ballad of Baby Doe*) to musicals (*Kiss Me Kate*), film, television, and even Off Broadway (*The Golden Apple*). Lerner was impressed with this "sedate little lady with a vast classic background," who appeared immediately to grasp what they were all working toward. Hayna Holm, Lerner later admitted, "almost made me lose my fear of choreographers."

With this position filled, Hart began to push for the libretto. On a mid-November Friday he phoned Lerner to inquire about his progress on the book; he was informed that the score was nearly complete and that Lerner had everything set in his head for the libretto. He should be able to finish the book in about three days of work, he thought.

"If you have any plans for the weekend," Hart said, "cancel them."

Lerner was, in a word, "astonished."

He was even more so when he learned that he and Hart were to travel to Atlantic City, then a luxurious resort center on its way downhill, best known for the Boardwalk, six miles of hotels, shops, and amusements. In the middle of November it was a ghost town: when, on their arrival, they found a hotel with an inexpensive penthouse, there were fewer than ten people on its register, counting themselves.

Hart outlined his plan: Not only would Lerner complete the book, but they would go through the entire show together, scene by scene. This worked out well, for each was geared to his own clock. Lerner's early rising gave him time to write before Hart awakened and had breakfast; after that they would work from around noon until three or four. Hart would read the script, the two would talk over his show-wise suggestions, and then they would walk along the Boardwalk and talk some more. Lerner later described those four days in Atlantic City as the "most delightful I ever spent. Moss never failed you." They returned to New York with the libretto to *My Fair Lady*, and Lerner was ready "for the battle to come."

In her autobiography, *Kitty*, Kitty Carlisle Hart recalled once asking her husband why, considering his efforts that weekend, he had not received credit as, perhaps, co-author of the book. In his reply, Hart was indifferent, satisfied to be known solely as the director. It remained for Lerner to put matters in perspective. In an interview published a year after the musical opened, a *Life* reporter suggested that though the songs were of course a great factor in the show's success, the book was equally important, and Lerner deserved all the credit he had garnered.

Lerner laconically demurred, reminding the interviewer, "There was a fellow named George Bernard Shaw."

And so, after Atlantic City, it was back to Loewe. By early December they had found another Doolittle song, "Get Me to the Church on Time," for Stanley Holloway's big second-act number. They now needed a similar statement for Higgins. They had agreed that in this particular song Higgins should reveal, insofar as it was possible for him, his true feelings for Eliza—it was to be a non-love love song, in other words. As it turned out, Shaw himself once again provided the idea for their song.

In the fifth, and last, act of *Pygmalion* Eliza has a fiery encounter with Higgins, during which she makes it plain that she intends to leave him now that their experiment in phonetics is over. He has up till now shown no concern for her future or her feelings, and she is apprehensive about what is to become of her as a well-spoken ex–flower girl. She tells him, "You'll have to do without me" (a cue for a previous Eliza song).

When Shaw's Higgins realizes what is about to occur, he sheds some of his arrogance and admits, "And I've grown accustomed to your voice and appearance. I like them, rather."

Eliza coldly suggests that he turn to the photo album he has compiled and, as for her voice, he has it on a recording "on your gramophone. . . . When you feel lonely without me, you can turn it [the machine] on. It's got no feelings to hurt."

Higgins's reply to this uses the words "voice and face"; with a lot of imagination, and a little compression, Lerner now had a title to give to Loewe: "I've Grown Accustomed to Her Face." Like "I'm an Ordinary Man," the song is emotionally ambivalent, oscillating from the lyrical to the explosive—interspersed with a brief monologue as Higgins contemplates the prospect of Eliza's marriage to the silly, lovesick Freddy (a denouement that Shaw projects in the play's last word on the subject), which he predicts will bring her crawling back to him, "in tears and rags." With its complex structure—it is definitely not a standard popular song—"I've Grown Accustomed to Her Face" did not simply evolve, as did so many other Lerner and Loewe creations, from the title; it is, in fact, two separate songs with spoken texts. Loewe's melody to the main portion of the song is simple but shapely and expressive; it is clearly the product of close work, and one of the finest elements in *My Fair Lady*'s score. It is this part of the song that in time became a "standard," one of the most frequently performed and recorded songs of the period.

With rehearsals approaching and their creative juices finally flowing, they decided on Eliza's exuberant song in the first act, when she expresses her happiness over getting the "Rain in Spain" exercise correct. That tango leads to a show-stopping moment when she, Higgins, and Pickering dance together. Alone, she diminishes the bitterness of "Just You Wait" with a song that intimates her suppressed feelings for Higgins, "I Could Have Danced All Night." Loewe conceived a melody around the title in a day; the next day Lerner brought him back the completed song. Although he loved the joyful, sweeping melody, Lerner was unhappy with one line in his lyric, "My heart took flight": he had a "special loathing," he said, for songs in which the heart performed anthropomorphically. He assured Loewe that he would find a better line eventually, but he never did (a failure that does not seem to have damaged the song's eventual popularity).

At last they were ready for rehearsals, which were set to begin just after the first of the year. But toward the end of December, Loewe was looking poorly, and his condition worried Lerner: The composer appeared to be in pain and could barely stand upright. Lerner, always careful about his own health (to the point of making sure there was a scale everywhere he went so he could watch his weight), insisted that Loewe see his doctor, who had him immediately admitted to a hospital for an appendectomy.

According to Lerner, Loewe was "furious" at this, despite the obvious necessity for surgery. For years afterward, he accused Lerner and his doctor of placing him in the hospital "under false pretenses"; evidently a man, even an intellectual, who could believe in ghosts could just as readily believe that he had not been as ill as he felt. Lerner did not elaborate on his collaborator's peculiar attitude; there would be other warning signs as their work went on.

By January 3, Loewe could hobble around as everyone assembled for, as Lerner phrased it, the "battle to come."

While his fellow countrymen and young countrywoman spent Christmas with family and friends, one of the most formidable combatants arrived in New York three days before the holiday: Rex Harrison. Lerner believed that it was his professionalism, his dedication to his craft above all else, his striving for perfectionism that brought him in early. Julie Andrews, in contrast, preferred to spend Christmas in Britain, taking her young brothers to a traditional holiday pantomime, and would appear, as per contract, on the third, when rehearsals officially were to begin. To Lerner this seemed "unprofessional," but he forgave her; she was not yet a star, whose primary obligation was to the play, not family. (This very attitude would in fact serially and unhappily contribute to the unraveling of Lerner's private life.) He temporarily overlooked the fact that she had not undertaken any new assignments while waiting for the rights to clear and the play to be written. She may have been a relative newcomer compared to the high-strung Harrison and the self-assured Holloway, but Lerner would soon come to admire this seemingly composed, always prepared young professional, herself destined for stardom.

Over Harrison's arrogant professionalism lay a mantle of thin skin or, to stretch the metaphor a bit, easily ruffled feathers. As the fact of the impending production of *My Fair Lady* became more definite, he grew increasingly intimidated by the thought of standing on stage and attempting to sing; up to the night the musical opened in New Haven, he was by turns frightened and tyrannical.

The first read-through of a show, particularly a musical, traditionally mixes nervous excitement, apprehension and expectation, reunions and introductions, and, inevitably, yes, hype. In this instance, the press was invited by master press agent Richard Maney, with the first hour or so to be given over to interviews and general mingling. It had been almost four years since Lerner and Loewe had done a Broadway show, though Lerner's Academy Award had kept his name relatively current; Hart, for his part, had not had a play on Broadway for several years, though he, too, had brought back a degree of glitter from Hollywood for his work on *Hans Christian Andersen* and Judy Garland's *A Star Is Born*.

Rex Harrison was always good for copy; a veteran of Broadway successes such as *Anne of the Thousand Days* (during whose 1948 run he and Lerner had first met) and the pre-London *Bell, Book and Candle*, he was probably best known in the United States for his film work, beginning with *Anna and the King of Siam* (without music) and *The Ghost and Mrs. Muir*.

Of the rest of the cast, Julie Andrews was remembered for *The Boy Friend* and a recent television appearance in a musical based on Maxwell Anderson's *High Tor*, starring Bing Crosby and Nancy Olson (Mrs. Alan Lerner). Stanley Holloway was familiar to American audiences mainly through his film roles in *The Lavender Hill Mob* and Laurence Olivier's *Hamlet* (as the gravedigger); in 1954 he had also been seen as Bottom in the Old Vic's production of *A Midsummer Night's Dream* at the Metropolitan Opera House. Yet another Briton, Cathleen Nesbitt (cast in the minute role of Higgins's mother), had made her Broadway debut forty-five years before and had since appeared in Dublin, in London, and in a handful of undistinguished plays in New York.

Press agent Maney did not, for the moment, have much to work with, and there was no unusual excitement as the press milled about, studying sketches for the costumes and sets. On the stage were a couple of long tables facing banks of folding chairs; there was no scenery and only a work light illuminated the bare boards. After about an hour, the women and men of the press were ushered out, leaving only those directly connected with the show— except for Kitty Carlisle Hart, who was regarded as part of the company by marriage and shared love of the theater.

Moss Hart sat at the middle of the center table, flanked on either side by the various technicians as well as his assistants (one of whom was his brother Bernard), producer Levin, designers Smith and Beaton, stage manager Samuel Liff, choreographer Holm, and musical director Franz Allers (a Lerner and Loewe standby since *Brigadoon*). To one side of the stage were Loewe at the keyboard and Lerner beside him.

The principals sat in the first row of chairs facing Hart, the secondary actors took the second row, and the rest of the cast settled into the remaining chairs. After his introductory talk, Hart called out the stage directions, the cast members read their lines, and, on cue, Lerner and Loewe performed the songs in the first rough reading of *My Fair Lady*.

During the course of act 2, Lerner became uncomfortably aware of a clouding of the Harrisonian visage. The first act had engendered delight and zeal among all the cast, but as the second continued, Harrison's voice lost volume, and his face grew longer. Between "You Did It" and "I've Grown Accustomed to Her Face," he felt, Higgins got lost. It was true: Eliza sang, Freddy sang, Eliza and Freddy sang, Doolittle sang—but what did *Higgins* do? Hart and Lerner agreed with their star and decided to give his character another song in act 2. Loewe was not terribly happy with the idea, thinking his work was done, but he arranged to meet Lerner the next morning so the two could "begin staring at each other."

Musical-theater lore abounds in anecdotal tales of how this or that star was born or song created. It has often been said of Richard Rodgers, for example, that it took him only as long to compose a melody as it did to play it: instant composition. Ira Gershwin, so the story goes, almost invariably worked from his brother George's tunes, while Cole Porter and Irving Berlin are purported to have composed words and music simultaneously. Good stories all, but not necessarily true.

When Loewe and Lerner stopped staring at each other and came up with an idea for the additional Higgins song, they got its title, too: "Why

Can't a Woman Be More Like a Man?" (later retitled "A Hymn to Him"). In foraging for a possible concept, Lerner recalled an incident that had occurred during a before-dinner walk on Fifth Avenue with Harrison, in which the conversation had centered on their multiple marriages and the handicaps associated with them (Lerner was on his third marriage and Harrison on his second, while also involved with Kay Kendall).

Harrison had stopped abruptly and exclaimed, in a voice that Lerner said carried for yards, "Alan! Wouldn't it be marvelous if we were homosexuals!?" A bit disconcerted by the glares of passersby, Lerner could only reply, "I don't think so." But he remembered the remark when, a week or so later, he conceived the title "Why Can't a Woman Be More Like a Man?"

Harrison told a somewhat different story. It featured the same cast, same street, same song—but with an additional pedestrian, Nancy Olson Lerner. In his posthumous autobiography, the actor maintained that the three of them were strolling along Fifth Avenue on their way to the Pierre Hotel when, feeling ignored, Nancy Lerner lashed out at her husband and, according to Harrison, "scream[ed], 'What you really mean, Alan, is why can't a woman be more like a man?'"

However the song was inspired, it was completed just in time for the second week of rehearsals, and approved and admired by both Hart and Harrison, who, when initially informed of the theme, "roared with laughter." On hearing the finished "Hymn to Him," he simply said, "Quite right! You're absolutely right"—it was a good expression of his own view of the sexes.

Harrison, because he was unfamiliar with how musicals worked, was given special attention during evening rehearsals. Hart had adjusted the traditional rehearsal schedule; while he still complied with the rules of Actors Equity, calling the cast together for eight and a half hours a day (with an hour and a half off), he began at two in the afternoon instead of the more typical ten in the morning, and went until eleven at night. That way, he thought, the cast would be less fatigued for the next day's work.

Hart took Harrison in tow during the seven-to-eleven shift the first week, staging his numbers while the others were off in different parts of the theater going through their scripts and songs. (Holm's dancers learned their steps in another theater.) Musical rehearsals can often be cacophonous, with the sound of voices and pianos echoing in from stage, basement, and dressing rooms; an outsider would be hard put to make sense of it all. But Hart was aware of the disparate pieces of his production and of how and where, one day, they would seamlessly fuse.

Taking it upon himself to look out for the interests of his countryman Bernard Shaw, Harrison carried a paperback copy of the Penguin Books *Pygmalion* with him at all times; if a line did not seem Shavian enough to him, he would call out, "Where's my Penguin?" to check up on that cunning Alan Lerner. Once he was assured of the authenticity of the lines, the rehearsal could continue. Lerner took this for a week, and then one day, when Harrison called for his Penguin, a stuffed specimen acquired by Lerner at a taxidermist's was handed to him onstage. That ended the actor's consultation of his Penguin, though the stuffed bird found refuge in his dressing room for the run of the show.

On one occasion, he inadvertently snared the wily author. In the fifth scene of act 1, just before the "Rain in Spain" number, Higgins, in a rare show of understanding, gently tells Eliza, "I know you're tired. I know your head aches. I know your nerves are as raw as meat in a butcher's window," and then launches into a diatribe on the beauties of the English language and what they are striving for. Harrison, duly impressed, said, "That's a damn fine speech," and inquired as to its Shavian source.

"I wrote it," Lerner admitted. Harrison exhibited some displeasure in his expression, but he did not insist that Lerner's contribution be excised. However, "from then on," Lerner later exaggerated, "he lost respect for [the passage] and seldom got it right."

Concluding from this that veracity was not the best policy where his nit-picking star was concerned, Lerner changed his approach. From then on, whenever Harrison came to an unfamiliar line and snapped, "Is that yours?" Lerner would assure him that it had come from the Great Man himself—if not from *Pygmalion*, well, then, from one of the prefaces, or an obscure essay, or even a letter. Harrison was suitably mollified. (Some years later, in a London interview, he would state that in all of *My Fair Lady*, only six lines were Lerner's!)

Harrison's temperament was not the only source of irritation. With Hart spending so much time with Harrison, and then later with Julie Andrews, Stanley Holloway felt neglected and, before the show packed up for tryouts, threatened to leave the cast; Hart had to take him aside and explain that because he was an experienced musical professional, he did not require the careful handling of a nervous star in his debut musical role or a young girl in her first major Broadway part. A happy Holloway quickly withdrew his resignation. Yet another disaffected Londoner was Harrison's old friend Robert Coote (Colonel Pickering), who was unhappy over the placement of Higgins's new song, "A Hymn to Him." At this point in the musical, Eliza has just walked out on Higgins, and Pickering dominates the scene with a longish phone call in which he tries to get Scotland Yard to begin the search for her (the call is merely alluded to in Shaw's play).

The assertion of Higgins's song during this scene, with the repetition of the question "Why can't a woman be more like a man?" interrupted Coote's telephone monologue. Originally, the interruptions had come only in the form of Higgins's revelation, while Pickering describes her for the Scotland Yard inspector, that he had noticed such details as the color of Eliza's eyes and hair; the addition of Harrison's song at this point, in Coote's mind, spoiled his single significant speech in the show. This mishap he attributed to Harrison, not to Lerner (who conceived it), and for some time he was rather frosty in his relationship with his quondam friend.

A daily diversion imported from England was soon introduced by Holloway: tea time. At four every afternoon, time out was called while Julie Andrews prepared tea for the Britons in the company—herself, Harrison, Holloway, Coote, and Cathleen Nesbit—and anyone else who wished to join. It was a civilizing if strange touch, since American show people were more attuned to another custom: drinking a scalding-hot liquid called coffee out of paper or foam cups.

By the second week of rehearsals, certain practices were in place, feathers were unruffled (except for Harrison's, from time to time), and preparations had begun for the out-of-town tryouts. The show would need to have some sort of title (none had yet been chosen from among the suggestions) for the newspapers in New Haven and Philadelphia. Producer Levin said any old name would do, citing as an example the uninspired tryout title *Away We Go* for the musical that became *Oklahoma!* in New York.

"Why don't we just take the title that we all dislike the least?" Lerner offered—and that was *My Fair Lady*.

The week was also devoted to coaxing the cast out of chairs and onto the stage (or "getting it on its feet," in trade jargon) and to testing the actors' memory (referred to as "getting the script out of their hands"). It was during this period that Julie Andrews exhibited a problem: She knew all the words, but something was missing in her projection of Eliza Doolittle. Harrison, obviously unhappy with her, at one point blew up and stalked out of the theater, snapping something about the "bitch" (one of his cherished synonyms for females at the time; the other—applied to both sexes, but female in origin—was one that Shakespeare never used, nor Shaw) and swearing that if she showed up for the next week of rehearsals, he would "quit the show," another popular locution among theatrical types.

Hart canceled rehearsals to allow him to work with his Eliza without other members of the company around. As he had done with Lerner that November weekend on the New Jersey shore, he took her through the complete play; "he bullied and pleaded, coaxed and cajoled. He made me Eliza," Andrews remembered. She was furious, frightened, and crushed, but after a couple of sessions, she had truly mastered the part. Now, as Lerner noted, the only trouble was her quite proper speech. "To assist her," he wrote, "we found an American phoneticist [actor Alfred Dixon] who did in reverse offstage what Higgins was doing on stage."

Even Harrison noticed the change, and as rehearsals resumed, all went reasonably smoothly. Lerner was never overly concerned if things seemed a bit ragged in what he called the "down week" (that is, the third); after the initial excitement of discovering a new work had worn off, enthusiasm often picked up again when all the elements were brought together—dialogue, songs, dancing—and all the members of the cast could see and hear what everyone else had been doing over the past several weeks. Invariably, the reception was appreciative—in Lerner's view, suspiciously so: he checked off the lines that got excessive laughs, for experience had shown him that what amused the cast and crew at this juncture would not necessarily tickle a paying audience. He then prepared a few alternative lines, just in case.

As the time approached for the beginning of the show's out-of-town tour, Lerner sensed another Harrison tempest in the offing. From its inception, the actor had not liked the idea of having to stand watching, with nothing to do, while Julie Andrews sang "Without You" at him. Hart had so far sidestepped the problem by skipping the scene during rehearsals, even going so far as to omit it from the complete run-through before everyone and everything set out for New Haven. A possible Harrisonian eruption was thus temporarily avoided, and all else went well enough—though the songwriters and director worried that the repetition of Holloway's zestful "With a Little Bit o' Luck" twice in the first act was less than successful. Lerner made a note to look into that in New Haven.

The company arrived in Connecticut on a Monday, production manager Samuel Liff having come up earlier to "hang the show" (i.e., place the sets), and conductor Franz Allers to prepare the orchestra, made up of local talent built around a core of musicians from New York. En route to New Haven by train, Hart decided it was time to tackle the "Without You" problem. He took a seat next to Harrison and told him that Julie Andrews was going to sing the song either "with or without you on the stage." If he insisted on being offstage while she sang, Hart said with a no-nonsense edge in his usually gentle voice, "you will look like a horse's ass if you leave the stage when she begins . . . and return when she has finished."

So strong had been Harrison's objection to the song, indeed, that he had refused even to listen to an idea of Lerner and Loewe's that would focus attention on *him* while Andrews sang. Hart now asked him to extend a little courtesy and see how they proposed to stage the scene. Harrison agreed.

While the sets were being put in place at the Shubert, the company began a week of rehearsals in a nearby hall. When Hart called for a run-through of the vexatious "Without You," Lerner and Loewe waited apprehensively: Would Harrison come out onstage? He did, and they demonstrated their additions: a line of dialogue (Higgins's "You brazen hussy!") and eight lines for *him* to sing, thus interrupting her at the climax of the song (not to mention filching her applause):

> *By George, I really did it!*
> *I did it! I did it!*
> *I said I'd make a woman*
> *And indeed I did! . . .*

With this problem solved, rehearsals could continue—at least, that is, until the next battle: Rex Harrison vs. the orchestra. During the weeks in New York with piano accompaniment, and the few days with the orchestra in the rehearsal hall, with conductor Allers by his side, Harrison had felt relatively at ease. In preparation for a Saturday-night preview performance, however (with the official premiere scheduled for two days after that), a Friday-night rehearsal was called with everything in place, including the sets and, for the first time, the orchestra in the pit. Thirty strong, the musicians were located somewhere below Harrison's now cold feet, and hidden partly under the stage.

In the midst of singing "I'm an Ordinary Man," he stopped abruptly, stepped down to the apron, glared at Allers, and demanded, "Can you hear me?"

"Yes," Allers replied, "I can hear you."

"What?!"

"I can hear you," he repeated.

"*I* can't hear *you*; how can *you* hear *me*?"

Harrison returned to the song as Allers cued the orchestra. After his next line, there were a couple of bars of brass.

He stopped again. "Take that out," he shouted.

"Take what out?" Allers inquired.

"That *yah, ta, ta, ta, tah!*"

"You'll get used to it," the conductor assured him.

"I will never get used to it," Harrison snapped. "It's absolutely ridiculous for a man to be standing up here singing his lines with a symphony orchestra blasting away down there!"

Hart, ever the peacemaker, promised Harrison that he would be able to rehearse alone with the orchestra on Saturday afternoon, before the premiere. The additional rehearsal time helped; the actor calmed down and admitted that he was ready to go on. But with the Shubert sold out for that evening's preview, yet another storm struck—this time a literal one.

On February 4, 1956, "the night of our opening in New Haven," Julie Andrews recalled, "there was a blizzard, a snow blizzard, and it was terrible. People wondered if anybody would show up at the theater. The amazing thing was that millions of people, it seems, came from New York. They drove through the snow in limousines and so forth."

For a brief time, Lerner and others in the company saw this natural near-catastrophe as a godsend. What the brave souls who had come from all points through the snow did not know was that late that afternoon, Rex Harrison had announced, with finality, that he would not go on that night. After insisting that he needed at least another day of rehearsals with the orchestra before the Monday-night premiere, he had locked himself in his dressing room with his penguin, announcing, "I never liked musical com!" Opening curtain was now only about three hours away, and sturdy souls had already started out from New York—those "dear shits" (as Lerner and Loewe called them) who were as eager to witness a flop as to see a success.

The impossible weather would, they hoped, give them a way out without their having to reveal the truth about Harrison's defection; then, too, of course, they could always fall back on that blanket excuse "technical difficulties" (which they would learn in fact existed in this instance). They canceled the performance and had the news broadcast regularly over the local radio station.

No less furious than the snowstorm itself, however, was the reaction of the Shubert's house manager on being informed of their decision to cancel. Lerner noted, with apprehension, that the man was livid; he was also vocal. By

six o'clock, two hours before curtain was due to go up, a mob had formed outside the Shubert in the sleet. They had not heard any radio bulletin. The
manager confronted Herman Levin, Hart, and Harrison's agent, threatening
to reveal the true reason for the cancellation: the fact that Rex Harrison had
deserted the company. The revelation could seriously damage Harrison's future—in the American theater, at least.

The agent began pounding on Harrison's dressing-room door, shouting
deprecations and repeating the manager's threats. That and, according to the
actor, his sense of loyalty to the cast changed Harrison's mind again, and he at
last emerged. The company had in the meantime been dismissed and now
had to be reassembled from movie houses, bars, and, as Kitty Carlisle Hart
recollected it, health clubs. Miraculously, all returned to the theater in time.

When the curtain rose, at eight-forty, the house was full. Lerner stood,
paced, fretted. The "technical difficulties" came when the twin turntables
onstage moved too slowly and curtains snared on the set. To the lyricist's surprise, the song they had considered shortening, "With a Little Bit o' Luck,"
brought down the house; Holloway had carried it off. But Harrison's "Come
to the Ball" was, in Lerner's words, a "disaster in three-quarter time." "On the
Street Where You Live," for its part, seemed to mystify the audience and the
song was greeted with dead silence. After a lengthy ballet dubbed "Decorating Eliza," an obviously overlong (twenty-five minutes too long, by Lerner's
watch) first act ended. Despite all the day's disasters, however, something was
clearly going right: Even Harrison managed to suppress his anxiety, and in
Julie Andrews the theater had a glorious new star.

The second act went perfectly, and when the curtain descended, the audience erupted with applause; all stood and cheered and cheered. Excitement, congratulations, and general commotion carried the cheering
backstage and into the dressing rooms, where Harrison was at the center of it
all, now beaming and relieved. Lerner was jubilant but concerned, considering the morning after even as he basked in the genuine enthusiasms of the
"dear shits," who recognized a hit when they saw one. He did feel a bit guilty
about an earlier encounter with one of them, an agent, who had made the
mistake of asking him how things were going. In his agitation, Lerner had
come back with, for him, an out-of-character show of ego: "I have no idea of
what the reaction of the audience will be," he snapped, "but I genuinely believe it's the best musical I ever saw." He would be joined by multitudes in his
innocent arrogance.

All concerned met on Tuesday morning to discuss cutting act 1 and to decide the fate of "On the Street Where You Live." Only Lerner retained a fondness for this song, whose melody he liked (and Loewe detested) and whose "flagrantly romantic" lyric, he believed, fitted the slightly foolish Freddy just right. They set that matter aside for the moment to deal with the more critical problem of shortening. Out came "Come to the Ball," "Say a Prayer for Me Tonight," and the ballet "Decorating Eliza."

As for "On the Street Where You Live," Lerner felt that the real difficulty was that the audience had no idea who it was who was singing, or why: In the previous scene, the one in which Eliza commits her gaffe with the racehorse at Ascot, Freddy is dressed just like all the other men, with nothing to differentiate him from them. Lerner solved the problem, and saved the song (which would become one of the most popular from the score), by simply rewriting the verse in which Freddy refers to an incident at the home of Higgins's mother:

> When she mentioned how her aunt bit off the spoon,
> She completely done me in.
> And my heart went on a journey to the moon,
> When she told about her father and the gin.

To further acquaint the audience with the character's identity, Lerner also provided the lovesick Freddy with additional dialogue: When Higgins's housekeeper answers the door, he repeats his name and explains, "If she doesn't remember me, tell her I'm the chap who was sniggering at her"; with the closing of the door, Freddy bursts into the chorus of "On the Street Where You Live." Loewe wrote new music for the revised verse, and the reworked song had its debut on Thursday night when it momentarily stopped the show. (First heard on "Your Hit Parade," that purveyor of success and profitability in popular song, on June 2, 1956, the song achieved the number-one spot on August 4 and remained on the Hit Parade for no less than fifteen weeks, vindicating Lerner and pleasing the dubious Loewe).

"On the Street Where You Live" was Freddy's one big musical moment in *My Fair Lady*. In the play and the musical he is a marginal character, a representative—to Shaw as well as Eliza—of the British upper classes. He does not work, lives off his mother's money, and is infatuated with Eliza. In his afterword to the play, Shaw dismisses "happy endings," thus Eliza rejects Higgins and marries the simpering Freddy. In the musical, Lerner has her leave Higgins, go off with Freddy briefly, and finally return to Higgins—Lerner's major contradiction of Shaw. Lerner, ever the romantic, could not avoid a happy ending.

After shifts and cuts occasioned by its week in New Haven, *My Fair Lady* was ready for its next stop, Philadelphia, where only minor polishing was required. The "superb" reviews were a source of both delight and worry: Richard Maney, the show's press agent, not without minor hyperbole, reported that the

> out-of-town hysteria swept Broadway like a flash fire in a mesquite patch, and sent ticket brokers into tribal snake dances. So feverish were the reports of the show's magic that producer Herman Levin, authors Lerner and Loewe, and director Moss Hart broke out in cold sweats. Such superlatives, they felt, could boomerang. They might develop a "this had better be good" resistance in New York audiences. More than one show, they recalled, had been victimized by the excessive zeal of volunteer press agents.

Variety's "Hobe" opened his review of *My Fair Lady* with a similar observation after the premiere at the Mark Hellinger Theater on March 15, 1956. His was but one of a unanimous collection of practically ecstatic assessments.

That night, as was his way, Lerner paced in the back of the theater and backstage. (He once acquired a pedometer to gauge this compulsion and found that in one night he might walk two miles going nowhere.) A preview audience the night before had been most gratifyingly responsive, but he remained skeptical, later recalling that "until that opening night was over my name was angst." It began, that night, with further feeding of his anxiety: The first-night audience seemed too quiet, too reverent. The songs were generously applauded, but the laughter was slight—not an untypical reaction, according to Lerner, though considering the advance hoopla, not exactly what they had expected, either.

As Lerner paced, Loewe observed the stage with equanimity. With the singing of "Wouldn't It Be Loverly?," the first scene ended to appreciative applause, and Moss Hart hurried over in a state (*frantic* was the word that came to Lerner's mind).

"I knew it," he blurted. "It's just a New Haven hit. That's all. Just a New Haven hit."

Smiling, Loewe suggested that if "Mossie" did not recognize the "biggest hit that has ever come to New York," perhaps he could use a drink. By the time they returned from a nearby bar, one of Loewe's frequent havens for a drink and a smoke between musical numbers, "With a Little Bit o' Luck" had stopped the show. And it grew: "The Rain in Spain," Richard Maney recalled with a publicist's zeal, was so enthusiastically received that "three horse players and two TV comics, mooning over their pastrami in Lindy's on the corner, bolted into Fifty-first Street, fearful that there'd been an explosion in the subway."

"The cheering at the first act curtain routed the last of the dissidents," he continued, "those skeptics who had argued that an adaptation of *Pygmalion* was strictly for eggheads, that a musical without kiss, caress or display of feminine pelf could not survive in a community conditioned to naked nymphs, double entendres, and outhouse humor." While this encomium was drafted for a special advertising supplement to the *New York Times* (published four years after the event), it was in fact entirely true.

The final curtain brought the audience to its feet, hands above heads, demanding several curtain calls. Hart had been wrong about the New Haven hit, and Lerner and Loewe had been right. *My Fair Lady* was the best musical Lerner had ever seen, the biggest hit that had ever opened in New York, a unique mix of all the ingredients that make for a successful show: producer, book (not forgetting, of course, Shaw), lyrics, music, director, cast, choreography, sets, costumes, lighting, and musical direction, with additional behind-the-scenes musical contributions from arrangers Robert Russell Bennett, Phil Lang, and, for the dances, Trude Rittman. An almost miraculous fusion of these discrete talents into virtually a single creative unit brought forth one of the most perfect musicals ever staged.

"Don't bother reading this review now," began Walter Kerr's commentary in the next morning's *Herald-Tribune*. "You'd better sit right down and send for those tickets to *My Fair Lady*. First things first.

"Are you back? Well, almost the most enchanting thing about the new musical at the Hellinger is watching it grow, like Liza Doolittle, before your eyes." He made special mention of "With a Little Bit o' Luck" (which was "most engaging"; even by this point, he said, it was already obvious that the audience was seeing a "good show, if not a great one"), "I'm an Ordinary Man," "Just You Wait," and "The Rain in Spain." "After that," Kerr claimed, "you couldn't have stopped *My Fair Lady* if you'd . . . invited the authors of *Buttrio Square, Hit the Trail,* and *Carnival of Flanders* to work over the second act" (the reference was to a trio of recent major flop musicals whose combined runs had added up to a grand total of seventeen performances). Kerr went on to applaude in print virtually everyone in or connected with the show, especially those who had "hurled song after song from the Lerner-Loewe treasure chest into the . . . auditorium. Pace, taste and triumphant good humor rolled on into the night." He concluded with further accolades for Julie Andrews and Rex Harrison, "both of them together finding humor and honesty in a brilliantly purposeful score."

Second only to Kerr in his sensitivity to musicals was the *Post*'s Richard Watts, Jr., who began his review with an allusion to the "glowing tryout notices," thanks to which the audience had been prepared for "something notable and would have been satisfied with nothing less. Happily, this is just what they found."

He went on to devote a paragraph to Shaw's contribution to this success:

> His tale of the arrogant and selfish expert on phonetics, who bet he could turn a Cockney flower girl into a lady, has an unsentimental chilliness about it that keeps romantic gush at a distance, but, with just a slight push from his adapters, his story is given the proper warmth for a musical play without losing the Shavian spirit, and his wit, irony and comic imagination mingle superbly and comfortably with the songs and dances.
>
> This doesn't in any way mean that Mr. Lerner and Mr. Loewe thereupon had a soft job on their hands. If the music and the lyrics, as well as the editing they had to do, hadn't possessed the proper mood and the necessary sort of wit to go with the original *Pygmalion*, I hate to think what might have happened.
>
> Mr. Lerner's lyrics are witty, polished and intelligent, and they also have the great merit of sounding as if they belonged in a work stemming from the Master. Mr. Loewe's music is bright, gay and charming, and it has the enormous value of being a perfectly integrated score that belongs to the book as completely do the lyrics. I won't try to single out any favorite numbers.

While Kerr and Watts were the most musicianly of the critics, it was the *New York Times*, then as ever, that would provide the last word—or rather, the first, as it was invariably to the *Times* that the company first turned on the morning after. A drama critic for the paper since 1925, Brooks Atkinson was also a former college English teacher, news reporter (during the Second

World War he had been sent to China and the Soviet Union), and erudite author of books ranging from biography to travel. His was a powerful voice on Broadway.

"Bulletins from the road have not been misleading," he began. "*My Fair Lady* . . . is a wonderful show. . . . [It] is staged dramatically on a civilized plane. Probably for the first time in history a typical musical comedy audience finds itself absorbed in the art of pronunciation and passionately involved in the proper speaking of 'pain,' 'rain' and 'Spain.'" From there on it was clear sailing, with praise for all—even though Harrison, according to Lerner, "flew into a blinding rage (which, of course, passed quickly) because he felt the *New York Times* had not given me my due."

Atkinson followed his daily review with a Sunday sequel that gave the company great pleasure during the daylong recording of the cast album at the Columbia Records studios on Thirtieth Street. (Lerner's old friend Goddard Lieberson, who supervised the session, would soon learn that he had engineered a very wise investment indeed.) The subhead of Atkinson's Sunday essay should have satisfied even the hard-to-please Harrison: "Shaw's *Pygmalion* Turns Into One of the Best Musicals of the Century." The piece asserted that though

> in the new musical comedy, the hero and heroine never kiss . . . as a musical play, *My Fair Lady* is one of Broadway's celestial works. Although it includes the familiar elements of book, songs, dance and spectacle, it dispenses with bromides of showmanship and stands on its own feet as a theatre creation.
>
> Mr. Lerner has not only adapted the Shaw play without cheapening it; he has also written new scenes and lyrics that carry the story into new dimensions.

Atkinson's final words on the subject were, "In taste, intelligence, skill and delight, *My Fair Lady* is the finest musical play in years."

By the time *My Fair Lady* finally closed, on September 29, 1962—after a run of six and a half years and 2,717 performances—it had received more than its share of plaudits, including the New York Drama Critics Circle Award and the League of New York Theatres Award (called the Tony in honor of Antoinette Perry) for Best Musical. Tonys went also to Harrison, Loewe, Lerner, Hart, Hanya Holm, Herman Levin, Oliver Smith, Cecil Beaton, and Franz Allers. The Best Actress award that year was given to *Bells Are Ringing*'s Judy

Holliday instead of Julie Andrews, but Andrews nonetheless had a solid stage and film career ahead of her. (Disappointingly, in the good if rather unexceptional film version of *My Fair Lady*, Eliza is portrayed by a stronger screen name, Audrey Hepburn, with vocals dubbed by Marni Nixon—an oversight comparable to that represented by the filming of *Gypsy* without Ethel Merman. Ironically, when the Academy Awards were handed out in 1965, Rex Harrison won for his Professor Higgins and Julie Andrews for her title role in *Mary Poppins*.)

For years *My Fair Lady* held the record as the longest-running show in New York (its London run, featuring most of the original cast, lasted almost as long—2,281 performances), only to be overtaken by *Hello Dolly!*, which opened in 1964. The original cast album became an immediate best-seller; by 1978, as Lerner indicated in *The Street Where I Live*, CBS's $400,000 investment had brought in more than $42 million for Columbia Records, which produced the score in a number of languages, including Spanish and Swedish, for release wherever the show appeared. Revivals continue to be successfully staged, and the 1964 film version, though flawed, was also popular.

After the opening, the Lerners invited a few friends to gather in a room they had taken over at "21." Present were the Harts, Harrison, Goddard Lieberson and his wife, the former ballerina Vera Zorina, Irene Selznick, and others. By two in the morning Lerner was euphoric, even "numb," but not from drink: He cherished the joy of his friends, he said, even more than he did the ecstatic reviews. He was somewhat suspicious of success, believing that it "steals your defenses and leaves you on top of the world, stark naked." By 1960, however, with *My Fair Lady* enjoying its fourth anniversary on Broadway, he had changed his view a bit and could say, "I have no particular nostalgia for failure"—he was thinking of *What's Up?*, *The Day Before Spring*, and *Love Life*—"but success teaches you more. You learn from a failure what you've done wrong, but a success shows you what you've done right."

By the time he and his wife got back to their apartment after the party at "21," Lerner knew that *My Fair Lady* was a success writ large.

As they entered the elevator, he said, "What a night!"

"Did you like my dress?"

"Beautiful . . . beautiful," he replied.

9

—w—

PARIS

Lerner's and Loewe's divergent reactions to their unqualified achievement were characteristic: While Loewe took off for Paris and its chemin-de-fer tables, then proceeded to Cannes for a summer of more gambling and gamboling with the young beauties of the port, Lerner barely stopped to catch his breath.

Four days after the premiere of *My Fair Lady*, he spoke at the Grolier Club of New York, as a guest of the Shaw Society of America. (His subject was, unsurprisingly, "*Pygmalion* and *My Fair Lady*.") Unlike his partner, he was anxious to begin working again, though he had certainly earned a rest and had been a most neglectful husband during the writing of the musical: By this time, a sense of uneasiness had crept into his marriage to the very domestic Nancy Olson. He explained away his work-compulsion by recalling something Lorenz Hart had once told him during one of their card games at the Lambs Club: "To be a writer you must be brutal."

He clarified Hart's attitude, so much like his own:

He didn't mean you must hurt people. He meant you must be ruthless with yourself, you must concentrate on your writing to the exclusion of everything and everyone else, you must devote

yourself to learning it, improving it, working at it constantly without ever giving yourself an out, without ever settling for less.

In Lerner's view, his creative marriage to Loewe took precedence over everything and everyone else.

Loewe, however, was not then the least interested in work. Lerner had
promised Arthur Freed, who had flown in to Philadelphia to see *My Fair Lady*,
that he would consider the idea of doing a musical film adaptation of Sidonie
Gabrielle Colette's 1942 novella *Gigi*; at the time, he had been too preoccupied with his new musical to give it much further thought, but he told Freed
he would be in touch as soon as things settled down. With *My Fair Lady*
Lerner and Loewe had found the perfect working formula, especially for writing about someone else's characters. *Gigi* would be just right for them, but it
would have to wait until Loewe was finished with his French fling.

As *My Fair Lady* grew fatter at the box office, Lerner began to be annoyed at being asked what could he ever do to top it. According to one source,
it was his unsympathetic mother's only query after the obvious success of the
premiere—the one spoiling moment of the otherwise memorable night. In
April he was surprised to read in the *Times* that he and Loewe had abandoned
work (never begun) on a musical version of *Saratoga Trunk* (three years later
Edna Ferber's book would be produced—and be a dismal failure—as a musical with songs by Harold Arlen and Johnny Mercer).

By May the Lerners were back in their New York retreat, where they bus-
ied themselves with committee work in support of Adlai Stevenson's second
and, as it would turn out, again unsuccessful bid for the presidency. Also active on the committee were conductor Mitch Miller, author Charles Samuels,
and Joseph Fishkin, president of the local school district. Despite his having
suffered a serious heart attack the previous September, Dwight D. Eisenhower had announced his candidacy that February. Lerner's choice, the artic-
ulate and intellectual Stevenson, stood little chance against the Republican
"Peace and Prosperity" campaign; by this time the irresponsible behavior that
had fueled the flames of Stevenson's first run, the witch-hunting of Senator
Joseph McCarthy, had ended in the latter's emasculation by the Senate (with
the help of correspondent Edward R. Murrow and Boston attorney Joseph L.
Welch). For Lerner, some of the sparkle had gone out of politics with Mc-
Carthy's official condemnation.

In August, with the election still some months away, Lerner flew out to the West Coast to meet with Freed. Since his last stay there, when he had worked on the never-produced *Green Mansions*, Hollywood's musical scene had begun to deteriorate. Fewer musicals were being shot, and even the usually bountiful MGM had become budget-conscious; television was taking its toll, and the Beatles were just around the corner.

Since *Brigadoon*, the Freed Unit had produced only three musicals: an original called *It's Always Fair Weather* (1955), *Kismet* (also 1955), and Cole Porter's *Silk Stockings* (to be released in the summer of 1957). Of the other studios' memorable 1955 musicals, two were filmed Broadway hits (*Oklahoma!* and *Guys and Dolls*), while another, *Hit the Deck*, borrowed only the title and some of the musical numbers from that Broadway show. Disney's cartoon *Lady and the Tramp* featured songs, Fred Astaire's *Daddy Long Legs* was mild entertainment, and two of that year's other films were musicals only insofar as they were more or less accurate biographical portraits of vocalists Ruth Etting (*Love Me or Leave Me*) and Lillian Roth (*I'll Cry Tomorrow*), with scores consisting of songs associated with the two women and depending largely on nostalgia. From 1955 on, original musical film production in Hollywood dwindled.

When Lerner arrived in Los Angeles in the summer of 1956, the writing was evident on MGM's fading walls. The "only thing that had not changed," he found, "was Arthur's enthusiasm." The producer was deep into the *Gigi* project, and had been for almost two years now: It was no small task to get the story of a young courtesan-in-training past the morals squad of the Production Code office. What Freed had not realized until after he acquired the rights was that Colette's widower, Maurice Goudeket (his wife had died in 1954), had already sold the musical rights to producer Gilbert Miller, who was planning to adapt the stage version by Anita Loos (in which Audrey Hepburn had starred in 1954). Freed's announcement that Alan Jay Lerner was working on a film musical adaptation of *Gigi* raised an outcry in New York; it cost more than $87,000 to buy out Miller, Loos, and company.

With the sybaritic Loewe for the time being uninterested and unavailable, Lerner instructed his agent, the redoubtable Irving P. Lazar, to make it clear that he was to do the screenplay and nothing else. Disappointed, Freed prevailed upon Lerner to communicate with Loewe in Cannes, but the composer's answer was still negative.

Skirting the subject of songs and lyrics for the moment, Lerner and Freed turned to the casting, an important consideration for Lerner while he fashioned his script. Who would be Gigi? Lerner believed that Audrey Hepburn, having established herself on stage in the role, would be fine for the screen version, but Freed was thinking of someone more authentically Parisian: Leslie Caron, who had appeared in half a dozen films since their *An American in Paris*, including the winsome *Lili* and *Daddy Long Legs*, opposite Fred Astaire. For the sophisticated former boulevardier, uncle of the story's youthful male protagonist, there was, they agreed, only one choice: Maurice Chevalier, one of a handful of performers whom Lerner had dreamed of working with. To realize his dream, Lerner created a character who does not appear in Colette's story: Chevalier would portray the film's worldly wise narrator. As Gaston, the second-generation man-about-town, Lerner wanted to cast the Englishman Dirk Bogarde, "one of the best screen actors alive," who had a "serviceable singing voice" and the skill "to play a bored man and not be boring."

Before he left California, Lerner "reluctantly" consented to do four songs with someone other than Loewe, provided that Freed make a strong bid to get Chevalier to star and Cecil Beaton to design the sets and costumes. Back home in New York, he began writing the screenplay and spotting the songs, but as he finished the first draft, he resolved "to have one last whack at Fritz," arguing that the least he could do "was read the bloody script." He also suggested that for ambience, Loewe could hardly do better than Paris for writing the score.

The first point, Loewe conceded, was reasonable, and the second enticing. According to Lerner, Loewe had returned to New York in November 1956 and, since he had promised to read the script, dropped by to visit. "Fritz took the script home with him, and bright and early the next morning he telephoned to say he loved it and wanted to do it." Lerner was relieved, for he had promised Freed that if Loewe refused again, he would work with another composer.

There was jubilation over this news in Freed's offices in Culver City, and Freed at once wrote Loewe to express his delight and gratitude. The composer replied that he, too, was "delighted . . . especially as I just read the script and found it enchanting. Alan and I are raring to go, and I have a feeling that we will come across with a lulu of a score."

Although the script was still only in rough form and he was not yet happy with it, Lerner sent it off to Freed, confident that the producer would be able to make something of it. As it turned out, however, MGM's story department was not impressed by Lerner's effort. *The Street Where I Live* amusingly recounts one of its author's frequent, rather oblique conversations with Freed during a short trip to Hollywood.

> LERNER: . . . What about the script?
> FREED: Do you want to do it [referring to a proposed Irving Berlin film, *Say It with Music*]?
> LERNER: You have it [*Gigi*].
> FREED: MacKenna wants to talk to you. [Kenneth MacKenna was head of the story department.]
> LERNER: What about?
> FREED: Don't pay any attention to him.
> LERNER: Didn't he like it?
> FREED: How about some lunch? I've got some ideas about Maxim's [one of the settings in *Gigi*].

All through lunch that day, Freed made no mention of the subject Lerner was willing him to broach: the *Gigi* script. Then, as he rose from the table, Freed confided that he had to return to his office to discuss Chevalier's contract. An astonished Lerner could only ask, "Does he want to do it?" "Why not?" was the producer's response. "It's a great part for him." And he moved on to another subject.

Apparently, *Gigi* was on.

In March 1957, after seeing off the second road company of *My Fair Lady*, Lerner and Loewe set off for Paris. They had a script that was close to final, they were certain of Chevalier, the dependable Vincente Minnelli was set to direct, and they already had one song title, "Thank Heaven for Little Girls." In this first song, at the film's opening, Chevalier would address the audience, set the scene, comment briefly on marriage—or, rather, on the Parisian indifference to it—and introduce Gigi, the ugly duckling being groomed to enter the family business by her great-aunt, an elegant courtesan. It is Aunt Alicia's plan to make a stunning young woman of this awkward girl, who is first seen—as Chevalier sings—playing with her schoolmates. In just a few moments, Lerner has thus effectively established the mood, creating a blend of sophistication and naïveté that is beautifully enhanced by Cecil Beaton's costumes and use of the setting (the Bois de Boulogne), and Minnelli's camera work. Chevalier is delightfully insouciant; a man of the world, a retired roué, his amiable, smiling, wise Uncle Honoré sets the tone for the rest of the film—an ingenious concentrated feat of writing by Lerner, given that no such character exists in Colette's story. It is Lerner's Honoré who, as narrator, sometime participant in the action, and vocalist, unifies the plot, from fade-in to fade-out.

When Lerner and Loewe landed in Paris, the weather was foreboding—nothing new for Lerner, whose every previous experience of the French capital had likewise featured uncomfortably dank and dark conditions. When the estimable E. Y. Harburg composed the words to "April in Paris," Lerner grumbled, he had clearly never been there (it was true). He would change his mind about the weather when, later, it became steamy and glowing.

In preparation for their first visit with Chevalier, the songwriters went to work on "Thank Heaven for Little Girls." Although they were not yet finished by Easter weekend, they hired a car and were driven to the little town of Le Zout, in Belgium, where Chevalier was singing in a nightclub. They arrived in time to enjoy the seventy-two-year-old performer's "captivating and adroit" act. Lerner was especially impressed by the fact that when he met with them after an hour and more of singing and strutting, the older man exhibited no sign of fatigue. They talked about *Gigi*, and Chevalier expressed his eagerness to hear a song—any song—unaware that he had just given Lerner the idea for another.

Chevalier, alluding to his age, admitted that he was now too old for wine and women; only song remained to him. Philosophically he told them, "All I have left is the audience, but I find it is quite enough." Months later, as they were finishing their score, Lerner recalled this remark and recast it as "I'm Glad I'm Not Young Any More."

Back in Paris after their meeting with Chevalier, they completed "Thank Heaven" and began another song for him entitled "I Remember It Well." Curiously, Lerner borrowed from himself for this lyric. In *Love Life*, the long-wed protagonists sing a duet in which they reminisce about their marriage, he getting the facts wrong and she correcting him. The melody in the earlier play seems rather humdrum for Weill; undoubtedly it was Lerner's lyrics that dictated the rise and fall of the tune. Both words and music become more sophisticated in *Gigi*, where the singers are Chevalier and his former lover, played by Hermione Gingold (as Gigi's grandmother), and the tone is more humorous than sentimental. Lerner obviously did not want to waste a good idea on a forgotten show:

"I Remember It Well"

LOVE LIFE	GIGI
HE: *It was late at night,*	HE: *We met at nine.*
SHE: *It was six-fifteen.*	SHE: *We met at eight.*
HE: *You were dressed in white.*	HE: *I was on time.*
SHE: *I was dressed in green.*	SHE: *No, you were late.*
HE: *Ah, that's right!*	HE: *Ah yes! I remember it*
I remember it well.	*well.*

Both lyrics thus turn on the man's mistaken recollection of the time of day and the dress worn by the woman. But whereas in the earlier song, the final section of the chorus is a dual declaration of love despite the husband's faulty memory, the *Gigi* version has a subtler point. When Gramma assures Honoré that he is not getting old, reminding him of his youth, his gaiety, calling him "A prince of love/In ev'ry way," a smiling Honoré responds, "Ah yes! I remember it well," lending a poignant air to a gently amusing song.

With two songs completed, Lerner called Chevalier, who lived in a village outside Paris; he arrived at their working suite in the George V promptly, as promised, at three in the afternoon. As Lerner later recalled it, they sang him the songs, and he listened politely, thanked them, and then left, taking the music and lyrics with him.

Their one question was, had he liked them or not?

The next morning he called and asked if he might come again that afternoon at three. The wound-up Lerner could only say to Loewe, "Oh, Christ! What's wrong?"

But not only did Chevalier love the songs, he even asked Lerner for another rendition of the release of "Thank Heaven for Little Girls" ("Those little eyes so helpless and appealing . . ."), saying that he preferred the other's phrasing to his own. The astonished ("touched" would be a more apt adjective for Lerner) writers again demonstrated the number for an attentive Chevalier. Again profuse, sincere thanks, "and off he went into the gray Paris afternoon."

Around this time, Freed called Lerner and asked him to see Audrey Hepburn, who also happened to be in Paris, at the Hotel Raphael. Her film career had been launched in small parts in English films such as *The Lavender Hill Mob* and *Monte Carlo Baby*. She was then enticed to Hollywood to appear opposite Gregory Peck in *Roman Holiday*, for which she received an

Academy Award. Her appearance in the dramatic version of *Gigi* (for which she had been chosen by Colette herself) had initiated a brief stage career. She did better in films and had recently completed the musical film *Funny Face*, with Fred Astaire.

Lerner had his doubts about Hepburn's desire to portray Gigi again, but he called her anyway, and they arranged to meet. He was right: she was not interested, though she turned him down graciously. He reported her answer to Freed, who, unruffled, asked him to fly to London to talk with Leslie Caron, now living there with her husband, Peter Hall. This fitted in with Lerner's plan to talk with his friend Dirk Bogarde vis-à-vis the role of Gaston.

He visited with Bogarde first, eager to walk him through the part of the bored young bon vivant who himself must not be boring. The actor liked the sound of it and promised to see about getting released from his current contract with film producer–magnate J. Arthur Rank.

Not having seen Leslie Caron since the filming of *An American in Paris*, Lerner was taken aback to find that she had lost her "adorable" French accent and now "sounded more English than the English." He was further surprised to learn that she had only recently appeared in a failed London stage production of *Gigi*. He understood now why their initial moments together had been tense: She wished to know how he planned to interpret the character. He asked her the same question; getting no reply, he explained that the plot of the film *Gigi* would center on the evolution of a girl into a woman and not on the education of a professional mistress. She brightened and merely said, "Oh!"

Taking that as a favorable reaction, he inquired as to her interest and availability; she was interested, and she was available.

"Good," he said, "I'll see you in Paris," and he left.

Part of his task, at least, had been accomplished: They had their Honoré and their Gigi, but for the time being, no definite Gaston.

At the end of April, as Lerner and Loewe were working on a song for the moment when Gaston begins to realize that his mistress is cheating on him, Freed and Minnelli arrived. Freed took an entire floor in the Hotel Raphael, where he established Arthur Freed Productions, Inc., France; the Minnellis— Vincente, his French wife, Georgette, and their two-year-old daughter, Tina, along with Georgette's parents—settled into a suite below the songwriters' work and living quarters on the top floor of the George V. In a city not yet given over to the science of air conditioning, working conditions were not always pleasant.

"Fritz and Alan were operating out of a room upstairs from mine," Minnelli wrote of that stay in Paris. "They spent sweltering days at a rented piano, both of them in their underwear, trying to get relief from the heat by taking many cold showers. The songs gradually took shape—and charming ones they were—the last being 'Gigi' with all its lovely patter." The knowledge that France was suffering through its hottest weather in twenty years was little consolation.

While Minnelli ranged across Paris searching for shooting locations, Freed and Lerner discussed the revised script and the songs. Lerner was taking greater liberties with Colette than he had taken with Shaw: The character of Honoré, for example, does not exist at all in the story and appeared only briefly in the play; Lerner's development of the character, and Chevalier's portrayal, were a happy invention. As for Gigi's mother, a significant figure in Colette's original, she is all but eliminated from the film, heard a couple of times as an offstage voice obtrusively singing scales but never seen. Lerner also chose to focus more sharply on the relationship between Mamita (Hermione Gingold) and her granddaughter Gigi.

For added atmosphere, Lerner and Loewe wanted as much of the film as possible to be shot in Paris—both interiors and exteriors. Despite the increased production costs, Freed, after some coaxing from Minnelli, agreed. He was taking a chance, but he was still a power in Culver City.

Shortly after Freed's arrival, they learned that Rank would not release Dirk Bogarde. With this disappointing news, as Lerner put it, "J. Arthur Rank became the face on my dartboard."

Meeting one day in Freed's suite in the hotel to discuss casting, dipping wrists in ice buckets to stay cool, they decided to ask the striking, regal Isabel Jeans to portray Aunt Alicia, the retired courtesan who teaches Gigi. No one appears to have been bothered by the fact that two of the key roles in this very French film were to be filled by two very British women. The Mamita character, they felt, while sympathetic, should reveal no trace of sentimentality, and Hermione Gingold would not disappoint. For her part, Alicia was proud, calculating, a little icy, but still beautiful—Isabel Jeans would be perfect.

"But what about Gaston?" Lerner kept asking. Freed assured him that all would work out, for he had approached Louis Jourdan, best known in the United States for his work in the popular *Three Coins in the Fountain*, a nonmusical whose Academy Award–winning title song had been performed on the soundtrack by Frank Sinatra.

Lerner conceded that Jourdan was a personable young man, he was French, he had the Gastonian look—but could he sing? This little technicality worried the actor as well, but when he joined the group in Paris, Lerner was delighted to discover that he was not only musical but possessed of a passable voice, better than Rex Harrison's. For Lerner, the greater challenge now lay in Gaston's depiction of a prematurely world-weary young man who seems to suffer from terminal boredom.

The difficulty was brought home to him one day when he, Jourdan, and Minnelli all met for lunch. In discussing the film, especially the role he was to play, the actor, smiling expansively, mused, "You know what I love about the character of Gaston?"

"What?" Minnelli asked.

"He's so bored!"

Gloom settled over the table, mystifying Jourdan. Both writer and director wondered, as Lerner put it, whether he could "play boredom without falling into the trap"—that is, without being boring himself.

Minnelli and Lerner escorted their companion back to their hotel, all the while discussing how to handle the part. Lerner found Jourdan rather serious— "usually more serious than the topic of conversation warranted." The more time he spent with the actor, the more he came to realize he would have to rewrite the part for him. In the end, Gaston's ennui remained but was tempered by anger, mostly at himself, for being bored. This vacillation, Minnelli later observed, "was what made the character, removing the unsympathetic aspect and giving us an attractive protagonist."

With the Gaston character firmly in mind, Lerner and Loewe provided Chevalier and Jourdan with a "buoyant duet" (Lerner's term) appropriately entitled "It's a Bore." As his ebullient uncle points out some of life's delights, Gaston dismisses them as boring—even the trees, green this year, last year, and next. In the preceding scene, Gaston is first shown in his luxurious apartment (actually the Musée Jacquemart-André, which permitted the filming only after long, agonizing negotiations), listening, bored, as an automobile salesman describes the features of two of his most expensive cars. A butler enters and tells Gaston that his uncle is waiting, then inquires if the young man purchased a certain stock; when he says yes, he is informed that it has gone up. "I thought it would," he replies indifferently.

As Gaston is about to leave the room, the salesman asks him about the car. Deliver it in the morning, he is told, and bring the bill. "Which one?" he asks. "Either one," Gaston says, and he exits. Having thus deftly established the young man's character, Lerner underlined it with "It's a Bore."

Chevalier waits for his nephew downstairs because he does not wish to run into Gaston's father—his brother—a bore who is "unique" in that "he was born at the age of five." By the end of the song, more a longish dialogue than a tuneful exchange, Gaston is so bored by the prospect of his impending lunch in the park with some boring people that he stops the carriage and heads for the home of Madame Alvarez, variously known as Grandmama or, as he calls her, Mamita. He is not bored in her company, enjoying the wisdom of the older woman and the antics of her granddaughter Gigi.

Lerner and Loewe felt that a song was required for this "recognition scene," in which Gaston realizes that the duckling has turned into a swan and that he has finally, truly, fallen in love. The rest of the score was coming along well, but the writers were stalled after several attempts at the recognition song, which was also to serve as the film's title song. Five other numbers were complete by the middle of July, with shooting set to begin in early August. The Freed Unit had begun assembling in Paris, bringing together the several technicians and others essential to the film, among them the irreplaceable troubleshooter, diplomat, and all-around musician Lela Simone, who had worked in the past with both Freed and Minnelli. She was joined by director of photography Joseph Ruttenberg and musical director André Previn. A composer, pianist (jazz and concert), and conductor (popular and concert), Previn had been educated in Germany and brought to the United States at the age of ten, at the beginning of the Second World War; he had inaugurated his Hollywood career at age seventeen in 1946, as a conductor and composer of background scores. Both composer and lyricist were thrilled with his being chosen as musical director (the orchestrations were assigned to yet another reliable, Conrad Salinger). Lerner considered Previn "one of the most gifted musicians I ever encountered, one of the most amusing, and also one of the most mysterious"—"mysterious" mostly in his work methods, which Lerner would witness firsthand when they later collaborated on a musical. Previn, it seems, was capable of carrying on a conversation and working at the same time, peppering his talk with witty anecdotes while he scribbled on paper, only to finish by handing Lerner a completed song, plus the piano part.

With all the Freed forces gathered and deployed, Lerner believed it was time to find the musical "Gigi." Three months had already been spent searching in vain for a song idea; by mid-July, when he and Loewe met for yet another day's work, the weather had turned lovely. Loewe was at the piano, "dressed in the Byronesque costume in which he always works—his baggy underwear; as for Lerner, as he liked to tell it, he "was sitting on the john," reading a newspaper. Loewe's hands moved over the keyboard and found a melody.

Dropping his paper, Lerner shouted, "My God! That's beautiful." He dashed into the living room, "my trousers clinging to my ankles[,] . . . like a man on tiny stilts," and demanded that Loewe repeat what he had just played. In his excitement, he paced, stumbled, fell, "and almost broke my jaw on the coffee table." As the bruised Lerner reclined, Loewe continued with the melody's development, and in less than an hour the tune was virtually complete. (That it wasn't *entirely* finished gave the often-frustrated lyricist some small satisfaction; he noted smugly, "For once, the last two lines took the composer three days to write.") They had their "Gigi" at last; the final two songs could wait until their return to Culver City, in September.

"Gigi" is a complex song, both words and music, decidedly not Brill Building, the Tin Pan Alley of the time. It consists of four sections in which Gaston vacillates among conflicting feelings for Gigi, whom he has just left in a fit of temper. Stamping along the streets of Paris, furious, he dismisses her as a "babe!/Still cavorting in her crib," and "Just a snip!/Making dreadful baby noise;/Having fun with all her toys." In the next section the music softens, as does his irritation as he recalls a weekend spent with Gigi and her grandmother; then the mood shifts again, back to the music of the first section, and he is once more irate, declaring her a "scamp and a brat." With the return of the second-section music, he finds himself confessing that in a new dress of which he had not approved, "She looked surprisingly mature/And had a definite allure." After another brief spell of anger, Gaston suddenly realizes what is happening to him, clearing the way for an entirely new section in which, to a new melody, he wonders where the little Gigi he has known for so long has gone. This fragment serves as an introduction to the fourth, or main, melody—the beautiful line that brought a hobbled Lerner out of the bathroom in a trice.

It is this last section alone that has become known as "Gigi"; the other three parts are rarely performed, save perhaps for the introductory six lines, which are sometimes sung as a kind of truncated verse. The tune itself is quite simple (in contrast to the complex structure of the complete song), composed in the key of C and in four/four time; it is even in thirty-two-bar popular-song form. Unconsciously, perhaps, Loewe had gone and written a popular song—and popular it would indeed become. Many critics, reviewers, and others have pointed out that "Gigi" could easily be a Rex Harrison leftover from

My Fair Lady, and it is undoubtedly a close relation to "I've Grown Accustomed to Her Face," in both theme and content. This similarity led to a temperamental near-disaster during filming.

Like all the songs shot in the streets—Chevalier's "Thank Heaven for Little Girls," for example—"Gigi" was prerecorded by the vocalist with piano accompaniment only. The piano was on one track, the voice on another; the orchestration would be added later, in the studio. After a few rehearsals with Previn at the piano, Jourdan, a nervous vocalist at best, did several "takes" of the song. He was not happy with any of them, but Lela Simone believed they had a good one. Freed, accompanied by Minnelli, came down to the recording studio to hear the playback and listened, pacing, as Jourdan's voice came out of the speaker.

When the recording ended, without thinking—as often was his wont—Freed turned to Simone and said, "Sounds like Harrison in *My Fair Lady*."

Likewise not thinking, she agreed, "That's just what it is."

Without saying a word, Jourdan left the studio.

Sensing that something was wrong, Simone hurried after him and coaxed him into a bar for a drink. She tried to explain that the producer had been referring to the song itself, not to Jourdan's interpretation of it, but he was not convinced. He took Freed's remark as a criticism—and he was going to quit the film. In desperation, Simone pleaded with the actor to talk things over with Minnelli before making a final decision.

Jourdan agreed, and he and Minnelli talked, in what film historian Hugh Fordin characterized as a "lengthy conversation" that ended the crisis.

The filming of Gaston's "soliloquy," as it was often called, was an elaborate undertaking. As Minnelli visualized it, the camera would pick up the angry Jourdan storming out of Mamita's apartment and then follow him through the streets, across boulevards, and past fountains as he lip-synched to his recording of "Gigi." Near the close of the scene, Minnelli included a shot of him seated on a bench in the Jardin de Bagatelle, with a pond in the background and, in the pond—Lerner was horrified to observe—a few graceful swans.

The presence of the swans, he argued, was distracting; the audience would watch them and not hear what Jourdan was singing. For the moment, however, the scene stayed. (When work moved to California, Lerner objected again and this time prevailed. After the first preview, with Minnelli back in France on another film, the lyricist tried to persuade the MGM executives that the swans were bad for the song; he and Loewe even offered to pay

$50,000 toward reshooting. The studio agreed with his argument and, to the songwriters' relief, actually paid for the refilming of the close-up. But as fate would have it, not one foot of the reshoot was used in the final cut: Minnelli's original version, swans and all, remained off the cutting-room floor and in the film. The effect is not quite so drastic as Lerner made out, but once noted, the birds all but steal the scene.) Lerner took some small consolation in the knowledge that one of the swans had bitten Minnelli.

As the crew's Paris stay was winding down, with the bulk of the score complete, MGM's vice president and director of publicity, Howard Dietz, arrived with his wife, designer Lucinda Ballard, who had designed the costumes for Lerner and Weill's *Love Life*. In addition to his high-level position at MGM, Dietz was half of the celebrated songwriting team of Dietz and (Arthur) Schwartz. Freed arranged an audition of the score for the Dietzes, which was also attended by Freed's wife, Renée, set designer and costumer Cecil Beaton, Minnelli, and Lela Simone. Seated beside Loewe on the piano bench, Lerner occasionally joined his partner in some four-hand piano playing, and in his distinctive husky voice sang all the songs they had written in Paris, plus one salvaged from *My Fair Lady*, "Say a Prayer for Me Tonight." (In fact, Lerner did not care for the latter, which he thought sounded like a cello solo; Loewe agreed but added that it was a "very nice cello solo." He played it for Freed and Minnelli one evening when Lerner was not present, and the next morning it was voted into *Gigi*, three against one.)

By the time the last note sounded, Simone was relieved; she told Hugh Fordin that "all of us were elated," and that even the Paris heat seemed bearable. Dietz's exit line, however, shook their confidence: Taking Freed's hand, he said, "Arthur, this will be the most charming flop you've ever made!"

With their work in Paris finished, the songwriters made plans to return to New York and from there fly to California for further filming in September. Although Lerner nowhere mentions it in his book, his life had changed over that half year in France, during which he had been an absentee father and husband. Even before his departure in March, his marriage to Nancy Olson had turned sour; tired of her domesticity, he was as bored as Gaston. Always romantically adventurous, he was taken with a petite, pretty young woman he met one evening at a party, the aristocratically named Micheline Muselli Pozzo di Borgo. Only about thirty but already highly regarded as an attorney, she was of Corsican birth and claimed Napoleonic ties—a curious assertion given that the most celebrated member of the family was one Carlo Andrea Pozzo di Borgo (1764–1842), likewise Corsican but an ally of Pasquale Paoli, a bitter enemy of the Bonapartes'. (Carlo Andrea served as head of the British-backed government from 1794 until 1796, when Corsica's reconquest by the French forced him to flee to Russia. His entry into the diplomatic service there enabled him to make further mischief contra Napoleon by promoting the 1805 Russo-Austrian Alliance against the Little Corporal, but when, two years later, Napoleon and Czar Alexander I signed the Treaty of Tilsit, Pozzo di Borgo felt an urgent need to retire from diplomatic duty for a while. When the Russians and French took up warring again in 1812, the Corsican returned to the service; following Napoleon's abdication, in 1814, he was appointed Russian ambassador to France, in which capacity he exhibited an excessive sympathy toward the restored Bourbon monarchy. His bias became so blatant that he was eventually transferred to London.)

Lerner, whose knowledge of French history was shaky at best, once told an interviewer that Micheline's "great-great-great-grandfather was Napoleon's godson." He also proudly reported that "she was the youngest person ever admitted to the French bar. She was only twenty, but already she'd won her master's degree at the Sorbonne. Later she became a specialist in international divorce." Micheline was most helpful to him, he said, in translating English into French. In due time she would give him a crash course in her particular specialty.

Over the course of Lerner's long stay in Paris, while he was seeing a great deal of Micheline Muselli Pozzo di Borgo, his long-distance marriage literally dissolved. Even as his sojourn began, in the spring of 1957, Nancy Olson returned to acting and appeared opposite comedian Tom Ewell in *Tunnel of Love*. During the play's tour, the *New York Times* printed an item from Milwaukee: Nancy Olson had separated from "her husband, Alan Jay Lerner," who had informed the *Times* that the separation had occurred about a month before, in July. Early the following year, when the time came for Lerner to head to California for the previews of *Gigi*, he would be accompanied by the next Mrs. Lerner.

In the meantime, he had also found another infatuation, this one in London, where he and Loewe stopped en route to the United States. On leaving his hotel one day, he spotted the "most extraordinary automobile I had ever beheld": a convertible Rolls Royce (the first of its kind, he would soon learn). After lunching with theatrical producer Hugh Beaumont, on their way to the airport, and California, Lerner and Loewe took a detour through the Rolls Royce showroom on Conduit Street. The salesman knew about the special new convertible but informed Lerner that it would take a year to make him one; undaunted, Lerner asked for a color chart, then specified a royal-blue Rolls with a beige top. To the salesman's amazement, the American then proceeded to talk his reluctant companion into buying one, too. Loewe protested that he simply did not need, or want, such an example of excessive conspicuous consumption; Lerner replied that he might not want one at that moment, but once Lerner's was delivered, "you'll be sore as hell. Pick out a color."

Halfheartedly, Loewe pointed to a gray on the chart.

The transaction—which had taken, according to Lerner, less than five minutes in all—was now complete. To the still-astonished salesman, he said, "That's it. The gray one for Mr. Loewe and the blue one for me." (Lerner's own favorite variant on what would become a Conduit Street near-folktale about the two rich American madmen had Loewe whipping out his check-book, once the decision was made, and saying, "I'll get this. You paid for lunch.")

As they left, Lerner told the salesman that Louis Dreyfus, head of the U.K. division of Chappell Music, would confirm their order and attend to the payment. When Dreyfus was advised of this shopping spree, he amusedly re-assured the salesman that yes, he had indeed sold two Rolls Royces in a single day. (According to Lerner, the man was promoted to manager for this distinctive display of high-pressure salesmanship.) Such impulse buying was not atypical of Lerner, a compulsive and princely shopper from New York to Beverly Hills. Burton Lane once observed, "Alan spends more money than some countries."

September found the songwriters back in Culver City to complete their score ("The Night They Invented Champagne" and "I'm Glad I'm Not Young Any More") and study the "dailies" from the Paris filming. Lerner was particularly unhappy with Jourdan's "She's Not Thinking of Me," which had been shot in Maxim's. As he watches his mistress (played by Eva Gabor) dancing, laughing, flirting, and generally enjoying herself, Gaston *thinks* the words to the song but does not actually sing them out loud—it is his expression, in conjunction with the Lerner lyric, that tells the audience that Liane is decidedly not thinking of *him*.

Lerner strongly objected to the absence of close-ups in the scene. "How can an audience know a song is being sung in someone's head if one cannot see the head?" he wondered. When Freed returned to California, just prior to the completion of filming in Paris, Lerner broached the subject of this seemingly un-Minnelli-like oversight. Freed assured him that the close-ups were

---

undoubtedly on their way from Paris with the rest of the film, but by the following week, when the film arrived, an anxious Lerner was unhappier still: Minnelli simply had not shot any close-ups of Jourdan in Maxim's. The scene was beautifully done, but in Lerner's opinion it was "pointless": If the audience had no idea who was singing, the song made no sense.

Freed agreed; the four days' worth of film from Maxim's was scrapped, and the scene reshot. By this time Minnelli was unavailable (he had gone back to Paris to work on a Rex Harrison–Kay Kendall film), and Charles Walters had to be hired at considerable cost to fill in as director of the sequence. A section of Maxim's, down to the color of the paneling, had to be re-created on the MGM lot; long-stemmed glasses had to be flown in from Paris; and the lighting had to be carefully matched to that in the salvaged original film. At the end of October 1957, with this final scene at last complete, production on *Gigi* closed down and postproduction work began. With the previews not scheduled until early the next year, Lerner and Loewe were free to return to their private lives.

While Loewe reembraced his customary indulgences, Lerner turned to the serious matters of divorce and remarriage. During the final stages of his work on *Gigi*, he took a house in Santa Monica, where he lived with his daughters with Nancy Olson, Jennifer, then five, and Liza, four; this lessened some of the pain of separation and pending divorce. Loewe bivouacked in a penthouse atop a hotel overlooking the Sunset Strip in Hollywood, where they worked.

Every day, Lerner drove the fifteen miles to Loewe's hotel in a convertible (not yet the Rolls Royce, which was still in production). One interviewer noted that "Lerner has acquired a becoming beachboy's bronze. Loewe's sun-drenched terrace would give Loewe the same effect effortlessly [, but] if he's considered it, he's decided it doesn't suit him." The lyricist announced that after *Gigi*, the team would begin work on a musical version of *Father of the Bride*; next would came a straight dramatic production of Jean Anouilh's *Ornifle*, starring Rex Harrison as a lyricist. In the end, neither project came off, though for a moment it looked as if Lerner and Loewe intended to follow in the footsteps of Rodgers and Hammerstein, now involved in the production of nonmusical plays by others.

For November and December, while *Gigi* was undergoing editing and cutting, and the orchestration was being added to the vocals and background, Lerner returned to New York. After moving from one luxurious hotel to another, he finally settled into an equally plush apartment in Sutton Place. The divorce now final, Nancy Olson and her two young daughters found an apartment on the less exclusive Upper West Side.

By the time Lerner and Loewe went west once more for the previews of *Gigi*, in January 1958, their twosome had become a threesome: The lyricist had taken his fourth wife, she of the supposed Napoleonic linkage, the previous November in New York. The *Times* had carried a simple announcement on December 2, 1957, under the heading "Alan Jay Lerner Weds Lawyer": "Alan Jay Lerner, author of the book and lyrics for *My Fair Lady*, and Micheline Muselli Pozzo di Borgo, a lawyer, were married here last Friday." He couldn't have been happier.

All concerned (with the exception of Minnelli, still filming *The Reluctant Debutante* in Paris, and the major members of the cast, who had already returned to their homes abroad) gathered at the Granada Theatre in Santa Barbara on January 20. According to Freed Unit historian Hugh Fordin, Lerner termed the event a "disaster." In spite of the fact that an overwhelming majority of the audience (88 percent) rated *Gigi* between "good" and "outstanding," the creators, even the ebullient Freed, thought it a mess. Adrienne Fazan, the film's editor, told Fordin that "Lerner and Loewe . . . were just dumbfounded. 'That's not the film we wrote,' they said."

In Lerner's view,

> The picture was twenty minutes too long, the action too slow, the music too creamy and ill-defined, and there must have been at least five minutes (in the theatre that can seem like five hours) of people walking up and down stairs. . . . The [audience-reaction] cards, on the whole, were quite good, which confounded Fritz and me. . . . The ride home from Santa Barbara was not unlike the ride home from any funeral.

As was their practice, the partners put off any discussion until the next morning. After a night's rest, Lerner recalled, they arose, ordered breakfast and much coffee, and lighted the first of many cigarettes. Lerner doubted that mere cutting would be sufficient; rewriting was required. The "I Remember It Well" duet by Gingold and Chevalier, for example, warranted scrapping and refilming, he felt. As for Conrad Salinger's orchestrations, Loewe found them "too lush and Hollywooden," as Lerner put it; with his theater experience,

Loewe preferred a leaner, Broadway sound. Lerner agreed, though he knew revised orchestration would necessitate rerecording, a further drain on the already overdrawn budget.

Having agreed on what their position would be, the songwriters set out for Culver City. Some of their suggestions had already been anticipated by Kenneth MacKenna, a member of Freed's staff. The character-establishing scene in which a bored Gaston buys an automobile while his uncle waits for him downstairs did nothing for MacKenna, and could, he thought, be eliminated (it was not); Caron's "I Don't Understand the Parisians" was overlong and "would benefit greatly by being cut in half." For him, too, the Maxim's sequence lacked "dramatic quality and in some ways was disappointing musically" (Lerner agreed heartily on this point). Finally, like Lerner, MacKenna felt the film as a whole was fifteen to twenty minutes too long.

By the time Lerner and Loewe got to the MGM lot, Freed had studied MacKenna's memo. Although he affected good spirits for their benefit, he was, according to Lerner, "obviously as depressed as we were." After comparing notes with them and agreeing with their assessment, Freed toted up an estimate of what it would cost to implement the necessary changes: more than $300,000, or one third of *Gigi*'s original budget. Now they were even more depressed than before. There was nothing more for them to do except approach studio head Benny Thau for further discussion; they arranged to meet with him in his office at noon.

With Lerner leading, they explained what they thought was wrong with the film, and Freed then informed Thau how much it would cost to cure what Lerner called its "artistic ills." The studio head agreed that the film needed reworking, but the figure concerned him. "Mr. Thau did not say no," Lerner later remembered, "but the way he did not say yes meant no." Following a contingency plan conceived before the meeting, Lerner and Loewe now made a startling suggestion, one that was probably unique in the snarled annals of Hollywood: they offered to buy 10 percent of *Gigi* for $300,000. Thau's only reply was a promise to call the main office in New York.

Joseph Vogel, head of the New York office and Thau's superior, wanted to fly in and see the film for himself. Following another preview—about fifteen minutes had by now been cut—he let it be known that the studio did not permit outsiders to invest in its films; besides, he said, he thought *Gigi* was just fine as it was, and no more work was required. As they broke for lunch, the unhappy songwriters asked to have another audience with Mr. Vogel that afternoon; in the meantime, they contrived another ploy.

Lerner led off their afternoon session with an even more surprising offer than his first: He wanted to buy the print of *Gigi* for three million dollars. "Vogel, Thau and Arthur turned to stone," Lerner noted. According to Lerner, Vogel asked that the writers give him a little time to discuss this new twist with Thau and Freed; excusing themselves, Lerner and Loewe sought relief in the men's room. Where, Loewe queried, could they possibly get three million dollars? From Bill Paley, maybe, Lerner supposed.

"My boy, he's not an idiot. Who would make such an offer?"

"*We* just did," Lerner said.

"That's because we don't have three million dollars. Bill Paley has. That's a big difference."

Troubled, they returned to the room where the meeting was being held. Lerner was now almost in a panic: What if MGM accepted their offer?

Although Lerner would not later recall Vogel's precise words, their gist was heartening: He was impressed by their sincerity and feeling for *Gigi* (as he has been impressed, too, by *My Fair Lady*), and his respect for them left him no alternative but to come up with the additional funds needed to turn it into the film that Lerner and Loewe so passionately envisioned. (Writing a decade and a half later, Thau did not remember the incident in quite the same way: He recalled only Lerner and Loewe's wanting to invest in the film, not their offering to buy it outright.)

They had won, but the revisions would not be easy to accomplish. The dispersed cast would have to be flown in from Paris, London, and New York for reshooting, and Charles Walters would have to stand in for the absent Minnelli—all of this after Lerner made a few additional cuts, revised some dialogue, and reworked a lyric here and there. A former dancer who had come to Hollywood to direct, Walters had supervised sequences in two Judy Garland movies, *Presenting Lily Mars* and *Meet Me in St. Louis*, and directed *Easter Parade* and other film musicals including *Summer Stock* and *High Society*. His assignment on *Gigi* was to refilm Jourdan's "Soliloquy" and "She's Not Thinking of Me," Gingold and Chevalier's "I Remember It Well," and a few other odds and ends (quite literally, in one case: At Lerner's suggestion, Chevalier provided a softer rendition of his last line in the film, the closing lyric of "Thank Heaven for Little Girls").

Walters was especially inflexible when it came to Jourdan's soliloquy, the shooting of which consumed two full days. This exasperated Previn, who complained that after twenty takes or more, "no one could remember what it was about Take 1 that was any different or less good than Take 19." He and music editor William Saracino worked for hours on this single sequence, only to have film editor Adrienne Fazan insist, following another preview, that the Minnelli version be reinserted.

On March 3, after thirty-five days (twelve more than scheduled), the revised *Gigi* was ready for its fourth preview, this one in Encino. The changes worked. "By the grace of God," Lerner wrote, "all the steps we had taken had been in the right direction. The reaction of the audience dramatically changed from appreciation to affection." The eleven days of reshooting had put the project more than $400,000 over budget (for a total cost, according to Hugh Fordin, of $3,319,335), but for now it all seemed worthwhile: Speaking for himself and Loewe, Lerner ecstatically pronounced the film "at long last *Gigi*." Besides the cost overrun, however, there was another *but*: Encino was not New York or even Peoria.

Lerner was in London looking after the English production of *My Fair Lady* when *Gigi* premiered at the Royale Theatre in New York on May 15, 1958. The Royale was a legitimate theater, not a film house: Before opening *Gigi* at an enormous movie theater, Freed wanted to present it as a special event, almost a Broadway show, even to the extent of having reserved seating.

Two days before the film's premiere, Lerner had suffered anxiety and depression upon reading a "dreadful" review in *Time* magazine. Soon after that, however, came the New York notices, all favorable. Bosley Crowther of the *Times* opened on a familiar note:

> There won't be much point in anybody trying to produce a film of
> *My Fair Lady* for a while, because Arthur Freed has virtually done
> it with *Gigi*, which had a grand premiere at the Royale last night.
> But don't think this point of resemblance is made in criticism of
> the book, for *Gigi* is a charming entertainment that can stand on
> its own legs. It is not only a charming comprehension of the spicy
> confection of Colette but it is also a lovely and lyrical enlargement
> upon that story's flavored mood and atmosphere.

New York, it turned out, was even more affectionate than Encino.

Lerner saw the finished *Gigi* a week later, when it was screened at the Cannes Film Festival. Unhappy with the French subtitles—musicals invariably did poorly in foreign markets since it was difficult effectively to translate song lyrics—he set about reworking them. In time this care would be extended to several other languages, making *Gigi* the first American film musical to be so treated. A new soundtrack was produced for each country, with songs dubbed by singers of the appropriate nationalities (Chevalier did his own vocals again for the French version). Historian Hugh Fordin has written that "Lerner played an important part in the subsequent success of the picture abroad"—a success that rendered *Gigi* historically unique, especially so in that it came at the end of the era of the grand, lush, carefully crafted screen musical. It was close to the end, as well, for the Freed Unit, which would make but one more musical, *Bells Are Ringing*, starring Judy Holliday and still playing to standing-room-only theater audiences when *Gigi* opened in New York.

Gigi would make further history when Academy Award time came around in April 1959. No less than nine Oscars were lavished on the film, beginning (or ending, in traditional Oscarcast fashion) with the Best Picture Award. Minnelli was named Best Director, while Joseph Ruttenberg won for his color cinematography, Preston Ames and Keogh Gleason for their art and set direction, André Previn for scoring, Cecil Beaton for costume design, and Adrienne Fazan for film editing.

Alan Jay Lerner was a double winner, taking home Oscars as writer of the best screenplay based on material from another medium, and (with Loewe) for Best Song, "Gigi." Lerner did not intend to go through the usual Oscar routine, in which the winner thanks "everyone from the head of the studio to his uncle Julius in Pittsburgh"; he would say only one simple sentence and get off. This he did. When his name was announced a second time, he repeated the sentence—"Thank you"—and added "again."

Loewe, for his part, stole the show. Only recently recovered from a severe heart attack, he slowly mounted the steps to the stage and, after a dramatic pause, accepted the statuette with the words, "I want to thank you from the bottom of my somewhat damaged heart."

Curiously, none of the cast received awards, except for Chevalier, who was given a special Oscar for his lifetime contribution. With a little fudging, *Gigi* could thus be said to have won ten Academy Awards, the most bestowed upon any film up to that time. (In 1962, *West Side Story* would win ten fudge-free Oscars.) Only two other musicals released in 1958 are worth mentioning, both adaptations of successful stage shows: *South Pacific* (which won an Oscar for Best Sound) and *Damn Yankees*. As an original film musical, *Gigi* was one of the last of a dying breed.

The Academy Award sweep did not end the *Gigi* saga. Despite its cost overrun, the film grossed more than $13 million (including the box-office take from its 1966 rerelease); its soundtrack albums in English and French were best-sellers; NBC Television paid MGM a generous $2 million for a two-time airing; and it is today available on videocassette.

Some fifteen years after it opened, in another historical twist, *Gigi* became the first film musical to be turned into a stage musical. Lerner himself made all the necessary revisions to accommodate the change of medium—no camera techniques to fade in and out of scenes, no location shooting in the streets of Paris—and he and Loewe expanded the score with four additional songs. The new version of *Gigi*, a joint effort by the Los Angeles and San Francisco Civic Light Opera companies, was produced by Arnold Saint-Subber, who had earlier been associated with the Broadway productions of Cole Porter's *Kiss Me Kate* and *Out of This World* as well as Harold Arlen's *House of Flowers*.

Gigi opened in California in May 1973 and premiered in New York's cavernous Uris (now Gershwin) Theatre on November 13 of the same year. A fine young singer named Karin Wolfe appeared in the tile role; Alfred Drake portrayed Gaston's uncle, Agnes Moorehead was cast as Gigi's aunt, Maria Karnilova was Mamita, and Daniel Massey played Gaston. There were atmospheric settings by Oliver Smith, costumes by Oliver Messel, new orchestrations by Irwin Kostel. It proved to be a qualified flop, closing in February 1974 after only 103 unprofitable performances.

The final irony came when *Gigi* won the Tony Award for Best Score of the 1973–74 season. By then Broadway, like Hollywood before it, was musically on its way down. There being no musical that year with an original score that it deemed worthy, the Tony committee instead selected a regenerated film.

10

—ﷳ—

EXIT: FRITZ

IN THE LATE WINTER OF 1958, while the finishing touches were being added to—or taken from—their film *Gigi*, with nothing left for them to do in Hollywood, Lerner and Loewe returned to New York. Loewe moved into his favorite haunt, the Algonquin, and Alan and Micheline Lerner took up residence in their Sutton Place apartment. The collaborators then turned their energies to the forthcoming London production of *My Fair Lady*, scheduled to open, with most of the original New York cast, at the Drury Lane at the end of April. Lerner and Loewe, Moss and Kitty Hart, and Herman Levin planned to leave late in February for casting and rehearsals; Micheline Lerner had already gone on ahead to take care of some business in Paris.

Lerner was startled awake early in the morning a week before their scheduled departure—he recalled it as being three o'clock—by the telephone. It was the night manager of the Algonquin, calling to tell him that Loewe, experiencing severe chest pains, had just minutes before been taken to the Medical Arts Center on West Fifty-seventh Street. After calling his own doctor, a heart specialist named Milton Kramer, Lerner raced to the hospital, where he found Loewe extremely pale, obviously in respiratory distress, and very weak. He insisted that his partner be placed in an oxygen tent, but the hospital staff demurred, the consensus being that it was not necessary. Lerner, no stranger to hospitals after his father's long illness, raised a fuss, and to keep the peace, the medics complied with his demands.

When Dr. Kramer arrived soon after, he determined that Loewe had suffered a massive coronary. He could not yet predict his chances of survival; they should have a better idea of that in another three days or so. It instantly struck Lerner, as it had on the death of his father, that "life is finite." Studying the drawn face of his collaborator, he felt certain he could face his own death, "but not that of others—especially Fritz's—and I was shattered." He spent most of the night at Loewe's bedside, even though he realized there was nothing he could do.

By the end of three days, though still in the oxygen tent, Loewe was improving slowly and out of danger; however, he would have to remain in the hospital for several weeks at least. Reassured, Lerner was free to fly to London (with side trips to Paris) for the *My Fair Lady* preparations.

The musical's widespread fame had had Londoners in a state of excited expectancy since long before the rehearsals even began; as early as the spring of 1956, just weeks after the show's New York premiere, the original cast albums were being smuggled into Britain by ship stewards and airline attendants, to be sold at an enormous profit. One London newspaper went so far as to count down the days to the opening, as if it were an event tantamount to Christmas—as indeed, at least for the ticket sellers, it was. As April 30 approached, the excitement only grew.

Fuel was added to the fire early on, with the surfacing of a long-smoldering internal feud. Among the first to arrive of the original cast was Stanley Holloway, who was met by avaricious members of the British morning press. Perhaps at their urging, he blasted Rex Harrison (likely with good reason) for his insufferable rudeness, ego, and, worse, unprofessional behavior. Harrison, then in Paris with his new wife, Kay Kendall, read Holloway's remarks and blew up; no less angry with the press than with Holloway himself, he refused, for a time, to grant any interviews at all. When he did finally consent to one, it was with the *London Times* and resulted in a piece that Lerner found "fair and interesting." It was in this interview that, to Lerner's delight, the actor stated that except for Lerner's "six lines," all the dialogue in the musical was Shaw's.

An apology and the usual "misquoted" disclaimer ended the Holloway-Harrison feud, and the show went on without further incident. The reviews—some reserved, most favorable—assured *My Fair Lady* of a successful run of

2,281 performances, the longest ever at the Drury Lane; in October 1963 it would set out, with a different cast, on a six-month tour of Britain. With *My Fair Lady* off to a fine start in England, Lerner crossed back to Manhattan; he was restive.

By the summer of 1958, Loewe was released from the hospital to suffer through a further recovery period at the Essex House, under the stern eye of what Doris Warshaw Shapiro called a "ferocious nurse." Once rid of her, he spent the rest of the summer on the Riviera, despite the necessity, at least for a while, of exercising unaccustomed restraint in his way of life. As he told one newsman, his heart attack had caused him to reconsider his excesses: "I drank from five at night until five in the morning. I smoked three, four packs of cigarettes a day. It was a senseless, futile existence" (he skipped over his other "senseless" former activities—gambling and availing himself of the company of pretty young women). By October, thinner, a bit wan, he was back in New York.

Relieved by his friend's recovery, Lerner soon acquired a new anxiety: What to do next? He remembered that when they were in Philadelphia with the New York–bound *My Fair Lady*, in a moment of group elation (knowing they had a hit on their hands), he, Loewe, and Hart had vowed that they would all collaborate on the next Lerner and Loewe musical. Lerner was now confronted by two questions: What musical, and would Loewe be able and willing? He and Hart, especially, spent a great deal of time reading, looking for a new idea.

The idea was supplied one morning by Lerner's production manager, confidant, and close friend, Stone Widney (better known as Bud), who had come east to work on *Paint Your Wagon* with Lerner in 1951, when he was fresh out of UCLA, and had been with him ever since. Tossing a copy of that Sunday's *New York Times Book Review* onto his boss's desk, he said, "Lerner, here's your next show."

Lerner had read the "glowing" review the day before, but it had not sparked any great interest in him. If Bud saw something in it, though, he reasoned that it might be worth looking into, and he sent one of his assistants out to buy a copy of the book. Meanwhile, Moss Hart phoned to ask if he had read the review of a book entitled *The Once and Future King* in Sunday's *Times*; Lerner promptly sent for another copy. A hefty (more than 600-page-long) reworking of some of the Arthurian legends by one T[erence] H[anbury] White, the book took its title from King Arthur's hypothetical tombstone, whose inscription, according to one of the earlier compilers of the legends, Thomas Malory (fl. 1470), read: *Hic jacet Arthurus—Rex quondam, Rexque futurus.*

Born in Bombay, White was a former English schoolmaster, writer, and poet. Reclusive and eccentric, according to author-teacher P. J. Keating, he "led a life that alternated between moods of wild bohemianism and intense self-destructive loneliness, and for long periods of time was isolated from human society, finding consolation in hunting, fishing and a strange collection of animals he kept as pets." Lerner later described the author as a "large, shaggy man with a great white beard." He was a charmer, a witty conversationalist with that "far-off look in his eye of a poet—a poet who wishes he were somewhere else."

White's version of the story of Arthur, Guenevere, and Lancelot captivated Lerner not least because it was, in Keating's description, an "idiosyncratic handling of the Arthurian cycle combining great knowledge of medieval life, colourful fantasy, casual brutality, deep pathos and modern slang." The first volume in the series, *The Sword in the Stone,* had been published in 1938, with other volumes following regularly thereafter, and the complete quartet being issued in a single volume in 1958. British novelist-critic David Garnett (himself an author of a fantasy, *Lady into Fox*) concisely called it "one of the curious classics of English literature," by a writer with a "genius for recreating the physical conditions of the past." Children who read it, Garnett advised, "will learn far more than all the historians and archeologists could tell of what England was like in the Middle Ages." White's is, however, hardly a book meant for children, what with its intellectual allusions, its anachronistic whimsy, and, in the portion that Lerner would select for adaption, its adultery.

The Sword in the Stone's playful, deft prose is peppered with period lore and terminology, its tone established practically on the first page. Two men, Sir Ector and Sir Grummore, are drinking and talking about Sir Grummore's "quest" (the knight's raisons d'être: doing single combat and rescuing damsels in distress). Sir Grummore says, "Good port this."

"Get it from a friend of mine," he is told.

"But about these boys," Grummore asks, referring to Ector's natural son, Kay, and the illegitimate Arthur, called Wart. "How many of them are there, do you know?"

"Two," says Sir Ector, "counting them both, that is."

"Couldn't send them to Eton, I suppose?" wonders Grummore.

Here White addresses the reader: "It was not really Eton that he mentioned, for the College of Blessed Mary was not founded until 1440, but it was a place of the same sort. Also they were drinking Metheglyn, not port, but by mentioning the modern wine it is easier to give you the feel."

Two chapters later, the major character of Merlyn, who will be Wart's tutor, complainingly asks as he draws a heavy water bucket from the well, "Why can't they get us the electric light and company's [i.e., running] water?" *The Once and Future King* is replete with such anachronisms, and this intellectual frolicking enchanted Lerner.

When Loewe arrived at their office, Lerner suggested that he read the *Times* review. He did and said, "You must be crazy. That king is a cuckold. Who the hell cares about a cuckold?"

Lerner disagreed, arguing that people had cared about Arthur for more than a thousand years. Loewe dismissed that as English and American romanticism, the fantasy of two nations of "children." Lerner respected his collaborator's sophisticated, Viennese point of view—in Austria, as in Paris, a deceived husband was regarded as a figure of fun, a fool to be derided, not a hero.

Lerner sent out for yet another copy of the book, which Loewe would never finish reading. Lerner and Hart's enthusiasm was so persuasive that after much talk, Loewe checked with his physician and then told Lerner, "My boy, I'll try it one more time. But if it's too tough or if I start to worry so much I can't work the way I want to, the next will be my last."

All three together came to a curious decision once they were embarked on their new venture: They would also act as the producers of the musical. When their attorney, Irving Cohen, began researching the rights, he learned that Walt Disney had already acquired *The Sword in the Stone*, which tells the story of Arthur (or Wart) as a boy, and was not interested in selling its interest in the book (Disney's cartoon version would be released in 1963). This was not a problem for Lerner et al., however, as they intended to focus on the story of the triangle formed by the adult Arthur, his queen, Guenevere, and Lancelot, and to trace its devastating effect on their lives, on the celebrated Round Table, and on Arthur's dream of a better world. Once the rights were secured, the novice production team had no difficulty persuading CBS once again to put up the $400,000 backing.

The producers' lighthearted working title, *Jenny Kissed Me*, eventually gave way to *Camelot*, a name more in keeping with the musical's hopeful but somber conclusion. For his libretto, Lerner drew primarily on the last two books of White's novel, concentrating on Arthur's dreams, the dissolution of his idealistic Round Table, and, even more centrally, his unhappy marriage and his love for both his wife and Lancelot, who unwittingly destroys that marriage. There is no secondary plot in Lerner's book; White's account of Lancelot and "Elaine the fair" (and their son, Galahad) is not reproduced here, nor is the legend of the Holy Grail. Rather, Lerner trimmed the plot down to those characters and incidents the he believed were essential to the story he wanted to tell in the musical; even so, it teemed and sprawled. His Arthurian legend retained White's theme of the "clash between Might and Right" in Arthur's wish to put knighthood to a constructive use: Instead of dashing around seeking bouts, his valiants would follow a "new order, where might is only used for right, to improve instead of destroy." Arthur, in Lerner's words, deflates the speciousness of chivalry when he realizes that it is, in fact, armor that makes the knight:

> Only knights are rich enough to bedeck themselves in armor. They can declare war when it suits them, go clod-hopping around the country slicing up peasants and foot soldiers, because peasants and foot soldiers are not equipped with armor. All that can happen to a knight is an occasional dent. Wrong or right, they have the might, so wrong or right, they're always right—and that's wrong. Right?

Lerner visualized Arthur as a kind of innocent, "ingenuously charming" and so lovable that an audience—he hoped—would "forgive him anything, follow him everywhere, even over the hot coals of tolerating his wife's infidelity." He believed that the legend of King Arthur was "far more than a mere love story," and that if the knightly feats and jousts, and the magic of Merlyn and Morgan le Fay (both of whom appear only fleetingly in *Camelot*), were eliminated, it would become evident that "there lies buried in [the legend's] heart the aspirations of mankind."

Camelot was not to be what Rex Harrison referred to as "musical com." Such a rendering of the milieu had already been accomplished by Rodgers and Hart, in their 1927 adaptation of Mark Twain's *A Connecticut Yankee in King Arthur's Court*; entitled simply *A Connecticut Yankee* (with a book by Herbert Fields), it was the most successful Rodgers and Hart musical of the twenties, with a run of 418 performances. Taking its satirical tone from Twain's novel (while omitting his anticlerical views), it was both a musical and a comedy, with most of the action occurring in a dream.

Lerner wanted to take a more serious approach. "All of this," he admitted, "may seem far removed from the light entertainment of a musical play [, but] it is not. It is the hidden guide, the silent voice that is heard when creative decisions are made." *Camelot*, for Lerner (and, to some extent, for others), would prove to be a succession of dark and darker chasms.

When work began on the project, in the winter of 1958, according to Kitty Carlisle Hart, the plan called for Lerner and her husband to collaborate on the book, but then Lerner suddenly decided to write it by himself (he does not mention this in his autobiography). Hart was disappointed but took the rejection with his customary good grace. His wife consoled him negatively: *Camelot* could not possibly be another *My Fair Lady* (whose book she was certain was partly his though he had gone uncredited), and in any case it would be easier for him to serve as director and behind-the-scenes play doctor. When they received an early draft from Lerner, she recalled, both she and her husband found it hopeless. (The question arises, if the highly professional Hart deemed the script impossible, why did he stick with the project?)

The production trio agreed that it would help to have a cast in mind. Lerner immediately thought of Julie Andrews, then living in London, for Guenevere; she readily agreed. For Arthur, Hart suggested Richard Burton; as a musical quantity, he was unknown, but Lerner insisted that all Welshmen could sing and swore he had heard Burton do so at a party at Ira Gershwin's home in Beverly Hills. And to play the bumbling Pellinore (or Pelly), the king who could not find his kingdom, they simply called Robert Coote (still in London's *My Fair Lady*), whose assent was prefaced with the simple appraisal, "My favorite book." Soon after plans to produce *Camelot* were announced, Roddy McDowall called Hart from Hollywood and all but demanded the part of the deliciously evil Mordred, Arthur's illegitimate son (who in some versions of the legend is a product of incest). When Lerner and Hart met with him, they explained that the part was small (though critical), for Mordred does not appear until act 2, when he sets in motion the mischief that will send the plot downhill. A former English child star (at twelve he had been in the fine *How Green Was My Valley*), McDowall was still something of a name, though by 1959 he had pretty much dropped out of films to concentrate on stage and television work. At the Stratford Shakespeare Festival, he acted in *Julius Caesar* and *The Tempest*; he was also preparing to become an exceptional photographer.

Hart and Lerner advised McDowall that Mordred was not a star part, and that consequently (speaking now as producers), there was not much in the budget for the Mordred player. But McDowall persisted, and the part was his. Now their only problem was finding a proper actor for Lancelot, the good knight who starts out holier than everyone. They gave up in New York and shifted their efforts to France—logically, they thought, since Lancelot was supposed to be French. The search proved fruitless there, too; France's major singing actor, Yves Montand, was not right for the role.

Even the British actor, Laurence Harvey, who could have projected the Lancelot Lerner had in mind, auditioned for them, only to reveal a singing voice that was too deep. Although he announced publicly that he would appear as Lancelot, Harvey did not get the part. He did, however, proceed as if he had been hired, going so far even as to take voice training (his business manager billed the *Camelot* management eight pounds for the lessons, which said management refused to pay). Interestingly, when *Camelot* opened in London in August 1964, Harvey starred as King Arthur, with a much lightened tenor and to great success.

According to Lerner, they did not find their Lancelot until the final day of auditions in the spring of 1959, when a "young man suddenly appeared on the stage in blue jeans (unfamiliar garb at the time)." Possessed of a fine French name—Robert Goulet—he was on his way to Toronto (a French Canadian!), but his luggage was somewhere between Bermuda and New York. He certainly looked the part (despite his informal attire) and soon proved that he had a fine voice and could read dialogue. He was, in fact, American-born, but he had studied at the Royal Conservatory in Toronto, been a disc jockey, and appeared on a weekly television show in Canada as well as in stage productions. In Lerner's assessment, he "had a superb baritone voice, was undeniably handsome, and he looked like Lancelot."

With all his major characters cast, Lerner could now concentrate on the libretto and songs. While Lerner's Guenevere, Arthur, Pellinore, and Mordred seem true to their traditional Arthurian models, his Lancelot is something of an anomaly. The character of Lancelot is in fact a latecomer to the stories of the Round Table, an immigrant from a thirteenth-century work called (appropriately enough) *Lancelot*. He first appears in his new context in a poem written in the next century, "Le Morte d'Arthur" (predating, and not to be confused with, the classic work of the same title by Malory). Malory's version, like later and often illustrated editions of the Arthurian legends, was short on textual description, so that the reader's image of knights, including Lancelot, would depend largely on any accompanying illustrations or plates. The drawings and paintings of Arthur Rackham and N. C. Wyeth would have graced the boys' books of Lerner's youth, and it is likely that these influenced his creation of *Camelot*'s Lancelot. (Writer Gene Lees, in his biography of Lerner and Loewe, suggests a different interpretation, blaming Lerner's Lancelot on a personal vendetta. Painting Lancelot as very handsome, vain, and selfish was his way, "consciously or unconsciously," Lees claims, of lashing out at his French wife, Micheline. In truth, Lerner's book bristles with moderate Francophobia.)

It is perhaps curious, considering the source of his libretto, that Lerner ignored a passage in White's book in which Guenevere "liked [Lancelot's] broken face, however hideous it was, and Arthur asked her to be kind." But this was no description of Robert Goulet, who more closely resembled the Lancelots of illustrated books for boys; and besides, *Camelot* was to be a romantic musical, not a documentary. With Goulet in the cast, Lerner and Loewe were ready for work.

As it turned out, it would be an unusually peripatetic collaboration. Over the approximate twenty-one months that they worked together on the songs, Lerner and Loewe averaged a thousand miles a month in deference to Loewe's desire to spend some time (often several weeks) in Cannes, some time in New York, and some time (mostly winters) in Palm Springs, California. By June 1959 they had completed half a dozen songs and were in Paris for an interview; Lerner was still working on the script as they composed the songs. It was slow going. By the following April Lerner was back in New York, the show was called *Camelot*, and half the score was ready. He was interviewed by Joseph Wershba of the *New York Post*. "I am constantly at war with what I think I want to do and what I eventually wind up doing," he told Wershba. "The characters dominate. We have to understand them completely before we even try to put words in their mouths or set music to their words. I have to find the characters; I just have to fall in love with them. That's why there are always new problems—and that's why we are always in a sweat."

He returned yet again to Lorenz Hart's advice about having to be brutal in order to write for the theater. And again, with a little variation, he explained what Hart had truly meant: "He meant that you would have to make sacrifices in your life, that you even had to be fanatical about your work. I'm probably a fanatic myself. . . . But quite often it's fanatics who produce some of the best things in our culture—a benign fanaticism, may I say."

On a different topic, he admitted that he had become disenchanted with the American political scene. "I'm a Democrat, but not out-and-out organizationally. And if there were another Wendell Willkie. . . ." He left the sentence hanging. The Democratic presidential candidate that year was his old Choate and Harvard contemporary John Kennedy; Lerner would sit back and wait.

He was disappointed, he told Wershba, in how American society relegated writers to second-class citizenship, both financially and spiritually. "If I weren't also a lyricist I would not be able to retire on my earnings as a playwright," he said.

In Europe [since his recent marriage he had been spending six months a year in Paris], writers are respected for the honor they bring to the country. Here, there is no affection or respect for our artists. If an Arthur Miller or Tennessee Williams walks into a public place, he's looked on as a "celebrity," or character—or freak, not as a man who has raised the stature of America in the eyes of the literate world.

But let me remind you: nobody today knows who financed Shakespeare's plays. And as [James] Thurber says, a nation in which a Congressman can seriously ask, "Do you believe the artist is a special person?" is a nation living in cultural jeopardy.

Nostalgically, he recalled his years at Harvard:

My faculty adviser gave me this advice when I asked what courses I should take: "If I were you," he said, "I would major in all the things that will be useless in your future work. Study all the things that will enrich your life which are not directly related to your career."

I never took a course in English or play writing. That's something you pick up as you go along in your work. And, oh! the shock of recognition years later, when you pick up a book that you had studied poorly in college days, and tell yourself—"I must read that now!"

The interview took place in Lerner's office, a suite on the fortieth floor of the Waldorf-Astoria ("I love working in hotels," he said.) There was one firm, set rule: When he was working, there were to be no interruptions, no interference. The exception, Wershba noted, was Michael Lerner, child of the lyricist's fourth marriage, now a year and a half old. "That's how I get my vacation on the job," Lerner told him. "Michael's around."

Despite his fondness for his wife's native France, he asserted that an "American really can't work in Paris—or in any other country but his own. He begins to lose the national identity of his work. He can't tell if it's American. Once I asked Micheline what she thought of something I had written. Her answer was: if you're no longer sure, it's time to go back home." He emphasized Micheline's significance in his life by saying about her, "[she] understands my work processes and is very sympathetic." In the near future she would give him cause to revise that statement.

During the early phase of the writing of *Camelot*, when he had rented the Château de la Garoupe in Antibes on the Riviera to be near Loewe, and with his forty-first birthday approaching, he considered the subject of age in a conversation with writer Pete Martin. "I don't regard myself as very old," he confided,

> but I'm old enough to know this: The older a writer gets, the harder it is for him to write. This is not true because his brain slows down. It's because his critical faculties grow more acute, and he finds it harder to please himself. If you're young, you have a sense of omnipotence. You're sure you're brilliant. You're an egg-head with two yolks, and even if youth is secretly frightened, it assumes an air of outer assurance and plows right through whatever is before it. As I grow older, I judge success by only one standard: Have I successfully avoided humiliating myself?

The two men were in a large room overlooking the "turquoise-blue Mediterranean sea with diamond wave caps"; in another part of the house were Lerner's children, daughters Susan (from his marriage to Ruth Boyd), Liza, and Jennifer (Nancy Olson) and young Michael, tended by a nurse. The conversation turned to creative paralysis; Lerner spoke of a poetic playwright (whom he did not identify) who, having tried and failed to "find words which could say more than words can possibly say," had stopped writing. Martin offered a similar tale about an illustrator who would do countless drawings, only to have the third or second one selected. Her reaction, too, had been simply to give up and stop working.

Lerner's response to this was, "Perfection can be incurable."

Switching gears, Martin asked Lerner about the similarities between the plots of *My Fair Lady* and *Gigi*. The librettist conceded the point.

"Were you aware of that resemblance when you began *Gigi*?"

"No," Lerner admitted. "Like a husband with an unfaithful wife, an author is the last to know when the plot is two-timing him."

Martin now turned to Lerner's work in progress, which he didn't imagine would "carry even a faint echo of *My Fair Lady* or *Gigi*."

"That's true," Lerner said. "White's book started by being an imaginative, poetic, humorous retelling of the stories which grew up around Arthur. He ended by writing about the human spirit."

"That's pretty high-sounding," Martin admonished. "Do you think the same people who loved *Brigadoon*, *Gigi*, *Paint Your Wagon* will be able to tune in mentally and emotionally on this new one?"

"It's not as high-sounding as it may seem," Lerner assured him. "We're taking White's material and reshaping it to our needs. . . . There's nothing wrong with a musical play which has a philosophical attitude, a thesis. The audience may never be aware of it, and you are aware of it only when you are writing it." He offered no further information or comment on the half-completed *Camelot*.

At summer's end, all the Lerners and Loewe returned to New York until the winter winds signaled that it was time to pack up again and settle in Palm Springs. With the coming of spring 1960, and with dates set for *Camelot*'s premiere (originally slated for November 17) and first rehearsals (September 3), it was time to put down roots and dig in for the final push. Each collaborator took a house at Sands Point, Long Island, north of Port Washington and about an hour's drive from Manhattan. It may have been too far from Manhattan for Micheline; she was bored on the island's elegant North Shore, known also as the Gold Coast, with its mansions reminiscent of the F. Scott Fitzgerald era. It was simply not metropolitan enough for her. Restive, she interfered with Lerner's work with Hart as well as with Loewe, voicing her opinions on everything, much to her husband's discomfort. She neither understood their work processes nor was sympathetic. Lerner's nerves "frayed" (his word) and his work suffered and dragged.

A great deal was at stake here. Columbia Records (CBS) had invested $400,000 in the show, and there was more. The March 27, 1960, issue of the Sunday *New York Times* included a lavish sixteen-page supplement celebrating the fourth anniversary of *My Fair Lady*. Heavily illustrated (with many pictures in color), it included articles by humorist-cartoonist James Thurber, Ira Gershwin, Cleveland Amory (Harvard, Class of '39), Anita Loos, Bennett Cerf, et al. Color pages featured the multiple recordings in their several languages; color portraits of the various Elizas and Higginses were provided, as were photographs of mandatory scenes from the musical. The back cover carried an advertisement for *My Fair Lady*'s New York production, as well as satellite shows in London, Oslo, Stockholm, Melbourne, Copenhagen, and Helsinki.

All of page thirteen (which Lerner considered to be a lucky number) was devoted to the announcement that Richard Burton and Julie Andrews were to open on November 17 in *Camelot*, based on T. H. White's *The Once and Future King*. Of the facing page, half was devoted to publisher Chappell & Co.'s advance advertisement for *Camelot*'s score, and the other half taken up by a proclamation from the O'Keefe Centre (of Front and Yonge Streets, Toronto, Canada):

> The O'Keefe Centre for the Performing Arts . . . opens October the first, 1960 . . . and has pleasure in announcing its opening attraction will be the world premiere of the Lerner-Loewe-Hart production of *Camelot*. During its first season the O'Keefe Centre is also proud to present the Herman Levin production of *My Fair Lady* . . . and takes this opportunity to extend congratulations on the fourth anniversary of *My Fair Lady*.

Within four weeks, mail orders for tickets (evening orchestra seats went for $9.40, balcony seats for $4.80) had reached $250,000. (By the time the musical arrived in New York, a bit late, the advance ticket sale would amount to more than $3 million). Even as he worked as librettist-lyricist, Lerner's other title, that of coproducer, gave him cause for contemplation, what with Columbia's sizable investment and the flourishing box office. He knew that the latter was in large measure a testimonial, sight unseen and sound unheard, to the creators of *My Fair Lady*. There was pressure on all sides.

In March, with half the score complete but the book not yet finished, Lerner hoped to find the requisite solitude (with Loewe, of course) at Sands Point. By June he realized that was not to be, however, as his and Micheline's marital "discussions" became both fortissimo and frequent.

He was thus relieved when, one day in mid-July, his wife announced that she had had enough of Long Island and would take their son, now two, to Europe for a short time. Although he would miss Michael, Lerner expected that the peace and solitude would speed up his work on *Camelot*: September was approaching inexorably, and he was still mired in act 1. Only a couple of days after Micheline and Michael left, he caught the rhythm of his working style and "was writing away furiously."

A week later Micheline Muselli Pozzo di Borgo Lerner, whose name nowhere appears in Lerner's *The Street Where I Live*, struck. She and Michael would remain in France; if Lerner wanted to see his son again, he would have to come to them. Shocked and sickened, Lerner, by his own account, was paralyzed. He slumped in a chair near the phone for three days, weeping uncontrollably and unable to muster the strength to get up and go to the bathroom. In mental disarray, he imagined that he would never see Michael again.

Curiously, no one called him during these three crucial days, not even Loewe. (Lerner assumed that his collaborator thought he was working on a lyric at the time—ironically, as Lerner notes in his book, "If Ever I Would Leave You"—and was waiting for *his* call.) Eventually he realized that he needed help, that his breakdown and inactivity could jeopardize the careers and work of a great number of good people. In desperation, he called Moss Hart and as calmly as possible informed him that he was having a little trouble, just some writer's block, nothing serious. He recalled the name of one of Hart's analysts and wondered if perhaps he might know of someone nearby whom Lerner might see now and then. He said nothing about his wife's defection or his neurotic paralysis. Hart was happy to give him the name and number of one of the country's most respected analysts, then on the staff of Johns Hopkins University; he, in turn, referred Lerner to a psychiatrist he respected who happened to be vacationing in nearby Great Neck, less than four miles distant.

Lerner pulled himself out of his "grisly chair," bathed, and raced to Great Neck, though "how I got there without killing half the population en route was a miracle." Hollow-eyed, pale, and shaken, he met with the doctor, who concluded that he needed more than a sympathetic listener and prescribed what Lerner termed some "pills of unusual potency." He was to begin with four a day and increase the dosage gradually until he was up to twelve daily; the doctor suggested that he drop by every three days so he could monitor the effect of these unidentified pellets on his patient. The lyricist soon felt good indeed, and within a couple of days could call Loewe to tell him he had completed "If Ever I Would Leave You."

By the end of the week, he was able for the moment to put aside his concern for his son and concentrate on *Camelot*. He spent all of August on the book working night and day, with little sleep; on the last day of the month he sent the completed script out to be copied, and it was in the hands of the cast on September 3, when rehearsals began. The first reading presaged the troubles to come: Lerner's weighty libretto required more than three hours to get through, even without scene changes or intermission.

They had less than a month to prepare for the previews and the grand opening of the O'Keefe Centre. This latter was in itself another form of risk: *Camelot* would be the first production in an unknown, untried venue. As it turned out, the O'Keefe was not a kind hall, creating problems for all concerned with sets, lighting, staging, and, not least, sound.

Lerner admitted that he and his coproducers had selected Toronto for the premiere of their musical for two reasons, "both bad." When plans for *Camelot* were first announced, the producers were approached by the O'Keefe Centre's manager, Hugh Walker, who made them an offer they could not possibly refuse: If they premiered *Camelot* at the Centre, they could have the theater—*gratis!* And not only that: The Centre would also cover all the expenses of transportation—for people as well as scenery and other trappings—housing, and so on. So, money constituted the first reason—that and the fact *Camelot* was a heavy show to move around, with cast, sets, and costumes.

The second reason, as unrealistic a rationale as could be imagined, was the producers' desire to avoid the influx of "dear shits" from New York. Opening in practical secrecy, they felt, would allow them to hammer their little monster into shape in peace before tryouts in Boston. But they were operating here on two illogical concepts. First of all, Toronto is as readily reached by plane from New York as Boston. And second, they could hardly expect the O'Keefe Centre's public-relations staff not to trumpet the opening of their multimillion-dollar theater, especially with a new Lerner and Loewe musical previewing there.

In fact, an American producer-impresario named Alexander H. Cohen had been hired to handle the introduction of the new theater (the unrefusable offer had been his idea). Cohen's wide experience and contacts made him an ideal choice for the job. He had begun on Broadway as coproducer of the play *Angel Street* in 1941, and produced his first musical, *Of V We Sing* (a mediocre wartime effort), the following year. After a lax period, he had come back with *Make a Wish*, produced in partnership with Jule Styne and Harry Rigby and featuring songs by Hugh Martin and Ralph Blane; it did a little better than *Of V We Sing*. Cohen had also worked with musical personalities including Victor Borge, Maurice Chevalier, and Marlene Dietrich, as well as comics Nichols and May. Alexander H. Cohen knew his way around Broadway, and Alan Jay Lerner was to hold him personally responsible for flying planeloads of "dear shits" up to *Camelot*'s out-of-town (out-of-*country*) tryout. Although Cohen himself believed that Lerner eventually forgave him for doing his job, there is no mention of him in Lerner's book—an ominous sign.

After too few rehearsal days in New York, Lerner began pruning the book, and they had what he considered to be a "brilliant run-through." Then *Camelot* and company hit the road, which would prove rocky indeed. While the technicians wrestled with the O'Keefe's acoustics, the stage, and other problems, Lerner, on his psychiatrist's advice, weaned himself off his "magic capsules." He was now down to four a day and was supposed to eat slowly and frequently, but two days before the opening, set for Saturday, October 2, he forgot the pills and "returned to the normal, pre-opening diet of black coffee in soggy containers and infrequent, indigestible sandwiches."

Reenter Micheline Lerner, with her mother and Michael. It was a bad time for additional tension, but his fourth wife had, as Lerner put it, "decided to return to fight another day."

As the frenzy in the theater increased, so did the population of Toronto as Cohen arranged for planes to come in from New York and even London. He wanted the "dear shits" to see, and spread the good word about, the O'Keefe Centre. The attendees were primarily show people, but no doubt scattered among them were curiosity seekers who, Lerner apprehensively sensed, had come in hopes of seeing Lerner and Loewe fall on their artistic faces. Cohen made sure, too, that the press—print, radio, and television—would be there. Toronto had already begun to evolve into what it is today, a clean suburb of New York; by Saturday, virtually the entire world was aware of that night's premiere of *Camelot* in the O'Keefe Centre for the Performing Arts. As darkness fell on October 1, 1960, Hollywood floodlights lit up Front and Yonge streets, and spectators lined the sidewalk.

Backstage, an anxious, strained, and jumpy Alan Lerner was trying, unsuccessfully, to turn down the volume on his wife's berating him for not bringing her mother to the theater. Ten minutes before curtain time, Doris Warshaw Shapiro saw Micheline Lerner seated on a high stool in a gorgeous silk gown, her lovely blond hair cascading to her bare shoulders, pointing a delicate finger at her kneeling husband, who admitted it was his fault that he had neglected to send for her mother. He pleaded for forgiveness, saying he had not been thinking clearly (he rarely did on opening night). Everyone connected with the show was housed in one or another hotel within easy walking distance of the theater. True, Mrs. Lerner's mother may have been a bit old for that, but as the more logical Shapiro mused, "Why didn't the daughter bring the mother?"

The curtain rose to a full, expectant house (the O'Keefe seated 3,200) at 8:15. It came down for the final time, according to the *Variety* reviewer, at

12:25 the next morning. Lerner estimated that the show had run for four and a half hours, an understandable exaggeration given the conditions, personal as well as professional, that he had to endure that night. But now they all knew the show was in trouble; after all, hadn't Moss Hart, in a rather inexplicable before-curtain speech, told the audience, "You're going to be a lot older when you get out of here tonight"?

Taking his cue from that gratuitous but all-too-true warning, one of the Monday-morning critics referred to *Camelot* as "*Götterdämmerung* without laughs"—the single line that Lerner found vexatious, another example of the self-consciously witty critic getting his exercise by dancing on the playwright's grave. On the whole, however—all things considered—the Toronto critics were quite kind and, it appeared, tried "to be as constructive as possible."

The review that would be most crucial did not appear until Wednesday, five days after the premiere, in *Variety*. By this time Cohen had flown his planeloads of guests back to New York, where word had begun to spread: *Camelot* was hopelessly sore afflicted. The reviewer ("McStay") began with the truth: "Obviously the present stage version of 'Camelot' is not the one that Broadway is going to see in finished form." The show, he suggested (echoing a legion of others), was "in for sharp editing," with its four-plus hours needing to be trimmed to about two and a half. But he found the "entire conception" to be so

> colorful in production values and costuming that heart-breaks [will be] inevitable in the necessary cutting.
>
> When Alan Jay Lerner, who did the book and lyrics, and Frederick Loewe, who wrote the music, put their discarded material—as adjudged by Moss Hart—in the future file, it should be marked "don't forget!" The librettist has some memorable dialog, although betimes some of it sounds a bit too topical and contemporaneous.

McStay had high praise for cast, costumes, and choreography, though he found "unsightly . . . the ten mikes fronting the stage, with the O'Keefe Centre's acoustics favoring the principals or the choral groups in kneeling positions. The new theatre seats 3,200 which does present an acoustic and projection problem." Loewe agreed, though *his* major criticism was that the orchestra was all but inaudible.

By the time they saw the encouraging *Variety* review, the three coproducers were well into the task of cutting about an hour and a half from the show. Hart had begun trimming while they were still in New York. The first thing to go was Hanya Holm's second-act animal ballet, set in the magic forest of the sorceress Morgan le Fay. Although Lerner considered it one of Holm's "most brilliant choreographic creations," he reluctantly agreed with Hart that its excision would improve the timing of the play. Hart had questioned, too, a long (twelve-minute) song in which Goulet, as Lancelot, musically expatiated on the subject of his quests, but with characteristic thoughtfulness, he judged it best to wait and gauge its effectiveness before an audience. "The Quest" was jettisoned almost as soon as the new round of cutting began, on the Sunday morning after the opening.

Under growing pressure, Lerner, Loewe, and Hart (especially Hart) managed to delete another twenty minutes or so—not enough, but a beginning.

The next day, Monday, the revisions were rehearsed by what could only be called a sympathetic and cooperative company—agreeable, helpful, uncomplaining. That night the curtain fell at midnight. While eating supper after the performance, his head full of further revisions, Lerner suffered a spell of dizziness, then another. Alarmed, he called the hotel physician, who diagnosed hemorrhaging (from a bleeding ulcer) and immediately admitted him to the Wellesley Hospital. Lerner agreed to go but informed the doctor that he could not stay in for more than three days, as he had important—critical—work to do. The doctor nodded, filled a hypodermic, and gently injected Lerner, who awakened four days later, on Saturday, the eighth of October. That was only the beginning.

Anxious to get back to the theater, Lerner demanded to know when he could be released. In a week, he was told—provided that he rested during that time and saw no one associated with *Camelot*. Still, he had a phone and was permitted a call or two a day to keep minimally informed. He took hope from Hart's message that things were working out, though they still faced the midnight-curtain handicap: He was loath to touch any of the writing without Lerner's approval. "I also learned," Lerner later wrote, "that somehow Moss was keeping the company together and the spirits from falling. How he did it I will never know."

He was happy to learn on Thursday that if he continued to improve, he would be released on Saturday, the fifteenth. It was with anticipation and relief that he packed his little bag on Saturday afternoon and, accompanied by a nurse, walked to the elevator. He turned while they were waiting and saw an occupied hospital bed being rolled into his former room; in the elevator the nurse told him that the patient was Moss Hart, who had suffered a severe heart attack, his second in ten years.

A shaken Lerner steadied himself against the elevator wall, finding the news unbelievable. In near shock, he returned to the Royal York still weak in the knees. *Where do we go from here?* he asked himself. He missed the Saturday matinee.

Loewe, who had been carefully guarding his own heart and nerves from the very beginning, spoke to the cast after the performance, wanting to inform them of Hart's condition before the rumors started and grew (a common show-business occurrence). He explained that though Hart was very ill, he was not on the critical list; meanwhile, he said, Lerner had been released, and as soon as he was able, the two of them would attend to the task of preparing the show for Boston.

That night, preoccupied with Hart's absence and wondering how they could go on without him, Lerner saw a shorter, and improved, *Camelot*. Hart had managed to subtract an hour, but the show was still thirty minutes too long, and to Lerner's dismay, the stripping-away had served to emphasize the weaknesses of his book.

When Hart was strong enough to see his wife, he asked her to tell Lerner to take over the direction until he was out of the hospital; he thought it would be a mistake to bring in another director at this difficult moment. This was a touching display of trust, but for Lerner it was also a burden: Rewriting was one job, directing quite another.

No one seconded Lerner's reservations more vehemently than Frederick Loewe, who deemed it an impossible idea. Lerner's loyalty to Hart made him reluctant to search for a replacement director, but Loewe was in favor of finding someone with a fresh outlook, an objective approach. Besides, he pointed out, how could Lerner be in the hotel working with him and supervising the cast in the theater simultaneously? Lerner admitted he was right, but it did not resolve the problem. He assured Loewe that he would think about hiring a new director. This issue would eventually lead to the dissolution of the team of Lerner and Loewe.

To demonstrate his good intentions, Lerner suggested that they call Jose Ferrer in Beverly Hills and ask him to take over the show's direction; Loewe agreed, but Ferrer was busy directing the film *Return to Peyton Place*, and was unavailable. Loewe was not much appeased. Nor was he happy about Bud Widney's increasing role in the production and his frequent conferences with Lerner (never a problem before, these were now a source of irritation for the composer). Widney had even taken over the coaching and rehearsing of the replacement actor playing Tom, whose character had a touching final scene with Arthur. With Loewe, this presumption rankled, too (as show business goes, by the time *Camelot* reached New York, there would be a third Tom).

Seeking support among the cast, Lerner first approached Richard Burton and Julie Andrews, who understood (he did not tell them of Hart's request, only asked for their help) and were sympathetic and encouraging (Lerner's words). Burton, cheerily and with great skill, even became a de facto assistant director, with help from the British drama coach Philip Burton. (Richard Burton, born Richard Jenkins into a large Welsh coal-mining family, had been taken under Philip Burton's professional wing as a teenager. The elder Burton proceeded to educate and train the young Welshman, who, in his midtwenties, became one of the Old Vic's youngest Hamlets. In gratitude, he took his mentor's name.)

A womanizer and heavy drinker, Burton was a company favorite; his devoted followers included the young Goulet and another newcomer, named John Cullum, his understudy in the Arthur role. Burton's high spirits, professionalism, and relaxed manner amid the continuing changes were beneficial to the company's morale. Julie Andrews, for her part, was even-tempered and flexible and, as she had done during *My Fair Lady*, brightly presided over the company's tea concession. Only Loewe avoided Lerner and smoldered. Still, he, too, was professional: When his collaborator needed him, he was there.

Rather than subject the company to myriad alterations (and since he sensed that several scenes were going well), Lerner decided to "apply a cleaver to the second half of the second act," while leaving the very last pages—with Arthur and the boy Tom—untouched. The scene in question (act 2, scene 7) originally included dialogue between Arthur and Mordred as they look out the window of Arthur's study into the courtyard, where the executioner is preparing to burn Guenevere for her adultery (staged by Mordred, with the connivance of Morgan le Fay). Mordred is gleeful, but Arthur cannot bring himself to give the signal to set the fire. Lerner excised most of the dialogue, and then he and Loewe refashioned their song "Guenevere," cutting even that so that just the chorus, "in quasi-oratorial fashion," carries the plot, questioning Arthur's indecision and expressing his hope that Lancelot will arrive in time to rescue her. This deft revision speeded up the scene and advanced the plot brilliantly.

These last changes were inserted and rehearsed near the end of the week, on a Thursday and Friday, though none was yet introduced into the actual performance. The final Toronto curtain descended on Saturday, October 22; Lerner ruefully clocked it at 11:50. The sets were struck and bags were packed as the *Camelot* caravan prepared to leave for its next stop: Boston. Only the irreplaceable Moss Hart remained behind.

Eight train cars were required to carry the costumes, the props, and the company, more than two hundred strong. Lerner recalled that the scenery was transported in vans that made the move look, from the air, like the pioneers' opening of the West. However they did it, the cost of moving *Camelot* from Toronto to Boston to New York was estimated at thirty-five thousand dollars.

Even as the sets were being fitted onto the stage of the Shubert, and Lerner and Loewe and others were settling in at the luxurious Ritz-Carlton, the vultures were converging with Mordred-like glee and expectancy—and with them, two sharp reporters from *Time*, assigned to do no less than a cover story on the show.

Time's writers caught some of the tryout-town frenzy in their observations of the collaborators at work:

> Lerner joins Loewe at the piano as they work together on four new songs, including one called "The Seven Deadly Virtues," plus the problems of telescoping four Act I scenes into two, straightening out Act II, deepening Mordred's villainy—all of which requires new lines, new musical bridges, and scenes long enough to allow complicated scene shifts.

The estrangement of Lerner and Loewe went unnoticed by the reporters, though they dutifully noted (adhering to *Time*'s fondness for facts), that Lerner had taken suite 1004 and Loewe was two floors up, in 1204. Across the hall from 1004 were Micheline and Michael Lerner, the latter with his own phonograph, on which he listened to French music (they detected and identified a work by Debussy). For his comfort, Loewe shared 1204 with, as revealed in *Time*, a "current, 24-year-old friend; he calls her 'baby boy,' she calls him 'baby bear.'" They dug no deeper on this; her name was, in fact, Tammy.

Loewe, they reported, was "short, lean, with the sallow skin of the heart patient. [He] is 59 and looks it." Lerner fared better, despite the medication he was taking for his still-present ulcer; possessed, they said, of an "unweathered complexion, Lerner is 42 and could pass for a graduate student." His precarious health, his explosive marital situation, and, not least, the shambles of *Camelot*—all were artfully concealed behind his schoolboy demeanor. Of course, he did smoke, always had, constantly, "twirling the ignited cigarette in his fingers like the active end of a turboprop." It was acknowledged, too, that "Lerner is a bit of a hypochondriac, makes a fetish of weighing himself daily; he buys a new scale wherever he goes, probably owns the largest collection this side of the Office of Weights and Measures."

Lerner and Loewe, in sum, "are marvelously meshed, and Fritz even goes so far as to say of Alan, 'I love him.'"

By now it was obvious to everyone but the reporters that Loewe's declaration dated from another time and place. They could no longer do the work required of them without tension and unspoken criticisms. It had always been their practice to work closely together, without witnesses, but in an effort to mollify and ingratiate himself with his wife, Lerner now informed Loewe that Micheline would sit in on their work sessions. For the composer this seemed an unfathomable incursion into a very private creative communing; it had never happened before. (The fourth Mrs. Lerner now expressed an interest in the theater, whereas in the past she had held mere show business in contempt.) Loewe, furious, threatened to add Tammy to their audience. The breach deepened; there was barely a Lerner and Loewe anymore.

Burton's virtual direction, Bud Widney's constant presence at Lerner's side, and now the introduction of Micheline—it was all too much for Loewe, who had thus far maintained an icy calm, and his distance. Late one night he got so angry that Doris Warshaw Shapiro, still Lerner's protective assistant, believed him fortunate not to have suffered another heart attack. Still, somehow, the collaborators managed to labor on, expanding Roddy McDowall's role with "The Seven Deadly Virtues" in the first scene of act 2 and giving Guenevere a musical farewell to Lancelot (just before they are caught in her room by the scheming Mordred), "I Loved You Once in Silence."

The problem lay in that second act, Lerner knew, but he could not find a solution. As *Time* facetiously put it, "everyone was rewriting *Camelot*. Bit players were suggesting changes to chorus girls. Even floor waiters appeared to have a new second act under their silver dish covers." Scene designer Oliver Smith, who had also joined the rally round Lerner, went so far as to suggest that the entire second act be abandoned and the first elaborated; he believed that Lerner had written two conflicting shows. Too late, he realized that in "*Camelot*, the first half was joyous and romantic. But the second half told the story of disintegration of the Round Table, and it became pure drama. Unfortunately, there is no way of making a downhill story go uphill."

But Lerner could not agree with that assessment. One night, alone—Julie Andrews once referred to the miserable collaborators as the "loneliest men in town"—he realized that his dramatic goal consisted in the final three pages of the libretto. Arthur has lost everyone and everything, and has bitterly concluded that he and his dream of a world of right and justice have failed. Then, one night, on the battlefield where the Round Table and its symbolism will be destroyed, after Arthur has wished Lancelot well in the battle to come and bade a loving farewell to Guenevere (who has entered a nunnery), *A young lad, about fourteen, appears, from behind the tent. His name is Tom.*

A stowaway on one of the ships to France, Tom, though not yet even a page, wants to be a knight. He has never actually seen a knight, but he knows of them from the "stories people tell."

Arthur's eyes light up, and his spirit rises; he asks Tom what he knows about the Knights of the Round Table.

"I know everything, Milord. Might for right! Right for right! Justice for all! A Round Table where all knights sit. Everything!"

Gently, Arthur instructs the boy to avoid the battle and return to England "to grow up and grow old." But first he must do what the king tells him, in apposite lyrics sung to the tune of "Camelot":

> *Ask ev'ry person if he's heard the story;*
> *And tell it strong and clear if he has not:*
> *That once there was a fleeting wisp of glory*
> *Called Camelot.*

The slightly dotty but faithful Pellinore now arrives with Arthur's famous sword Excalibur, which the king uses to dub the boy "Sir Tom of Warwick." The confused Pellinore then reminds Arthur, "You have a battle to fight."

"Battle?" Arthur replies. "I've won my battle, Pelly. Here's my victory." (The "Camelot" theme here builds to near crescendo.) "What we did will be remembered. You'll see, Pelly. Now run, Sir Tom!" (Thomas Malory was a Warwickshire man; this was one of T. H. White's fanciful contributions to the legend.)

Again he shouts "Run, boy!" as the music swells fully and the curtain descends.

Loewe was not convinced. He continued to press for a new director; neither he nor Lerner, he believed, could judge any longer what worked and what did not. As one theater historian has observed, "When a show is really in trouble on the road and gripped by desperation, fear and fatigue, there comes a time when any change appears to be an improvement, but that may not be true. Different is not necessarily better."

His nerves raw, his stomach churning, Lerner could not even guess what the reception might be for the preview, to be followed the very next night by the official opening. While some revisions had yet to be implemented, many were already in place, and all the excision in the second act would at least make the show shorter.

When the curtain came down at 11:35, it was not because of libretto length, but because of audience reaction—laughter in the proper places and show-stopping applause. "It was time for the champagne," Lerner exulted. But the premiere the next night revealed that they had celebrated too soon: There remained the problem of length, though it was a better show than Toronto had seen. They still had a long way to go, and some rather painful decisions to make.

During the musical's first week in Boston, author T. H. White arrived from his retreat on Aldernay, in the Channel Islands, to view what Lerner had wrought. This large, bearlike, Viking-bearded man intimidated Lerner, who tried to warn him about the conversion of book to play: In fact, there was not really much left of *The Once and Future King*, other than its essence (which had been in the public domain for centuries) and the three precious pages at the close of the show.

White appreciated Lerner's concern and understood his position. He was also, to the other's relief, "enthusiastic and encouraging and magnanimously gave me free rein to do whatever I thought was best for the play."

And so he began again, rewriting over half of the first act (which revision required a new song for Julie Andrews) and discarding or rearranging most of the second (necessitating a new opening set). It was a complex process, with the cast having to perform one version even as Lerner rewrote it. After a couple of days' rehearsal (in this Lerner had Widney's assistance as well as Burton's), the changes would go into an evening performance to be studied. Then it was on to the next shift. This routine would continue for a month as the three-week Boston stay was extended a week to prepare for New York—a delay that, needless to say, caused the rumors to dance along Broadway.

By the third week, Lerner had begun to worry about the new first-act song that Guenevere needed to replace her eliminated farewell scene with Lancelot. In it she must tell him to leave on his quest, but at the same time she must let him know how much his leaving will affect her. It had to be bittersweet—and most important, brief. All Lerner could come up with was a possible title, "Before I Gaze at You Again"; he gave this to Loewe, who quickly turned out a melody (the song as it finally was lyricized is a mere eighteen lines long). Lerner knew he could not complete the lyric in Boston, and the following week, the fourth, would mean the "freezing" of the show—that is, no more could go in, no more could come out. The cast needed a stable book in preparation for the previews before the premiere.

Lerner confronted the unperturbable Julie Andrews with his "outrageous request": Would she "consent to perform a brand-new song at the first New York preview? 'Of course, darling,' she said, 'but do try to get it to me the night before.'" (Writing on the road as *Camelot* lurched to Manhattan, and in his hotel room, he managed to have it finished *two* nights before.)

As the Boston run was coming to an end, Lerner became aware that he was rarely seeing Loewe, who spent most of his time either in his suite with Tammy or hovering like a wraith at the back of the Shubert. When the show closed after the final Saturday-night performance—still a bit unwieldy, still troubled—he sensed that he and his beloved Fritz had each taken a wrong fork in the road and would never find their way back. "It must have been as much agony for him as it was for me," he later supposed.

While Widney and Burton prepared the cast in its new setting, Manhattan's Majestic Theatre, Lerner sequestered himself in the hotel to finish "Before I Gaze at You Again." On Tuesday afternoon, he and Loewe demonstrated it for Julie Andrews (Loewe had had the foresight to have an orchestration arranged, implicit evidence of his trust in Lerner the lyricist). According to Lerner, their Guenevere "sang it through and thanked us profusely."

When they had a bare-stage, no-costume run-through on Wednesday evening in preparation for the first preview on Thursday, Lerner witnessed what he later said was the most memorable, most moving performance of *Camelot* he ever saw. Without the impressive Oliver Smith sets and the dazzling Adrian–Tony Duquette costumes, the show was simpler, more intimate (he felt), reflecting, with theatrical magic, the thesis of his book. He would never forget that performance. For the first time, he was unaware of the show's top-heavy opulence; the sets and costumes were beautiful, he admitted, but they fattened *Camelot*. (In a sense, it was no longer his choice to make: Audiences, after *My Fair Lady*, had come to expect lavish trappings in a Lerner and Loewe musical.)

Then, all at once, it was time. On Thursday, December 1, an appreciative, expectant preview audience saw a performance that Lerner pronounced a "perfect joy." Everything went remarkably well—and, as expected, Julie Andrews had her new song down pat. The following night was a benefit, and benefit audiences were always unpredictable; often as not, they wanted their extra money's worth. Only a few minutes into the show, however, Lerner was convinced that this more critical audience was "even better than Thursday night's." As he paced the back of the theater, he wished only that Moss Hart, still recuperating in the Toronto hospital, could be there with him. (Had he been there, Hart might have been better able to prepare him for the reviews they would read after the Saturday premiere.)

One of the two loneliest men in town spent the early part of Saturday watching the final preparations, mostly involving lighting, for that night's performance. Loewe was not around, and Lerner himself was generally ignored. Late in the afternoon, tired, he forced himself out of his seat and climbed the steps to the stage, where a young stagehand was sweeping up. For some inexplicable reason, Lerner patted the man's shoulder and said, "Good luck, kid."

The stagehand assured him that he—Lerner—did not need any luck: "There's too much love on the stage."

Deeply touched, Lerner thanked him, left the theater by the back door, walked down the three steps into the alleyway, and burst into tears.

That evening, after giving the cast a brief speech about the vagaries of first-night audiences—"an autograph hunter's paradise"—he took his usual pacing position, alone in the rear of the Majestic Theatre.

It did not go well. The responses, the laughs, the delighted applause that had bolstered them during the previews—all were now missing. During intermission, Lerner sought the solitude of the manager's office, alone again. Goulet's "If Ever I Would Leave You" got the second act off to a good start: It stopped the show. But that was it. The show *was* long. Lerner felt chilled. "The curtain calls were well-applauded," he recalled, "but it was all too clear there was no excitement in the house."

The mandatory, factitious, backstage postcurtain celebration was subdued, but even so, it was livelier than the audience's reaction had been. As he made the traditional rounds of dressing rooms, distributing his appreciation among the cast, Lerner sensed their disappointment and again assured them of the venerable treachery, and ambiguity, of the first-nighters (another show-business folk belief). But they all knew that already. Noël Coward added to the festivities with his sotto voce accolade, "Mahvelous, darling, mahvelous," but the papers had yet to be heard from: Because of the Saturday-night opening, with the Sunday *Times* already on the stands, there would be a longer-than-usual wait for the first reviews in Monday's early editions.

Contrary to his usual practice, Lerner joined everyone at the ritual opening-night party at Luchow's, a restaurant dating back to Victor Herbert's time; located on Fourteenth Street near Irving Place, it was about as far as one could get from Sardi's to wait for the reviews. Press agent Richard Maney was ready at his post near the *Times*. Once again, Lerner made the rounds, then went to his table and, according to his account, began drinking in preparation for the words from the press (a not very salutary activity in view of his recent hospitalization).

As soon as the *Times* review was available, it was phoned in to Luchow's. The reviewer, Howard Taubman, was a former *Times* music critic who had recently taken over the drama spot from Brooks Atkinson. Taubman was not happy with *Camelot*, finding it "unfortunately . . . weighed down by the burden of its book. The style of the storytelling is inconsistent. It shifts uneasily between light-hearted fancy and uninflected reality." Lerner's lyrics were, he conceded, "fashioned cleverly" (that's all?) and Loewe had "written some pleasant tunes." He proceeded to wax musicological. "Fie on Goodness!," sung by the knights, smacked of Friml; Mordred's "The Seven Deadly Virtues" was inventive but had been set to the wrong rhythmic accompaniment. Recognizing "Guenevere" for what, in fact, it was—a song that the "authors undoubtedly use to replace a lot of narrative"—he dismissed it as an "oratorio without a trace of genius." His kinder words were reserved for the cast, the sets ("visually, *Camelot* is never anything less than a thing of beauty"), the costumes ("royally lavish and impeccably tasteful"), the choreography, and the lighting. He professed himself unwilling to fault Lerner, Loewe, and Hart for "not attaining the heights of *My Fair Lady*," but in the end was unable to resist: "It cannot be denied that they badly miss their later collaborator—Bernard Shaw."

Although he was assured that the review contained plenty of good quotes that could be extracted for advertising, Lerner was nonetheless "crushed." There was worse yet to come.

Taubman himself followed up with an essay in his Sunday column in which he underlined the problem of experiencing virtually two shows in a single evening in one theater. He suggested that either the entire musical should have been composed in the spirit of the light and airy first act, or else the more serious approach of the second act should have prevailed, with its focus on the Arthur-Guenevere-Lancelot triangle. Lerner had not developed a "consistent point of view," and this, according to Taubman, was the show's major flaw. The other problem was money: The advance sale had reached a record-breaking $3 million. "Blame Broadway for this," the *Times* critic concluded, "if you like. But remember that Broadway has seen to it that *Camelot* need not fret about financial security."

Taubman believed that *Camelot* looked better—costumes, sets—than it played in Lerner's book. Also, because of the advance-ticket sales, the musical was rushed to Broadway before its time. "Clearly no expense has been spared," Taubman opined in his follow-up Sunday column. "And here we arrive at a clue to the insuperable hazards Broadway sets for its children once they put a big production in motion. With costly contracts signed, countless theatre parties spoken for, innumerable commitments involving thousands of dollars made, how is it possible to pause in Toronto or Boston or Philadelphia? Who has the courage to take stock and say the point of view is muddled and the show must be redone even if it requires a year?"

This was, in part, true (of *Camelot* as well as other shows) and easy to proclaim from the safety of a desk at the *Times*. And, too, Taubman had no idea of what had occurred in Toronto and Boston.

The play's author fretted through the night, however. Every time the phone rang, another pronouncement was heard. Walter Kerr of the *Herald-Tribune* found it "mixed," while John Chapman of the *News* registered a "rave"; Robert Coleman of the *Daily Mirror* reported that "Lerner set out to pen a serious satire . . . and missed the boat." And so on.

As the results came in, as if on some election evening, Lerner shriveled and, characteristically, Loewe shrugged. One reviewer referred to *Camelot* as "Costalot"; few could resist the temptation of comparing it to *My Fair Lady*. (*Variety* would not publish until the following Wednesday, but Hobe's first sentence seemed to sum up the general verdict: "To vary a phrase of a generation ago, *Camelot* is beautiful and not very bright.")

Miserable, with a wrenching stomach that he was not quite inebriated enough not to feel, Lerner left Luchow's and went home. On Monday morning, when he learned that there was no line at the Majestic ticket box office, he realized that even if the show were deemed a commercial success, for him it was an artistic failure. He even discovered that William Paley had called a couple of his attorneys to get an appraisal of the show's chances; their opinion was that once the large advance had been accommodated, the musical that was born in December would expire in May (how exactly this was determined, Lerner never knew). Based on this prognostication, CBS hurried to release the original cast album.

Discouraged, Lerner left town.

He spent several weeks at a Swiss ski resort, mostly sitting in the lobby with the (other) injured downhillers. In February he returned to a "bleak *Camelot*," rested and ruddy but no happier. In that brief time, however, something good had occurred: Moss Hart, too, had come back to Manhattan. They saw *Camelot* together, and Hart suggested that they go to work—an all but unprecedented move, since shows are rarely reworked three months after their premieres, when all the reviews are in and word-of-mouth has done its damage. Hart made Lerner realize that the consensus was true, and the critics had been right, and he himself had unconsciously rejected their views because he was standing too close up and not far enough away. Inspired by Hart's professional objectivity, Lerner spent a week at the typewriter, cut a choral number, and deleted another song—and found that the show played much better.

But to what end, he wondered, once the ominous month of May came around and Paley and his grim doomsayers proved right?

And then came what Lerner called the "miracle," in the form of television variety-show host and part-time columnist Ed Sullivan. His was the most successful Sunday prime-time show then on television, and its secret was simply this: It provided something for everybody, from circus acts to ballet. From time to time he devoted portions of the show to popular songwriters such as Harold Arlen, Rodgers and Hammerstein, or Cole Porter. He now wished, in celebration of the fifth anniversary (in March) of *My Fair Lady*, to devote a full hour to the works of Lerner and Loewe. His timing could not have been more propitious.

When Lerner and Loewe met with Sullivan to discuss the content and form of the show, Lerner suggested that rather than doing a run-through of their "top hits," as was Sullivan's usual practice, they might devote a good portion of the hour to *Camelot*. Whenever a new musical opened, the customary thing was to present a song or two to plug it; Lerner's novel idea was to offer, instead, a hefty group of songs—no less than, say, twenty minutes' worth. Sullivan agreed.

When the time came, Andrews, Burton, and Goulet appeared in their costumes, in approximations of the stage settings; Burton sang "Camelot,"

Andrews "The Simple Joys of Maidenhood," Goulet "If Ever I Would Leave You," and Andrews and Burton together "What Do the Simple Folk Do?" They were, as Lerner put it, a "smash."

The next morning he was awakened by a phone call from the Majestic's excited manager, who urged him to come by the theater to see what was happening at the box office for himself. Lerner dressed and hurried over to West Forty-fourth Street. For the first time since the show's opening the previous December, the box-office line stretched halfway down the block. The Sullivan show had wrought a miracle.

When the new audiences saw the refurbished *Camelot*, the curtain came down at eleven-fifteen to riotous applause. "The people came up the aisles raving," Lerner wrote. "*Camelot* was finally a hit."

And it went beyond the merely financial aspects (though William Paley could rest easily on that account as well). The audience response inspired the cast, whose performances became more electric, more alive, less tentative. A hit indeed, the show ran for two years and was subsequently successfully toured (and revived). *Camelot* also did reasonably well in London, lasting 518 performances with Laurence Harvey as Arthur, Elizabeth Larner as Guenevere, and Barry Kent as Lancelot. The original cast album sold in the millions, and there were two other recordings as well, one by the London cast and the other of the soundtrack to the unfortunate film version, heavy-handedly directed by Joshua Logan and released in 1967. Even Lerner did not care for the film (with its often bloated close-ups, in wide-screen Panavision, no less!), for which he provided a slightly revised script. Its three Academy Awards—for art-set decoration, scoring, and costume design—were not enough to prevent the film *Camelot* from being a financial failure.

Broadway's *Camelot*, in contrast, could be counted a success. There were Tonys, too, for Burton, Oliver Smith (for scenic design), Franz Allers (as musical director), and Tony Duquette and (Gilbert) Adrian (for the costumes). For this last, the award came posthumously.

Once MGM's most celebrated costume designer (dressing the likes of Harlow, Garbo, and Shearer), Adrian had retired from Hollywood due to poor health. Early on, Moss Hart had suggested him as the right man for the job of designing costumes for *Camelot*. Happy to be doing something again, he had produced some sketches based on a reading of White's book; all were delighted with his fanciful work, and he became one of the first to join the company. When, eight months later, he died of a heart attack, his widow, Janet Gaynor, proposed that the producers hire his protégé, Tony Duquette, to finish the work. An established set designer whose credits included the "Adam and Eve" sequence for the filmed *Can-Can* and opera and ballet designs for the San Francisco Opera, Duquette completed the costumes in keeping with his predecessor's original conceptions.

When the *Time* team (Joyce Haber and Henry Grunwald) descended upon the Boston tryout of *Camelot*, they tossed off a phrase that would be often repeated (even by Lerner), to the effect that *Camelot* "had very nearly turned . . . from a musical into a medical." Beginning with Adrian's death, they compiled a list of casualties: Lerner's bleeding ulcer, Hart's coronary, and assorted other illnesses, including Burton's virus (which affected his voice), Goulet's "company cold," and Loewe's influenza. They had to dig deeper to find the wardrobe mistress's husband who dropped dead in New York, the chorus girl who stepped on a needle onstage, the chief electrician's bladder trouble. They quoted one of the stage managers as saying, "We are all quitting. We will be replaced tomorrow by hospital orderlies."

With *Camelot* revived thanks to Hart, all seemed well in the spring of 1961. Everyone could relax; Lerner went off to Europe again, his marriage once more in good repair. When he returned, it was to a splendid five-story town house at 42 East Seventy-first Street, with a 100-by-60-foot garden and sixteen rooms (eight baths) that Mrs. Lerner, predictably, began filling with Napoleonic antiques. One evening, as the two friends discussed their next project, Hart unselfishly suggested to Lerner that they do a nonmusical; Lerner, touched, rejected the idea, feeling Hart could do a much better job without him. For his part, he had already begun to contemplate a musical future that did not include his longtime collaborator.

Like Loewe, the Harts had taken a fancy to Palm Springs and bought a home there; when the New York winter began to seem too inevitable, they headed for California. In December Lerner received the call that was to cast the "musical into a medical" legend in stone: On December 20, 1961, Moss Hart suffered his third, and last, heart attack in the driveway of his home in Palm Springs. His death, at the age of fifty-seven, Lerner bitterly classified as "anything but senseless cruelty."

As for Loewe, he made it clear that he and Lerner were finished. In the future he would confine himself to his pleasure palaces, in Cannes, in Paris, his home in Palm Springs, or anywhere else he did not have to work. His attitude in general was revealed in a story told by Ira Gershwin, who opened his door to Lerner's erstwhile collaborator one evening at around eleven o'clock (Gershwin was a night owl).

"How was the party?" Gershwin asked (he knew there had been one, but he rarely went to parties, if he could get out of them).

"Oh," Loewe told him, "I just had a late dinner at Romanoff's."

"Didn't you go to the party?"

"Yes, I was there on time. They said seven-thirty."

"What happened?"

"Well, I thought dinner would be served at about eight-thirty or nine. But it was ten o'clock before I found myself standing with a large plate in a long line waiting to get at the buffet. It was too dull and I put the plate down and said to those near me, 'Sorry, but I'm too old and too rich for this kind of thing.'"

And with that, he had left.

11

—⁂—

"HOW TO HANDLE
A WOMAN?"

I N APRIL 1960, when Lerner and Loewe were about midway through the
score for *Camelot*, a curious item appeared in the *New York Post*, announcing the future collaboration of Lerner and Richard Rodgers. That composer's
flourishing partnership with Oscar Hammerstein II would not end until that
August, with the lyricist's death from cancer, but by April it was already evident that Hammerstein would not write again, and he retired to his farm in
Bucks County, Pennsylvania, to wait out his life. The final Rodgers and Hammerstein musical was the triumphant *Sound of Music*, of the year before.

Loewe had not yet officially bowed out of his collaboration with Lerner,
and *Camelot*'s Toronto troubles still lay in the unknown future, but if this pre-
mature item bothered him, he made no mention of it. Lerner was taking him
at his word that the "next will be my last"; like Rodgers, Lerner liked to keep
working.

The *Post* noted that the new collaboration would not begin until "late
this year or early in 1961," by which time each would "finish other commitments so they can start working together." Lerner had to complete *Camelot*,
and Rodgers was engaged in creating the score for a thirteen-hour (over
twenty-six weeks) television special called *Winston Churchill—The Valiant
Years*.

They had three possibilities in mind, the *Post* reported: one "based on the life of French fashion designer Chanel" and the other two "too vague to mention." As Rodgers put it, "We met and had a drink. Then we started having lunch together and decided to go to work." Rodgers said no to the Chanel musical (Lerner would return to it nine years later, with André Previn as composer), but he liked Lerner's thought of doing a musical about extrasensory perception and reincarnation. (Rodgers also had an idea of his own, for a musical—words and music—on the still-sensitive subject of interracial love, inspired by a television appearance by the very glamorous Diahann Carroll. He did not suggest this as a vehicle for Lerner because he wanted to use another librettist, his friend Samuel Taylor.)

The press announcement led to a flurry of excitement both on Broadway and in the music business. In interviews, each carefully spoke well of the other. Lerner was optimistic, saying that after their mutual lawyer, Irving Cohen, brought them together—he knew their creative drives, it was a natural!—"we discovered that we talked the same language. . . . We realized we had the same attitudes toward the theatre, the same ideas about casting, management, and [the] breaking of theatre molds."

In his autobiography, *Musical Stages*, Rodgers echoed the same sentiment: "From what I knew about Alan, his general philosophy and attitude toward the musical theatre seemed closest to mine of any lyricist then active on Broadway. . . . Even more important to me was the kind of theatre he had come to represent. It had taste and style, and it 'said something.'"

Since nothing was generally known of the dissolution of the team of Lerner and Loewe, the new collaboration was treated as a feat of triangular geometry—almost like an affair. Writing from Cannes, in April 1961, Art Buchwald alluded to this reaction in his column in the *Herald-Tribune*: "When lyricist Alan Lerner and composer Fritz Loewe got a divorce after producing such successful offspring as *Brigadoon*, *My Fair Lady*, *Gigi*, and *Camelot*, Mr. Lerner immediately found happiness with Richard Rodgers and their marriage was announced in all the papers."

Buchwald interviewed Loewe on his yacht, a few miles offshore from Cannes, while, according to the imaginative reporter, the composer kept an attentive eye, through binoculars, on his (convertible) Rolls-Royce. He was in good humor, asserting, "I came back to the Riviera because I know they love me for my money, and not myself."

Buchwald's inevitable query about Lerner's new alliance elicited a not-unexpected reply: "How can I be bitter when I don't want to work?" Loewe asked him. "I am a great admirer of Richard Rodgers and I think it was inevitable after Oscar Hammerstein's death that Lerner should become Rodgers' partner." He hedged the truth a little when he said he had learned of the collaboration only on reading about it in the papers; the *Post* item had appeared almost exactly a year earlier. In answer to the reporter's question "Have you seen Mr. Lerner since the breakup?" Loewe poignantly answered, "No, but all I can say is, even if we don't talk to each other, we'll always be good friends."

Expectations for Lerner and Rodgers were high, and goodwill widespread. For all the fine words, though, one was missing: *compatibility.*

In *Musical Stages*, Rodgers reveals something of himself when he admits that he had been following Hammerstein's advice to "always collaborate with a younger writer"—for he was more than fifteen years older than Lerner. Seniority would, he thought, give him the upper hand. Richard Rodgers was businesslike, punctual, in charge, and confident of his place in the American musical theater. Work came easily to him; once, when asked how long it had taken him to write "Oh, What a Beautiful Mornin'," he replied, unsmiling, "How long does it take to play it?"

After his non-skiing holiday in Switzerland and some time in Paris, Lerner returned to the United States for the fifth-anniversary celebration of *My Fair Lady* and the unexpected, miraculous salvaging of *Camelot.* In March 1961 he and Rodgers began work on *I Picked a Daisy* (later retitled *On a Clear Day You Can See Forever*), the story of Daisy Gamble, who seeks help from a psychiatrist to stop smoking. In the course of her "treatment" we learn that she can predict phone calls, read minds, direct the loser to a misplaced object, and make flowers grow just by talking to them—in short, she has extrasensory perception. Further, while Daisy is under hypnosis, we learn that under the name Melinda she lived before, in the 1700s. The major plot twist has the psychiatrist falling in love with the eighteenth century's Melinda, not with the twentieth's Daisy.

It was a beginning; there were discussions and some music but few words. A peculiar news item dated May 3, 1961—only two months later—had Lerner working on *Coco*, the show about fashion designer Chanel that Rodgers had rejected. For him it was a form of déjà vu.

Rodgers had previously worked with two other lyricists, both masters—very different, but masters nonetheless. Both had presented problems for the disciplined, systematic composer.

Lorenz Hart had been capable of working very quickly, even under difficult conditions (e.g., backstage during tryout troubles). His work was distinctive: witty, literate, at times mordant (a quality often attributed to his own unhappy personal life), perfectly rhymed. With Hart, Rodgers composed some of his finest (for some critics, *the* finest) songs, literally hundreds of them. But Hart was wonderful only when he could be snared—or found. (In one anecdote, probably true, Rodgers managed to get Hart out to his Connecticut home for some work. Not in the mood, Hart, according to popular-music historian Jack Burton, "bribed Dick's daughter to hide him in her playhouse, located in a maple tree and completely hidden by the foliage, after swearing her to secrecy.") Hart's eccentricities and unreliability finished their rich collaboration even before his early death.

Rodgers would find that while Alan Lerner had no recourse to tree houses, there was the ubiquitous jet airliner.

Hammerstein, unlike Hart, was not eccentric, and he was reliable. By the time he and Rodgers decided to work together, he had already suffered a long succession of flop Broadway shows, two each with Sigmund Romberg and Jerome Kern, including (with the latter) the beautifully scored but short-lived *Very Warm for May* (1941). *Oklahoma!*, the first of the Rodgers and Hammerstein musicals, was produced in 1943.

But even Hammerstein, according to Rodgers, had a flaw. During one of their rare work sessions together, Rodgers confided to Lerner, "Do you know what Oscar used to do? He would go down to his farm in Bucks County and sometimes it would be three weeks before he appeared with a lyric. I never knew what he was doing down there. You know a lyric couldn't possibly take three weeks." (Lerner did *not* know.)

In Alan Jay Lerner, Richard Rodgers was getting a little bit of Hammerstein *and* Hart; in Rodgers, Lerner was emphatically *not* getting an easygoing, hedonistic Frederick Loewe.

Rodgers soon learned to his dismay that his new collaborator was not a nine-to-five man, nor could the composer "understand why, once having made an appointment, [Lerner] would often fail to show up or even offer an explanation"—the Hart part—"or if he did arrive, why the material that was supposed to be completed was only half finished"—the Hammerstein part. Very little was accomplished on *I Picked a Daisy* through all of 1961. "Devoting so many unproductive months to this enterprise was extremely frustrating, particularly at this stage of my career," Rodgers explained (he was then sixty and suffering from cancer of the jaw; he knew he had little time to waste).

While Lerner struggled with book and words (and wife—a difficulty

Camelot, Act I, Scene 1: Guenevere (Julie Andrews) meets Arthur (Richard Burton), unaware of his kingship and that he is the man she was sent to Camelot to marry. (*Photofest*)

Lerner, Andrews, and Burton backstage on the opening night of *Camelot*, December 3, 1960, before the disheartening reviews came in. (*Photofest*)

On the set of the film *Camelot* (released in 1967) with its Guenevere, Vanessa Redgrave. Directed by an unsympathetic Joshua Logan, the screen version fared poorly. (*Photofest*)

Micheline Mussell Pozzo di Borgo Lerner, the fourth Mrs. Lerner, with her husband and their two-year-old son, Michael, about to board a flight to Paris soon after the opening of *Camelot*, December 1960. Their marriage, already a shambles, would close with an ugly court battle in 1965. (*AP/Wide World Photos*)

Richard Rodgers and Lerner in April 1961, when they began their collaboration on a new musical called *I Picked a Daisy*, scheduled for production in the fall of 1962. With virtually no work done, Rodgers withdrew from the collaboration in July 1963. (*AP/Wide World Photos*)

Participants in NBC's hour-long television production *The Broadway of Lerner and Loewe*, February 1962: Maurice Chevalier, Robert Goulet, Julie Andrews, Richard Burton, and Stanley Holloway. (*Photofest*)

Burton Lane, who collaborated with
Lerner on the film *Royal Wedding* and
the Broadway musicals *On a Clear Day
You Can See Forever* and *Carmelina*
(ASCAP)

New York's Dr. Bruckner was John Cullum as the
analyst who falls in love with Daisy's (Barbara
Harris) alter-ego from the eighteenth century,
Melinda. (*Photofest*)

On a Clear Day rehearsal with
Barbara Harris and Louis
Jourdan, the show's original
Dr. Mark Bruckner. Jourdan was
fated to leave during the Boston
tryout. (*Photofest*)

A month after the premier of *On a Clear Day*, Lerner escorted Jacqueline Kennedy, widow of the former president; the pair met with Barbara Harris backstage after a performance. At this time, Lerner was seeing Mrs. Kennedy's sister-in-law Jean Kennedy Smith. (*Photofest*)

Lerner on the set of the film of *On a Clear Day*, with Barbra Streisand (*center*) in the role of Daisy and Yves Montand (*far right, with back to camera*) as Dr. Bruckner. The film's director, Vincente Minnelli, stands at far left. (*Photofest*)

Jack Nicholson, who had a minor role in the film *On a Clear Day*, encounters Daisy on the roof of her building, where she talks to her flowers to make them grow. (*Photofest*)

Katharine Hepburn at a rehearsal of *Coco*, in which she starred in the title role as Coco Chanel. With music by André Previn, *Coco* had a good run thanks to a strong score and cast—especially Hepburn. (*Photofest*)

Herman Levin, who had produced *My Fair Lady*, encounters Lerner in a music store in 1973. Lerner had just converted his screenplay *Gigi* into a Broadway musical in November 1973. The theatrical *Gigi*—starring Alfred Drake, Daniel Massey, Karin Wolfe, and Agnes Moorehead—ran barely one hundred performances. (*Courtesy of Warner-Chappell Music*)

An unidentified admirer enjoys Leonard Bernstein's music from his and Lerner's *1600 Pennsylvania Avenue*. (*Photo by Sam Siegel, courtesy of the Estate of Leonard Bernstein, via the Music Division, Library of Congress*)

The troubles of *1600 Pennsylvania Avenue* were evident in late February 1976: It opened in Philadelphia, suffered through changes there and in Washington, D.C., and then lasted seven performances in New York. At a rehearsal, Bernstein and Lerner show the strain. (*Photo by Henry Grossman, courtesy of the Estate of Leonard Bernstein, via the Music Division, Library of Congress*)

Shortly after their marriage in August 1981, Lerner and his eighth wife, English vocalist-actress Liz Robertson, appeared on CBS television in *An Evening with Alan Jay Lerner*. They sing "I Remember It Well." (*Photofest*)

Liz Robertson, with co-star Len Cariou, in *Dance a Little Closer*, the musical created for her by her husband. It sadly opened and closed on the same night, May 11, 1983. (*Photofest*)

In March 1985, Alan Jay Lerner was honored by his colleagues in the National Academy of Popular Music with the presentation of the Johnny Mercer Award. With him are actor Hal Linden (*left*), the evening's master of ceremonies, and Edward M. Cramer (*center*) of Broadcast Music Corporation. (*Courtesy of Edward M. Cramer*)

Rodgers was not aware of), Rodgers could stand the waiting around no longer; he returned to the interracial love story and began working with Samuel Taylor. What remained of 1961 was not wasted; by December the Rodgers-Taylor *No Strings* was ready for a long tryout period before its opening in New York on March 15, 1962. The musical was innovative not only for its romance (between Diahann Carrol, as a fashion model in Paris, and Richard Kiley's floundering author) but also for its use of musicians onstage (there was no pit band) and swift scene changes made by the dancers before the audience's eyes. Although the reviews were mixed, *No Strings* enjoyed a better-than-average run. Not only did Rodgers, in partnership with Taylor, produce the musical; he also, significantly, wrote his own lyrics.

With *No Strings* nicely on its way, Rodgers was ready to move along on *I Picked a Daisy*. While Rodgers had been on the road with his musical, Lerner had not managed to accomplish much—"just bits and pieces," Rodgers informed one reporter. He could understand some of Lerner's preoccupation, given the announcement, the previous September, that Warner Brothers had paid $5 million for the screen rights to *My Fair Lady*, with Lerner signed up to adapt the screenplay from his own script.

Finally, on Labor Day weekend in 1962, Rodgers was told by Lerner on Friday that since no one would be around, he could devote the entire weekend to *Daisy*. Saturday morning, just as he was about to leave for his country home, Rodgers phoned his collaborator, only to be informed by a woman with a rich French accent (not Mrs. Lerner, but one of several people who kept the house running) that Mr. Lerner was in Capri, in the Bay of Naples.

Rodgers attributed Lerner's "not liking work" and wishing "to show his independence" in part to his own rigidity: As the elder collaborator, he surmised, he had to be challenged by the younger man. (This was rigidity indeed, for Loewe had also been the older member of a team.) But even after he and Lerner went their separate ways, Rodgers kept to Hammerstein's rule of thumb. His final shows were all written with junior collaborators—Stephen Sondheim (*Do I Hear a Waltz?*, 1965), Martin Charnin (*Two by Two*, 1970), Sheldon Harnick (*Rex*, 1976), and Charnin again, with Raymond Jessel (*I Remember Mama*, 1979)—all with unfortunate results.

The quasi-collaboration with Lerner dragged into 1963; some progress was made, for it was announced that *I Picked a Daisy* would star Barbara Harris and Robert Horton, with Gower Champion to be involved as director-choreographer. There was another interruption when, in May, Lerner was asked to stage a birthday celebration for his Harvard classmate, now president, John F. Kennedy; it would be his forty-sixth (and tragically last) birthday. Lerner, like so many others, had renewed his interest in the Democratic party during the early years of the youthful Kennedy administration and helped with an occasional rally in New York.

The celebration was to be held in two ballrooms at the Waldorf; it would be an elaborate affair (at a thousand dollars a plate). With only a couple of weeks to line up the entertainment and arrange for staging and lighting, Lerner would have no chance to work on lyrics. This time Rodgers had had it.

The first word that emerged was that the production of the musical had been "postponed until the fall of 1964"; then the July 17, 1963, issue of *Variety* announced the end of the Lerner-Rodgers collaboration and *I Picked a Daisy* because of, in Rodgers's words, "incomplete lyrics." Later he would concede in his autobiography that "as any songwriter will tell you, writing lyrics is more demanding than writing music," but for now that hardly mattered: For Rodgers, the long-drawn-out, unproductive noncollaboration was over.

Lerner was relieved as well: Rodgers's attention to what he himself considered to be boring business details interfered with his muse. But he had other, more urgent matters on his mind. He hoped to go on with the *Daisy* musical, but with whom? Then, too, there were serious problems in the Lerner town house on East Seventy-first Street. Micheline was feeling left out. He was spending too much time, she believed, on the town with theater people and others, and not enough with her (during this period, beginning in 1960, he was president of the Dramatists Guild, and did some work for the National Hospital for Speech Disorders and the New York Osteopathic Hospital, and was active in the American Society of Composers, Authors and Publishers).

The Lerners did not see eye to eye on the Social Life. His was filled mostly with his work, while hers was more conventional: She was driven to the hairdresser in their Rolls-Royce and gave occasional formal luncheons in their beautifully decorated home, which he would dutifully attend. When Mrs. Lerner was photographed at a Cardin showing at the French Consulate, Mr. Lerner, as the cliché would have it, was conspicuous by his absence. Her glittering Sunday-night parties were worthy of coverage in the society columns and required gowns from Dior, jewelry (often a gift from her husband), the best wines, servants.

Micheline Lerner began confiding her discontent to a diary. At around the time Lerner was occupied with the Kennedy birthday fund-raiser, she made a tantalizing reference to a young (then twenty-seven-year-old) man they had hired as their son's piano teacher. "One has to defrost Peter [Zorin]," she wrote in May 1963. Later, a warmed-up "Peter called me 1,000 times today. He comes after dinner and I have two husbands instead of one." An entry from the end of July found her in near panic: Peter had, she believed, revealed "horrors" concerning her to her husband. As she put it, she and Zorin had certain secrets that would permit Alan to be awarded Michel (as their son's name was spelled at the time) in the event of a divorce.

By August, Lerner was spending more time, even living, in his Waldorf offices. Turning back to *Daisy*, he considered the possibility of working with Burton Lane again—and, by happy coincidence, Lane, too, had been thinking about the musical on learning that Rodgers had backed out. Lane had been away from Broadway since *Finian's Rainbow* (1947) but was now back in New York after some unhappy experiences in Hollywood. After *Royal Wedding* he had worked with Ira Gershwin on the disappointing *Give a Girl a Break* (1952), with Dorothy Fields on a television musical, *Junior Miss* (1953), and with Harold Adamson on an Esther Williams aquatic film musical called *Jupiter's Darling* (1955). Since then he had not found a libretto that caught his creative fancy, but Alan Lerner's excursion into things otherworldly sounded intriguing to him.

He knew what to expect from Lerner after their experience together—drawn out, with unexplained Lerner absences—on the writing of *Royal Wedding*. Lerner might be elusive, but he was a brilliant lyricist, and after three works based on the efforts of others, he had now returned to writing his own libretto, on a potentially fascinating theme.

After some preliminary communication, Lerner and Lane met in Lerner's Waldorf suite (whose elaborateness effectively eliminated it from the "office" category). In September the lyricist outlined the story and even brought out some of the fragments he had written for Rodgers. Lane wanted to begin again from scratch. He felt that a song with a lyric by Lerner and music by Rodgers was a Rodgers-Lerner song; in addition, in a postbreakup interview, the composer had made veiled allusions to possible legal action (though in the end none occurred). As far as Lane was concerned, *I Picked a Daisy* was promising, and the new collaboration was on.

But Burton Lane would soon learn to his irritation and dismay that he had unwittingly walked into a complex situation. It was like a triple-voiced fugue. He was aware initially of what seemed to him to be the major theme: the writing of the new musical. The second theme, as yet unknown to him, would affect the first discordantly—this was the hornet's nest inside the house on East Seventy-first Street—while the third, one Dr. Max Jacobson, purveyor of methedrine, would color the entire composition. Lane was in for a very difficult two years. A preview of the work schedule to come would be glimpsed in December when Lerner and his wife slipped off to Acapulco, in historic southern Mexico; if this was an attempt to reconcile, to renew their once-romantic marriage, it was, as Lane would learn, a drastic failure.

Like a good many other show people, including singers and performers ranging from playwright Tennessee Williams to sportscaster Howard Cosell, Alan Lerner had been enthusiastically advised about a physician who accomplished miracles for the creative artist. Dr. Jacobson's office was only a block or so away, on East Seventy-second Street near Third Avenue, and being treated by him was quite the "in thing"; no one seemed to know exactly what it was that he gave them, but whatever it was, it enabled the "patient" to shed fatigue, work for days without sleeping, and, in a phrase that would surface soon, "feel good." (During the thirties, another doctor had flourished among the gifted, but he was an analyst. Dr. Gregory Zilboorg's patients included people from the arts, the ballet, the theater, and music [George Gershwin, for one]. It was thought quite chic to be under Zilboorg's supervision; it was said that though you did not have to be neurotic to see him, you might end up that way. He did a good deal of psychological damage before almost losing his license in the latter part of the decade.)

On the "Coast," the use of "pep" pills for stimulation and sleeping pills for the opposite was so commonplace as to be virtually ubiquitous; no one considered it an addiction. As early as 1940 it was widely known (even reported in *Life* magazine) that pianist-wit Oscar Levant drank countless cups of coffee and countered their effect with a nightly sleeping pill. By the time he arrived in Hollywood to stay, in the fifties, his drug intake was damaging.

But Dr. Jacobson did not give out pep pills, he treated his patients hypodermically—perhaps he was dispensing massive doses of supervitamins? In truth, he was not.

Methedrine is a drug of the amphetamine group, a stimulant that raises blood pressure, relieves fatigue, and eases the need for sleep; among its effects are mental alertness, a touch of euphoria, sharpened concentration. For a time amphetamines were widely used to curb the appetite of patients wishing to lose weight; they were also given to hyperactive children and prescribed to treat narcolepsy. This was regarded as a helpful and nonthreatening protocol when administered under medical, or sometimes psychological, supervision.

Quite soon, however, its use on overactive children would come under attack, as it was discovered that methedrine could not only be addictive but also cause heart and gastric problems. Dependence on it over time led to the psychological necessity for an increased dosage, which could in turn result in hyperactivity, insomnia, and irritability. (Addiction was particularly prevalent among athletes and truck drivers, who needed respectively to be alert and to stay awake over long hauls.) Amphetamines came to be known as "uppers," "bennies" (from the trade name Benzedrine), and, in the form Lerner was given, "speed."

Dr. Jacobson was medically imaginative; he mixed his methedrine with other substances, among them calcium, according to Doris Warshaw Shapiro, still Lerner's assistant, who became one of Jacobson's "patients" and often watched him prepare her shots. For his part, Lerner was probably unaware of what it was that he was taking into his veins; all he could tell Shapiro was that it made him feel "good" and "strange." After Jacobson treated her for an inner-ear infection, Shapiro herself likened the drug's effect to an orgasm.

Lerner sincerely believed that Jacobson's injections were salutary and not in any way hazardous—hadn't the good doctor intimated that he had treated President Kennedy on one of his trips to New York?—and unhesitatingly recommended him to employees and friends. He believed in Dr. Jacobson, so much so that he hung a life-size photograph of him in his workroom.

Now partnered by Burton Lane, and with chemical assistance from his doctor, Lerner was able to begin again on the new musical. The composer, since he had not heard any of Rodgers's melodies, felt he could set lyrics germane to the plot, especially one of his personal favorites, "What Did I Have That I Don't Have?" in which Daisy sings about her two selves, and the brilliant "Come Back to Me." But before the real work could get under way, something had to be done about Mrs. Lerner. She was lavish with money, took acting lessons, loved Tiffany and Cartier. Lerner resented her, and she, he eventually averred, regarded him as a "cheap musical-comedy writer." The inevitable explosion flared in mid-May 1964; the fallout would fill the newspapers for as long as it took to write a show. But this was not a musical, and it was certainly not a comedy.

Lerner struck first. Annoyed with her shopping habits, her demands, her interrupting his work on *Daisy* to discuss her acting and to confiscate cash for her forays onto Madison and Fifth avenues, he cut her, literally, to the quick. A few calls later, Mrs. Alan Jay Lerner all too quickly learned that her charge accounts at all the best places had been closed.

She made the next vindictive move, no less petty than his: She had the locks changed on their house on East Seventy-first. On May 14, 1964, the presses began to roll: She hired an attorney and filed for a separation in New York's Supreme Court. Her chosen legal representative, Roy M. Cohn, of Saxe, Bacon, and O'Shea, stated that she had taken this step because of her husband's "cruel and inhuman" treatment, to which charge Mrs. Lerner added, via the *New York Post*, that of "neglect."

Cohn was a master of cruel inhumanitarianism. He had earned an unflattering notoriety in the early fifties as chief counsel to Senator Joseph McCarthy in his fateful attack on the United States Army and its "subversives." Cohn had been only twenty-five then, but his behavior at the time, as exemplified by his tour of U.S. overseas libraries with his friend-assistant G. David Schine, had, in the words of David Caute, "made America the laughingstock of Europe." The son of a judge but an indifferent student (at Columbia University), he was feared as an unscrupulous, shifty, sleazy lawyer who was always out to win and didn't much care how he did it.

When the news began breaking, one of Lerner's (unnamed) friends was quoted in the *Post* as saying, "This is certainly no surprise. This has been brewing for months and months."

Lerner spent that first night in his Waldorf suite downtown, but he had a plan. The next morning, early, he returned to his block and entered the building adjacent to his, Tunisia House, which opened at around eight o'clock in the morning for diplomatic business. He managed to make it to the fifth floor without being challenged. Tunisia House's roof was on the level of his own; a short leap and he was home. He quietly opened the door leading into the top floor and made his way downstairs, where, as the *News* graphically reported, he surprised Micheline, "clad in a silk brocade lounging coat over her negligee as she was tending their five-year-old son, Michel." The ensuing argument reached the street, and a doorman put a call in to the Sixty-seventh Precinct; soon two police cars were parked at the curb.

Lerner insisted that it was his house and he would not leave. He stood his ground as other forces arrived; besides the sergeant and three patrolmen, there were no less than six lawyers, according to the *News*—"three to a side." As Lerner stubbornly sat, the situation took its legal course: Cohn obtained a show-cause order charging that Lerner had not been home "between September 1963 and last January"; Lerner's attorney, the skillful and respected Louis Nizer, argued in vain. Justice Thomas A. Aurelio upheld the order barring Lerner from his home.

The *Journal American* found the battle amusing, depicting Lerner as a poor little rich man who had only

> three expensive homes to go to last night, but not his palatial Napoleon-decor mansion at 42 East 71st Street. . . . Mr. Lerner this early A.M. had his choice of any of his other three homes: a luxurious Paris apartment, a large home on the French Riviera, or at the Towers of the Waldorf-Astoria, where the prolific writer also maintains an office and apartment. Expensive, of course.

It was the stuff of a thirties society comedy starring Cary Grant and Katharine Hepburn, and fun to write about. The tabloids assigned reporters to keep an eye on the battling Lerners; eventually they would get around to the couple's bewildered, emotionally bruised five-year-old son. In the center of the battleground were the two Ms: Michael and money. Taking into consideration Micheline Lerner's petite attractiveness, of course, the press also had a fine time working the phrase "fair lady" to the point of banality.

A couple of days later, when Lerner had the chance to speak for himself, he told Justice Aurelio that he wished to be permitted into his home to continue his routine of breakfasting with his son between seven and eight in the morning.

"I think it's an ugly hour," Aurelio ruled.

Nizer objected to some of the "scandalous" charges made by Mrs. Lerner, ranging from "drug addiction" to "tax evasion" (both of which would come to haunt her husband).

Cohn argued that Lerner had abandoned his home in September 1963 (three days later, Micheline Lerner would move that date ahead a month, adding that she suspected her husband of having hired a detective to follow her for the past year, and also of having had her room wired).

Justice Aurelio granted Lerner the right to visit his son between the comelier hours of one and five P.M. on Mondays, Wednesdays, and Fridays, and from ten in the morning to five in the afternoon on Sundays.

Mrs. Lerner's demands were to the point: She wanted exclusive use of the residence, custody of their child, and $5,000 a week to sustain her way of life, plus $50,000 for legal fees (a day later, no doubt after Cohn reexamined his conscience, the last figure was raised to $75,000). By the end of the month, quiet settled over the battlefield as legal papers were shuffled and certain money matters were discussed. Lerner continued to be barred from his home, but Micheline Lerner's award was limited to a more modest $1,500 a week (still a record sum at the time) and $15,000 in legal allowances.

The issue of cash heated up again early in June, when Nizer stated that Mrs. Lerner "had mulcted this man out of over a half million dollars" and "shipped several hundreds of thousands of dollars off to Switzerland!"

Mrs. Lerner's other attorney, Joel Stern, denied that his client had received $163,000 from her husband in 1963.

Nizer countered with his firm belief that Lerner was "being deprived of his Constitutional Rights by being denied access to a property he owns."

The month of June ended with Lerner still locked out and Mrs. Lerner somehow managing to get by on her $1,500 per week.

On July 2, 1964, the Appellate Court reversed Aurelio's decision, ruling, "The possession of the marital home is restored to the defendant." Two weeks later, there was surprising news from California: The *New York Times* reported that the Lerners had reconciled and taken a cottage at the Beverly Hills Hotel. Deprived of the marital convulsions of the Lerners, the tabloids were forced to resort to such mundane stories as the arrival of the Beatles to promote their film *A Hard Day's Night* (the group's impact on the American musical scene would afflict Lerner); the presidential campaign then under way (Barry Goldwater vs. incumbent Lyndon Johnson); and the Communist (i.e., North Vietnamese) attack on American ships in the Tonkin Gulf, which would give Johnson the opportunity to escalate U.S. participation in a civil war in Southeast Asia. With the Lerners at peace, the other news concerned the readers more; but the Lerners would be back.

The August "reconciliation" barely lasted until September, when Michael Lerner was due back in New York for the beginning of the school term. Instead of returning east, his mother chose to remain in California and enroll him in a school in Beverly Hills. Lerner's attorneys swiftly issued a subpoena demanding to know why Mrs. Alan Jay Lerner should not be held in contempt of court "for failing to grant her husband visitation rights to their child." This tactic did not work; on October 30, Justice Charles Marks allowed Michael to stay in California and refused to order a contempt citation for Micheline. Suddenly it seemed as if all of the New York court system had turned on Lerner, who early in December was ordered to pay back alimony ($9,000) plus $7,500 in legal fees. He won a single small victory when his wife's $1,500 weekly allowance was reduced to $850; however, the judge, Justice George M. Carney, seized the occasion to lecture the defendant, decrying his "unwarranted withholding of personal items [clothing, etc., that his wife needed in Beverly Hills]." Carney regarded such actions as "picayune, vindictive and ill-befitting a man of [Lerner's] status." Thus did 1964 come to an inglorious close.

And with very little work done.

Between December 1964 and March 3, 1965, when the official *Lerner v. Lerner* proceedings began, Lane and Lerner managed to get some work done, though in Lane's opinion not enough. When their project (now called *On a Clear Day You Can See Forever*) was announced, its opening was tentatively set for mid-April 1965, but by March there was not even enough of a score for rehearsals, so those, too, were postponed. Barbara Harris stayed with the show, but Horton and Champion could wait no longer. Lerner wanted to produce it himself, but Lane argued him out of it, suggesting that they instead approach the successful musical production team of Cy Feuer and Ernest Martin, who accepted the offer. Their fine record included *Guys and Dolls*, *Where's Charley?*, *Can-Can*, *The Boy Friend*, and *Silk Stockings*, as well as a flop or three, but they were professionals and knew their musical theater. Dancer-choreographer-turned-director Bob Fosse agreed to direct.

Further delays eventually discouraged both producers and director (not to mention the composer, who often considered dropping the whole thing): Fosse withdrew and went on to direct the successful *Sweet Charity*, and Feuer and Martin switched to *Skyscraper*, another of their few failures.

While Burton Lane fretted, his collaborator was again faced with litigation, which once more took a predictably ugly turn. On March 3, 1965, with Mrs. Lerner absent, Cohn, taking over from Stern, repeated the allegations: cruel and inhuman treatment and desertion. Nizer countercharged her with the same plus an "adulterous act" committed during the hypothetical California reconciliation. All charges, in turn, were denied.

When she appeared in court on March 5, Micheline Lerner testified that her husband was addicted to the "vitamin" injections given him by Dr. Max Jacobson, which he insisted enabled him to "write quicker"; he often became violent, bit his nails, and had lost 30 percent of his vision. In answer to Cohn's question, she also said that they had been having "sex problems," adding that these were "on my husband's part." She all but canceled out the latter claim by accusing him of having an affair with a former airline attendant (who had left the airline to become a member of his secretarial staff) and, further, the next day, of "associat[ing] with disreputable persons, including homosexuals" (something quite difficult to avoid in the arts, and especially the theater). Cohn was working this angle hard, even going so far as to offer publicist Harvey Mann, a friend of both Lerners, a considerable sum (according to Mann, a hundred thousand dollars) to sign an affidavit to the effect that he and Lerner had had a homosexual affair; even with additional importuning from another of her battery of attorneys, Marvin Mitchelson, Mann categorically refused. Word nonetheless got back to Lerner that Mann had signed, and Lerner never spoke to him again. (The sequel to this comprised a double irony. When the case was finally settled—it would, for one reason or another, drag on into the 1970s—Cohn sued Micheline Lerner and asked Mann to testify against *her*; Mann refused again. And Cohn, a notoriously homophobic crusader against gay rights, would vehemently deny rumors of his own homosexuality before dying of AIDS in 1986.)

On the stand Mrs. Lerner spoke of an incident that had occurred in Acapulco in December of 1963, when, she said, Lerner had beaten her "all over," as she put it—"arms, legs, everything."

"What have I done?" she pleaded.

"You looked at me with disgust at the pool this morning," she recalled his answering. "If you open your mouth, I'll kill you."

Little was made of this story by the Nizer team, who instead attempted to deflect attention onto Mrs. Lerner's profligacy in the better shops of Manhattan. Over a period of seven months she had, according to Nizer, spent $500 on cold cream, $400 on thirty-three pairs of gloves, and $12,000 at Christian Dior. The largest figure was $71,000 for jewelry—a gift from her husband. This last could not be held against her, of course.

On March 6 Nizer tried a new strategy: He introduced into evidence Micheline's diary dating from 1963, two years before, when this latest round of troubles had first erupted.

Cohn objected, claiming that Lerner had "swiped" the diary, but he was overruled.

An uncomfortable Micheline had to revisit references to the necessity of "defrosting" her son's piano teacher and to her fear that he had revealed some unfortunate "horrors" that could be used against her in a divorce case. Her entry for July 26 confided that Lerner's fingernails "repel me. . . . His horrible fingernails tried to caress my leg. I have lost the habit of making love and certainly the desire."

Mercifully, the curtain finally came down on all this (as one newspaper not very originally put it) when, on March 8, the combatants agreed on an out-of-court settlement; on June 25, in the neutral zone of Las Vegas, both signed a separation agreement. Mrs. Lerner would do well financially, with a lump-sum payment, plus alimony and child support—and as many of the Napoleonic furnishings from the house on East Seventy-first Street as she could carry.

Lerner sold the house and moved into a hotel; secretly, during the litigation period, he had acquired a fine mansion on Center Island in Long Island Sound, near Oyster Bay. He could work there, see his friends, and be with his new love.

12

—⚭—

FOREVER . . . AND EVER . . . AND EVER . . .

BURTON LANE, under normal circumstances, is a congenial man, blessed with a quiet—though at times acerbic—sense of humor that announces itself with a twinkle and the suggestion of a smile. He is a giant of a gentle man—unless his anger is aroused. Over six feet tall, free of portliness and paunch, he towered over Lerner. Possessed of sensitive, sizable hands that might have been the envy of a Rachmaninoff, he is a pianist in the tradition of Gershwin (if not quite in that composer's virtuoso category), with a sure touch and a rich chordal sense and a flair for sophisticated rhythms. His pleasant, informal baritone makes him a superior interpreter of his own songs as well as those of other songwriters whose work he admires, including Gershwin, Arlen, et al. Many a professional popular singer could learn from Burton Lane (he was among the first to recognize the promise of Frances Ethel Gumm, later Judy Garland). His talent, his humor, and his high temper threshold sustained him through two busy and successful decades in the musical jungles of Hollywood. In the early 1960s he decided that working on Broadway again would be exhilarating and exciting, and would give him an opportunity once more to get truly and fully involved in the creative process.

He soon realized, however, that "working" with Alan Jay Lerner on *I Picked a Daisy* would be more irksome, more frustrating, and more protracted than anything he had experienced during their *Royal Wedding* collaboration.

More than a year had gone by since Rodgers's defection in the summer of 1963, with Lerner having accomplished little during the litigious 1964 and early 1965. Still, before the actual trial began, in March, the lyricist completed a version of *Daisy* (not yet retitled *On a Clear Day You Can See Forever*), dated February 22, 1965.

The springboard was the script he had given to Rodgers almost two years before. Lerner's note to his (non)collaborator, undated, suggests that he had finished it around the turn of the year 1963. "I hope," he wrote to Rodgers, "what will come between these covers will make this one of the happiest of your many happy years. Affectionately, Alan."

Rodgers's *I Picked a Daisy* file also contained a copy of the first two scenes, with Lerner's written promise to send along the rest of the script, which he felt still needed cutting, "in a day or two." How happy Rodgers may have been with the complete script is not known: while the story is in the file, there are no lyrics, only song cues and titles. (The exception is "It's Lovely Up Here," present in two versions plus a manuscript copy in Lerner's neat hand.)

In this early (Rodgers) version, the first act runs to seven scenes; the later (Lane) script stops at six, as does the final book, as produced and as published by Random House. The second act, for its part, would undergo much rewriting. The one common element in all versions (though with minor title changes) is a pair of songs, "It's Lovely Up Here" and "What Did I Have?"; these were retained in the film version as well despite drastic plot permutations.

The basic story never changed much from Lerner's original idea: A young woman with a gift for extrasensory perception, wishing to stop smoking, sees a psychiatrist, who hypnotizes her and finds she has lived before, in another time. When the analyst falls in love with this "other," long-dead woman, his patient, Daisy, in effect becomes her own rival.

Daisy's fiancé, Warren, balances her free spirit; a graduate student ("top two percent") being wooed by various industries, he is so pompously self-assured that he has formulated complete plans for his future, right up to his and Daisy's burial, even before his graduation.

Several other important secondary characters who appear in Lerner's early draft would later get moved around or even, in some instances, moved out. For example, Lerner felt that the analyst, Mark Bruckner, required another professional to serve as a foil and to help fill in the audience on the theoretical proceedings. In *I Picked a Daisy*, this function is performed by the skeptical Dr. Conrad Fuller, who believes neither in Daisy's extrasensory powers nor in her reincarnation; in *On a Clear Day*, the task is taken over by a formidable array of fellow psychologists, all members of Mark's family—mother, brother, and assorted cousins and uncles—and all in regular disagreement with one another's views.

The contentious presence of this latter group enabled Lerner to needle psychiatry and its practitioners. In one scene, the doctor advises his secretary, "Keep those papers under lock and key . . . especially with my brother around. He's been an analyst so long, he invades privacy instinctively." Or this, in a discussion of the fortunes to be made practicing their trade in the United States: "Neurotically speaking, it's extraordinary what this country has accomplished."

One trenchant line in this vein made it into *On a Clear Day* from *Daisy*. When the analyst's dabbling in ESP and reincarnation makes headlines, he is discharged; his colleagues (not to mention his family) are appalled that he can have been so unscientific. His wry comment to his brother is, "You know who will be hardest hit? The sweethearts of Sigmund Freud." While this awful pun would be spared, some of the rest of the antipsychiatric humor would have to be abandoned when most of the Bruckner family was cut out of the show in Boston.

One character besides Daisy and Dr. Bruckner appears in all versions of the musical: the Greek shipping tycoon Themistocles Priapus. (Lerner was engaging here in some not-so-subtle wordplay: In Greek and Roman mythology, Priapus is the male god of gardens and procreation; the name consequently alludes to the phallus. It is difficult to know exactly what Lerner was getting at here, since Priapus's brief scene at the opening of the second act is not in the least priapic; but given that the mythological Priapus is generally depicted as short and ugly, with an exaggerated phallus, it is possible that Lerner did indeed base his character, as some believe, on Aristotle Socrates Onassis, who was himself short, not at all handsome, and noted for his enormous sexual appetite. On the way to Broadway, the character underwent an alteration: He became Themistocles Kriakos, a name free of any erotic connotation.)

Lerner's major structural problem was the play's ending, of which he had three. In the Rodgers *Daisy*, the final scene is set in Dr. Bruckner's office and features a regression. Daisy, turned Melinda, takes up a stringed, lutelike instrument of the sort that the eighteenth century called a hurdy-gurdy (not to be confused, as Lerner points out in his script, with the modern barrel organ) and plays a song; just moments before, as Daisy, she had not even recognized the instrument. To the momentarily doubting Bruckner, this performance proves that reincarnation exists. The play ends with the doctor's rejecting Priapus's offer of millions for research (plus the guarantee of his own reincarnation), as he refuses to allow Daisy to be exploited. Lerner concluded this script with the coda:

END OF ACT TWO AND THE BEGINNING

The early (late February 1965) Burton Lane *On a Clear Day* script has a different ending. Upset by the doctor's infatuation with Melinda, and with the fact that he has been exploiting her for his experiment in reincarnation and his newfound love for her, Daisy decides to get as far away as possible. When she arrives at the airport, she is dismayed to see that the name painted on the nose of the airplane she is supposed to board is *Trelawney*. Remembering that Melinda, in another century, had gone down on a ship of the same name on her way to America, she refuses to board and warns the other passengers ("I was killed on the *Trelawney* once"), upsetting the airline personnel. She is considered loony; in desperation she sends for Dr. Bruckner, who convinces everyone that she may be right. After the flight is canceled, an inspection reveals a mechanical problem that would have caused the plane to crash on landing. She has proved herself. When one of the mechanics asks, "What is she, Doctor, a witch?" Bruckner replies, "Almost two hundred years old." They leave the airport, arm in arm, to a reprise of the title song. This was the ending that Lerner used for the Broadway opening of the show.

The film version, released five years later, was revised by Lerner to include what might be termed an inconclusive conclusion. The basic plot is intact, and Daisy is still the same vulnerable, lovable eccentric, but there her doctor has had a slight character change. Following his singing, literally from the rooftops (that is, skyscraper tops), "Come Back to Me," he and Daisy are reunited in his office: She has come to tell him to stop communicating with her by having virtually everyone she sees in the streets of New York—men, women, children, dogs, sing the same song, in his voice. As the film ends, their conversation takes a peculiar turn, and the audience learns for the first time that the doctor is married and plans to return to his estranged wife. Daisy reassures him that one day, in the next century, they will be married and living happily together, with only their names changed. She has given up on her ambitious graduate student and decided to marry the son of one of her father's wives (briefly and laconically played by Jack Nicholson). Earlier in the film, there is a characteristic exchange of dialogue between him and the student, who wonders about him, for he seems to do nothing but lounge around Daisy's flower-packed roof. Doesn't he work?

"I don't have to," comes the reply.

"Why not?" Warren asks.

"I'm rich."

With the doctor evidently packing to go back to his wife, Daisy leaves and exits the building. After bursting into "On a Clear Day," as the film ends, she appears to be singing in the clouds. The significance of this is generally lost on the audience.

This equivocal ending had its beginnings back in the summer of 1963, when Lynn and Burton Lane, visiting at Lake Saranac, first read that Richard Rodgers had given up on *I Picked a Daisy*. Lane, familiar with the musical's plot from having read news items about it since 1960, regarded it as a "good premise" and decided to write to Lerner to find out more about it. He posted his note, then checked in with his New York phone answering machine and got the message from Lerner asking him to call.

Calling the lyricist from a side-of-the-road booth, Lane listened as Lerner walked him through a general outline of the script and read him the lyric to one of the songs, "What Did I Have?" Exclaiming, "Sounds marvelous!" Lane promised to see him as soon as he returned to Manhattan.

Marvelous was not the word Lane would have used, however, for the reincarnation sequences. "I hated the past," he has said. He believed that these scenes should be presented mysteriously, even "impressionistically," not realistically; the audience should be uncertain as to whether these events actually happened or were merely imagined by Daisy. To underscore this, he also proposed that Dr. Bruckner remain onstage during the Melinda sequences to give the audience a dramatic base: Daisy and Melinda were—if the reincarnations were real—the same person.

He had another idea for the character of Melinda, to lighten the eighteenth-century scenes. Why not make her a great leader, he suggested, the activist opposite of the compliant Daisy, a woman who somehow "made this country what it is"?

Lerner rejected the notion, and Lane gave up on it.

The jarring litigation that began early the next year interrupted the new partners' plans (primarily Lerner's) for several months. Then, after four acrimonious months, came the unanticipated news that the "reconciled" Lerners were living together at the Beverly Hills Hotel.

During this spurious truce, Lerner felt free to return to his musical. He invited the Lanes to California and, with Micheline, met them at the Los Angeles air terminal. Lane got in beside Lerner in the front seat of the car, and Lynn Lane climbed in back with Mrs. Lerner. As they pulled away from the curb, Mrs. Lerner, out of the blue, confided in a whisper, "My son is going to be my piggy bank."

On a Clear Day, Lynn Lane realized, was in for another interruption. Her prediction was borne out the next month, in September, and her husband was forced to sit on his hands through the rest of 1964 as the Lerners went public yet again with their marital problems.

About four months after Lerner delivered his script to Burton Lane, during another temporary marital truce between the Fighting Lerners, it was announced that an office had been taken at 4 West Fifty-eighth Street by Montfort Productions and the Clear Day Company. Lane's spirits picked up, for it appeared that they were at last in business. He was not happy about Montfort Productions, however, for the name was merely a front: Lerner had decided once again to act as his own producer.

The Fifty-eighth Street office served as a business center under the supervision of Irving Squires and Ronald Lee, a way to take the burden off Lerner in the fiscal and logistics departments—somewhat to the relief of the more and more restive Burton Lane. Lerner was then living in the town house on East Seventy-first Street, and some of their work was done there, in the workroom on the second floor, with its large cork bulletin board that he used to keep track of his fluctuating script. He also retained the Waldorf suite with its piano room and desks for his other staff: His close friend and assistant Bud Widney, the publicists, and Doris Warshaw. Besides acting as his confidante and part-time secretary, Warshaw (later Shapiro) joined him in regular visits to another significant (to him) address nearby, the office of Dr. Jacobson, on East Eighty-third Street. Lerner continued to believe in, and convinced Warshaw of, the efficacy of the doctor's "vitamins," which enabled him to function under pressure and without rest. During the final phase of the writing of *On a Clear Day*, they would make regular, even frequent, visits to Jacobson's office.

Even before the Clear Day office was established, Lerner and Lane had made some progress on the songs. Although reluctant to tread in Rodgers's tracks, Lane found a couple of early (i.e., *Daisy*) lyrics he liked, namely "What Did I Have?" and "It's Lovely Up Here." With the show's new title in mind, he fashioned a soaring melody to the uncompleted lyric. But, as sometimes happens in the fluid process of songwriting, one of Lane's melodic turns did not conform to the original lines, and Lerner had to attempt to accommodate it with a revision; it would take him eight months to find the last two lines to "On a Clear Day," as Lane fumed.

It had been going on for too long—ever since the initial Feuer–Martin–Bob Fosse period, when so little had been accomplished that Lane had considered dropping out at least a dozen times when no lyrics were forthcoming. Lerner "very seldom wrote anything with me," Lane recalled. "As I played he made notes in his tight, constipated handwriting—so small I couldn't read it." More often than not, the lyricist would leave with a promise to have the words ready soon.

Lane, like Rodgers before him, found Lerner elusive. On one occasion they worked over a tune just before a weekend; Lerner listened, made his diminutive scribbles, and assured Lane he would have a completed lyric "by Monday." On Sunday, the composer decided to find out how things were going and was told that his lyricist had gone to Paris.

"What happened to that wonderful lyric?" he murmured.

Earlier in their collaboration, Lane had not been so philosophical. One March day in 1965 he made a definite appointment with Lerner: 10:00 A.M. at the Seventy-first Street town house. Promptly at ten he arrived, was admitted, and went up to Lerner's workroom. Lerner was not in; papers were strewn all over the place, even on the floor.

Eleven o'clock and still no Lerner.

By eleven-thirty, Lane was "going out of my mind." Why not, he thought, find the lyric himself (if he could) and head for home? A stack of papers on the floor caught his attention; curiosity got the better of him, and he began shuffling through them. The letterheads startled him: the White House, the State Department—"I should have made notes," he later regretted—endorsements, all, of the good Dr. Jacobson. (On March 5 Micheline Lerner had stated in court that her husband was addicted to shots given him by a certain Dr. Max Jacobson; distressed and guilty, Lerner had been spending his days attempting to prove his doctor's worth in high places. He had evidently met with some success.)

At around 12:20, just as Lane was writing a note to leave for him, Lerner came in, all apologies: "I had to go to the dentist." He asked for some sandwiches to be brought in.

Lane was eager to discuss the new lyric, but when he turned around, there sat his lyricist, fast asleep. Having had enough for that day, he left, but not before penning a curt note: "When you wake call me."

When no call had come by late evening, he phoned Lerner. He was not home.

"Call him at Dr. Jacobson's office," Lynn Lane suggested. It seemed unlikely that Lerner would be there at this hour, but Lane tried anyway. A man answered—obviously the doctor, to judge from the slight German accent.

"Can I speak to Alan Lerner?" Lane asked.

"He will call as soon as he's finished his treatment," he was told.

Soon after, a remorseful Lerner called. Lane was not in the best of moods, considering the long wait, no lyric, no call as requested, and, besides, "You fell asleep on me this afternoon."

"He gave me the wrong shot," Lerner blurted; he had forgotten his excuse about the dentist.

There were more surprises to come. Troubled, as ever, by Lerner's procrastinations, Lane thought perhaps he could get one of the lyricist's close friends to talk to him. He phoned producer Norman Rosemont and explained the situation. But instead of offering to speak to Lerner, Rosemont launched into a tirade of purest vitriol against him, and Lane realized that the problem was his alone. (Given Rosemont's stated low opinion of Lerner, Lane was baffled, after the withdrawal of Feuer and Martin as producers, to learn that Lerner's coproducer on *On a Clear Day* would be none other than Norman Rosemont, who spent most of his time, however, in the background.)

Lane, as Doris Warshaw remembered during this time, was a "tall, gloomy, attractive man." There was good reason for gloom: Auditions were scheduled for June, and rehearsals for late July. June was almost upon them, but there was little in the way of songs to rehearse. In addition, Lerner was still polishing the script, which he promised to have ready in time for rehearsals. According to Doris Warshaw, it was a period of daily visits to Dr. Jacobson, during one of which her employer completed a song he had been working on for months.

This particular number was critical to the plot; entitled "Melinda," it is also graced with one of Burton Lane's most haunting melodies. In it Dr. Bruckner expresses his doubts about the existence of Daisy's two-hundred-year-old alter ego, Melinda, who he says is "just a mirage" in a dream world.

Lerner concluded the first stanza with the doctor's realization that Melinda is "dealing [him] lies, before [his] eyes," and began the second stanza with his declaration, "There is no Melinda!" He had written himself into a corner, and had a mere eight lines to get himself out of it and counteract the sense of the first verse. It should lead into the moment of revelation—

the nexus that playwright Maxwell Anderson had referred to as the all-important "recognition scene" of a play. By the last lines, Bruckner would realize that indeed there *was* a Melinda, thus closing the song with a positive, mystical twist.

The idea came to Lerner, according to Doris Warshaw, in Jacobson's office, following a "treatment." He lay back, glowingly warm, his head clear. Concerned about "Melinda" and Lane's obvious anxiety over the show, he had brought a copy of the unfinished lyric with him. As he relaxed and concentrated, he spoke the words "Don't go, Melinda." He sat up, smiling. He had found his recognition scene in the third line; the rest was easy. Melinda, Bruckner concedes, is no dream:

You and I know that long ago
Before the dream there was you.

It was the last Tuesday in May; there was still the script to finish, as promised, on Friday, May 25. He immediately threw himself into revising the second scene of act 2. Lane was pleased with the completed "Melinda," but he soon became aware of yet another source of delay.

During his John Kennedy birthday production, Lerner had met and been attracted to the President's sister Jean. Like him, she was married, and apparently unhappily so. Her husband, Stephen E. Smith, was a highly regarded member of the Kennedy team and had distinguished himself as a behind-the-scenes manager of the political campaigns of John, Robert, and Edward Kennedy. This last would later say of Smith, "He was the wisest adviser, the most skillful campaign manager, and the best friend that any of us ever had."

Jean Kennedy had married Smith in 1956, when both were in their late twenties. Like her, he came from a wealthy family. He graduated from Georgetown University with a degree in history, then joined the family business, Cleary Brothers, Inc., which operated tugs and barges in New York Harbor and on upstate New York canals. Having learned the financial side of the business, he moved to the Park Agency, which he eventually headed. He became acquainted with the Kennedys as manager of a three-hundred-million-dollar investment fund. When he joined the Kennedy campaign, in 1959, his role was more managerial than political: He served as business manager, fund-raiser, and office manager. Writer Theodore H. White described Smith as quiet and unobtrusive, "slim, soft spoken, absolutely discreet and business trained." But apparently he was not discreet enough, for there were rumors and gossip about his philandering. For Jean Kennedy, there was no Camelot. The youngest Kennedy daughter, she was the mother of four, two girls and two boys.

During Lerner's struggle with *On a Clear Day*, once his separation was temporarily settled and Micheline Lerner had taken their son to California, he and Jean met frequently at the Seventy-first Street house. They also found a peaceful retreat at Lerner's secret home on Center Island in Long Island Sound. Despite these pleasant distractions, Lerner had a script ready, a week late, on Friday, June 4.

On that day, several of the production principals met in the Lerner town house: Lane, director Robert Lewis, choreographer Herbert Ross, designer Oliver Smith, and, as always, Bud Widney and Doris Warshaw. Lewis and Lerner had first met when Lewis directed *Brigadoon;* since 1947, he had directed plays as well as such musicals as Marc Blitzstein's *Regina*, Harold Arlen's *Jamaica*, and, in London, Bernstein's *Candide*. Ross had made his Broadway debut as choreographer (replacing George Balanchine) for the Harold Arlen–Truman Capote musical *House of Flowers* and continued with the Schwartz-Dietz *The Gay Life*, Stephen Sondheim's *Anyone Can Whistle*, and Harold Rome's *I Can Get It for You Wholesale*.

Mimeographed copies of the script were distributed. Although it pleased Lane to be holding a real script in his hands at last, he was unhappy to learn that Lerner had not yet decided on the play's conclusion, beyond the ordained reprise of the title song.

With customary aplomb, Lerner assured Lane and the others that such "details" could be worked out during rehearsals and the tryout. There was enough here for the auditions, now scheduled for late June and July; August would be rehearsal time.

The meeting over, Lerner casually informed Doris Warshaw that he would be taking a four-day holiday before the auditions began: He and Jean Smith planned to fly off to Venice. Considering the time that would have to be spent airborne, it seemed a wildly romantic use of a handful of days.

On his return from Italy, Lerner faced another personal crisis: His mother, remarried and now Mrs. Edith Lloyd, was seriously ill following a series of strokes. Dutiful if reluctant, he briefly visited her in her Park Avenue apartment for a regular dosage of guilt: Unlike his father's, her illness did not affect her tongue. He fled as soon as he could and returned to *On a Clear Day*.

When rehearsals began, in August, he was still undecided about the ending; nor were all the songs completed, a sore point with Lane.

Some months earlier, when the casting of the male lead had first come up, Lerner had suggested Maximilian Schell, a young Austrian who had made a memorable impression in the film *Judgment at Nuremberg* (Academy Award, 1961), followed by roles in several less-distinguished films. The year before his name was mentioned in connection with *On a Clear Day*, he had appeared in the slick caper film *Topkapi*.

Schell was in Paris at the time, so Lerner was dispatched to audition him. Lane's first question when he returned was, "Can he sing?"

"He sings beautifully," Lerner assured him. But Lerner's word, in this instance, was not assurance enough. A group consisting of Lane, Cy Feuer and Mrs. Feuer, Ernest Martin (Feuer and Martin were then still the producers), and Bob Fosse (still director) flew off to Paris. After some searching, they managed to secure a place to audition the actor—the well-appointed apartment of one of the banking Rothschilds. Lerner had been right: Maximilian Schell could sing. "His voice," Lane concluded, "was OK. But he could not count beats, he was not musical." The consensus was that Schell would not be their Dr. Bruckner. (The fruitless trip was not without its hazards: As the disappointed quintet drove off to dinner, their cab was rammed by another, causing drastic damage to the vehicle but no serious injury to either passengers or driver.)

Once back in the States, they continued the search for their doctor. After a couple more rejections, they settled—Lane somewhat reluctantly—on an old Lerner favorite, Louis Jourdan.

Lane was happy that Barbara Harris had kept herself available through the show's long gestation period, but he had his doubts about Jourdan's vocal ability. The actor had proved himself adequate, if with a small voice (and microphones), in *Gigi*; singing onstage was quite another matter. For the moment, however, composer went along with lyricist. William Daniels was cast as Daisy's proto-yuppie fiancé, Warren Smith (he was to make a greater impression as the lead in the musical *1776* four years later). The Greek stage and film star Titos Vandis (best known in the United States for his role in the popular *Never on Sunday*) was to play the part of the soon-to-be-renamed-Kriakos. Aside from performing an energetic ethnic dance that enlivens the opening of act 2, the Kriakos character served mainly to carry one of Lerner's resourceful, if obvious, plot contrivances. Having accumulated a good share of the world's wealth, the tycoon decides to buy into the doctor's theory of reincarnation; once it has been determined whom he will return as, he will leave the money (less a generous amount for Dr. Bruckner) to himself. In short, he will take it with him. (When he later revised the book for his screenplay, Lerner essentially wrote the character out.)

The reincarnation theme was dramatically troublesome. Critic Walter Kerr would later indicate that in fact (once again!), Lerner had written two plays, one set in the eighteenth and the other in the twentieth century. The British Melinda, with her marital and legal vicissitudes, is the antithesis of the American Daisy, with her smoking habit and tedious fiancé. The flashbacks continued to make Lane uneasy. He believed that to make it clear that a kind of fantasy was occurring, the costumes and settings should be simple, not elaborate and realistic, as Lerner had conceived them; if the dream sequences were presented in a dreamlike mode, he thought, the audience would have less difficulty following two musical plots. Despite his misgivings, Lane demonstrated his versatility in creating music that is Georgian in both tone and form.

A sybaritic, brawny first-act dance called "At The Hellrakers'" ("the best-known wine and wench club in London"), would suggest something out of *Tom Jones* to both Walter Kerr (*Herald Tribune*) and Hobe Morrison (*Variety*). Hobe, going even further, would detect the influence of *Zorba the Greek* (a recent film with music) in Vandis's dance in act 2. The *New Yorker*'s reviewer would provide additional clues to Lerner's sources by bringing up, in a passing reference, the name Bridey Murphy, subject of a best-selling book entitled *The Search for Bridey Murphy*, a purported nonfiction account of a woman's experiences during reincarnation. Such references were expected and would not discomfort Lerner; what concerned him was the future reception of a musical that was now in rehearsal without a full score (lyrics, that is) or a final scene.

The main lead—Daisy—was assigned to Barbara Harris and, Lerner asserted, was a part written for her. Described by theater historian Stanley Green as "round-faced, sandpaper-voiced actress specializing in 'kookie' characters," she had made her Broadway debut in Arthur Kopit's comedy *Oh Dad, Poor Dad, Mama's Hung You in the Closet and I'm Feelin' So Bad*. She had also recently completed two films, *A Thousand Clowns* and *Oh Dad, Poor Dad*. . . . *On a Clear Day* was her Broadway musical debut.

As rehearsals progressed during August, Burton Lane continued to doubt the choice of Jourdan as their lead. But Lerner once again prevailed, and Lane waited, uneasily.

With August almost over, Lerner slipped out of rehearsal one day to rent a yacht—nothing conspicuous, merely a comfortable eighty-five-foot vessel with a crew of five. His plan was to travel by sea up to Boston for rehearsals and tryout, accompanied by Jean Smith. They could nip out of New York undetected and anchor in Boston Harbor; they would have privacy, and he would have a quiet workplace (only a few on his staff knew about the yacht) and a haven from the press. Like everyone else connected with the upper echelons of the production, he would also have a suite at the Ritz-Carlton, not far from the Colonial Theatre, but he would not have to spend a great deal of time there until after the preview and opening.

Burton Lane continued to deplore the lack of a finished score: "We never had a score," he protested as the frenetic shambles was frantically pulled together in Boston. During rehearsals, he and Lerner managed to write a lively song in which Daisy explains why she missed a meeting with her boyfriend's boss and his wife: She was with her doctor on the "S.S. *Bernard Cohn*" (the song's title and the name of the boat on which they circled Manhattan). It worked and stayed in the show.

In desperation, Lane recalled, he reluctantly took one of the *Daisy* songs, "Mom," and tossed off an inconsequential patter tune "to give the actors something to rehearse in Boston." (To his chagrin, one of the Boston reviewers actually called it the best song in the show; it was dropped before the Broadway opening.)

With the preview set for Monday, September 6, rehearsals continued even as the scenery and lights were being placed. This process, known as the "tech," usually requires about three days: As the actors are put through their paces, reading their lines, dancing, and singing, the technicians move the sets and the lighting crew prepares its charts in an effort to, as Lerner put it, "familiarize themselves with the flow of the play." These integrations of machines and people were especially complex in the case of *On a Clear Day*, with its between-centuries scene shifts. The "teching" took five days, not three; and even without a final ending in place, the show ran too long. Everyone, including the ubiquitous Dr. Jacobson, was generous with advice; Lerner decided to close with the happy ending at the airport and make revisions as necessary, based on the audience reaction.

At the Monday-night preview, the audience was restive, and there were some early exits. Lerner sensed, as did others, that somewhere in the middle of the second act the plot floundered—and the play as a whole was too long. Nothing could be done before the official opening the next night (September 7, 1965), but it was obvious that the Boston tryout would have to be extended to allow for dramatic repairs.

By the second night's performance, Lerner had managed to excise only five minutes, and Lane, more dissatisfied than ever with Louis Jourdan, had begun calling for a replacement who had a good stage voice. This was no simple matter, considering Jourdan's popularity at the time. Barbara Harris had received an adoring reception, but she, too, seemed distressed.

Her unease had begun soon after two *Newsweek* writers arrived to prepare a cover story about her, to be published the same week *On a Clear Day* opened in New York. The writers, Mel Gussow and Karen Gundersen, divided their assignment: He would concentrate on Harris and she on others associated with the show to fill out the article. Karen Gundersen was a Vassar graduate, bright, slender, attractive, and a determined and experienced journalist.

Lane noticed Barbara Harris's greater-than-usual edginess and learned that the presence of Karen Gundersen was making her uncomfortable. The precise cause was unclear; Lane believed it was because the writer was pursuing the actress too aggressively, while Gundersen herself thought it was because she seemed to be ignoring Harris. Since Harris was Gussow's job, not hers, this was indeed the case: She *was* ignoring her. The star assumed that gossip was being gleaned about her from the other members of the cast to spice up the article.

Lane felt that it was up to Lerner, as the producer, to defuse the situation, since there was already enough backstage tension around the show. Lerner confronted Gundersen with the problem, which, in turn, upset *her.* She tried to explain the division of labor: Hadn't she, not long before, surprised him, Doris Warshaw, and Bud Widney by boarding the no longer very sequestered yacht to interview him? She was what would eventually be termed an investigative reporter; having exhausted all the usual channels looking for an interview, she had sought until she found him. Lerner was impressed with her assurance, her demeanor, and, not least, her beauty, and convinced by her argument, he invited her to dinner. (The final outcome of the contretemps was decided by the Boston critics: Once the reviews came in, the cover story was canceled, and a lesser piece on Harris was published instead. For Lerner the incident would have a more important, personal sequel.)

When they met the next day, Lerner led Lane to believe that he had taken a dislike to the *Newsweek* reporter and that Barbara Harris could relax. But they still had the problem of the show's half-hour overtime.

Lerner shut himself up, away from his collaborator, to discuss possible cuts with Widney. Two days after the opening, after some agonizing, they decided to eliminate most of the doctor's bickering psychiatric family. Of the five ancillary Bruckners, only two remained, both in minor roles. But this eliminated only ten minutes.

After watching a few more painful performances, Burton Lane decided that Jourdan must go. Lerner preferred to be evasive; he was in a difficult spot, for he and Jourdan, besides being colleagues in more than one troubled venture, were friends. And, too, Louis Jourdan was an International Star.

It was nonetheless clear that the Boston tryout had intensified the Frenchman's handicaps. In the previews and the performances that followed, Lane (and others) found Jourdan "strained[;] he didn't come across." Worse, the continuing revisions, even minor changes, presented a memorization problem for him: "He couldn't learn them," Lane averred. He had trouble with English and had to learn dialogue and lyrics, according to Lane, "by rote." This affected the plot as well as his songs.

Despairing of their star, Lane pressed Lerner harder. Wavering, he asked whom Lane had in mind. Lane's choice was Hal Linden, who had made his debut as a replacement lead in Bells Are Ringing a few years before; not only did he have a fine voice, Lane reported, he could also act (years later Linden would star in the successful television series Barney Miller). Lerner objected that Linden was "too Jewish." How about another member of the chorus, John Cullum? He was not quite what Lane had in mind, but he was a reasonable compromise. The composer was tired of stress and wanted the score finished in time for New York.

John Cullum was a graduate of college and regional theaters as well as Off Broadway's Phoenix Theater. He had made his Broadway musical debut in Camelot, in the small role of Sir Dinadan and as understudy to both Richard Burton and Roddy McDowall. He had a modest Broadway and film reputation, having appeared in Richard Burton's stage production of Hamlet (as Laertes) and, as On a Clear Day was under preparation, just completed his part in the massive film Hawaii, starring none other than Julie Andrews. He may not have had the star quality of a Louis Jourdan, but he did have a rich baritone voice that suited Burton Lane's well-formed melodies.

Jourdan, however, did not want to leave, and he had a contract. It devolved on Bud Widney to call Jourdan's agent and promise a generous settlement. After some friction, the agent agreed. Cullum went on one night as Dr. Marc Bruckner, and Louis Jourdan and his wife left Boston the very next day. She was not all he took with him: The New York Times reported that Jourdan was "being paid for not working more than Mr. Cullum is getting for working. In settling Mr. Jourdan's contract, the producers agreed to pay him $2,700 a week for 18 months. If he is not employed during this time he will get $4,000 a week, which would have been his normal salary. Mr. Cullum is getting $1,200 weekly."

When Jourdan left, Doris Warshaw believed, a "certain classiness went out of the show." Disheartened, she sensed that Lerner was no longer in control of the musical's direction. The strain was obvious in Lerner's "bitter look around the mouth," she thought, and his petulance when he was offered a suggestion or criticism (ordinarily taken with good grace and humor). He would skip rehearsals and then pace through the entire evening performance, wondering if his afternoon's revisions were working. By the time the show packed up for its delayed New York premiere, the consensus was that the changes were not enough to save it. Doris Warshaw, by then virtually estranged from the man she had worked for and with and worshiped for years, felt he was "mad at everybody" and was "sabotaging the show." She recalled set designer Oliver Smith's grim comment as he observed the effect of Lerner's changes on the play: "It's been destroyed."

Lerner was not deliberately "sabotaging" *On a Clear Day*; rather, he was desperately attempting to fuse the two musicals into the one that he had conceived two years before, and to devise a suitable, romantic, and, most important, *believable* finale. The frequent presence of Dr. Jacobson was not as salutary as he believed. (When *On a Clear Day* premiered in Manhattan, on October 17, 1965, Doris Warshaw was in a hospital, being detoxified at the insistence of her husband, Bert Shapiro. He had always been suspicious of Jacobson. Doris Warshaw Shapiro, who had worked for Lerner since the summer of 1954, from the inception of *My Fair Lady*, now left his employ after more than a decade and returned to California with her husband, a filmmaker. Although she would remain friends with Lerner, with *On a Clear Day* everything had changed.)

On the musical's opening night, the *New York Times* was ready with a first-night article to go along with Howard Taubman's critique. The piece provided some vital statistics: It was the season's costliest show (at $600,000) with an advance sale of $1.2 million. No matter what Taubman wrote, *On a Clear Day* would be around for a while.

This was small consolation to Alan Lerner, who paced back and forth in his customary place at the back of the orchestra section of the theater. In the *Times*'s Milton Esterow's description, the "short and lean, fastidiously dressed" Lerner "occasionally looked at the stage. When Barbara Harris, the co-star, was doing a number, he seemed somewhat like Prof. Henry Higgins carefully studying and admiring Eliza Doolittle." He went on to quote the lyricist as saying, "I listen to everything the audience reacts to, comparing it with other audiences."

When asked how he felt, Lerner replied, "I don't feel a thing." Esterow sensed that this was said with an attempt at a smile that did not, however, show.

He spotted Burton Lane in the last row, on the aisle, unconsciously singing along (sotto voce) with the cast. Lane now and then left his seat to stand in the rear near his collaborator, laughing with the audience, tapping out a rhythm. Lynn Lane told Esterow that her husband was "petrified."

The reporter's *Times* colleague the next morning came to the point in his second paragraph, following a mildly negative first: "The most admirable assets of the musical, which arrived last night at the Mark Hellinger Theater, are the songs and the leading lady."

Reading the reviews in the morning papers at the opening-night party at Luchow's was unsettling, especially for Lerner the librettist (Lerner the lyricist generally came off quite well). Backstage, after the curtain came down at ten o'clock (it had risen at 7:16, the *Times* remarked, instead of the announced 7:00; *On a Clear Day* was a most carefully chronicled theatrical event), there was the usual backstage effusion. One woman embraced Lerner, gushing, "Alan, you should be thrilled to death!" Others cried, "Darling, you were wonderful!" or "I adored it." Director Robert Lewis read aloud a telegram containing the encomium "On a clear day, you'll run forever." Esterow overheard yet another prediction: "The critics will love it."

Seated at Lerner's table at the party were his friends Mr. and Mrs. Arthur Schlesinger, Mr. and Mrs. Louis Nizer (his attorney), Mr. and Mrs. Irwin Shaw, and Vera and Goddard Lieberson (whose company had not bought into the show; the cast album would be issued by RCA Victor). Also at the table were, as the *Times* put it, "President Kennedy's sisters, Mrs. Stephen E. Smith and Mrs. Peter Lawford." Esterow reported that when they met Lerner backstage, the sisters "shook [his] hand," and noted, too, that Mrs. Smith had invested fifteen thousand dollars in the show. Soon after, the Smith-Lerner romance faded.)

By around midnight the *Times* had appeared, and a couple of the television critics' views were in. Someone said that they "had some good things and some bad things to say." To this Lerner could only reply, "It sounds like quotable reviews." Resignedly, he then shrugged and added, "From the time the curtain comes down it's a crapshooter's world."

Burton Lane, meanwhile, was in no mood to be philosophically fatalistic; he was fuming. When he and his wife arrived at Luchow's, they found that someone—he was certain it was Lerner, with whom he had exchanged few words since Boston—had given them a table adjacent to the kitchen. This was followed by a peculiarly infuriating incident. After the *Times* was in, general manager Irving Squires came to the Lanes' table and said to Lane, "Howard Taubman hated you."

Lane had read Taubman's review and knew it had kind words for the songs, singling out "On the S.S. *Bernard Cohn*" ("a happy evocation of a New York scene") and "Ring Out the Bell" ("has an eighteenth-century elegance") and discerning a Pucciniesque quality in the melody of "She Wasn't You." With quiet fury, he asked, "Which Howard Taubman are you talking about? Who the hell put you up to this?"

Squires retreated to another part of the room, and the Lanes left.

In Lerner's crapshooter's world, it was soon obvious that *On a Clear Day* was not a winner. Morrison, of *Variety*, was the least quotable. "*Clear Day*," he wrote, "has a good advance sale—reportedly about $1,175,000, representing approximately 11 weeks at capacity. Unless it sets and builds on strong word-of-mouth comment, it's a questionable bet for a long run, or at least enough to recover its investment. It's doubtful for the road, an uncertain prospect for stock and dubious film material."

He was right and he was wrong. *On a Clear Day* lasted for 280 performances, unprofitably, but it did glean a few stock performances, and in 1969 it was made into a lackluster film. Lane was able to convince a friend at Paramount to acquire the screen rights, but his effort almost ended there; Lerner, however, also had a friend at the studio, its head at the time, Robert Evans, a former juvenile actor turned executive. Howard W. Koch, formerly a Paramount vice president, was assigned to the film as coproducer with Alan Jay Lerner.

In what director Vincente Minnelli called a "bit of off-beat casting," Barbra Streisand was signed to play Daisy. No less odd was the choice of Yves Montand as Dr. Bruckner.

In the four years since *On a Clear Day*'s stressful premiere, Lane had avoided Lerner; when they did meet, he was cordial but generally mute. With *On a Clear Day* on Paramount's 1969 production agenda, he was prepared to write new music to fit the screen requirements, but when he spoke with Lerner's agent for the film, Irving P. Lazar (better known in Beverly Hills as Swifty), he was told, "Alan doesn't want you."

Lane had signed a very binding contract with the Clear Day Company; he was the one and only composer of the musical, in whatever medium.

"Let's find another writer," Lane replied. End of discussion. In the end, Lane would compose the music for two new songs, for in revising the book into a screenplay, Lerner would jettison about half of the musical's score.

Some of the revision was suggested by Minnelli. Like almost everyone else, he found the

> regressions [Lane's "past"] the weakest part of the play. I perhaps felt they should visually overwhelm the audience [this ran counter to Lane's view]. Barbra's past incarnation of Melinda actually wasn't much of a story . . . an artist she posed for, a lover's jealousy, and sudden death.
>
> We decided to come into it in a backward way. We first showed her trial, which ended in a verdict of death for treason, before explaining what it was all about. [This is one of the more perplexing elements of the film.] I hoped in this way that suspense would be created, so that the audience couldn't wait to get back to the regressions.

Minnelli's usual impeccable filmic instincts failed him here. He advised—*insisted* might be more apt—Lerner to set the regression sequences in the Regency period of the early nineteenth century, rather than in the original eighteenth. His reasoning was that "one thing the sequence didn't need was actors in white wigs."

He was enchanted by Barbra Streisand's Melinda, "stunning in a white décolleté dress and turban, studded with beads and diamonds, with pearls dripping from her forehead." The Regency sequences were filmed at the Royal Pavilion in Brighton, England; their lushness added to the cost of the film, which Minnelli noted had the highest budget of any he had ever directed.

Lane spent some time in Hollywood to observe the production and was upset to find, on receiving a copy of the screenplay, that Lerner had reinserted their "Who Is There Among Us?" from the original *I Picked a Daisy*, a song that Lane had rejected out of hand because the lyric made no sense to him.

He went to coproducer Koch and demanded, "What is this song doing here?" Howard Koch had no explanation, except to say that it was in the script. Lane told him, "I didn't know what it meant when I first saw it, and I still don't know what it means!"

But "Who Is There Among Us?" remained and was recorded for the soundtrack by Jack Nicholson. Lerner suffered through the session, only to have Nicholson approach him and ask, "What does the song mean?"

Apparently happy with the take, Koch played it for Streisand when she came on the set. She listened with evident pleasure; when it was over, she turned to Lane and said, "It's a lovely melody, Burt. What does the lyric mean?"

"Howard knows what it means," Lane replied. "Ask him."

The song was eliminated from the final cut of the film.

Lane returned to Manhattan, where yet another anomaly surfaced in Central Park. Lynn Lane and a friend happened by the zoo when Minnelli was shooting a scene one day; to their surprise, they saw Barbra Streisand dressed as a leopard. When Lane heard this, he confronted Minnelli: Someone was rewriting the book. That leopard scene was completely alien to the mood of the play—was it another regression? How did it get in? He had a right to know.

Indicating Barbra Streisand, Minnelli said, "She wanted it that way." That scene did not make the final cut, either.

Never mind the film's non-ending, with the doctor going off to see his wife and Daisy floating in the clouds; it was clear that Streisand was no Barbara Harris, and Montand looked slightly pained throughout. And, worse, it lacked the Minnelli magic. As the director himself honestly put it, "It was not my greatest musical success, but neither was it Paramount's greatest musical failure."

Lerner and Lane agreed on one thing: *On a Clear Day You Can See Forever* was not much of a film musical.

13

—⁓—

NO FAIR LADIES

I F *On a Clear Day* was not much of a success, at least it was over, and as ever, Alan Lerner had to get on to the next project. No dweller in the past, he could nonetheless find some consolation in the haunting glow of *My Fair Lady* (and it would haunt him for the rest of his professional life). On Broadway and just a few short blocks from the Mark Hellinger with its faltering *On a Clear Day*,) the film *My Fair Lady* was in its second year at the Criterion Theatre. Still there was a twinge: *Lady* had begun its now-legendary run at the Mark Hellinger in 1956.

A little recovery, some rest, and the first of many phone calls to Karen Gundersen (it would be a surprisingly long courtship), and he was ready for the next event.

Three weeks after the miserable *Clear Day* premiere, Lerner jauntily attended a Career Club fashion show at Stern's department store. More to the point, however, was the announcement, published in the *Times* for November 7, 1965, that he had formed a partnership with Danish-born British producer Frederick Brisson (best known as the husband of Rosalind Russell and shaper of her career). He and Lerner, according to the item, were "convinced" that a "lively, funny musical" could be fashioned (so to speak) around the half-century career of Gabrielle Chanel— "Coco" to such friends as Cocteau, Picasso, and Stravinsky—the celebrated fashion designer and innovator, best known in the United States for her perfume No. 5.

A little checking into the *Times* file would have disclosed that this was not a new project, but one that Richard Rodgers had rejected five years before in favor of *I Picked a Daisy*. (Lewis Funke, who wrote the article, speculated on a possible composer for the show, naming Burton Lane; he obviously was unaware of, or did not want to refer to, the Lerner-Lane estrangement.) Lerner was drawn to the drama of this woman who, with the eruption of the Second World War, had given up her house of couture in Paris and gone into retirement, only to decide in 1953, at the age of seventy, to make a comeback. She was a pioneer in her field, a most independent woman who had nonetheless had several lovers, and her long, interrupted career afforded dramatic movement back and forth through time.

Lerner had resumed work on his book in the spring of 1961, *Camelot* having been mended by a recovered Moss Hart; soon after that, and following the show's fortunate revitalization thanks to Ed Sullivan, he returned to Paris, where in May it was reported that he was working on a play he called *Coco*. By then he had already written a bitter letter to Loewe breaking off their collaboration (which, in fact, Loewe had already accomplished); now, in 1965, when he took up *Coco* again, he and Burton Lane were definitely finished.

As he considered finding a new songwriting partner, he remembered the inventive musicianship of the youthful, often funny André Previn and their work together on both *Gigi*, which Previn had conducted, and, more recently, the film version of *My Fair Lady*. Previn had received Academy Awards for his work on both.

About a decade younger than Lerner, Previn was born in Berlin in 1929 and studied music in the conservatories there and in Paris. At ten he had fled Germany with his family and come to the United States; as a teenager he had gone to Hollywood, where his uncle the conductor-composer Charles Previn was an important figure in the film and concert worlds. At seventeen, Previn had begun scoring musicals at Metro-Goldwyn-Mayer; he was also active as a pianist, both concert and jazz, having formed his own trio and recorded jazz interpretations of the music of such composers as Fats Waller, Harry Warren, and Harold Arlen. In 1950 he scored his first important film, *Three Little Words* (based on the lives and works of Bert Kalmar and Harry Ruby); he was by then all of twenty-one. Renowned as a fine arranger, pianist, and conductor but not as a songwriter, he composed individual songs that enjoyed scant commercial success. (With his second wife, lyricist Dory Langdon, he wrote the interesting but little-known "Second Chance," "Where, I Wonder," "Control Yourself," and "Change of Heart," among others. As a lyricist Langdon is underappreciated, though she worked with such outstanding composers as Johnny Green, James Van Heusen, and Harold Arlen; her collaboration with Previn would end when he left her for actress Mia Farrow.)

When Previn and Lerner met, he was known primarily as the composer of the songs for the Gene Kelly musical *It's Always Fair Weather* (1955), after which effort he had returned to scoring and conducting (*Porgy and Bess*, 1959, and *Irma la Douce*, 1963, both Academy Award winners). As for his sole "musical" experience, he told author Hugh Fordin that Betty Comden and Adolph Green, his lyricists on the Kelly film, had "initiated me into the mysteries of how to construct a musical. They pointed out the fact that the songs must be inevitable instead of the way they were inserted in other producers' films." (The film's producer, Arthur Freed, agreed with Comden and Green, who wrote film musicals based on their Broadway training—thus creating such masterworks as *Singin' in the Rain* and *The Band Wagon*.) Previn was harshly honest in his appraisal of his own contribution to the score: "I don't think that too many of the songs [in *It's Always Fair Weather*] were very good and that's because I was too intent on having them sound clever or well arranged and all that," he confessed to Fordin. "I just wasn't a good enough songwriter to divorce those two things."

As he pondered the partnership question, Lerner kept more or less busy with his presidency (since 1960) of the Dramatists Guild and his memberships on the boards of the American Academy of Dramatic Arts, the National Hospital for Speech Disorders, and the New York Osteopathic Hospital. He frequented the Lambs Club, as usual, and also the Players, downtown. He looked in on ASCAP meetings and played an occasional round of golf (weather permitting) at the Sands Point Golf Club near his Long Island home. And in those winter months of 1965–66 he frequently called Karen Gundersen.

After some discussion with his producer partner Brisson (who continued visualizing his wife, Rosalind Russell, in the role of Coco), Lerner put in a call to André Previn, who was elated by the prospect of working with the creator of *My Fair Lady* and quickly agreed. The fact of the new Lerner-Previn collaboration was announced late in January 1966, with *Coco* projected to open in New York sometime during the 1966–67 season.

Inevitably, there were interruptions and delays.

First, of course, Previn lived in Los Angeles and Lerner in New York,

London, or Paris; then, too, though the proposed musical and the name of his collaborator had been publicized, the lyricist had other projects on his plate that would contribute to his younger coworker's frustrations—for example, his promise to write the screenplay for *Camelot*. Previn, too, had offers for screen scores (during his several waits, he would score the films *Thoroughly Modern Millie* and *Valley of the Dolls*).

Lerner plotted his book for *Coco* even as he worked on the *Camelot* screen treatment during the spring and summer; he also began seeing Karen Gundersen regularly. *Coco* troubled him, and he almost gave up, meeting with Brisson to admit that he "just couldn't get hold of it." He felt guilty for tying up the musical for five years. Brisson asked if there might be some new approach for him to try—perhaps he could focus on the story of a determined has-been, a woman alone in an industry dominated by men, who at seventy staged her own revival in a world different from the one she had ruled over before the war?

Lerner began talking about certain ideas—using film for flashback, for example. Coco would reject men; she would once again make her mark in the world of Paris fashion. As he had done frequently in the past with others, Lerner now talked himself into continuing with the project.

In the fall he flew off to Los Angeles to work on *Camelot* and with Previn on *Coco*. They spent a good deal of time in Previn's spacious home, according to one interviewer, who quoted Lerner as saying, "This is good working room for us, we both need pacing space." The new partnership was doing well when Lerner's life turned another corner. After more than a year as a bachelor—his longest period single since his college days—Alan Lerner married Karen Gundersen in Santa Barbara on November 15, 1966, after which the couple enjoyed a honeymoon in Bimini, in the Florida Straits, the supposed location of the Fountain of Youth. At the time, Lerner was forty-eight and his bride thirty-one. They returned to New York for the holidays, planning to return to Hollywood after the New Year for the filming of *Camelot* and, for Lerner, further work with André Previn.

The pattern was established: Work on *Coco* continued between other projects, with postponements of rehearsals and openings. The film *Camelot* set back the original date of 1967, then another interruption pushed the premiere to early 1968, but that was not to be, either. This time the higher priority was the screening of *Paint Your Wagon*, which Lerner had also agreed to produce. His collaboration on this latter film with Arthur Schwartz had not worked out, despite some writing's having been accomplished (Schwartz's son, writer–radio personality Jonathan, warmly recalls one of their songs, "Over the Purple Hill"). Lacking a composer for the additional songs the film might require, Lerner approached Loewe in Palm Springs; the years since *Camelot* had lessened the pain of their breakup, and Loewe was a friendly host to Lerner and the new Mrs. Lerner. But he was not in the least interested in contributing to a screen version of *Paint Your Wagon*, and the thought of working with Producer Alan Jay Lerner again was inconceivable to him. They parted on good terms, but Lerner still needed a composer.

It was simple, he realized: His collaborator was in nearby Los Angeles, the insufficiently employed (that is, on *Coco*) André Previn. (As Lane had learned, it could be difficult to get a finished lyric from Lerner, but only five songs were needed for the new script, and much of the work was done in the producer-lyricist's office at Paramount.)

As *Coco* was again put on hold, however, the mere five songs became the least of *Paint Your Wagon*'s afflictions, all of which added to the film's cost. Lerner, with director Joshua Logan and production designer John Truscott, led an expedition to scout for a dramatic setting for the film. They had reached a consensus: Both *Brigadoon* and *Camelot* had been maimed by being shot on sound stages rather than on location. Several weeks were spent searching for the ideal spot for their No Name City (aka Rumson): northern California, the obvious choice since that was the setting of the play, would not do; nor would anyplace they saw in the state of Washington. They moved on and, as writer George Scullin put it in the film's colorful *Souvenir Book*, into Oregon "before coming at last to the breath-haltingly beautiful Wallowa National Forest, some forty-seven mountain miles northeast of Baker, Oregon[, where] Lerner's party found everything Nature could provide. The rest they had to provide themselves."

Among the first things they would need was a proper roadway, so graders were unleashed on the old Eagle Valley Trail for purposes of transportation. Where the valley widened, set director James I. Berkey built Tent City, with No Name City a mile away, on the banks of Eagle Creek. Here pioneers had actually made a stop on the historic Oregon Trail.

Then, Scullin wrote, once the location was set,

eight forty-foot vans, making a round trip a week between Los Angeles and Baker [the writer omits mention of the extra forty-seven miles], were but part of a fleet of trucks needed to haul in the inventory of merchandise needed to stock the saloons, hotels and stores called for in the production schedule. In a film called *Paint Your Wagon*, there naturally were painted wagons, plus 250 horses to draw them, as well as saddles and harnesses, a blacksmith and harness-maker, and enough holsters to handle the teams, as well as fifty recalcitrant mules, twenty-eight huge oxen imported from Massachusetts, and an assortment of sheep. A crew of fifty men were needed to dish out the hundred bales of hay consumed daily by the livestock, to build fences, supply water, and run down strays.

The realistic fact behind some of these statistics is that much of the livestock spent its time munching hay and waiting to be filmed, as the animals and their handlers rested, almost on vacation, at the expense of Paramount Pictures.

"Even the mongrel dogs seen in the film," Mr. Scullin reported, "had to be especially trained in Hollywood to play their roles to perfection, including one hound who was schooled to bite Lee Marvin on cue. . . . Then of course, there were the bull and grizzly bear."

Adding to the expense was Lerner's passion for authenticity: The most lavish attention . . . was devoted to the Grizzly Bear Saloon, where some $20,000 was spent on the sculpture of the female figures that adorn its exterior, $4,000 for the century-old nude ornamenting the bar and another thousand for the stuffed grizzly. As a final note of authenticity, there were 400 antique bottles that graced the bar, and which were purchased from collectors in and around Baker.

The terrain, while providing spectacular backdrops, was rugged. If a scene was to be shot away from the valley sets—to "open up the play"—transportation could be problematical. If a truck could not make a climb, a jeep was used; if the jeep wasn't up to it, the mules were put to work. Failing that, helicopters were employed, as they were to bring in some of the cast from Baker, where they were housed. Others suffered the forty-seven miles by bus. (The Lerners were luckier: Paramount provided them with a jet for regular flights to Los Angeles to catch up on the amenities and for Lerner to add a word or two to the slowly developing score of *Coco*.)

Visitors to the isolated scene of the filming included, notably, Max

Jacobson and Ed Sullivan. Sullivan was there to scrutinize the proceedings as a possibility for his television show; he was filmed with a bouyant Lerner and a rather dour Joshua Logan. (In choosing the latter as his director, the former had apparently learned only half a lesson from Logan's deplorable filmed *Camelot*.) For Lerner it was all exhilarating: The exciting mountains, the river, the forest, the primitive accommodations as of old, the rolling stock, the helicopters—he had never experienced such adventure before.

Then, too, there was the weather, with icy rain falling as the shooting stretched into overtime and ran out of summer. Production designer John Truscott, a thirty-year-old Australian who had just won an Oscar for his *Camelot* costumes, had arrived on the set with special-effects technician Maurice Ayers the previous March, after the snows melted. The bulk of the filming was done during the summer, after the ground was prepared by two hundred construction workers with help from the U.S. Forestry Service; this special site work was done in accordance with what Lerner called his "first directive": "Build me a city solid enough for a set but which will completely collapse on cue." Ayers described the effort:

> There was a labyrinth of underground rivers. This meant we had to fill the entire area with tons of earth so we could begin work with ground solid enough for the building to sink into, as well as [to] house a maze of eight-foot-high underground tunnels which . . . trigger the demise of a city.
>
> The safety problems were gigantic. . . . Since the fissures extended the length of the [thousand-foot-long] main street in both directions, had they opened suddenly and by accident, we'd have faced a major disaster!

Having worked in special effects for over three decades, Ayers was in awe of Lerner's conception, telling him, "Full-sized controlled destruction of a city is something I've never known before in this industry." This pleased Lerner, who returned the compliment (if Ayers had meant his remark as such): "I know of no other instance in which an entire city has been destroyed without an optical illusion process such as double exposures and the use of miniatures. The sequences in *Paint Your Wagon* in which No Name City is destroyed are absolutely fantastic!"

This may have been true, but it had little to do with a musical.

A parody publication called the *No Name Gazette*, published on the set, carried an item headed "City Elections Postponed Again; Lerner Withdraws Hat from Ring." The article read:

> The long campaign of the *No Name City Gazette* to establish some form of law and order in this town has again been rebuffed, this time by Mr. Top Hat himself.
>
> As our faithful readers know, your editor is of the conviction that only the man in charge of the gold that lured us here can lead us out of the chaos that currently exists. That man is Alan Jay Lerner, and we spell his name out in full.

The "editor" (George Scullin) used a telling phrase, "the man in charge of the gold," and a word, *chaos*, that summed up the making of *Paint Your Wagon*. The production consumed more than the two months or so allotted for location filming, stretching the shoot to close to four months. There seemed to be no true schedule, nor a careful budget (at around $20,000,000, it was the most costly film musical of its day). It was as if Lerner, who certainly controlled the deficient Logan, had become a sort of D. W. Griffith, Cecil B. de Mille, or even Orson Welles, unleashed in an extravagant wilderness. This excess would not pay off at the box office, nor, for the most part, with the critics.

The final expense, once all the forces had returned to Hollywood for the interior shooting, lay in restoring Eagle Creek to its original state—returning it, as Mr. Scullin put it, "to the deer and the elk from whom it had been temporarily borrowed."

In August, as the finishing touches were being applied to a marred *Paint Your Wagon*, Lerner turned fifty. Karen Lerner had a special gift fashioned for him by *Camelot*'s codesigner Tony Duquette: a miniature stage peopled by characters from all his musicals. On the right was a tiny figure representing the elusive *Coco*, which finally seemed to be nearing completion.

But there was yet another interruption. A few days after his birthday celebration, the *Times* announced that Katharine Hepburn had agreed to appear in the title role of Alan Jay Lerner's new musical, *Coco*, production of which had, however, been postponed to allow Lerner to work on the screenplay (again for Paramount, as part of a multi-screenplay contract) of *On a Clear Day You Can See Forever*. The film was scheduled to begin shooting early in December 1968.

He was due back in New York for a dinner in honor of his silver anniversary in the theater, to be given by the Academy of Dramatic Arts at the Waldorf on February 9, 1969. (Curiously, subtracting twenty-five from sixty-nine does not yield a year in which Lerner had a show on Broadway. Having made their Broadway debut with *What's Up?* the previous year, Lerner and Loewe spent 1944, the year being commemorated, working on *The Day Before Spring.* In any event, the academy's questionable arithmetic mattered less than its determination to express appreciation for a member of its board of governors.) He flew in from California a few days before the event, landing practically in the teeth of the worst snowstorm of the winter of 1969. By the night of the dinner, fourteen inches of snow had blanketed Manhattan. Of the expected fifteen hundred guests, only half managed to make it through the slush and drifts (among them the Rex Harrisons—his new wife was stage and screen star Rachel Roberts—who flew in from Italy). As the time neared for the ceremonies to begin (cartoonist Al Capp was to serve as emcee), with the Waldorf-Astoria's Grand Ballroom only half filled, passersby were invited in to the party.

"Suzy" (Aileen Mehle in real life), master of the boldface beau monde roster for the *Daily News,* reported on the intrepid attendees and what the women wore. She further dropped the names of some who were *not* there. "Mr. and Mrs. George Backer," she wrote,

> invited forty people and almost everyone showed up except the Leland Haywards, who were snowbound in the country. . . . At the Backer table [was, among others,] Mrs. Wyatt Cooper [Gloria Vanderbilt], all in black with a Queen Elizabeth black ruff, ruffled pants, and pounds of glittering necklaces, belts, rings, and bracelets.

She described Karen Lerner as an "extremely pretty brunette" dressed in pink silk crepe and "jeweled hither and yon." She also spotted the "Kennedy sisters, Mrs. Stephen Smith and Mrs. Pat Kennedy Lawford."

At Lerner's table were the Rex Harrisons, Mr. and Mrs. Gardner Cowles (of *Look* magazine), actress Lee Remick, and Mayor and Mrs. John V. Lindsay. "Mary [Lindsay] looked soignée in a skinny black crepe dress with no back and strands of brilliants."

Representing the world of the musical theater were "Phyllis Newman, precious in pink, with her dear husband" Adolph Green, Roger Edens (formerly of the Freed Unit, now defunct, at MGM), lyricist Betty Comden, "and so on and on and on."

Speeches were made by Harrison, Senator Jacob Javits, and the celebrated Alan Jay Lerner, who Suzy thought did "well and wittily." To round out the evening, entertainment was provided by vocalist Constance Carpenter (who had succeeded Gertrude Lawrence in *The King and I*), Van Johnson (featured in the film *Brigadoon*), and Harvé Presnell (who had spent some time with Lerner in Oregon during the filming of *Paint Your Wagon*); Diahann Carroll, too, sang, "in a white beaded dress cut down in a deep V," and Lerner himself did a number from *Coco*. "Alan wore a black velvet smoking jacket and a black velvet bow tie. Last night he was called a poet," Suzy concluded. "That he is. Also a lyrical genius. But you knew that."

Not listed among the snowbound, but nonetheless absent, was Frederick Loewe. Also Burton Lane.

With screenplays, and tribute, out of the way, Alan Lerner could devote himself to finishing *Coco*. When producer Brisson first suggested that his partner switch his focus to the septuagenarian Chanel's life in the fifties, there was little to go on in terms of plot or character, aside from the unexpected return of the strong-willed older woman to the fashion world she had dominated some years before. The decade since this triumphant comeback had, however, brought real changes in the social scene, especially with the advent, in the United States, of the so-called Women's Liberation movement. Betty Friedan fired the opening shot with the publication of *The Feminine Mystique* (in 1963), to be followed three years later by the formation, appropriately enough in Friedan's hotel room in Washington, D.C., of the National Organization of Women (NOW). The battle was joined in the press, in further meetings, and eventually in more books on the subject as women declared their independence from Man.

These developments gave shape to Lerner's book, in a sense forcing him to discard his predilection for fantasy and the past in favor of the contemporary reality of a troubled world. While *On a Clear Day* had been set nominally (and partially) in the present, it had never left the realm of the romantically fantastic; the new heroine of the filmic *Paint Your Wagon*, in contrast, with her independence of mind and her duplicate husbands, was definitely a Modern Woman, but she was stranded in the 1890s.

Source material aplenty could be found in the fashion columns of the newspapers and in *Women's Wear Daily*, the *Variety* of the fashion industry. There were two French biographies of Coco (and Lerner was fluent in French), Pierre Galante's *Mademoiselle Chanel* and Claude Baillén's *Chanel Solitaire*; both were published in English after Chanel's death, in 1970.

Coco has two plots, the first devoted to the designer's own story and the second revolving around two young lovers, Noelle and Georges, who cannot agree on a woman's "proper" place in the world. Coco herself, of course, sides with and advises the young woman—who hopes to become a wealthy model—and, in her loneliness, practically adopts her as the daughter she has never had. Coco's dramatic conflicts are thus played out in the various arenas of business, the heart, and her own overwhelming ambition. (An additional theme is that of age, a subject Lerner himself was facing in his fifty-first year; he was no longer the perennially youthful Harvard lad.)

Simply stated, *Coco*'s book poses two basic questions: Will Coco make it, and will she interfere in the uneasy romance between Noelle and Georges? The ghost of Jerome Kern's *Roberta* (1933) seemed to hover in the wings of Lerner's play. The work of lyricist-librettist Otto Harbach (based on a novel by Alice Duer Miller), Kern's musical was likewise set in a Paris fashion salon—with the highlight of the evening being an elaborate fashion show. Lerner judiciously scuttled his plans for a similar scene.

He dedicated the first act to delineating the character of Coco through her determination to return to the fashion business, interweaving some flashbacks relating to her affairs and her devotion to her father (who abandons her) with the introduction of the two young lovers and their disagreements. Preparations meanwhile proceed for the presentation of Chanel's new line, amid problems between the designer and her assistant, Sebastian, who despises her. As the first-act curtain descends, Coco, having rejected Sebastian's fanciful, vulgar creations and made the designs hers again, is ready for her second debut.

Soon after the curtain rises on the second act, it becomes apparent that the showing was a disaster, and the reaction of the Paris fashion critics devastating. Coco is depressed; there have been no sales, and her money is dwindling. The tide of gloom is reversed, however, with the appearance of four American buyers—from, as the song goes, "Orbach's, Bloomingdale's, Best and Saks"—who care nothing for the French critics' opinion and want all of Coco's line, as much as she can supply. The designer becomes a raging success. With the business going well, she turns her attention to Noelle, even going so far as to select a new home for the two of them to live in, only to learn that the young model and her lover, against all the older woman's urging, will marry.

The play closes with Coco's resigning herself to a life of loneliness, pleased with herself for not becoming sentimental and softhearted or dependent on anyone else. As the curtain comes down, she is her old assertive self again and has begun to design Noelle's wedding gown.

Consensus held that there was a paucity of plot in Lerner's script, a criticism that surfaced early in the creation of *Coco*. Brisson had difficulty convincing Chanel that she could be the subject of a musical (musical theater does not flourish in France, as Lerner frequently noted). She became more agreeable when he mentioned that Hepburn would star, only to lose interest again when he clarified matters by informing her that he was referring to Katharine, not Audrey. Chanel had in mind a more glorious and glamorous depiction of her early years: Katharine Hepburn, she asserted, was too old (Coco was by this time in her early eighties, and Hepburn her midfifties).

When Brisson brought Lerner to meet her, the feisty couturiere asked how he intended to handle her story. (She had no idea who Lerner was until Brisson explained that he had created the libretto and lyrics to *My Fair Lady*; she remembered the film but claimed to have detested the Cecil Beaton costume designs. Beaton was to do the costumes for *Coco*.)

Lerner answered her query by summing up his plot as the story of a strong woman who sacrificed everything—love and family—to leave her mark on the world. She commented that it sounded more like a tragedy than a musical comedy.

But she nonetheless consented, and the work went on.

Composer André Previn and choreographer Michael Bennett both found the book lacking even as the production threatened to swell monstrously (Beaton was in charge of the sets as well). Previn, new to the musical theater, deferred to his collaborator but remained uneasy about the show. As he later told Lerner and Loewe biographer Gene Lees, "*Coco* was not very good. In fact, I disliked it a lot." He admitted that he himself did not "do a very good job." (He was being too hard on himself, for there is a lot of good music in *Coco*; a brilliant musician, Previn is an outstanding conductor, pianist, arranger, and orchestrator, though it may be true that he is not an outstanding songwriter.)

Previn's greatest frustration while working with Lerner on the *Coco* score was catching his collaborator, who seemed constantly on the run. After the *Times* reported in September 1968 that Katharine Hepburn was to star, further postponements occurred while Lerner attended to the film versions of *Paint Your Wagon* and *On a Clear Day*. And Previn once threatened to lock Lerner in a room until he emerged with some finished lyrics.

Despite such interruptions, the score was ready for rehearsals in the late summer of 1969 and the out-of-town tryout, all of which went smoothly enough. However, the juvenile lead, Don Chastain (selected by Lerner and approved by Hepburn), noticed during this period that as Lerner stood in the wings he would nervously pop something into his mouth, then chew; he'd then remove his white glove and chew on his fingers, which were "chewed raw," Chastain recalled. "They looked like hamburger." Not only did the show concern Lerner; his marriage to Karen Gundersen was coming apart.

Coco opened in New York on December 18, 1969, at the Mark Hellinger; to await the critical words, Lerner took a room at "21." If he was expecting— or hoping for—a good reception to erase the bad taste left by the critics after *On a Clear Day*, he was to be disappointed: The word was bad, with Previn singled out as a special target.

Theater historian Gerald Bordman summarized the treatment in his *American Musical Theatre*: "What its fate might have been," he writes of *Coco*, "but for the presence of Katharine Hepburn in the title role is unpleasant to contemplate." He compares the show to another musical biography, *Jimmy*, allegedly the story of New York's popular Mayor Jimmy Walker, which closed in less than three months. "Like *Jimmy*," Bordman asserts,

> This slightly romanticized biography of the great fashion designer, Gabrielle "Coco" Chanel, was framed in a highpoint of Miss Chanel's life, her attempted comeback after World War II. But unlike *Jimmy*, the frame was expanded and actually embodied what unsubstantial plot there was. . . . A trite subplot injected a love interest between one of Coco's protégées and a young man. Alan Jay Lerner provided the book and lyrics, with the rhymes outshining the libretto as usual. The songs were by André Previn, a well-known young composer and conductor. They were undistinguished. Neither Chanel nor her associates were called upon to create the costumes; Cecil Beaton was enlisted for the chore. His dresses and gowns were as disappointing as the show itself. His gowns seemed far too feminine to suggest Chanel's elegant, slightly masculine lines. The show's obvious prop remained Miss Hepburn, who was on stage virtually from beginning to end, coasting through on her unique glamor.

(Soon after Hepburn left the show and was replaced by Danielle Darrieux, *Coco* closed, having run for 332 performances. It cost close to a million dollars, but according to Lerner, it "made a sizeable profit and the accounting department of Paramount Pictures, who financed the play, totted up the final figures with black ink.")

Lerner may have produced an amorphous book, but besides some brilliant lyrics, it contains several witty one-liners (mostly assigned to the acerbic Hepburn) reminiscent of the social comedy of Noël Coward. In one instance, provoked by the petty nastiness of her troublesome (and very blatantly homosexual) assistant, Coco observes, "There's no bitch like a man, is there?"

Speaking about fashions, she suggests, "What God has wrought is often better bought." Also, "God was marvelous with the big stuff, but He had no eye for detail." And one more: "Do you know why fashion is so atrocious these days? Because men are making fun of women."

In an effort to convince her protégée-to-be to become a model, she confides, "The wages of sin don't compare with what you can make in the dress business."

She disparages love and marriage: "Love isn't blind, it's short-sighted. . . . The one thing a man says [that] a woman can believe in is: I don't want to marry you." Man changes, she says, only "when the woman no longer needs, she becomes needed." When she no longer needs him, *then* he needs her.

Encapsulating her philosophy of the relationship between the sexes, Coco asserts that a "woman needs independence from men, not equality. In most cases equality is a step down."

Finally, perhaps affording a glimpse into his own view of one aspect of life, Lerner has his lead announce, "One doesn's get married to escape boredom, one gets divorced."

Possibly—though this is conjecture—some of Lerner's lyrics may likewise express his personal feelings. While it is true that the views stated are those of his characters, little effort is required to infer from them the author's own emotions and attitudes. Since the mid-1950s Lerner had been repelled by the new "youth music" and its effect on popular song and even the theater; as he wrote in 1955,

> There is a wider difference today between popular and show music than at any time I can remember. So much popular music today turns its back on melody and resorts to gimmicks, freak arrangements, trick voices, contests to see who can make the weirdest cacophony. The taste in popular music has deteriorated to the point of cannibalism; mere gutter sounds. This trend is

restricting the audience for show writers, because good show music is basically melodic.

In the decade that followed, as far as Lerner was concerned, not only the musical theater but American society itself began to unravel. "The 1960s in America," he wrote in *The Musical Theatre*, "was the scene of the greatest social upheaval of the century. The causes were partly historical and partly anatomical." The 1963 assassination of President Kennedy (which Lerner felt sure was not the work of a single gunman), the Vietnam war, the murders of Martin Luther King, Jr., and Robert Kennedy, and the rebellion of the young—all these constituted the "historical" causes, as expressed through rock music, while the "anatomical" cause was the baby boom after the Second World War, when the "maternity hospital became the most thriving assembly line in the world." It horrified Lerner to think that by the "mid-sixties . . . of all the people who were living on the planet Earth, over twenty-five percent were under twenty-five years of age."

This often estranged segment of the population, with its generation gap in hairstyle, dress, and music, had, he believed, a dreadful effect on popular song as well as, eventually, the musical theater. For him, the *"belle époque* of the musical theatre came to an end" following the production of *Fiddler on the Roof*, in 1964. A big show with a fine Sheldon Harnick–Jerry Bock score and a brilliant cast (including star Zero Mostel), it had become one of the longest-running musicals of its time, surpassing even the long-lived *My Fair Lady* by more than five hundred performances. Lerner deemed *Fiddler* "compassionate, moving, imaginative and humorous"—in short, just his kind of musical, a traditional one.

He was irked by the new wave, which arrived even before *Coco* eked out its run. The year before (1968) had seen the openings of *Your Own Thing*, somewhat based on Shakespeare's *Twelfth Night*, and the "American Tribal Love-Rock Musical," as *Hair* was billed; both were still on Broadway when Lerner's Chanel musical closed. Still in the future were the likes of *Godspell*, *Jesus Christ Superstar* (the serious beginning of the British invasion), and *Grease*.

There were other shows that Lerner admired after *Fiddler on the Roof*—among them *Hallelujah, Baby!* (by Jule Styne and Adolph Green and Betty Comden), *Zorba* (John Kander and Fred Ebb), *1776* (Sherman Edwards), *Promises, Promises* (Burt Bacharach and Hal David), and most of Stephen Sondheim's work—but musicals in general were fewer, and most of them he found unpalatable. The times were indeed a-changing.

Lerner's *Coco* lyrics were, he later said, the "most intricately rhymed I had attempted," and quite personal, if only subconsciously. His (or rather, Coco's) commentary on the generation gap, "The World Belongs to the Young," for example, contains this quatrain:

> *I want it all again and more.*
> *I want the world the young deplore.*
> *So peck away, sweet birds of youth;*
> *It's eye for eye and tooth for tooth.*

Hepburn's songs were primarily declamatory, dependent more on the sense of the lyric than on the melody, in deference to her voice (as she put it, "you all know damn well I can't sing"). Her delivery was spirited, precise, and audible, the perfect complement to her character's dry wit. In a long speech-song called "The Money Rings Out Like Freedom," the designer triumphantly declaims on how she became the celebrated Coco, quite by accident beginning the craze for women's slacks and that for the famed "basic black dress," which she wore in mourning for "Alex," dead "without a word of warning":

> *Alex gone!*
> *What a shame!*
> *What a hit that dress became!*

In another of the song's stanzas, she recalls that

> *One day*
> *In May*
> *The duke and I*
> *Let the tempers fly,*
> *And I told him whither to go and stay;*
> *So he invited to the next soiree*
> *A buxom bore for whom he'd bought*
> *A diamond bigger than a diamond ought*
> *To be;*
> *Did he.*
> *And I knew why:*
> *To make me cry.*

But I came wearing imitation junk,
So large and gaudy that her diamond shrunk;
The crowd went wild with the glass display;
And costume jewelry was here to stay!
What a coup!
What luck!
Tell the bank to send a truck!
Oh, the money rings out like freedom!

Near the close of the song, Lerner gave her a worthy pun: "With money to pay, oh, debt, where's thy sting?"

In one of the rhythm numbers, Georges attempts to get Noelle away from Coco's world; his song, "A Woman Is How She Loves," begins with the line "A woman is not her dress." Further on, a telling four lines may be a sly allusion to the lyricist's fourth marriage, his most recent but one:

Why should I care
If it's Cardin or Gucci
Or Lanvin or Pucci
Who makes what's left on the chair.

This song, like many of the others, sparkles with interior rhymes and turns of phrase. In the verse to "Mademoiselle Cliché de Paris," for example, Coco tells of her lover's swearing she is "one in a million," when she knows perfectly well that for him, she is "one *of* a million."

Somewhat reminiscent of a square dance, the song "Orbach's, Bloomingdale's, Best and Saks" celebrates salesmanship as it makes satirical reference to fashion and department stores. The buyers assure Coco that their versions of her designs will be "totally identical,/ in every way authentic,"

Except the colors run a bit.
The seams may come undone a bit.
The wool is made of plastic
And the plastic's made of glass;
And occasionally they go up in flame.
But they're practically, yes, practically the same.

In her enthusiasm over their enthusiasm, Coco exclaims, "Three cheers for Al Capone and the eagle on top of Peak's pike!" She has a spot of trouble, too, with the names of the stores, calling one "Orblooms" and another "Saking-dale's."

While Katharine Hepburn's voice was best suited to patter songs (she was heard more than any other vocalist in the cast, in seven numbers out of a score comprising fourteen), Lerner and Previn also provided her with two touching ballads, the title song and the defiant quasi-lament "Always Mademoiselle." In the latter, Coco resigns herself to living the rest of her life alone; despite some regrets, she proclaims herself grateful "that all I've been pregnant with is dresses." If her life is empty, still it could not be lived in any other way: "Right or wrong, I'm glad to be/Gabrielle Chanel."

In his Coco, Lerner had created a tough yet vulnerable character, an artist driven (like him) to excel in her professional life, virtually the only existence she had. The real Coco died the following year, in 1970, in her late eighties; by that time Alan Lerner had moved on to his next project.

For some time he had been pondering the possibility of taking a new tack, of treating a contemporary—and controversial—subject. In 1958 the Russian-born writer Vladimir Nabokov had caused a literary tempest in the United States with his novel *Lolita*. Originally published that year in France (but in English, the language in which Nabokov wrote it), it got off to a fine start by being banned both there and in Britain, though it was readily imported into the United States. In its original Olympia Press edition, at least, it met with no objections on the part of the U.S. Customs Office.

Three years later, G. P. Putnam's Sons published the American edition, to critical acclaim and best-sellerdom. A brilliant book, and one of the least pornographic ever to be advantageously and profitably labeled as such, it went through several editions and was made into a film in 1962. James Mason starred as Humbert Humbert, a middle-aged academic with a hopeless predilection for pretty young girls; his Lolita was portrayed by Sue Lyon, a "demure nymphet of fourteen or so," in Nabokov's description. Memorably cast as the villainous playwright Clare Quilty, Peter Sellers gave a remarkable performance under the direction of a pre–*Dr. Strangelove* and pre–*2001: A Space Odyssey* Stanley Kubrick. (Nabokov's reaction on seeing the film was to write and publish, in 1961, his own screenplay based on the novel. Although this version was never shot—Kubrick's film was not well enough received to warrant a remake—its wordplay would have fascinated Lerner; it could almost be called Lerneresque, in fact, and even has a title song.)

Lolita's theme had been daring for its time and was still so twelve years later; for Lerner, adapting it for the musical theater was a way of distancing himself from the Rodgers-Hammerstein and Lerner-Loewe traditional forms. Then, too, *Lolita* was perversely romantic, a satire that some reviewers read as a "joke on our national cant about youth," "or a cutting exposé of chronic American adolescence and shabby materialism." If this was not quite what Nabokov had in mind, there is nevertheless something particularly mordant in his portrayal of predatory women, of the American landscape cluttered with ugly motels, of academia—and all of these themes could serve as grist for the Lerner mill.

The project's timeliness, Lerner felt, would require a very contemporary collaborator. Restive after taking time off following *Coco*'s premiere, he considered his options and settled on a young (then thirty-seven-year-old) British composer best known for his striking "007 theme." Besides writing music for the popular James Bond films, John Barry, né J. B. Prendergast, had scored such movies as *Zulu, The Ipcress File, Born Free*, and *The Lion in Winter*, winning Academy Awards for his work on the latter two.

In May 1970, after a little searching, Lerner located John Barry at his home in Majorca, off the coast of Spain. When he called him and outlined his plan for a new musical based on Nabokov's novel, Barry was receptive. Although he had studied music from the age of nine and once contributed music to a West End production of the racy *Passion Flower Hotel*, the Yorkshire-born composer had never written a musical, and was intrigued by the idea.

In June the Lerners joined Barry in Majorca, where the two would-be collaborators soon found they were quite compatible. There was a further meeting, this time with Vladimir Nabokov, then living in Switzerland; he, too, approved of Lerner's approach, and the *Lolita* venture began. Following a stint back in Majorca, the partnership shifted to London, where Barry had a home and the Lerners took a suite at the elegant Dorchester Hotel. After eight months of compatibility and work, the score was ready in time for the backers' auditions. By late 1970 *Lolita, My Love* (the title borrowed from a line in the book) was ready for casting, rehearsals, and the usual out-of-town anguish.

Lerner's first choice for the Humbert role was his reliable friend Richard Burton, but Burton was tied up with film contracts, so the part went instead to the distinguished English actor (on stage and screen in both Britain and America) John Neville. According to the show's *Playbill*, Annette Ferra was cast as Lolita only after a "nationwide talent hunt in which more than 1,500 young actresses were auditioned." She was fifteen, from California, and already a veteran of West Coast musicals (notably *The Sound of Music*), films, and television, having made, as well, recordings and television commercials. Dorothy Loudon, an established comedian-vocalist with impressive credentials, was signed to appear as Lolita's predatory mother, Charlotte Haze (a part played by Shelley Winters in Kubrick's version). Humbert marries her to be near Lolita, whereupon she conveniently dies in a freak auto accident—after her husband's failure to drown her. Humbert's rival, Clare Quilty, also a nymphet fancier, was portrayed by Leonard Frey, a reliable graduate of experimental theater, musicals, and television.

Lolita, My Love glittered with great expectations. It was to be John Barry's first Broadway show, and John Neville's first Broadway musical; Argentinian director Tito Capobianco was likewise slated to make his Broadway debut, after a successful career in opera (he had directed more than seventy productions, including Stravinsky's *The Rake's Progress* for Juilliard). Lolita herself, Annette Ferra, would first step onto the Great White Way in no less than a star's role.

The musical opened at the Shubert Theatre in Philadelphia on February 16, 1971, and ran for eleven days before being "closed down for revisions." By the time *Lolita, My Love* arrived in Boston, its nineteen scenes had been condensed to fifteen, though its score was still intact. Other revisions included the canceling of two prime "firsts": Annette Ferra left the show and was replaced by her understudy (and member of the dancing ensemble), Jill Streisant, while Capobianco was succeeded as director by Noel Willman. Dan Siretta, who had been cast as Quincey in Philadelphia, was recast as choreographer in Boston; two other members of the cast, Mona Dahl and Neil McNelis, were let go. Clearly, *Lolita, My Love* was in severe trouble.

As further evidence of desperation, the post-opening-night dismissals were quickly followed by helter-skelter revisions. Between March 24 (the morning after) and March 26, Lerner frantically restructured the show. "Lolita," originally the opening song, was pushed to the end of the second act, and Lolita was given a new song, "Saturday," in the first. "Mother Needs a Boyfriend" and "Have You Got What You Came With?" were cut, and the first-act curtain was moved up to allow the act to close with Humbert's anguished "Farewell, Little Dream," in which he regrets his marriage to Lolita's mother and realizes that he does not have what it takes to "eliminate" her.

With the first curtain now falling in a more logical place, Lerner shifted the two songs that had formerly concluded act 1, "At the Bed-D-By Motel" and "Tell Me, Tell Me," to the opening of the following act. The first of these brings Humbert's nemesis, Quilty, back onto the scene as his rival for Lolita,

while the second returns the object of their mutual affection to the stage after she has been away—to Humbert's dismay—at summer camp (Nabokov
called it Camp Q, Lerner Camp Climax). In "Tell Me, Tell Me" Humbert
promises her,

> *I'll buy you bubble gum,*
> *Sandals and jeans;*
> *Perfume, potato chips*
> *And movie magazines.*

Only after Humbert seduces Lolita does he tell her that her mother is
dead. The fourteen-year-old and the forty-year-old then team up to get away
from Quilty (Humbert's idea), and the show becomes a kind of road musical
as they flee from New York to Ohio to Arizona. A new song, another Lolita
complaint, entitled "All You Can Do Is Tell Me You Love Me," was written
into act 2:

> *The kids in this town—*
> *Go out and you'll see—*
> *They're all having fun,*
> *Excepting for me.*

It is an aptly cruel song, sung by a child who is missing the activities of her
contemporaries, a young girl forced early into womanhood. "That corny refrain," she accuses,

> *You sing as you slip on*
> *My collar and chain.*
> *I've had it; it's over.*
> *I'm jumping the train.*

One especially critical number stresses the theme of escape and chase:
"How Far Is It to the Next Town?" is sung by Humbert, Lolita, and the chorus as Humbert seeks a place for them to hide from the degenerate but re-
lentless Quilty, who, in "That damn Mercedes/Will follow us if the next
town/Is halfway to Hades." Quilty at last catches up and lures the girl away for
a while, only to be himself tracked down and shot by Humbert. When Humbert finally finds Lolita, in Missouri—now a married, pregnant "Mrs. Dick
'Dolly' Schiller"—she refuses to come away with him. He gives her some

money and is then arrested for Quilty's murder; the transplanted "Lolita" concludes the show.

In fashioning his book, Lerner tried to stay close to Nabokov's published—but unfilmed—screenplay. His most drastic divergence was his ending. The novel and the screenplay end with both Lolita and Humbert dead—she in childbirth, along with her stillborn daughter, and he of a heart attack. Lerner felt this would be dramatically difficult to present onstage without a narrator (in the show, Humbert himself acts as chorus)—and besides, two deaths in one theatrical evening seemed quite enough, thank you.

Even so, however, the play does not conclude on a happy note. While the original novel was a huge success, the film was not, and Lerner's production even less so. Its major theme was easier to read about than to watch, and consequently the show did not fly in Philadelphia, or in Boston. Humbert's "nymphet" fixation—with so much of the conflict taking place in his troubled mind—was not the stuff of a musical, let alone a "musical com," despite the presence of many humorous lines in the libretto as well as the lyrics.

The score is "integrated" with a vengeance. Barry's music is more than merely "serviceable"; it is rhythmic, melodic, declamatory, versatile, ranging from the cynical view of love expressed in "Going, Going, Gone" to the charmingly Gallic, and satiric, "Sur les Quais," sung by the pretentious though not especially refined Charlotte (who pronounces "van Gogh" as rhyming with *bog*). "How Far Is It to the Next Town?," as infectious as it is rhythmic and tuneful, is a plot song so deeply ingrained in the libretto that it would make little sense even in a smart supper club. Then, too, there is Humbert's lecturelike "Dante, Petrarch and Poe" (especially brilliant for Lerner's lyric), which must have given the audience pause—particularly its less well read members. For a talk given to a small-town cultural group, Humbert chooses as his subject three "Poets enraptured and captured by creatures/ Barely pubescent." These poets, he informs his rather shocked listeners (excepting Quilty, who is enthralled), were infatuated with very young girls, all younger even than Lolita (Poe married his thirteen-year-old cousin, unhappily; Dante's Beatrice and Petrarch's Laura both died young, and the poets went on to marry others). This long, expository production number features soloists and chorus. In one exchange, Quilty sings,

> *Does that man imply*
> *There may be thrills*
> *I do not know?*

To which Humbert replies,

> *But Dante did,*
> *And Petrarch did,*
> *And Edgar Allan Poe.*

At one point, Quilty asks Charlotte,

> *Who is that viper*
> *Who likes them postdiaper?*

There are some true ballads here of popular possibility, the closest being two of the published songs, "Lolita" and the poignant "In the Broken-Promise Land of Fifteen," in which Humbert sings of his first lost love. But in composing their so-called Musical Production, Lerner and Barry made no real concessions to popularity. The show was literate, adult, musically sophisticated—and probably doomed from the beginning. There is no love in the story, only obsession.

After the various changes were instituted, a recording was made of the performance of March 26, three nights after the premiere. The audience is not terribly responsive, though there are some laughs and the performers are rewarded with applause, the most generous being reserved for Dorothy Loudon as Charlotte, and her zestful rendition of "Sur les Quais," an elaborate dance number. Leonard Frey's (Quilty's) "Going, Going, Gone" is well received, as are some of his snappish lines (when asked about his next play, he summarizes it as a love affair between a priest and a rabbi; a student at the Beardsley School for Girls is admiringly described as "youth as its youthist"). John Neville is appreciated for his vulnerability, pathos, and hopelessness, qualities projected even on tape. But the final curtain engenders no more than a reasonable round of applause, and it is a quiet audience that moves out of the theater to the sprightly sound of the orchestra playing a medley from the show. No one sings along.

A dispirited and frazzled company went on again the next night, March 27, 1971, for one more performance of *Lolita, My Love*. Producer Norman Twain decided to close down the following day, and as the sets were being dismantled at the Shubert, the cast members headed for home. There would be no Columbia Records original cast album, as projected; there would be no Broadway. It was a bitter disappointment for Alan Lerner, who made no mention, in either of his books, of his first out-of-town closing.

14

—ɯɯ—

BACK TO THE PAST—
REENTER: FRITZ

BOSTON WAS A HUMILIATING EXPERIENCE for Lerner, his first total debacle. When he and his wife returned to New York at the end of March 1971, his mood was not lightened by such news items as the nearly simultaneous convictions of Charles Manson, for the 1969 murders of Sharon Tate et al. in Los Angeles, and Lieutenant William Calley for the slaughter of civilians at My Lai, in Vietnam (President Richard Nixon had the latter freed while the verdict against him was "reviewed"). Antiwar protests were spreading into Washington itself. It was not a pleasant time in America, and Lerner was sensitive to its historical implications: All of these events, and especially the political mischief of the Nixon administration, weighed heavily on his mind.

Meanwhile, back on Broadway, the successful revival of Vincent Youmans's *No, No, Nanette* was still running, and early April saw the premiere of Stephen Sondheim's *Follies*—an "extraordinary endeavor," in Lerner's view, and one that "contained some of the most remarkable lyrics in the modern musical theatre." Then came *Godspell* and its flower children singing gospel à la rock, followed by *Jesus Christ Superstar*, a musical that evolved from the song and the album that introduced Andrew Lloyd Webber to the United States. While neither of these was his kind of show, Lerner was nonetheless impressed by their longevity if not by their songs. For him the sole redeeming quality of the new rock musicals was their "deafening ampli-fication, which made unintelligible lyrics beneficially unintelligible."

In this period in the history of the musical theater—the 1970s were a time of "Sound and Fury," in Lerner's view—the two most influential figures seemed to him to be the American Stephen Sondheim and the Briton An-drew Lloyd Webber, the former for "content" and the latter for "form." Lloyd Webber chose to compose in the "popular musical language of the day . . . contemporary through and through," noted Lerner, adding with a trace of bit-terness that, "form, in these particular times, is apt to cast a longer shadow than content." The Englishman, in short, wrote the sort of blockbusters that the critics mauled and the public flocked to.

(When the two men met, during one of Lerner's low periods and one of Lloyd Webber's highs, Lloyd Webber complainingly asked why people seemed to hate him right from the beginning. "Saves time," Lerner an-swered.)

As the late spring of 1971 approached, Lerner felt the need to put his *Lolita* disappointment behind him and move on to the next project. Ever since his cordial visit with Loewe in Palm Springs during the filming of *Paint Your Wagon*, he had been trying to think of a way to coax his old collaborator out of retirement, and he now sent him a film script to consider. He had been asked by attorney Joseph Tandet, who owned the rights, to write a film musi-cal based on Antoine de Saint-Exupéry's cult classic for children of all ages, *The Little Prince*, a fable about a mysterious visitor from another, tiny planet and an adult aviator who force-lands in the Sahara Desert. Lerner himself found the book captivating.

Pilot-poet Saint-Exupéry had won a wide American readership in the early 1930s with the publication in the English translation of his *Night Flight*. This effort was followed by *Wind, Sand and Stars* (1939), among others. Saint-Exupéry wrote poetically, philosophically, and at times mystically about flying, stars, and the desert; combining all three motifs, *The Little Prince* was its author's final work before his disappearance during a reconnaissance flight over the Mediterranean in 1944.

Saint-Exupéry's last dedication states that despite the fact that the lit-tle volume is dedicated to a grown-up, it is nonetheless a book for the young. The dedicatee, a "grown-up who understands everything," was at the time "hungry and cold" in Nazi-occupied France and needed cheering up. "All grown-ups were once children," it concludes, "although few of them remem-ber it."

The Little Prince tells the story of a very wise child and his search for the truth. After leaving his miniature planet, he travels through the galaxy meeting metaphorical characters before coming to rest on Earth, in the desert, and being further enlightened by a snake and a fox. His lost aviator friend, too, learns from his adventure—if, indeed, it ever happened. The tale's elusiveness, its hidden truths, its honest child's vision, its obvious generation-gap theme—all of these made it a perennial success among those who did not ordinarily read children's books, including high school and college students as well as adults.

Reminded of the book at a time when he thought the nation could use some wide-eyed honesty and its youth some sweetness and mystery, Lerner wrote a script and sent it to Loewe in Palm Springs. "He called me," Lerner recalled, "filled with his old excitement, and I went out to see him. . . . Eleven years slipped away and it was 'pre-*Camelot*' again." But then yet another attractive proposition presented itself.

Transplanted New York producer Arnold Saint-Subber (now simply Saint-Subber), counted among his production credits Cole Porter's *Kiss Me Kate* (with Leland Ayers) and Harold Arlen's *House of Flowers*, as well as plays by Neil Simon and Truman Capote. Saint-Subber now wanted to bring together the Light Opera companies of San Francisco and Los Angeles to present a staged version of *Gigi* in partnership with Edwin Lester. It was an intriguing idea: for the first time, a screen musical would be converted into a stage show, in a complete reversal of the usual practice. And best of all—at least for Loewe—it would require little work on the part of the reconciled collaborators.

In transforming the screenplay into a book, Lerner first subdivided the film into a play's two standard acts; he and Loewe then agreed to eliminate three of the film's musical numbers—"The Parisians," the "Gossip" segment, and the dreary "Say a Prayer for Me Tonight"—and compose a handful of new songs. One of these was actually an adaptation of an existing musical sequence, "A Toujours," which became an amusingly tough bargaining scene called "The Contract." The show's longest singing sequence, it is a variant on Lerner's "The Marriage Contract," from the early scripts of *On a Clear Day You Can See Forever*. In it a quartet stipulates, in song, the conditions under which Gigi will become Gaston's mistress. The discussants include two attorneys, Gigi's Mamita (Maria Karnilova), and her worldly aunt-tutor, Alicia, who proves to be a skilled negotiator. (In the play, Alicia was portrayed by an icy Agnes Moorehead.) Instead of Maurice Chevalier's "The Parisians,"

Alfred Drake as Honoré sang "Paris Is Paris Again," while Gigi (Karin Wolfe) was given three new songs, "The Earth and Other Minor Things," "In This Wide, Wide World," and "I Never Want to Go Home Again." The first of these contains some particularly poetic lines, such as

> I know about the earth and other minor things;
> Why caterpillars smile
> And summertime has wings.

The final line of "In This Wide, Wide World" serves as Gigi's acceptance of near-marriage with Gaston: "I would rather be miserable with you than without you."

With the plot left pretty much intact, four new songs were added, which came easily, as the old collaborators could work in comfort in Loewe's home in Palm Springs. (Lerner said there was less tension in the California theater scene—a blessing.) The cast was rounded out with Maria Karnilova and Daniel Massey as Gaston, and the refurbished *Gigi* was ready for its premiere in San Francisco in late July 1973, whence it moved south and then east to open at the formidable Uris (now Gershwin) Theater in New York on November 13 of that year.

The idea that had seemed so good on paper did not, however, work well on stage: the effervescent film failed to translate into a joyous musical. The voices were fine—or at least adequate—but the Minnelli touch was missing (the director of the play was Joseph Hardy; the dances and musical sequences were staged by the dependable Onna White), and the vastness of the Uris stage did little to bring out the intimacy that was needed to make Colette's story come alive. *Gigi* failed on Broadway, closing after 103 performances.

Still, the show had its consolations: Lerner and Loewe were reunited and writing as before, and as Steven Suskin noted in *Show Tunes*, "ironically, inconsistencies in the Tony Award eligibility rules allowed *Gigi* to win that year's award for best score."

The old-new collaborators were now free to return to *The Little Prince*. Much work had been accomplished on it the previous year in London, where the Lerners had let an apartment while Loewe stayed at the opulent Dorchester Hotel. They enjoyed laboring together over their little fantasy. "Writing a film does not have the sustained rigor of writing a play," Lerner observed. "There are no agonizing weeks on the road."

The months they spent on *The Little Prince* were a happy time, and Lerner believed that "Loewe had written a most beautiful score, filled with melody and bubbling with the innocence of youth." Seeing the world and the men in it through the unspoiled eyes of the young constitutes the main theme of Saint-Exupéry's slim book: Except for the pilot, who has rejected worldly ways, the adult characters do not come off well.

Lerner's screenplay follows the book closely, though he eliminated six minor characters and, for reasons of his own, added two others. The simple story begins with the pilot-to-be (who tells the story as an adult, offscreen) as a six-year-old aspiring artist who draws a boa constrictor that has swallowed an elephant; the grown-ups laugh, or jeer, and remark that all he has drawn— and badly, at that—is a hat. (The book is illustrated with Saint-Exupéry's own drawings, which form the basis, as well, for some of the visual materials in the film.) He gives up both drawing and trying to explain things to his elders, deciding that the best way to get away from them is to leave the Earth in an airplane. Choosing to live alone, he is careful not to speak of "boa constrictors, or primeval forests, or stars" when he is with adults; instead he sinks to their level and makes an effort to "talk to them about bridge, and golf, and politics, and neckties" (one of many lines of dialogue and narration that Lerner adapted word for word from the original).

While flying over the Sahara, the pilot develops engine trouble and is forced to land his plane. The next day, as he is preparing to repair the engine, a tiny blond boy wearing a long coat and brandishing a miniature sword materializes out of nowhere. The Little Prince asks the pilot to draw him a sheep. The Pilot (he has no other name) knows he is a thousand miles away from anywhere; where, he wonders, has the boy come from?

"When a mystery is too overpowering," Saint-Exupéry wrote (and Lerner used the line in his script), "one dare not disobey." Unable to draw a sheep, the Pilot reproduces his favorite childhood effort, which the Prince looks at and rejects as an "elephant inside a boa constrictor."

And so the story begins. For the opening segment, Lerner easily spotted song cues: "It's a Hat," for example, leads into a flying sequence called "I Need Air."

In time the Pilot learns the Prince's story, as the film moves from the Sahara to other, even more inexplicable places. Like the Pilot, the Prince has fallen to Earth—in the boy's case with the help of a flock of birds, who deposited him and flew away. His tale is in three parts, beginning with his departure from his tiny asteroid and his travels through the galaxy, with stops at other small galaxies where he encounters, in turn, a King, a Businessman, a Historian, and a General. (The latter two are Lerner's inventions; he eliminated a Conceited Man, a Tippler, a Lamplighter, and a Geographer, who added little to the story. The Tippler section takes up a couple of dozen lines in the book: He drinks because he wants to forget. Forget what? That he is ashamed. Ashamed of what? That he drinks. Of him the Prince observes, as he does after meeting the others as well, that grown-ups are very odd. Lerner made the same point with the remaining and invented characters.)

When the Prince's birds finally bring him to Earth (before he meets the Pilot), he encounters a Snake and a Fox. (Here Lerner jettisoned two of Saint-Exupéry's characters, a Railway Switchman and a Merchant, who seemed to him inessential.)

The final portion of the Prince's tale treats his finding the answers to the questions he has been asking (thanks to the Fox) and his metaphysical return to the stars—with "help" from the Snake.

His journey, we learn, was instigated by the arrival of a Rose on his little asteroid. She is beautiful, egocentric, and demanding. Saint-Exupéry's (and Lerner's) other symbolic characters are easy to identify, even if only by their names, but who does the Rose represent? She is the only female in the story (Lerner employs a few in the "It's a Hat" sequence, but only as part of the chorus), yet she does not seem to represent Woman. (In the film, Lerner has dancer-singer Donna McKechnie—later to star in A Chorus Line on Broadway—play the Rose enclosed inside the petals of a huge flower.) The Prince declares his love for her, and she, eventually, hers for him. But their "love" jars: He is a very small though wise and questioning boy, and she a full-grown but miniature woman. This may not have bothered a reader of Saint-Exupéry's book, but it would disconcert a film viewer.

In both book and film, the Rose's vanity serves as the catalyst for the Little Prince's search. At the moment of her blossoming one sunrise, the Prince exclaims, "How beautiful you are!" and she agrees. After some frustrating discussions, the Prince decides he does not understand anything; his minute world has lost its serenity. As he sadly tells the Pilot, "I was too young to know how to love her."

And so he embarks on his journey in search of wisdom and a way to return to his own "planet" and the Rose.

Considering its philosophical content and vocabulary, The Little Prince can hardly be categorized as a children's book; nor can the film, which was neither a success nor well received. In essence, the latter is a two-character piece throughout which allegorical secondary characters appear in cameos: a King who is extremely jealous of his borders and in need of a Subject (he being the only resident of the planet); a General whose reply to the Prince's question about the meaning of life is that "it is about dying" (Lerner's creation in a screenplay written in a time of war); a Historian whose job is "making up things"; and a Businessman preoccupied with counting the millions of stars he intends to claim. When the Prince queries the King and the Businessman, they counter with the words "You're a Child!" as the Prince flies off with his birds.

The Snake and the Fox are more important characters, though their parts, too, are in essence extended cameos; for the film, Lerner switched between the real animals and human actors. The Snake was portrayed by choreographer Bob Fosse (singing "A Snake in the Grass" in his last film appearance), while Gene Wilder played the gentle Fox, who leaves the Prince with a secret: "It is only with the heart that one can see rightly; what is essential is invisible to the eye." As the Rose has tamed the Prince, so the Prince tames the Fox, who further impresses on him that one becomes "responsible, forever, for what [one has] tamed." Here Lerner again retains Saint-Exupéry's text.

It is the Snake who assures the Prince that he has the solution to his problem and can return him to his planet and the Rose:

> *If you would like to cure the fever called life*
> *Get some relief from all the struggle and strife,*
> *The grandest medicine that I can propose*
> *Is under your nose:*
> *A snake in the grass.*
>
> *If you would like to leave this inhuman race,*
> *And take up residence up yonder in space;*
> *When you are ready to go traveling on,*
> *Sit right down upon*
> *A snake in the grass.*
> *One sting!*
> *Is quite enough to make you happy and free.*
> *One sting!*
> *And you'll discover how relaxed you can be,*
>
> *Posthumously.*

The music is a sinuous tango, and Fosse does the reptilian dance (he choreographed his own sequence) brilliantly. One Lernerian touch may have bothered purists: While Saint-Exupéry's Snake is a cobra, the one in the film is a boa constrictor (suggested by the Pilot's childhood drawing), a species neither native to Africa nor poisonous.

Ultimately, the tale is about death, and in this sense it cannot help but be disturbing. *The Wizard of Oz* is likewise a fable, but it is easy to accept the notion that Dorothy has dreamed her adventures in Oz and that by clicking her heels she can return home to Kansas. The Little Prince, however, must suffer a snakebite in order to return to his world. Even the romantic-mystic Lerner felt obligated to tone down the book's ambiguous and questioning conclusion for the ending of the film version.

After the Prince is bitten by the Snake, the Pilot carries him back to his repaired plane. The Prince comforts him but says he does not wish to remain on Earth. When the Pilot awakens the next morning (in the same position he was seen in after the crash), the Prince is gone. "My God!" he exclaims. "It never happened!" This is Lerner's line, not Saint-Exupéry's; the film suggests that it may all have been a dream after a concussion (like Dorothy's).

The Pilot gets the plane into the air; as he ascends, he hears the laughter of the Little Prince, to the music of the title song. Lerner's ending is more definite than Saint-Exupéry's, wherein the Pilot asks the reader, should he encounter the Prince in the desert, to "send me word that he has come back." Lerner's Pilot, for his part, knows that the Prince, with his "laugh [that] turned on the sun," still exists among the stars.

In the film, the Pilot is portrayed by Richard Kiley, whose career began in Hollywood in the early 1950s with parts in "B"-category gangster films. After his voice was discovered, he moved to Broadway to appear in such musicals as *Kismet, Redhead, No Strings*, and, as Don Quixote, in *Man of La Mancha*. Initially, Frank Sinatra was to play the Pilot, but Lerner objected, and prevailed, which turned the Lerner-Sinatra relationship frosty. (Some years later, during a party at Kitty Carlisle Hart's, Lerner saw Sinatra arrive for coffee, as did critic-columnist Rex Reed, who had recently panned the singer. "I tried to hide behind Alan Jay Lerner," Reed recalled. "'Are you kidding?' asked Mr. *My Fair Lady*. 'After I fired him from my movie, *The Little Prince*, I'm the one he'll punch first.' As it turned out, nobody got punched.")

Cast as the Little Prince was the young, diminutive (when Kiley kneeled, he was still the taller of the two) Steven Warner, who gave a remarkable and altogether winning and believable performance. Although some of this must be attributed to the work of producer-director Stanley Donen, much credit must also be given to the actor himself. Only six years old when he made the film, Steven Warner came from a nonprofessional family (both his parents worked in the London bus system) but revealed a wish to act and dance from a very early age. He attended a school in which the mornings were devoted to conventional studies and the afternoons to dramatics, voice, and dancing. Not among the seven hundred or so boys auditioned for the part of the Little Prince, he was instead discovered almost by accident when a scout for Donen saw a staged BBC Television mock audition in which the youngster offered what was termed an "irreverent" rendition of "Santa Got Stuck Up the Chimney."

Much of the action and most of the musical numbers were filmed during a six-week location shooting on the southernmost tip of Tunisia's Sahara Desert. In this forbidding and—for film technicians, at least—trying setting, Donen assembled Kiley, Fosse, Wilder, and Warner. The child actor was accompanied by his mother, Rita, a tutor, a dialogue coach, and a nurse (just in case).

Young Warner's musical and dancing talents are displayed in two of the film's most delightful sequences. Having run out of water, the Prince and the reluctant Pilot set off into the wasteland to look for more. The Prince sings:

> *Why is the desert so lovely to see?*
> *. . .*
> *There is a reason*
> *Lovely to tell*
> *Because the desert is hiding a well.*

After they discover the well (actually a studio-constructed stream, complete with waterfall), the music rises, and the two join in an athletic water dance, the Prince laughing his infectious laugh. (Lerner's lyric for this song is rich in both poetry and humor.) Together they sing the final refrain:

> *H_2O, oh, here's to you!*
> *Why was the desert so lovely before?*
> *Why was it lovely, but not anymore?*
> *Water was hiding*
> *No one could see.*
> *But now the water is hiding in me.*

The Prince's other number is a combined vocal duet (with the Fox) and dance. In "Closer and Closer," the Fox explains how gradually he and the Prince may become friends (the Fox, naturally, is extremely shy and suspicious: "You must have a gun, you're a human being," he says—Lerner's line). Here again Lerner got his cue for the song from the book, in which the Fox advises the Prince that if he wants to make friends with him, he must be patient and "sit a little closer to me, every day." This sequence is an exuberant song-and-dance, with Warner keeping in step (as he had with Kiley in the water dance) through a happy romp through the forest.

The Little Prince opened at the Radio City Music Hall on November 7, 1974, as part of its annual Christmas program. The film's reception was no cause for celebration; the most important reviewers seemed to agree with the Times's Vincent Canby, who deemed it a "very exasperating" piece of work. He objected to the adults' being referred to as "grown-ups," feeling that this gave away the attitudes of those responsible for the film. (This was the tail end of the "don't trust anyone over thirty" era.) He further thought it "too abstract and sophisticated, and too simple-mindedly mystic and smug to charm even the most indulgent children." While faulting both Donen's point of view and Lerner's screenplay, he concluded that the score was "full of lovely things that are a total waste in these barren circumstances."

The other critics mostly concurred, though many had little good to say even about the score. Donen, who had settled in London and had been away from the American film scene for some time (and from the musical film for even longer—since 1957), came in for a good deal of criticism.

Lerner's comments, too, were cold and bitter, as well as strangely dismissive. In On the Street Where I Live he devoted only a half page—one paragraph—to The Little Prince, explaining, "Unlike the theatre, where the author is the final authority, in motion pictures it is the director. And if one falls in the hands of some cinematic Bigfoot, one pays the price for someone else's ineptitude. In this case the price was high, because it undoubtedly was Fritz's last score."

The "Bigfoot" was, as Lerner caustically put it, "someone named Stanley Donen, [who] took it upon himself to change every tempo, delete musical phrases at will and distort the intention of every song until the entire score was unrecognizable." Notably, he makes no complaint about Donen's tampering with the screenplay, nor with the lyrics; he was upset primarily about the handling of the music for what would prove to be, historically, the last Lerner and Loewe score. Donen himself was not responsible, as Lerner well knew, for the arrangements and orchestrations (criticized by some as seeming too grand for so simple a story); rather, these were the work of Angela Morley. But Lerner's reference to Donen as a mere "someone" constitutes a rare public display of contempt for what the director let happen to their songs.

Stanley Donen had been around Hollywood musicals since 1943. A former Broadway dancer, in his midtwenties he codirected *On the Town* (1949) with his mentor, Gene Kelly, and two years later made his solo debut as director of Lerner's own *Royal Wedding*. He went on to work with Kelly again on the classic *Singin' in the Rain* (1952), followed by *Seven Brides for Seven Brothers* (1954) and *Funny Face* (1957), among others, in addition to such nonmusicals as *Charade* and *Two for the Road*, both starring Audrey Hepburn and both successful. He was hardly just "someone," but in Lerner's book he was an inept Bigfoot who had destroyed his beloved Fritz's final score.

The real problem with *The Little Prince* lies not so much in the treatment of the songs, which are in general beautifully done, but rather in the story itself. Just as *Lolita* was an experiment in literature designed to be read and not necessarily seen, *The Little Prince* was conceived as a morality tale to think about or discuss in class. Actually, very little happens in the story outside of the Pilot's flying and the Prince's progressing from planet to planet as he meets with the various characters, including the Snake and the Fox—and much of these scenes is devoted to philosophical talk. The songs wonderfully, and tunefully, heighten the talk and liven the film; along with the cast's performances, they are the best part of *The Little Prince*.

Lerner's great regret was that after the warm and wonderful time he and Lowe had working on it in their old informal manner—joking, teasing, enjoying their work—it was all, in his view, for nothing.

The year that they devoted partly to the writing of *The Little Prince* songs, 1972, also marked the beginning of a new phase in Alan Jay Lerner's personal life. In London, as in New York, the Lerners were regular theatergoers, and during one of their evenings out, Lerner experienced a change of heart. In July the *Daily News* announced that the "separation of the Alan Jay Lerners now seems to be permanent"; rumors had been flying back and forth across the Atlantic for some time as each partner in the now-tattered marriage sought solace elsewhere. "London newspapers," the *News* continued, "are already linking Alan with some English actress." The actress in question was Sandra Payne, who in time would become Mrs. Lerner number six.

The next month brought another announcement: Arnold Saint-Subber planned to produce a musical with a score by Alan Jay Lerner and Leonard Bernstein. For the moment, the working title was *Opus 1*. If it materialized, it would be Lerner's eleventh Broadway musical; only two more after that and he would have his thirteenth—his lucky number.

15

—⧈—

AMERICAN DREAMING

IN MARCH 1957, the Harvard Glee Club and University Band appeared at Carnegie Hall. In honor of the occasion, two of Harvard's most celebrated musical alumni, Leonard Bernstein (Class of '39) and Alan Jay Lerner (Class of '40), contributed a pair of songs entitled "Dedication" and "The Lonely Men of Harvard." The latter was described in the *Times* as a "rousing march," but at least one member of the Glee Club found the song puzzling; he suspected, he said, that the lyric might perhaps be a little satirical.

Satirical indeed; the *Times* quoted a portion of it:

> *We're the lonely men of Harvard;*
> *Alone, alas, alone, alack, are we!*
> *And that's the curse we share,*
> *It's the cross we've got to bear*
> *For our irrefutable superiority.*
> *And that's the curse we share;*
> *It's the cross we've got to bear*
> *For our indubitable, irrefutable,*
> *Inimitable, indomitable,*
> *Incalculable superiority.*

The collaboration of Lerner and Bernstein was such a historic occurrence that the placement of their tongues in their cheeks either went unnoticed or was deliberately ignored and forgotten. The rousing march would surface again some years later.

Like Lerner, Bernstein loved activity. In 1957, he had only recently finished a stint as professor of music at Brandeis University and was regularly associated with the Berkshire Music Center, also in Massachusetts. When he and his fellow alumnus joined to write the Harvard songs, he was working on a musical to be called *West Side Story*, and Lerner was basking in the glow of the year-old *My Fair Lady*.

In the interim between their Carnegie debut and Saint-Subber's announcement of *Opus 1*, Lerner had suffered mostly downs in the theater and was disturbed by what he regarded as the political downs in America. By 1972, when the idea for *Opus 1* was conceived, Lerner had strong feelings about the "megalomaniacal Lyndon B. Johnson," the "hollow, patriotic sophistry of Henry Kissinger," and just about anything or anyone connected with the corrupt administration of Richard Nixon—including his Vice President, Spiro Agnew, who used the White House as a drop spot for "financial transactions concealed by the tablecloth"; the escalation of the war in Vietnam; and, while he and Bernstein worked, the "incident" at the Watergate complex in Washington.

For his part, Bernstein had been inactive on Broadway since the very successful production of *West Side Story*, which Lerner had once summarily dismissed as a "message musical" that dealt in "teen-age rumbles and switchblade knives." (He was rather more generous in his book on the musical theater, where he pronounced it a work of "remarkable originality, pulsating excitement, dynamic and passionately beautiful music.") While Lerner collaborated with Loewe, Lane, and Previn, Bernstein was active as a conductor (in which capacity he spearheaded the reappreciation of Mahler), lecturer, teacher, and composer of the *Serenade* for violin and orchestra (1960), *Chichester Psalms* (1965), and the "Theatre Piece" *Mass* (1971). His announced return to the musical theater, especially with Alan Jay Lerner, was cause for excitement, talk, and speculation.

At the time politically compatible (though Bernstein was more active, more outspoken, and, in the view of men such as J. Edgar Hoover, suspiciously un-American), both Bernstein and Lerner were strongly anti–Vietnam war and anti-Nixon. Nixon's landslide reelection in November 1972 depressed Lerner, who had initiated the *Opus 1* project the previous August, a few days after the U.S. Air Force carried out massive bombing raids on North Vietnam as American ground troops fled from South Vietnam.

That September, the Nixon administration would begin to unravel when two former White House aides, G. Gordon Liddy and E. Howard Hunt, were indicted, with five others, for "conspiring to break into Democratic national headquarters in the Watergate complex" on June 17, three months before. The full import of this escapade would not be revealed until the following summer, by which time Lerner and Bernstein were well into *Opus 1*.

Lerner later explained his inspiration for the musical's book: "I started thinking about it after the last election. . . . The show deals primarily with those moments when people tried to take the White House away from us. . . . The White House seemed to be getting rather remote from the country." The play's title was now significantly changed to *1600 Pennsylvania Avenue*: Lerner had selected his musical target.

Curious, coincident events occurred in Lerner's life during the gestation of the show. Three months after the *Opus 1* news release, the *Times* ran a front-page story about the celebrity "patients" of Dr. Max Jacobson—among them Alan Jay Lerner, the late President John F. Kennedy, and Jacqueline Kennedy—which brought the good doctor, finally, to the attention of the New York State Board of Regents; after an unaccountable delay, his license to practice was revoked on August 25, 1975, when he was in his mid-seventies. Less than a month later, on September 17, 1975, the *Times* printed the extraordinary news that Coca-Cola was going into the musical theater business by backing Lerner and Bernstein's musical.

This unique investment came about through one of Lerner's golfing friends from his precollege years, a Westchester resident and then Harvard Junior named John Paul Austin. It was he who had convinced Lerner that he should go to Harvard instead of Princeton, as originally planned. Austin, too, had risen in the world and in 1975 was chairman of the board at Coca-Cola. A phone call to Austin's office in Atlanta and a reunion in New York—plus the invocation of the lustrous names of Leonard Bernstein and Alan Jay Lerner in connection with a musical to be timed for the Bicentennial—had sealed the deal. In the *Times* article, Lerner is quoted at length; Bernstein merely added, "we've been on this since 1973."

Coca-Cola's financing made the creation and production of their ambitious musical infinitely less irksome than would have been the case under almost any other circumstances. There were no backers' auditions, merely the circulation of the general idea among the company's upper echelons, the presentation of a few songs in Lerner's usual winning manner, and the signing of a check or two. Coca-Cola, unlike virtually every other backer of a show, was benign to a fault. And why shouldn't it be? It had Lerner, it had Bernstein, and those two could be counted on to come up with a fitting, Coca-Cola-funded celebration fo the two hundredth anniversary of the American Revolution and several of the country's presidents. It was a sure thing—wasn't it? (Other corporations, too, contributed to the Bicentennial celebration—as sponsors of Washington's fireworks spectacular, New York's "Operation Sail," and so on—but Coca-Cola took the cultural prize.)

Because of Bernstein's peripatetic professional life—conducting here and there, recording almost everywhere—Lerner himself could relax and work in the free-and-easy Lerner-and-Loewe style. Their *1600 Pennsylvania Avenue* was not scheduled to premiere at the new John F. Kennedy Center in Washington, D.C., until January 1, 1976, when it would begin the gala Bicentennial, so they were in no hurry. Not much work was done on the book in 1973, as Lerner was occupied with the staged *Gigi* from summer until winter of that year.

In January 1974, settled into his Center Island retreat on Long Island Sound, he began the new year by composing a charming foreword to his friend and fellow lyricist Howard Dietz's autobiographical *Dancing in the Dark*. The essay consists primarily of an appraisal of Dietz's contribution to American popular song, especially through his theater work in collaboration with Arthur Schwartz. But before treating his main subject, Lerner wanted to sound off about the current state of the theater (no charm) and of politics (no "star" quality—no Roosevelt or Kennedy). Using theatrical terminology, he dismissed Nixon, as compared to other presidents, as a kind of "Chicago company"—that is, second-rate—and "of the Capone era at that." Agreeing, Dietz wrote a brief note that Lerner liked:

> *When I received your introduction to my book I was in the hospital.*
> *When I finished reading the introduction I went home.*

Although he was theoretically at work on the Bernstein opus, Lerner's mind was as sprightly—and as restive—as ever; as he once said, "I always have plans—I'm effervescent with plans." The truth of this statement was revealed in March, when he received a copy of a chapter from a book being prepared by the composer, conductor, and director Lehman Engle, to be entitled *Their Words Are Music.* Lerner informed him,

I read your chapter [devoted to Lerner] with great care and great pleasure and heartily agree with every compliment. But I do have a problem.

The problem is that at this very moment I am in the process of preparing a book of my own lyrics for publication and I am covering some of the same ground—obviously not in exactly the same way—that you do.

He then went through Engle's list of twenty-three songs one by one, eliminating seven altogether, truncating others, and suggesting that he would prefer the inclusion of only the verse to "On a Clear Day," commenting, "Is it necessary to use the whole chorus? It would help me enormously if you did not." Engle complied, using both the dialogue that leads into the song and the verse itself, which is not included in the published sheet music. Lerner proscribed *Paint Your Wagon*'s "I Talk to the Trees" but permitted Engle to replace it with "How Can I Wait?" The problem was amicably solved, with Lerner concluding, "I am fully aware that this will complicate things for you, but I must tell you that I am going against my own lawyer by allowing this much. . . . Let's get together. . . . I do have some information that I cannot use which might be of use to you as a substitute for the space lost. Besides, it's always a joy to see you." He signed off with an "Aye."

As it eventuated, Lerner did not compile a book of his own lyrics, as had Oscar Hammerstein and Ira Gershwin before him. Later, in 1977, he would sign a contract with Viking Penguin, but no book ever resulted. His quasi-autobiography, *On the Street Where I Live*, whose dedication reads "To Fritz, without whom this would have been an address book," was published by Norton in 1978. It is skimpily autobiographical, concentrating primarily on the creation of *My Fair Lady*, *Camelot*, and *Gigi* and reproducing generous lyric selections from those musicals.

During this same period, in 1974, Leonard Bernstein took time out from his musical travels to rework his celebrated but quickly terminated 1956 "Comic Opera," *Candide*. Its original book, by Lillian Hellman and based on Voltaire, was revised by Hugh Wheeler; Stephen Sondheim provided additional lyrics, and Harold Prince brilliant staging. It opened at the Broadway Theatre on March 8 for a run of 740 performances (the first had lasted for only seventy-three). There was more: in May 1974 the New York City Ballet presented the composer's *Dybbuk* (with choreography by Jerome Robbins), based on a Central European folktale about a restless and destructive spirit who takes possession of the body of a living person. Bernstein was clearly thinking theatrically again.

While Lerner dabbled with his libretto and thought about doing a book of lyrics, he was confronted by his broken marriage to Karen Gundersen, from whom he had been estranged since 1972. She had since gone her own way, was now a television producer at NBC, and was willing to be reasonable about everything. In December Lerner flew down to Port-au-Prince, Haiti, where on the ninth he divorced Gundersen and on the very next day, December 10, 1974, married Sandra Payne.

While he was in London, late in 1972, working with Loewe on the *The Little Prince* score, Lerner had seen the young actress (then about twenty-five) and was taken with her. She was perky and pretty, with a wide grin. His marriage to Karen Gundersen was by then a disaster, primarily because of his obsession with his work and the ministrations of his Dr. Feelgood. The sprightly, vivacious Sandra, who was active on the stage as well as British television, enchanted him, and in December of 1974 he married her. But it followed the usual pattern: "It lasted eighteen months," she told a London *News* interviewer. "No bad feelings, we simply agreed the marriage was a mistake." But that year and a half would prove to be an adventure in strain, anxiety, and disarray.

With the holidays over and the next year's Bicentennial in the news, Bernstein and Lerner turned to their musical in early 1975. Lerner's plan was to set the story in the White House as seen through the eyes of "retainers" (i.e., black servants) below stairs. Bernstein liked that idea, but by July the first dissenting voice was heard, that of producer Saint-Subber. After a number of disagreements and flarings of temper, it was reported in *Variety* that the task of producing would be taken over by Robert Whitehead and Roger L. Stevens, with Saint-Subber retaining an unspecified "financial interest" in the show. And incidentally, the score was still in progress.

Saint-Subber later said, "I worked for two years on *1600 Pennsylvania Avenue*. . . . It wasn't working out well. I tried to get everyone to abandon it. After many fights, I left the production. I was so annihilated by that experience." He soon left for northern California, where he bred horses and dogs. "I loathed it," was his ultimate opinion of the musical he had helped to conceive.

In mid-September, after Coca-Cola came to the financial fore, the *Times* sent Mel Gussow to interview Lerner, who told him that the plot of the musical would center on the administrations of eight presidents, spanning the period from Washington (when there was no White House) to Theodore Roosevelt (in whose term it officially became The White House, with a capital T).

Gussow learned that though Lerner and Bernstein had been contemporaries at Harvard, they had not seen much of each other around campus. The university's then president Nathan M. Pusey had brought them together in 1957, when they had written an anthem at his request for the Glee Club. This would have been the acceptable "Dedication"; the derisive "Lonely Men of Harvard" was best forgotten—though not by the songwriters themselves.

Lerner was asked about the collaboration. "Naturally," he replied, "any time you're writing with a new composer or lyricist, you do influence each other, and you should, in order to produce a new voice of your own. With Lenny, I usually write the lyrics first. With Fritz I used to write the lyrics second."

He boasted of their having an "enormous amount of music, almost double the usual amount. There are close to thirty songs, or at least thirty manuscripts with titles on them. A few scenes are done all to music. I doubt if they will be in by the time we finish.

"We will not," he emphasized, "have a four-hour show."

Turning to his book, he explained, "The scaffolding has to be very strong to make the music work. The book is based on actual incidents. The life of the 'house' [i.e., the White House] was full of surprises for me."

As for said "house," he had not visited there since the Kennedy years, but was "looking forward to a return visit by the end of the next election." (More than a year before the interview took place, his bête noire Nixon had been driven out of office by the Watergate scandal, with Gerald R. Ford having subsequently replaced him. But by the next election, when a Democrat, Jimmy Carter, would at last reclaim the White House, Lerner would prefer not to be reminded of the place, no matter *who* lived there.)

Between that September and the turn of the Bicentennial year, the score was completed and a cast assembled. The assorted presidents were portrayed by Ken Howard, who had appeared in the Burt Bacharach–Hal David success *Promises, Promises* as well as Sherman Edwards's *1776* (playing Thomas Jefferson in both the stage production and the later film version). The presidents' wives were sung and acted by the British-born Patricia Routledge, a veteran of dramas and musicals on the London stage; she had made her New York debut in the Jule Styne–E. Y. Harburg failure *Darling of the Day* (1968), which had expired after only thirty-two performances but nonetheless won her a Tony as Best Actress in a Musical. The significant roles of the black servants, meanwhile—actually the major love interests—Lud and Thomaseena, or Seena, were assigned to two relative unknowns, Gilbert Price and Emily Yancy. Before the musical's opening in Philadelphia, a euphoric Leonard Bernstein predicted great things for these four members of his heavily populated cast. He thought the score was "enormous" (it was—practically an opera), the orchestra was the "best," and all in all, he was "terribly excited. . . . I've never been so excited by a show while I was doing it. I've never been so confident, so thrilled"—not even, he admitted, by *West Side Story* or *Candide*.

He believed that his and Lerner's musical expressed a "passionate love of country" and hoped it would serve to "rescue the word *patriotism* from the bigots." (The critics would beg to differ with that statement in a few days.) He grew expansive. "Subject matter of such stature," he said, "of such nobility, could lead to pretentiousness and sentimentality. But if there is anything I'm proud of it is that we have avoided those pitfalls. We're not preaching, we're just telling what we feel. I hope we achieved it without being dogmatic, pedantic or sermonizing.

"I've never felt this way about a show before," he reiterated. "I was worried out of my mind over *West Side Story*."

He had one objection: It had been suggested in print that Lerner's book owed something of its concept to the popular British television series *Upstairs, Downstairs*, a below-stairs, servant's-eye view of the goings-on in an upper-class English household. He and Lerner, he pointed out, had "been on this since 1973 and that was before 'Upstairs, Downstairs' was well-known." (In fact, that was the year that the series won its first of several Emmy Awards for excellence.)

In retrospect, his confidence seems curious; he cannot have been unaware of the problems of the production, first brought to their attention by a frustrated Saint-Subber and then early on in his tenure by director Frank Corsaro.

A former child actor on stage and in film, Corsaro, by 1976, was known as the dynamic director of such operas as Erich Korngold's *Die tote Stadt* and the American works of Carlisle Floyd (*Susannah*), as well as the heralded Houston Grand Opera production of Scott Joplin's *Treemonisha*. Also a playwright, he brought a wide range of experience to *1600 Pennsylvania Avenue*. But nobody listened.

"When I got the book," he later recalled,

it was not quite finished. I didn't like the basic premise—it was based on the assumption that everyone sees the White House as a symbol of America—and I fought with Alan for changes. But they'd been working on it for years and every time I made a suggestion, they said they tried it two years ago. . . . They had bullied each other into this very pretentious, chicly liberal approach to American history.

Lerner disagreed; when the company arrived in Philadelphia, he described the show, rather, as a "play about a play's rehearsal." His new opening number comprised the hopeful assertion that if they "rehearsed and rehearsed and rehearsed, 'It's [i.e., the show's] Gonna Be Great!'" He was cheered by the presence of a touring company of *My Fair Lady*, then housed in the Shubert and heading once again for Broadway.

But in fact, the musical had no plot—what critics call the "story line"—beyond the love story of Lud and Seena. The play consisted of a series of vignettes, set pieces, each making a political or, as Bernstein put it, "patriotic" musical statement. "Ten Square Miles of the Potomac," for example, was a long sequence in which the placement of the capital of the United States was to be discussed by George Washington and various state representatives. Each of the thirteen states would be happy to be the site, but Washington, interrupting the cacophonous arguing, suggests that it be located instead on the Potomac River, "a Northern town built on a Southern River. . . . Beneath a Southern sky filled with Northern lights/Southern grandeur and Northern rights." Rather than name this swampy site Federal City, all decide, with Washington modestly not demurring, on "Washington."

The scene shifts to Abigail and John Adams, the first to occupy the not-quite-completed White House. They are welcomed by servants, who inform them that while they have kerosene, the lamps have not yet arrived, and that the bedrooms are upstairs but the stairs have not been built, and that

> Oh, de cellar's full of water
> But all de wells is dry.

The point is obvious and mildly amusing; the next scene has Abigail Adams (Patricia Routledge) singing one of the finest arias of the play, "Take Care of

This House." She sings to the young Lud, who will remain in the house after she and Adams leave it. Lerner's allusion to Watergate is reasonably subtle:

> Be careful at night.
> Check all the doors.
> If someone makes off with a dream,
> The dream will be yours.

And so on, from one point to the next, through history, but with no coherent story. There is the inevitable burning of Washington by the British in the War of 1812, when, in 1814, the Capitol was destroyed. The British are depicted as thieving fools; when Lud asks, Why the fire? one Admiral Cockburn, who ordered the burning, boasts,

> Why? Simple.
> Primo, I have ordered it and were it not aflame,
> The officer in charge would leave here deader than he came.
> Secundo, not a brighter torch could there be,
> For Blackie, by tomorrow morning Washington, D.C.,
> Will be Washington, deceased.

Lincoln appears only as a shadow with a stovepipe hat, but he is addressed in "American Dreaming," in which he is informed that all the good he left behind is being swept away.

> Presidential honor is a loser's lament.
> Principal is something drawing seven percent.
> And notify the meek that they are out of the will,
> Just in case they are still
> American dreaming.

Lerner's subtitle for the show was "A Musical About the Problems of Housekeeping," but the major problems realized during the rehearsals and previews were structural. "In twenty-five words or less, nobody knew what the show was about," as a confounded and fatigued Ken Howard put it. And contrary to Lerner's statement the previous September, they now had a four-hour show—one with a message.

Finally, after a postponement or two for rewriting and cuts, *1600 Penn-*

sylvania Avenue premiered at Philadelphia's Forest Theatre on February 26, 1976. The attentive, kindly interviewers of the weeks before now turned on them. The *Philadelphia Inquirer*'s critic-interviewer, William B. Collins, whose review was headed "Two Giants Fall Flat in *1600*," found their history lesson appalling. "They look back," he wrote, "and see nothing but hypocrisy, chicanery, corruption. They are properly outraged at the denial of equality to the black race. They are so depressed that they have written a big, long musical that makes the rest of us feel as bad as they do."

Variety's appraiser agreed, adding, "The question is whether it belongs on a stage or a soapbox."

And so it was onward and downward to Washington. As Lerner rewrote, a stream of play doctors came in to advise: Mike Nichols, Arthur Laurents, Jerome Robbins. The last two were former Bernstein collaborators, Laurents since *West Side Story* (based on Robbins's idea of turning *Romeo and Juliet* into a gang-rumble musical) and Robbins since Bernstein's first musical, *On the Town* (also Robbins's idea, based on their earlier ballet together, *Fancy Free*).

The word was not encouraging. Nichols could contribute nothing, Laurents suggested closing down, and Robbins was characteristically caustic, recalling that he "let them pick my brains." (The "them" included producers Whitehead and Stevens, who were by now running short of backing.) "There was no book," Robbins judged, "they were rewriting it. It wasn't quite coherent. Scenes referred to [other] scenes that weren't there."

The final weeks in Philadelphia and the early days in Washington were frenetic. As Ken Howard remembered it, "It was the most painful and torturous experience I've had in the theater. There was a rewrite every day and we were doing new material every night." By Washington, Howard's role had been expanded to thirteen—Lerner's lucky number again—presidents. That his Washington rewrites were done at the Watergate Hotel struck some of the company as rather ironic.

More drastic changes also occurred in the capital. In the second week of March, director Frank Corsaro gave up and left the show, taking choreographer Donald McKayle with him. In desperation, the top echelon postponed the March 17 opening and sought help.

They were certain they had found what they needed in the person of a young black director named Gilbert Moses. He was reputed to be bright and innovative, though it was also common knowledge that he had been replaced as director of the previous year's Broadway musical *The Wiz* by director-choreographer Geoffrey Holder, who had also taken over for the choreographer, George Faison. The latter now accompanied Moses on his mission to save the Lerner-Bernstein show.

"The whole concept," in Moses's opinion, "was very obscure and one had to get rid of the original concept. It was not a concept one could build on. The original concept was Lerner's—I think at first he wanted to do it simply but somehow it just grew and grew into a monster. Once *we* [emphasis added] added Bernstein's music it became larger and larger." He believed, too, that the collaborators were "too old" (all of fifty-seven, with Lerner only a week Bernstein's junior) to contend with the revisions that were necessary—meaning the revisions *he* thought were needed—to make something of the unwieldy musical. One of the musicians who worked on the show recalls his shock at seeing a quite humble Leonard Bernstein's being lectured by Moses. It may have been done for the good of the show, and indeed, the excisions did tighten it somewhat, but it is unlikely that the producers could have found a less sympathetic fixer had they taken out a full-page advertisement in *Variety*. This blunder may be attributed in part to some of the criticisms of the show's anti-white orientation. The overall theme can be pretty much summed up in one line of dialogue in the show: "Y'all can stay with the white folks if you want. I feel safer with the snakes and alligators." At the same time, there were charges, as well, of black stereotyping (*Time* eventually branded the musical "racist").

It was hoped that Moses could defuse certain aspects of the musical, and also pull it together. He and Faison went to work, tearing out whole chunks of the show and locking Lerner and Bernstein out of the theater while they rearranged the "concept." It seemed hopeless. Moses suggested to Whitehead and Stevens that they close down, move the production to California, and start all over again. Coca-Cola was already pouring a hundred thousand dollars a week into *1600 Pennsylvania Avenue*—and now they were asking for more. California was definitely ruled out, and the grind continued.

The reworked show, now shorter by an hour, finally opened at the Colonial on March 24. It was kindly if not enthusiastically appraised by the *Washington Post*'s Richard L. Coe, an inveterate musical-theater aficionado. The paper's music critic, Paul Hume, managed to find good things in the score, singling out "The President Jefferson March," which Bernstein had appropriated, in revised form, from his *Mass* ("Prefatory Prayers"). In the song's lyric, Jefferson's erudition, adventurousness, and knowledge of the world are manifested in his introduction of his guests to such discoveries as waffles from

Holland, ice cream and an éclair from France, spaghetti from Italy, and brown Betty from Britain. Hume especially liked "Take Care of This House" and the tour de force "Duet for One," in which Patricia Routledge did indeed sing a duet with herself, playing two very different characters: the rather common wife of the outgoing president, Julia Grant, and the pretentious wife of newly elected President Rutherford B. Hayes, Lucy. Lucy sings:

> Démodée Julia Grant . . .
> Passée Julia Grant . . .
> Her three little chins are now out of style.
> Her charm has become sub-sublime.
> I'm told they are planning to travel a while,
> Seeing friends who are still doing time.

And Julia:

> Now they'll cheer Lucy Hayes . . .
> That dear Lucy Hayes . . .
> They'll worship her matchless cucumber skin;
> Her fingers like ancient bamboo.
> They'll dote on her lips so enchantingly thin
> That it's hard to believe there are two.

According to the New York Post, the musical "won enthusiastic acclaim when it opened officially last night in the capital." Another paper, however, noted a significant absence: Leonard Bernstein was not in attendance.

Evidently the "acclaim" was not as "enthusiastic" as the New York Post made out, for further defections followed. When 1600 Pennsylvania Avenue's curtain rose at the Mark Hellinger in New York on May 4, 1976—after no less than three months of troubled time on the road—Coca-Cola was no longer credited in the Playbill. And when the curtain went down on a reprise of the hopeful "Rehearse!" it was obvious that it was hopeless. Variety called it a "bicentennial bore," while Newsweek, in a show of scholarship, dismissed it as a "victim of myasthenia gravis conceptualis, otherwise known as a crummy idea." Time's Ted Kalem finished off his critique by observing, "The British burned the White House in 1812 [sic], and Lerner and Bernstein are running the fire-sale." The show itself was completely burned out by the end of the week, after all of seven performances.

"I'm so shattered by the whole thing," Leonard Bernstein sorrowfully told a reporter from *Women's Wear Daily*. "The score was fragmented, not at all what I wrote. I do hope to salvage some of it somehow." (He did adapt "Rehearse!" for a musical tribute to his friend the cellist-conductor Mstislav Rostropovich, turning it into a lively little piece entitled "*Slava!*," after the Russian expatriate's affectionate nickname.) However, Bernstein would never return to the theater, except to rework such earlier pieces as *Candide, Trouble in Tahiti,* and its companion piece, *A Quiet Place.*

Alan Lerner was equally disappointed, though in public appeared sanguine. "I am not discouraged," he said a few days after the closing. "If failure discouraged me, I would have quit long ago. . . . This sort of thing happens in the theater all the time."

The experience taught Coca-Cola's executives a costly lesson: The company lost more than a million dollars. Show business, they found, was no business.

If Lerner was, as he claimed, undiscouraged, he was nonetheless anxious to erase the failure, the tensions of—and his preoccupation with—which had rendered his marriage to Sandra Payne virtually a nonmarriage. Her career in television and the theater was in Britain, not in the United States, and she now returned to England.

Burton Lane, when he read of the obvious fate of *1600 Pennsylvania Avenue,* predicted to Lynn Lane, "Alan is going to call—in a day, a week, maybe a month. But he will call." Having recently completed work with lyricist Sammy Cahn on the songs for a Hanna-Barbera film cartoon called *Heidi's Song,* Lane was at liberty. In the decade since their falling-out over *On a Clear Day,* he and Lerner had begun speaking again; but Lane had not forgotten.

If not accurate on the timing, his prediction was precise on the caller. Lerner was no quitter, but to judge from the voice Lane heard on his answering machine, his onetime partner was more discouraged than he wanted to let on. "He was stammering," Lane recalled. "He seemed unsure of himself."

The composer returned the call and bluntly asked, "What do you have in mind?"

Lerner said he had a new musical in mind, and maybe they could talk about it. Lane agreed, but when they met, he brought with him a list of conditions under which their collaboration, if any, might work. He began by saying, "Alan, if you can't agree to, or keep to, this plan, let me know now, and no hard feelings."

In part, Lane's list read as follows:

Are you planning any trips?
What other things are you doing?
If there are any production meetings, I must be there at every one.
Once we start, we must stick with it; nothing will be left unwritten.
We will go into rehearsals with all lyrics complete.

Lerner—nervously, perhaps—assured Lane that he would comply with his wishes, and they were ready to begin. He had an idea, he said, for a musical based on Robert E. Sherwood's 1936 Pulitzer Prize–winning play, *Idiot's Delight*. (The popular 1939 film version starring Clark Gable and Norma Shearer is most notable for Gable's song-and-dance to Irving Berlin's "Puttin' on the Ritz.") Sherwood's pacifistic comedy was regarded as a prediction of what was to become the Second World War.

Lane was not so sure. Politically sensitive and sophisticated at a time when Syria was invading Lebanon and race riots were flaring in South Africa, he did not feel that this was the moment for a musical about impending war, especially with a nuclear cloud hanging over the world.

Lerner came up with another idea, an invocation of the past. Lane really did not like it very much, either, but he felt it was a "cute idea" that might be developed into an entertaining musical.

His inspiration was a 1969 film of no great distinction called *Buona Sera, Mrs. Campbell*. Gina Lollobrigida starred as Carmelina Campbell, whose American soldier husband, the father of her (now seventeen-year-old) daughter, was killed in the fighting in Italy during the Second World War. Remaining in her little village of Forino ever since, Signora Campbell has lived well, supported by her dead husband's family in America. She is respected in the village and prays daily for the soul of her husband, much to the dismay of a local café proprietor, the unprepossessing Vittorio, who is deeply in love with her. To his further dismay, she spurns him, despite the fact that unbeknownst to him, she herself returns his love. She cannot respond to his overtures because she has a secret.

Carmelina's idyllic but not especially happy existence is threatened when she learns that members of the military battalion that occupied Forino during the war are due to return, after eighteen years, to hold a happy reunion. All the village rejoices, except Carmelina. She reveals her secret to her faithful housekeeper: she is no widow. During the American occupation, she was romantically involved with three GIs, each of whom now believes he is the father of her daughter, Gia, and each of whom has been sending money to mother and daughter for seventeen years. Even she herself does not know which one is Gia's father. If all three return—and they do—she will be disgraced in the eyes of her neighbors and of Vittorio.

The romantic, happy resolution to this distressing situation is initially complicated when Gia, now a great beauty, learns that her father did not die in the war and that her mother has been living a lie. Each of the former soldiers, taken with the young woman's charm, is certain that he is the father. Meanwhile, the hapless Vittorio, having lately been happily encouraged by Carmelina, now finds her suddenly withdrawn and elusive. The second act culminates in Gia's elopement with a fisherman whom she does not love; the three "fathers," aided by Vittorio, intervene and return "their" daughter to her anxious mother. All is forgiven—even the town still admires and loves Carmelina—and once the Americans leave, she and Vittorio are to be married, as promised in act 1.

If not precisely the stuff of a forward-looking musical, it was nonetheless enough to stir Lane's musical imagination (with an occasional Italian inflection), while exercising Lerner's flair for delineating character and emotion economically and poetically.

But the dread year 1976, it seemed, could not close without a final interruption: Early in December, Micheline Muselli Pozzo di Borgo was awarded, by the New York Supreme Court, a judgment of more than $16,500 in "back alimony and child support." Her appearance was never conducive to work; and as ever, she would return.

As Burton Lane was looking forward to making a serious beginning on the show that would be entitled *Carmelina*, his friend the music publisher Buddy Robbins called. He and his wife were planning to go hear Mabel Mercer in a club; would Burt and Lynn like to accompany them? Lane, a devotee of Mabel Mercer, was pleased to accept. Robbins then asked if they would mind if he also invited Alan Lerner. Lane, of course, had no objections, and the date was set.

The Lanes joined the Robbinses at the club before Mabel Mercer came on. Lerner was late; they joked about his indifference to punctuality.

"Burt," Robbins then asked, "when is Alan leaving for Australia?"

"Australia!" a stunned Lane echoed.

When Lerner arrived, Lane inquired about the trip, and Lerner replied, "I told you about that."

"You did not!"

Lerner swore he had informed Lane and seemed genuinely surprised to learn otherwise. Lynn Lane was skeptical: "Alan was a very charming man, but he was a con-man—he never told the truth in his life."

There was nothing for Lane to do but wait; still, Lerner had broken one of the cardinal rules of their new collaboration. (At the end of January 1977, *Variety* reported that Lerner, along with composer-lyricist Stephen Sondheim and producer Harold Prince, had attended an International Music Theater Forum at the Sydney Conservatorium of Music.)

He returned to New York in time to participate in a tribute to Ira Gershwin at the Ninety-second Street YMHA's Lyrics and Lyricists series on February 13 and 14. Appearing with composers Arthur Schwartz and Burton Lane, the lyricist's sister Frances Gershwin Godowsky, and vocalists Nancy Dussault and Lee Roy Reems, he discussed lyric writing, especially as practiced by Gershwin (who "invented the word *baby*," Lerner said). He also told the filled house of his experiences during the filming of *An American in Paris*. Although Gershwin himself did not attend the tribute, his wife, Leonore, did, and via home recording Ira sang a duet with Burton Lane.

Although Lerner gave series producer Maurice Levine a few anxious moments—during the writing of the event's script, barely a week before the first Sunday-evening performance, Levine found that Lerner had left the country—he returned to participate in a rehearsal and the two presentations. Clearly suffering from stress, a bit edgy and talkative (he discussed his Bernstein collaboration with Lane and Schwartz), he wore white gloves whenever he was offstage.

In March he was again summoned to the State Supreme Court, this time to be lectured by Justice Beatrice Shainswit, who greeted with sarcasm his explanation that it was a hardship for him to maintain alimony and child-support payments. Justice Shainswit pointed out that "Mr. Lerner's position is that his wife must be penalized because in the eleven years since the divorce he has luxuriated in a lavish life-style." Continuing in the same vein, she noted that he had nowhere documented his poverty, "except [in] his concurrent confession that his income for 1976 has dwindled to a mere $250,000. . . . Mr. Lerner's claimed condition of poverty," the justice concluded, "could well be the envy of ninety-nine percent of the entire population." She decided to appoint a special referee to look into his "true assets and true income."

A week later, Lerner was seen at Lynn Redgrave's tenth wedding anniversary party at the Cachaca Club with Nina Bushkin, daughter of jazz pianist-composer Joey Bushkin ("Oh, Look at Me Now"). Although the twenty-five-year-old was then director of development at the Mannes College of Music, when Burton Lane first met her, he was certain she was still a schoolgirl. On May 30, Lerner took another trip to Port-au-Prince, where he and Nina Bushkin were married. The newspaper item noting this event made a point of specifying that the bride was twenty-five and the groom fifty-seven. (It amused Lerner to discover that he was two years older than his new father-in-law.)

Meanwhile, he and Lane worked on their new musical—slowly. It was not until January 13, 1978, that *Variety* reported that Lerner and Lane were "planning *Carmelina*." By then almost two years had slipped by since Lerner agreed to Lane's work rules, and Lane was once again resigned to the usual Lerner habits. His partner, he now learned, was at work on an autobiography.

Worry about his health also absented the lyricist from work sessions. Concerned about his excessive smoking (a nervous habit since his Choate days, and practically an occupational disease in the theater), he began seeing a hypnotist. When this failed to work, he tried acupuncture, the newly fashionable, ancient Chinese treatment for various ailments, including stress. There was some temporary improvement, but eventually he turned to cigarettes again.

As Lane had feared, they were not quite ready when rehearsals for *Carmelina* began. He tried to warn one of the producers, Roger L. Stevens, that they were beginning with an incomplete show, but Stevens was not interested. After Lane made it clear that he thought very little of Stevens's capabilities as a producer, acrimonious arguments, even threats, soon filled the air. (Stevens was not the only member of the production team; also involved were J. W. Fisher, Joan Cullman, and Jujamcyn Productions, a group of theater owners. In short, it was an instance of producing by committee.)

Carmelina is unique in being the only Lerner work to employ a colibrettist. Joseph Stein was best known for *Fiddler on the Roof*, based on Shalom Aleichem's stories of Jewish life—or rather, survival—in Czarist Russia (with a score by Jerry Bock and Sheldon Harnick); he had followed this up with his adaptation of the Nikos Kazantzakis novel *Zorba* (1968; score by John Kander and Fred Ebb). One of his earliest efforts was 1959's *Juno*, a musical setting by Marc Blitzstein of Sean O'Casey's *Juno and the Paycock*, which, though not a success despite being beautifully done, had marked the beginning of its librettist's association with ethnic musicals. Stein's joining him in preparing *Carmelina*'s book left Lerner more time for the lyrics. Like Lerner a devoted member of the Rodgers and Hammerstein school, Stein could be counted on to create what historian-biographer Stanley Green has called a "resolutely old-fashioned" musical.

In the wake such inexplicable (to Lerner) hits as *Jesus Christ Superstar*, *Grease*, and the concept musicals with virtually no plot, such as *A Chorus Line* (premiered 1975, still going strong in 1979) and *Dancin'*, such a retrogression required courage—though *Annie*, another old-fashioned enterprise (1977), had become a huge success. It was time, Lerner believed, for a return to a traditional music with contemporary overtones.

Bringing in the dependable Joseph Stein was, in fact, Burton Lane's idea. With rehearsals under way and neither a completed book nor lyrics in hand, he insisted that Lerner get some help, and Lerner agreed. The tryout took place in Stevens's home base of Washington, D.C., with the show proper finally premiering at the St. James Theatre on April 8, 1979. The majority of the New York critics were not kind.

All agreed that Georgia Brown was very fine in the title role, and most were impressed as well with the voice of the Metropolitan's former Don Giovanni Cesare Siepi, as her long-suffering, lovesick suitor Vittorio. His was the only authentic Italian accent in the show; Georgia Brown, for her part, managed not to sound too British (she had made a most triumphant New York debut in 1963's *Oliver!*).

Every reviewer pointed out the show's *démodé* character, from the songs (many of which were nonetheless admired) to the sets by Oliver Smith (which were not). These same critics were only too aware of just *how* new a musical could be, having seen the innovative Stephen Sondheim shocker *Sweeney Todd* on its opening only the month before. *Time*, for one, called *Carmelina* a fossil. The program note stated, "The time is 1961," but one wag retorted that it could just as well have been 1921.

Of the songs, two of the ballads, "It's Time for a Love Song" and "Someone in April" (particularly Lane's melodies) were generally appreciated, as was the trio sung by the putative fathers, "One More Walk Around the Garden," likewise a ballad. More rhythmic were the marchlike "Signora Campbell" and the Italianate title song. In "I'm a Woman," meanwhile, Lerner brilliantly expressed a feminist, almost defiant mood of the time (if one could get past the unfortunate rhyming of *gorilla* with *villa* and *killer*).

Carmelina closed after seventeen performances. Neither Lerner nor Lane fully agreed with the criticisms, and Lerner even believed that had he taken over the direction (from José Ferrer), he "could have turned that show around" in a week. Lane differed with him on that point, but he did feel their work could be salvaged, with revisions. He and Lerner went so far as to talk about staging a revival in London, but it never happened.

The experience took its toll. Prior to a tribute to be given to Lerner and Loewe by the Theatre Collection of the Museum of the City of New York, Lerner was interviewed in the Le Roy Hospital. As reporter Robert Wahls, of the *New York Post* delicately worded it, Lerner had had a cyst "removed from his bottom." The most recent Mrs. Lerner, Nina, who was present for part of the interview, fluffed her husband's pillow and rather pointedly said, "Alan likes to be babied even when he's not hospitalized." Lerner admitted that he liked plenty of attention. The benefit-tribute for him and Loewe, at this dreary time—given *Carmelina*'s recent closing—seemed as much a memorial as a celebration of his work. But a reunion with Loewe, who would come in from Palm Springs, would give him a cheering opportunity to recall their golden past.

The old collaborators arrived at the Winter Garden on May 15, 1979 (Lerner had left the hospital earlier), and were given the star treatment by such stars as Julie Andrews, Rex Harrison, Alfred Drake, Louis Jourdan, and others. Lerner admitted he was "touched and honored." With Loewe at the piano, he sang some of their songs, and passages from his recently published book, *On the Street Where I Live*, were read to an audience as star-studded as the roster of participants (in attendance were Gloria Vanderbilt, the Joshua Logans, Claudette Colbert, et al.). It was a glorious evening of nostalgia, but at the same time a final reminder that the days of Lerner and Loewe were over.

There was also the crumbling of the lyricist's seventh marriage. Burton Lane had sensed that a breakup was coming even "before we opened [*Carmelina*]." Before that could become the stuff of public speculation, however, Lerner's laundry would be subjected to further public airings as, late in October, Micheline Lerner descended yet again. A Manhattan judge named her the receiver of Alan Lerner's personal property; she was claiming more than twelve thousand dollars for the nonpayment of alimony and child support owed her for the previous July and August. The *Times* reported that Justice Hortense W. Gabel "showed some annoyance with Mr. Lerner, pointing out that three judges [had] tried to get him to meet his payments." His conduct, she said, "was outrageously contumacious of the judicial process."

On November 21, the *Post* ran a column with a succinct header: "4th Ex-wife Sues for Sixth Time." Justice Felice Shea ruled that Lerner's poverty plea was "unsubstantiated," and his fourth ex was awarded a very substantial fifty thousand dollars, plus an additional fifty thousand as bond. Such judgments were good neither for his finances nor for his health.

But still he left for Cleveland to appear at the Playhouse on November 28, in apparent good health and spirits, for an evening of his songs. It was a good evening, away from the strife he had left behind. He tossed off a characteristic line when he told a reporter that he regarded his own singing as "democratic" because he gave every note a chance. He also made a reference to a new musical he was working on with French composer Michel Legrand (*The Umbrellas of Cherbourg*, etc.), to be called *The Mountains of Peru*.

On returning to New York, he read in "Suzy"'s column in the *News*, in early December, that "Alan Jay Lerner and his seventh wife, Nina, have separated and their marriage is on the rocks, something I reported weeks ago might happen."

Lerner, she further confided, planned to "live and work in London." It was certainly true that the American political climate made him uncomfortable: in Teheran, Iranian "students" had seized the U.S. Embassy, taking more than sixty Americans hostage, while at home an actor, Ronald Reagan, was actually making a second run at the presidency (after winning only one electoral vote in the previous election). When Richard Rodgers died, later in the month, one newspaper repeated Lerner's remark, "Dick's got that pipeline to heaven that goes through him"—a gracious comment by the lyricist about one of his least favorite people.

By April 1980 Nina Lerner had engaged two divorce experts (even *Lerner* divorce experts), Marvin Mitchelson and Roy Cohn. She was quoted in the *Post* (on April 24, 1980) as saying of her husband,

> I loved him when I married him three years ago. I think at the time I thought because of my show business background, I was going to make the difference, . . . could change him.
>
> I didn't notice [his age] at all when we were alone together [she was by then twenty-nine, Lerner sixty-one]. Alan is very young at

heart. But when we were with his friends it became very obvious—
some of his friends are eighty years old.

Her attorneys constructed a rather desperate image of Lerner, who, it was claimed, offered her one half of his income to stay, then raised the figure to 70 percent. This was not true; she and Lerner had in fact made a private, more sensible agreement. But that would go awry, too.

With the plans for the divorce settled, Lerner—for once—had no one waiting in the wings. And, too, he was professionally at loose ends. He left for the comparative peace of Europe, though there would be more hands-across-the-sea strife in April 1981, when the indefatigably bellicose Micheline came up for air again briefly to demand more funding for herself and her attorney, Raoul Lionel Felder. They would get it.

Still, that year would bring a new magic into Lerner's life through the happy fortuity of *My Fair Lady*.

16

—⚍—

NUMBER 13

THE PROVIDENTIAL TRAIN of events began somewhere in the provinces of Britain with a 1978 revival of *My Fair Lady*, one of several since the musical's London premiere twenty years before. Late in 1979, when the show was set to open in London after the tour, Lerner was asked to guest-direct for the occasion. Happy to be doing something definite (and a sure success!), he accepted. The Eliza of this production was Liz (née Elizabeth) Robertson, a young London-born-and-bred singer-actress. Lerner was then living in Paris, trying to initiate a new work and getting nowhere with it; the flight to London was quick and simple, and it was pleasant work. It was not long before he was smitten with the latest Eliza.

Liz Robertson was not born into show business (her father, though musical, was a Port Authority of London policeman), but with her mother's encouragement, she evidenced an early ambition to appear on the musical stage. She began as a dancer with a group called the Young Generation, and at age twenty-one made her West End debut in the 1975 production of Sondheim's *A Little Night Music*. Before starring in *My Fair Lady*, she had also been cast in the Cy Coleman–Michael Stewart musical *I Love My Wife*.

The new *My Fair Lady* was a success, as was its star, whom its author soon began seeing regularly, at times taking time off from his work in Paris (which was still not going well). It was a tentative "courtship," what with his being on the verge of yet another failed marriage, their three-decade age disparity, and even a couple of inches' difference in their respective heights (she being the taller of the two—an important fact to both). He had practically made up his mind to return to New York, but their meeting and growing affection for each other changed his mind: Why not leave unproductive Paris and settle in London instead?

Once his divorce from Nina Bushkin was final, he moved to London and took a house in the historic Chelsea section, which one of its earlier residents, James McNeill Whistler, who lived across the street from Oscar Wilde, had called the "wonderful village." The area's artistic and literary associations (to such as Henry James and Thomas Carlyle) were attractive to Lerner, and it was there that he brought Liz Robertson following their marriage in a simple ceremony in Billingsworth, Sussex, on August 13, 1981. She was then appearing onstage in a new play, *The Mitford Girls*, at the Chichester Festival.

Accompanying the notice of the wedding was the news that Lerner had completed a screenplay for a new production of *The Merry Widow*. Earlier, in May, when he was still in Paris, it had been announced by producers Steve Paul and Larry Sugar that he was, in fact, working on yet *another* screenplay, this one entitled *Melissa*, and further, that he and Michel Legrand were collaborating on a "contemporary love story due for production in New York in the summer of 1982" (perhaps the same one mentioned in 1979, *The Mountains of Peru*). In the end nothing would come of any of these promises, except that Lerner would later write the lyric for a screen title song to be included in Legrand's score for *The Secret Places*.

It had also been reported, in August 1979, that he had again turned his attention to the adaptation of Sherwood's *Idiot's Delight*, and that his collaborator on the project would be Charles Strouse. New Yorker Strouse (born 1928) had reached Broadway by a roundabout traverse: After study at the Eastman School of Music (in Rochester, New York), he was awarded a scholarship to study with Aaron Copland at Tanglewood, in Massachusetts, then went on to France to study with the legendary Nadia Boulanger. These "serious" studies resulted in a symphony and a string quartet (as well as, much later, a children's opera entitled *The Nightingale*). Like so many other ambitious young musicians, Strouse soon learned that while awaiting his big break in the concert world, he could make his living in the world of popular music, and for a number of summers he took the Catskills route, writing revues for the well-known resort Green Mansions. He spent his springs and winters as a rehearsal pianist or accompanist. At Green Mansions he met writer-editor Lee

Adams, with whom he teamed up to contribute songs to Off Broadway revues beginning in 1955. Five years later, they collaborated on an affectionate spoof of the Elvis Presley craze (with a book by Michael Stewart); *Bye Bye Birdie* was an enormous success. Their next, *All American* (1962), was less well received, but it featured one of Alan Lerner's favorite songs, "Once Upon a Time." Although the Strouse-Adams partnership had its ups and downs, the peaks were memorable: *Golden Boy* (with Sammy Davis, Jr., 1964), *Applause* (with Lauren Bacall, 1970), and *Annie* (lyrics by Martin Charnin, 1977), which ran nearly as long as *My Fair Lady*.

Paying affectionate tribute to Lerner, Strouse recalled his first, embarrassing meeting with the lyricist when both were on a New York–to–Los Angeles flight.

> [Lerner's] face and fortune were well known to all of us in the musical theatre. Not only was I sure he wouldn't know me, but at this particular moment I had to go to him and ask him to lend me some money. For his was the only face I knew on the plane, and stupidly, having packed in a rush, I had boarded without my credit card or any cash.
>
> I introduced myself, and he was really quite gracious about it, and he lent me forty bucks. I've heard him tell this story, and as he told it, he loaned me ninety bucks. This is typical of him. Alan Jay Lerner never lies, but he lives in a world much larger and grander than most of us. . . .This is his charm. He lives the improbable dream, and more times than not, gets away with it. As a lyricist and playwright, he aims higher, hits bigger and (seldom) falls farther.

Annie was still running on Broadway and had recently opened at the Victoria Palace in London when Lerner phoned from that city to suggest that he and Strouse collaborate on a musical. Write with *the* Alan Jay Lerner, Strouse thought—who wouldn't say yes? After they agreed to the deal over the phone, Lerner flew to New York to read the composer his version of *Idiot's Delight* (the script was completed, but the songs had yet to be spotted).

Having prepared himself by reading Sherwood's original, Strouse had to admit that he did not quite get Sherwood's point, although it had been a popular play and movie and supposedly a dark comedy, ending as it did with the outbreak of war, Lerner's revised plot was woven around a much more devastating conflict—obviously, Strouse felt, something more disturbing was on Lerner's mind. Besides, Strouse believed, it had been conceived as a "Valentine to [Sherwood's] wife."

It took the composer some time to get to know his new collaborator. Lerner was, Strouse noted, "passionate and romantic"; like so many of the characters he had created, he dreamed of the "perfect world, the perfect woman. . . . I am much more of a realist than Alan. . . . You can imagine what a joy it is for a composer to work with such a man." He had, of course, heard the Broadway tales about Lerner's indifference to schedules and appointments; while he believed that Lerner never lied, Strouse did concede that he was a great "fabricator." Both Leonard Bernstein and Burton Lane warned him about this quirk, about how Lerner would make an appointment only to show up hours late with a good story, but Strouse himself had no trouble with this idiosyncrasy. "I understood" he said. "I am late sometimes, or forget—so it didn't bother me." And in this collaboration, unlike the one with Lane, the lyrics arrived on time. Lerner was especially anxious to fashion a musical for the woman he called "my first wife": The world situation that inspired his libretto may have been an unhappy one, but the period spent on writing *Dance a Little Closer* was a contented, creative time for Alan Jay Lerner. The Burton Lanes could see this, as could such other friends as Maurice and Bobby Baird Levine. Levine was the creator and master of ceremonies for the 92nd Street Y's long-running "Lyrics and Lyricist" series devoted to the authentic presentation of the works of the men and women who wrote the words to the great popular songs. He had met Lerner at the home of Kurt Weill in 1949, when Levine was the music director of *Lost in the Stars*. His wife, Bobby Baird, was a vocalist noted for her musicianship and projection of lyrics; she was one of Lerner's favorite interpreters and appeared with him at the Y. They, and others, agreed that he had finally found that ideal woman.

He had begun work on his adaptation long before its official announcement in the *Times* in August 1981; according to a good friend, the author, composer, and popular-music authority Benny Green, it dated from sometime before November 1979. When the two men met by chance one day in a London street, Lerner informed him that he had just been completing the libretto of what Green calls his "wry comedy about the imminence of a world war" when he heard on the radio that the "Russians had invaded Afghanistan, a confluence of events so startling that he wondered playfully if his writing of the text had had some malign telepathic influence over the Kremlin." This is exactly the sort of coincidence that would appeal to Lerner, who once said,

"The weight of evidence is that we all have a vast latent extra-sensory perception" (though he himself never claimed any such experience). Just as Sherwood's play had predicted the Second World War, his adaptation, set in what he termed "The Avoidable Future," warned of a Third.

If Charles Strouse did not quite understand *Idiot's Delight* the first time he read it, Robert Sherwood, who died in 1955, might himself have had a hard time following Lerner's adaptation. Aside from some "updating," the plot is left pretty much intact, though Lerner did introduce some character permutations and even name changes. Sherwood's third-rate hoofer, originally portrayed by Alfred Lunt, was named Harry Van; Lerner renamed him Harry Aikens. Playing opposite Lunt was his real-life wife, Lynn Fontanne, as Irene; in that role in the musical was Mrs. Lerner, more elegantly called Cynthia Brookfield Bailey. Eliminated altogether was the Sherwood character Dumptsy, whose name was no loss.

Sherwood's plot, à la *Grand Hotel*, brings together a group of not especially compatible people in a pretentious but not impressive hotel in the Italian Alps, near the Swiss and Austrian borders. From its windows, the management boasts, can be seen no fewer than four countries—plus an Italian military airfield. Gathered in the cocktail lounge are a wealthy munitions manufacturer accompanied by his probable mistress, a spectacular blonde (Irene/Cynthia); a German scientist on the verge of finding a cancer cure; an excitable radical labor agitator; a young English honeymoon couple; assorted Italian soldiers and the hotel staff; and, last, Harry, the third-rate hoofer, and his troupe of six "girls"—all blondes. They sing and dance (one is a bubble dancer, another a fan dancer), and Harry, too, sings and dances—badly—and plays the piano.

The plot, with war imminent, revolves around the efforts on the part of all the guests to get permission from the Italian government to leave for the invariably neutral Switzerland. Interwoven into this, besides some Sherwoodian disquisitions on the pointlessness of war, is the slender thread of Harry's certainty that he and the blond mistress have met before and had a brief fling (which he has never forgotten) in a cheap Omaha hotel. Although not then a blonde, the woman had been a masterful liar; Irene (Cynthia) likewise never tells the same story twice.

When war comes (after the Italian bombers from the nearby field attack Paris), all the foreigners are cleared to go, save for Irene, whose passport has expired and who herself has been abandoned by the munitions magnate because she knows too much about his business methods. Everyone flees, except the labor agitator, shot for treasonable talk, and Irene, who now has the whole place to herself. She has confessed to Harry that she is indeed the woman he fell in love with in Omaha, and after seeing his troupe off to Switzerland on the train, he returns to the hotel.

The play ends with the arrival of French bombers bound to retaliate for the bombing of Paris. As the sounds of war fill the air, Irene and Harry sing "Onward, Christian Soldiers," in Sherwood's final ironic comment. His title, too, served as a wry metaphor: Idiot's delight is another name for the game of solitaire.

Earlier, Irene bitterly congratulates the munitions maker, Weber, on "all this great, wonderful death and destruction, everywhere. And you promoted it!"

Weber, in turn, protests that he is merely the "humble instrument of His divine will," the servant of God, "who put fear in man."

"Yes," Irene replies, "that's quite true. We don't do half enough justice to Him. Poor, lonely old soul. Sitting up in Heaven with nothing to do but play solitaire. Poor, dear God. Playing idiot's delight. The game that never means anything, and never ends."

Lerner discarded Sherwood's title in favor of his own, *Dance a Little Closer*, though the original reference remains, in the song "Anyone Who Loves": "We're only living by the hour/While the sages with the power/Play their game of peace and war/With no shred of pity for/Anyone who lives/Anyone who loves." Then,

> *We're here surrounded by the night*
> *While God plays idiot's delight.*
> *Why can't there be a ray of sun*
> *That shines on anyone*
> *Who loves?*

Lerner has Harry address this song to the Reverend Boyle (his creation, not Sherwood's), who has just balked at presiding over what he regards as a perturbing marriage. Lerner's adaptation has its own Grand Hotel cast of characters: Weber, the "merchant of death," has become Dr. Josef Winkler, a mysterious diplomat with a decided resemblance to Henry Kissinger (not one of Lerner's favorite people); the newlywed English couple, meanwhile, has given way to another couple whom the reverend cannot bring himself to marry— two young members of an air crew, both men. These two transformations alienated the critics. John Simon, writing in *New York*, damned the "silly homosexual subplot—meant to be with-it and liberal, but actually . . . dated and patronizing." And further, he asked, "Who can believe a charming Kissinger?" (though in fact, Kissinger could be very charming indeed and was the darling of the rich and famous). Lerner's Dr. Winkler, described in the book as an "American diplomat. A genius," is an Austrian-American; Kissinger was born in Germany but fled that country with his family in 1938: it is a thin disguise.

As for Simon's objection to the homosexual subplot, a similar storyline had proved acceptable in Off Off Broadway and Off Broadway productions of the praised *March of the Falsettos* two years before, and would be even better received when *La Cage aux Folles* opened later in 1983, four months after *Dance a Little Closer*.

Lerner was excited about this, his thirteenth Broadway musical; thirteen, he maintained, was his lucky number. There were thirteen letters in his name. Besides, as in London, he would be directing his "first wife." It was a happy time for him.

In an interview given around this time, he emphasized that *Dance a Little Closer* was "primarily entertainment," and insisted that though he was "passionate about disarmament," his was not an antinuclear play. But it *was* a message play—just the sort of musical he and Loewe had disdained in their romantic golden years. The failed *1600 Pennsylvania Avenue*, too, had carried a message; *Dance a Little Closer* was intended as another march on Washington. (Even as Lerner worked in June 1982, more than eight hundred thousand protesters—men, women, and children—filled the streets of Manhattan and Central Park in a demonstration against nuclear proliferation, hoping, in the words of Coretta Scott King, to get the "message . . . through to the [Reagan] White House and Capitol Hill." The show of strength did not work.)

Lerner's most direct commentary on the administration's attitude and actions is a duet entitled "What Are You Gonna Do About It?" A young, excitable student (student protests and the Kent State killings were fresh in Lerner's mind as he wrote) is furious over the doctor's casual indifference both to the mobilization of NATO forces in the airfield below and to the Russian threat of attack. He addresses the one calm individual in the bunch, Harry, who explains that he is calm because what can he, or anyone else not in power, do?

> *What are you gonna do about it?*
> *Stand up on an Alp and shout:*

> *"Fellers go away.*
> *Don't wanna play."*
> *And they'll turn around and all go home.*
> *Exactly as you hope.*
> *And tomorrow I will be elected Pope.*

Unlike Sherwood's Harry, Lerner's is a cynic.

The student, Heinrich Holloway (another Lerner invention in place of Sherwood's left-wing labor leader), states the basic message of the play when he chides Harry:

> *How can you forget*
> *That any threat*
> *Is to us all?*
> *No one can hide*
> *Behind a wall.*
> *Is it games or something more?*
> *Can you see this could be war?*

(The doctor has dismissed the commotion on the field as mere war games. He professes to know nothing about what is going on—but if so, why is he there? When Cynthia pries, he answers, "A war? While I am on holiday? Of course not, *puuchen*." For all his surface charm, Dr. Winkler is duplicitous, cold, shrewd, an egotist.)

"Lerner's book and lyrics," the unsympathetic John Simon said, "are unable to create a single genuine character, let alone a believable relationship, and neither the love story nor the political tract has the slightest urgency, poignancy, or credibility." Douglas Watt, in the *News*, found the play "chilly, charmless and foolhardy." (Watt, it might be noted, was himself a songwriter and often reviewed popular music for the *New Yorker*.)

All of these assessments were, unfortunately, too true. Even the Cynthia character, described in the libretto as being "in her late twenties, English, beautiful and furred to the teeth," is not very attractive. She is a fraud, she is selfish, and her desire for "creature comforts" is not of the same stripe as that of Eliza Doolittle. In a flashback, the audience sees Harry and Cynthia in the cheap motel (Lerner's touch; there were few of these in Sherwood's time). They have spent the night together, and Harry is elated, singing "There's Never Been Anything Like Us!" He wants to go on, but Cynthia sings:

> The way to my heart
> Is through the lobby of the Ritz,
> With a diamond this big
> That my finger just fits.
> The way to my heart
> Is on a Concorde through the sky.
> Can you manage all that?
> [Harry answers no.]
> Then good-bye.

She admits she "likes" Harry. "You're what I want, Harry," she tells him, "but what I need, you're not." She knows about love and what it is worth: "I want the moon, Harry. You got the earth." She sings that she wants "Another Life"—with satin sheets, a maid, breakfast in bed—and wants, too, to be known and "to live so near the sky/So high I'll never hear a train go by."

It is not until the middle of the second act that the audience gets a glimpse of her compassion. In a long musical sequence, "I Don't Know," the Reverend Boyle, in a quandary, explains that he does not know what to do about the marriage request of Charles and Edward. Virtually all the cast joins in to voice its views—first Harry, then his troupe (the Delights), a stylish contessa, and, finally, Cynthia:

> Anyone who loves,
> People anywhere;
> Anyone who loves,
> They deserve a prayer.

She "bitterly" berates the "sages with power [who] play their game of peace and war," without a shred of pity to spare for anyone, and Harry concludes with some words to the reverend, telling him "We're here surrounded by that night/While God plays idiot's delight."

At the end of the play, Cynthia confesses that she feels about Harry as he has felt about her, but by this time the audience can barely believe it.

The most reprehensible character in the story is, of course, Dr. Winkler, who abandons Cynthia because she begins asking too many questions. When the border opens again, he leaves with the contessa, with whom he has been flirting a good deal throughout. Although he has an opportunity to do something about Cynthia's expired passport, he chooses to leave her behind.

When Harry learns this, he leaves the Delights on the train and returns to Cynthia in the hotel's lounge. Alone together, they sing "Dance a Little Closer" but are drowned out by the din of aircraft engines as the curtain comes down.

Variety's reviewer allowed that "Liz Robertson has sensual appeal, projects emotion and has a lovely voice," but found "Lerner's staging . . . heavy and blocky" and the play's construction weak. While suggesting that the "score could use more variety," he conceded that "there are several excellent songs." He did wish to point out, however, that the first three songs in the "second act have nothing to do with the main story."

This was something of an overstatement: Lerner had his reasons. In the first of these numbers, "Homesick," the Delights express their longing to return to the States, even if it means going back to such unlovely realities as Three Mile Island, the San Andreas Fault, and Love Canal (Watt, of the *News*, objected to the first and third references). The song is quite in keeping with the concerns of a traveling crew anxious to get home.

The next number, Harry's "Mad," is equally in character. It is, too, one of Lerner's most brilliant lyrics, though it is true that it could easily fit into any musical containing a character who wanted (or whom the lyricist wanted) to air his annoyance with current social irritants: Marilyn Monroe picture books, the Japanese (who "have made everything I own"), being a "digital dot" in a data bank, and the fact that [gangster] "Meyer Lansky died in his sleep." Harry even proclaims,

> *I'm mad at places*
> *I can't pronounce.*
> *I'm sick of bosoms*
> *That never bounce.*

Interspersed between his short-phrased, choppy rantings is a brief, almost dreamy responsorial commentary; in lovely contrast to Harry's angry, rhythmic calls, the responses are sung in harmony by the Delights. They know why he is mad—because "he's mad about her." "Mad" is an ingeniously conceived and constructed song, not so much a song or aria as an inventive musical dissertation.

The third song of act 2, while not directly associated with the main story, is nonetheless important to the plot. This is "I Don't Know (Anyone Who Loves)," which treats the topic of the homosexual marriage and in which, in the last section, Cynthia and Harry sympathetically agree (at last) on *something*. But the *Variety* critic missed that point, too.

He did state, with the customary authority of the "grave dancer," that "Alan Jay Lerner is trying to do too much . . . in a clinker that can't survive on Broadway." He could not resist the irresistible joke: "The alternate title for the show among unfeeling trade gagsters, *Close a Little Faster*, will likely prove accurate." By the time the review came out, in the weekly *Variety* dated May 18, *Dance a Little Closer* was gone.

Alan Jay Lerner's lucky thirteenth opened at the Minskoff Theatre on May 11, 1983; it closed the same night.

FINALE

C LOSING IN BOSTON during a tryout tour was bad enough; lasting only a single performance in New York was depressing and humiliating. The *Herald Tribune*'s headline was especially galling: "*Dance* a Little Too Close to Schlock."

Besides pillorying his libretto, Broadway insiders were hard on Lerner himself: consensus held that the librettist should not share the director's job (also implied was that the director should not cast his wife as the show's star). Then, too, he was too lavish with the sets, which comprised not only a double-tiered lounge (the main set) but also—and this was the source of the *Tribune*'s "schlock"—a suite for Winkler, a motel room, and even an ice-skating rink. All this added to production costs and to the size of the tech crew. (The rink served merely as a setting for a brief flirtation scene—on skates—between Winkler and the contessa, as Cynthia watches and then sings "He Always Comes Home to Me.")

The plot may not have been hopeful or sunny, but then neither was the state of the world or what appeared to be its no longer "Avoidable Future."

On the day of the show's first rehearsal, March 7, 1983, President Ronald Reagan made a historic evaluation of the Soviet Union, calling it the Evil Empire. The Russians' rejoinder was that this leader of the Free World and of a major military power had a "pathological hatred of Socialism and

Communism." Two weeks later, when *Dance*'s rehearsals were in full swing, the president unveiled his response: plans for a Strategic Defense Initiative (or SDI, derisively known as Star Wars among the scientific community) that would carry war into outer space.

The metaphor in Lerner's title had become chillingly timely: The two massive military camps were themselves now dancing close to the ultimate edge. When Sherwood's play first opened, his projected war was three years distant and an ocean away; Lerner's, in contrast, was imminent and horrifyingly close to home. The audience found this possibility as alienating as some of the more unappealing characters in the musical.

That had not been Lerner's intention, of course. He did want to express concern for the state of the world, but his dream was to avoid a dread future, not to chronicle it. He once said that he did not "believe that there is such a thing as 'realism' in the theatre. If there were, there would never be a third act." *Dance a Little Closer* might be no more realistic than *Oklahoma!*, but its implied message was all too real for its audience.

"Fundamentally," he once said, "I suppose I'm more interested in the dreams of man, which are eternal, than in the temporary perversions of those dreams called reality." His dream for a war-free world was rejected, but after all, it was only a musical. In his next work—and there always had to be a next work—he would return to dreaming, this time with just a touch of contemporary reality.

If the dismal failure of Lerner's *Dance a Little Closer* sent shudders through the music industry, the confirmation that year that he had left the American Society for Composers, Authors and Publishers (ASCAP) for its rival, Broadcast Music Incorporated (BMI), unleashed a tremor.

ASCAP had been founded in 1914 by a group of songwriters, music publishers, and, yes, lawyers to protect the copyrights of composers and lyricists, whose works, until that time, could be performed in hotels and restaurants without payment to the creators. It thrived on revenues from the compositions of Irving Berlin, Richard Rodgers, the Gershwins, Oscar Hammerstein, and others—the elite of American popular music. (Originally, two published songs entitled a writer to membership.) Soon the names of Aaron Copland, Leonard Bernstein, and Igor Stravinsky were added to the society's membership—in short, everybody who, musically, was anybody belonged to ASCAP. In 1941, Frederick Loewe became a member; Alan Jay Lerner joined in 1945.

The organization was a powerful force in the music industry—and a propitious one for the songwriters—from its inception until 1940, when the radio industry rebelled (just in time to keep Loewe's songs off the air). Arguing that they were tired of paying ever-rising royalties to a "monopoly" (which ASCAP was by default, being the only organization of its kind in the United States), radio stations across the country united in a boycott of ASCAP music. For more than a year, only music in the public domain was broadcast, and newly written popular songs as well as new film and show scores suffered, as did, in their own way, the quasi–folk songs of Stephen Foster. "Jeannie with the Light Brown Hair," according to historian and "Tune Detective" Sigmund Speath, "was literally played to death."

In 1940 BMI began signing young, unknown songwriters to generous contracts, and in time such songs as "I Hear a Rhapsody" and "High on a Windy Hill" (by vocalist Joan Whitney and voice teacher Alex Kramer) became popular, though radio's vaunted Hit Parade, in Speath's view, "utterly failed to live up to its title."

Finally, in 1941, following the intervention of the federal government, an agreement was reached and the deadlock broken, somewhat to ASCAP's detriment: It was forced to remit a large fee to a legal peacemaker, accept a reduction in royalties, and withdraw its potential infringement suits against the networks. BMI was here to stay.

The new organization, unloved by the Berlins, Rodgerses, Arlens, and others, encouraged the membership of young writers of country-and-western music (once disparaged as "hillbilly"), rhythm and blues, and its progeny, rock and roll. Eventually, as BMI grew, it moved into ASCAP's major territory, theater and film. In a changing music industry, ASCAP, home of the traditionalists, itself now changed, going so far as to open an office in Nashville and venture into country music, even rock. With time, too, the hostility between ASCAP and BMI faded, as did any distinction between their respective memberships—though ASCAP remains the giant in the field of theater and "serious" music as exemplified by Copland, Gershwin, and Gould (BMI does have Ives and William Schuman).

But by the 1980s Alan Lerner was angry at ASCAP and especially fed up with some of its lower-level, everyday executives. In need of funds, he found only unsympathetic ears among them. So in 1983 he packed up his songs and went elsewhere. His leaving shocked his peers in the society, such greats as Irving Berlin, Ira Gershwin, and Harold Arlen. Although the exalted "AA" classification (that is, in the highest royalty payment category) had long since been abandoned, the older hands remembered it and knew that like them, Lerner qualified; as such, he enjoyed a substantial portion of ASCAP's annual yield. It was Ira Gershwin who quipped, "As long as I have ASCAP, I won't have to pass cap." In his later years, Berlin checked in regularly with president Morton Gould to see how things were going, while Harold Arlen, for his part, served on the board and worried that something might go wrong. Lerner's defection from this trusted organization seemed tantamount to treason.

Lerner had his reasons, though, and he had earlier voiced them to friend and veteran publisher Tommy Valando. Regarded as a small publisher in comparison to Chappell and Warner Brothers, Valando was nonetheless admired within the industry as "aggressive." Among the songwriters he worked with were Sheldon Harnick, Kander and Ebb, and Stephen Sondheim. He lent a sympathetic ear to a quite bitter Alan Jay Lerner, and then he introduced him to BMI's president, Edward M. Cramer.

"Alan Jay Lerner, BMI," sounded great to Cramer, but he had to be careful. Was Lerner certain he wanted to move from ASCAP?

"I don't want to deal with them!"

"I'm not so sure you're making the right move. We would like to have you here at BMI, but I don't know what I can promise."

Still Lerner persisted, and Cramer happily agreed. He advised him, "Give us a six-month trial; if you are unhappy, you will be free to leave."

As one BMI composer put it, "BMI pays up front." An arrangement was worked out and approved by the BMI board, and Lerner was given a cash advance based on his ASCAP earnings of the year before—and against his future royalties. (When the news broke, rumor had it that the advance was more than a million dollars, a figure Cramer has denied: "Nonsense! Completely untrue.")

Thus temporarily relieved, Lerner could turn to his next project. After *Dance a Little Closer*'s instantaneous death, he and his wife returned to Chelsea, where he considered his next show, something with a lighter theme than corruption in the White House or impending nuclear war. He selected *My Man Godfrey*, a 1936 classic of the "screwball" genre. With a screenplay by Morrie Ryskind and Eric Hatch, the film had starred Carole Lombard and William Powell. In the eponymous role, Powell played a jobless "forgotten man" opposite Lombard's scatterbrained rich girl, Irene, who finds him in a city dump during a society scavenger hunt and hires him to be her butler (he would turn out to be a kind of American Jeeves).

During the Depression, such escapist screwball comedies and light-hearted/light-headed musicals had been extraordinarily popular. Such box-office hits as *Nothing Sacred, It Happened One Night*, and the Fred Astaire—Ginger Rogers screen musicals had brought in a great deal of money at a time when there was little of it to spend.

Lerner began by making a detailed outline consisting of fifty sequences, coinciding closely with the Ryskind-Hatch screenplay. He then divided these into ten scenes, the first three of which he substantially fleshed out, adding several lyrics. Scenes 4 through 10 exist in outline form only, though with indications for reprises and spots for new titles. One of these latter, "March of the Dollars," was to be sung in the mansion of Irene's millionaire father, himself quickly going broke and in need of saving by the astute Godfrey.

Lerner set his play in the present, not in the film's 1934, as is made clear in the opening song, "Got a Job?" That the idle rich or the "yuppies" of 1984—the year Lerner worked up his outline—participated in scavenger hunts is doubtful, but he left that in. Godfrey, too, remains a forgotten man (at the time of the film, he would have been a veteran of the First World War), homeless and out of work. In the play, the character was to be more complex than that embodied on film by the smooth, unflappable Powell. Lerner's was more of a social comedy than a screwball romp, the product of a darker vision in an era of Reaganomics and, in his part-time new homeland, Margaret Thatcher's reelection as Prime Minister.

Both the outline and the completed lyrics indicate that Lerner intended to make a political statement, one a good deal sharper than that delivered by the original film, with its depiction of the rich as money-grubbing and heartless yet shrewd fools. His opening lyric sets the tone in its lament that "Garbage Isn't What It Used to Be." With no "discarded caviar," no "half-smoked good cigar," it concludes, "Garbage isn't what it used to be/It's an insult to democracy."

"I've Been Married" has some fun with the cutesy names then common in society columns: those "weekends with Piggy and Deedee and Mousey and Mimsy," says Godfrey, were enough to make him want to tear everyone from "limbsy to limbsy." A further victim of the Lerner wit is "Miss Hilary Bacon of Beacon Hill," a "Back Bay bimbo with looks to kill."

Lerner was getting along well in his work when the Internal Revenue Service struck. The *New York Post* reported on July 9, 1984, that Lerner was suing Israel Katz, Milton Pearlman, and Sherman Saiger because they "left him with an IRS bill he shouldn't have to pay," as they had used Alan Jay Lerner productions as "a conduit for various business transactions totalling $430,000." The IRS was now demanding $215,000 from Lerner.

"It is not my income," he tried to explain in July 1984, "and they [i.e., the accounting firm] should have to pay the tax on it. I am a playwright and lyricist and not familiar with business affairs and taxes." It was a stressful burden that never seemed to go away.

When he returned to *Godfrey* during a temporary calm, he felt he was far enough along to begin searching for the right collaborator—preferably someone close at hand. He approached James Henning, of Chappell's London office, for suggestions.

Henning told him about Gerard Kenny, an American composer-pianist who was then living in London. In 1979 he had composed a hit song with lyricist Drey Shepperd, called "Love"; that same year they also collaborated on "I Made It Through the Rain," which became an exceptional hit for Barry Manilow. Just the year before, in 1983, Kenny had had yet another fine song in "Not Just Another Pretty Face"; he was working in London with British producer-performer Ned Sherrin on *Jack*, a musical based on the career of dancer-choreographer Jack Cole.

He sounded fine to Lerner, so Henning called and asked him if he would be interested in collaborating with an American lyricist on a musical.

"Has he done anything?" Kenny asked.

"Yes," Henning replied. "*Brigadoon, Paint Your Wagon, My Fair Lady, Camelot—*"

"Alan Jay Lerner?!"

Gerard Kenny was very interested indeed, and he arranged to come around to the Lerner home in Chelsea.

Born in New York in 1947, Kenny was a graduate of the College of Music at Hofstra University. He divided his time between composing and earning his living as a pianist; in England he was also busy making recordings. He met Lerner in October 1984.

"He looked great," he recalled. "Tan, very 'up,' in extremely good humor." Kenny noted the three Oscars on the mantelpiece. After some talk, he played some of his tunes for Lerner, who immediately took to calling him "my boy": They would collaborate on *My Man Godfrey*. Lerner had yet another idea in mind (as always), but Kenny rejected it as being "too downbeat" (though he could not later recall what it was).

Kenny remembered their working hard, no less than five days a week. He was impressed with the affectionate relationship between the Lerners. Lerner was obviously creating the part of Irene for Liz Robertson; for Godfrey they had in mind Alan Bates, who had made his reputation in such films as *King of Hearts, Far from the Madding Crowd*, and A *Day in the Life of Joe Egg*.

Collaborating with Lerner, for Kenny, was a pleasure. Even though he was an unabashed admirer of the lyricist, his view of a song was still respected; he was never made to feel that he was privileged to be working with a legend.

Then there was the day when Lerner said, "My boy, if only I can make it past sixty-seven." He was then sixty-six; Kenny later learned that Joseph Lerner had died at that age.

Their work having come along well since their October meeting, the collaborators made an official announcement of their partnership, which appeared in the *New York Times* in March 1985. They took time out briefly to come to New York, where on March 18 Lerner received the National Academy of Popular Music's Johnny Mercer Award, a coveted honor voted by the recipient's peers. He was photographed after the event with BMI's Edward Cramer, holding the plaque hailing him as a "lyrical combination of elegance, literacy and wit." (The word *elegant* certainly applied to the tuxedo he wore, with a then-oversized black tie.) He obligingly posed for another photograph with Cramer clutching the plaque; his smile is tight, and he looks all of his sixty-six years.

In celebration of Lerner's receipt of the award, *Daily News* writer Don Nelson wrote a short article for BMI's magazine, *Music World*. The piece gives a good overview of its subject's career and accomplishments, though it provides few revelations. Even *Dance a Little Closer* is acknowledged, if only as an example of the producer-author's willingness to discuss the weaknesses and strengths of a show, since "he has control of both functions." Nelson adds, "Lerner also has strong political convictions and they showed up in *Closer*, which was a plea for more understanding in the international community and against the possibility of nuclear holocaust."

The reporter goes on to note a detail that had piqued Kenny's curiosity during their work sessions. "Unless Lerner has changed his habits, he still wears white gloves while working," Nelson observes. "He starts out the first draft with pen and ink, and the gloves are to protect his fingers from any overflow. In his early career, he wound up the day with blue fingers and had a hard time scrubbing them clean." This was the same explanation Kenny had received when he asked about the gloves.

After the ceremony for the National Academy's award (also known as the Songwriters' Hall of Fame Award), Lerner and Kenny returned to London and *Godfrey*. In the December following Lerner's sixty-seventh birthday, work was interrupted yet again, by another honors trip to the United States. The board of the John F. Kennedy Center for the Performing Arts had initiated an annual awards ceremony in which six outstanding figures were singled out for their contributions to the arts. The board offered, and Lerner accepted; while the Kennedy Center was a bit too close for comfort to 1600 Pennsylvania Avenue (then housing President Ronald Reagan, not a popular figure in the Lerner household), he believed the Kennedy Award meant something. (Four years later, Leonard Bernstein would turn down a White House Medal from the Bush administration, as undoubtedly Lerner would have done as well had Reagan wanted to give him one.)

The ceremony, which took place at the center on December 8, 1985, celebrated the lifelong achievements of film actress Irene Dunne, comedian Bob Hope, opera diva Beverly Sills, choreographer Merce Cunningham, and, as a team, Lerner and Loewe. A radiant Liz Robertson was there to sing their songs. It was the last time the old partners would appear in public together: As Loewe happily flew off to California, and the Lerners returned to London, it became obvious that Lerner was not well.

Work stopped on *My Man Godfrey*, though Lerner was able to complete the manuscript of *The Musical Theatre*, which was published in Britain and the United States in 1986. The affectionate dedication reads "To Liz, who is all the music."

In February of that year, he began treatments for lung cancer in London, but when his condition worsened in April, he decided to enter the Memorial Sloan-Kettering Cancer Center in New York. There was no hope; he was suffering from the same affliction that had killed his father and took his brother Robert, an attorney-turned-impresario who produced several of his brother's shows in Mexico. More tragically, cancer had also been consuming Lerner's oldest daughter, Susan (Olch), from his first marriage, to Ruth O'Day Boyd.

It was a painful time, those few weeks at Sloan-Kettering. He was gaunt and weak, though alert and in remarkably good humor (at least in company). He enjoyed visits from friends, among them an old Harvard classmate, producer William Harbach. One visitor was surprised, toward the end of May, to come in one afternoon and find Lerner cheerfully ordering some special shirts from his London tailor. He would never wear them.

At 10:15 in the morning on Saturday, June 14, 1986, he died. With him were Liz Robertson; his son, Michael, in from Paris, where he was a correspondent for *Newsweek*; and his daughters Jennifer (Frasier) and Liza (Bibb), from his marriage to Nancy Olson. Susan Olch had been released from Sloan-Kettering and returned to Los Angeles, where she died soon after her father.

He was sixty-seven.

At the time of his death, the IRS was in pursuit of him, and had been since the previous February, when he first began cancer treatments. In June the suit was still pending; any further claims by the persistent wife number four would have to defer to the primacy of the U.S. government. But Lerner's "first wife," now his widow, found herself virtually penniless. She had their apartment in London (they had sold the house in Chelsea) but little else other than her considerable talent. She was alone and on her own.

"The only thing Alan left me," she would say with affection and without bitterness, "was a taste for champagne."

APPENDIX I

Works by Alan Jay Lerner

MUSICALS AND FILMS

This section lists all known songs by Alan Jay Lerner, primarily lyrics (and occasionally music), as well as screenplays by him. Other pertinent production information is also included. The songs in Broadway musicals often varied from town to town during the out-of-town tryouts and sometimes even after the shows' premieres; the list is as complete as possible—the better to give an idea of Lerner's prodigious productivity. The film versions of the Broadway musicals were different from the originals, with songs inevitably dropped or added; in each case, these differences are noted under the listing for the film. Note that in the first Lerner and Loewe collaboration, *Life of the Party*, Lerner contributed mostly to the book and may have polished some lyrics; the Detroit advertisements and reviews credit him only with the book.

1935
Gold and Blue (lyrics and music: Alan Jay Lerner; football song written at the Choate School)

1938
So Proudly We Hail
A production of the Hasty Pudding Club, Harvard University, Cambridge, Mass., March 29, 1938

Music: mostly by Bobby Parks
Lyrics: Alan Jay Lerner
Book: Nathaniel C. Benchley, Benjamin Welles, John Graham
Cast: Vinton A. Freedley, Jr., Alan Jay Lerner, and other undergraduates
Songs: Man about Town; Living the Life; Chance to Dream (music and lyrics by Lerner)

1939
Fair Enough
A production of the Hasty Pudding Club, Harvard University, Cambridge, Mass., March 1939
Music and lyrics: Alan Jay Lerner
Book: Lerner
Published song: From Me to You

1942
Life of the Party
Music: Frederick Loewe
Lyrics: Earle Crooker
Book: Alan Jay Lerner, based on Barry Connors's play *The Patsy*
Directed by Russell Filmore; choreography by Theodore Adolphus. Produced by Henry Duffy at the Wilson Theatre, Detroit, Mich., Oct. 8, 1942; 9-week run
Cast: Dorothy Stone, Harry Antrum, Louise Kirtland, Helen Raymond, Dean Norton, Dudley Clements.
(*Note*: Although Lerner is not credited with the lyrics, it is possible that he did some polishing. Songs mentioned in reviews are listed to round out Loewe's work: One Robin Doesn't Make a Spring; Somehow; No Olive in My Martini; Wearin' the Grin; El Rancho; Alone in a Crowd; I'll Tell the World.)

1943
What's Up?
Music: Frederick Loewe
Book: Alan Jay Lerner and Arthur Pierson
Staged and choreographed by George Balanchine; book directed by Robert H. Gordon. Produced by Mark Warnow at the National Theatre, Nov. 11, 1943; 63 performances.
Cast: Jimmy Savo, Gloria Warren, Johnny Morgan, Don Weissmuller.
Songs: From the Chimney to the Cellar; How Fly Times; A Girl Is Like a Book; Miss Langley's School for Girls; Ill-Tempered Clavichord; You Wash I'll Dry; Joshua; You've Got a Hold on Me; Three Girls in a Boat; My Last Love; Natural Life; Just Then; Love Is a Step Ahead of Me

1945
The Day Before Spring
Music: Frederick Loewe

Book: Alan Jay Lerner

Staged by John C. Wilson; book directed by Edward Padula. Musical ensembles and ballets by Antony Tudor. Produced by Wilson at the National Theatre, Nov. 22, 1945; 165 performances.

Cast: Irene Manning, Bill Johnson, John Archer, Patricia Marshall, Tom Helmore, Hugh Laing, May Ellen Moylan

Songs: The Day Before Spring; God's Green World; You Haven't Changed at All; My Love Is a Married Man; Friends to the End; A Jug of Wine; I Love You This Morning; Where's My Wife?

1947
Brigadoon
Music: Frederick Loewe

Book: Alan Jay Lerner

Staged by Robert Lewis; dance and musical numbers by Agnes de Mille. Produced by Cheryl Crawford at the Ziegfeld Theatre, Mar. 13, 1947; 581 performances.

Cast: Marion Bell, David Brooks, Pamela Britton, Lee Sullivan, George Keane, William Hansen, James Mitchell

Songs: Once in the Highlands; Brigadoon; Down on MacConnachy Square; Waitin' for My Dearie; I'll Go Home with Bonnie Jean; The Heather on the Hill; The Love of My Life; Jeannie's Packin' Up; Come to Me, Bend to Me; Almost Like Being in Love; The Wedding Dance (*instrumental*); Sword Dance; The Chase; There But for You Go I; My Mother's Wedding Day; From This Day On; Vendor's Calls

Brigadoon (Film Version)
Screenplay: Alan Jay Lerner

Directed by Vincente Minnelli; choreography by Gene Kelly. Produced by Arthur Freed, in association with Roger Edens, for Metro-Goldwyn-Mayer; released Sept. 8, 1954.

Cast: Gene Kelly, Cyd Charisse, Van Johnson, Elaine Stewart, Barry Jones, Hugh Laing, Albert Sharp, Virginia Bosler, Jimmy Thomson, etc.

Songs retained from the original: Waitin' for My Dearie; Down on McConnachy Square; I'll Go Home with Bonnie Jean; The Heather on the Hill; Almost Like Being in Love; The Wedding Dance; The Chase

1948
Love Life
Music: Kurt Weill

Book: Alan Jay Lerner

Directed by Elia Kazan; choreography by Michael Kidd. Produced by Cheryl Crawford
at the Forty-Sixth Street Theatre, Oct. 7, 1948; 252 performances.

Cast: Nanette Fabray, Ray Middleton, Jay Marshall, Holly Harris, Cheryl Archer, Gene
Tobin

Songs: Who Is Samuel Cooper?; My Name Is Samuel Cooper; Here I'll Stay; Progress;
I Remember It Well; Green-Up Time; Economics; Mother's Getting Nervous;
My Kind of Night; Women's Club Blues; Love Song; I'm Your Man; Ho, Billy
O!; Is It Him or Is It Me?; This Is the Life; The Minstrel Show: Minstrel Parade,
Madame Zuzu, Taking No Chances, Mr. Right [Takin' No Chances on Nothin'];
Locker Room; You Understand Me So; (*Not Used*: Susan's Dream; What More
Do I Want?)

Huckleberry Finn
Music: Burton Lane

Screenplay: Alan Jay Lerner

(In July 1951, Lerner and Lane completed the screenplay and several songs for this
never-made Metro-Golwyn-Mayer film, which was to have been produced by
Arthur Freed.)

Songs: I'm from Missouri; Huckleberry Finn; The World's Full o' Suckers; I'll Wait for
You by the River; I'll Meet You Down by the River; Pittsburgh Blue; Asparagus
Is Served; When You Grow Up You'll Know

1951
Paint Your Wagon
Music: Frederick Loewe

Book: Alan Jay Lerner

Directed by Daniel Mann; dances and musical ensembles by Agnes de Mille. Produced by Cheryl Crawford at the Sam. S. Shubert Theatre, Nov. 12, 1951; 289
performances.

Cast: James Barton, Olga San Juan, Tony Bavaar, James Mitchell, Marijane Maricle,
Gemze De Lappe, Rufus Smith

Songs: I'm on My Way; Rumson; What's Goin' On Here?; I Talk to the Trees; They
Call the Wind Maria; I Still See Elisa; How Can I Wait?; Trio (Mormons'
Prayer); In Between; Whoop-Ti-Ay!; Carino Mio; There's a Coach Comin' In;
Hand Me Down That Can of Beans; Another Autumn; Movin'; All for Him;
Wand'rin Star; Strike!; (*Not used*: Sh!, Take the Wheels Off the Wagon, What
Do Other Folks Do?)

Paint Your Wagon (Film Version)

Screenplay: Alan Jay Lerner; *adaptation*: Paddy Chayevsky

Directed by Joshua Logan. Produced by Lerner for Paramount Pictures; released Oct. 15, 1969.

Songs retained from the original: I'm On My Way; I Still See Elisa; Hand Me Down That Can o' Beans; They Call the Wind Maria; Whoop-Ti-Ay!; I Talk to the Trees; There's a Coach Comin' In; Wand'rin Star

Added songs (*music by André Previn*): The First Thing You Know; A Million Miles Away; The Best Things in Life Are Dirty; Gold Fever; The Gospel of No Name City; (*Not used*: Over the Purple Hill [music by Arthur Schwartz])

1951

Royal Wedding (Film)

Music: Burton Lane

Story and screenplay: Alan Jay Lerner

Directed by Stanley Donen; dances by Fred Astaire and Nick Castle. Musical direction by Johnny Green. Produced by Arthur Freed for Metro-Goldwyn-Mayer; released Mar. 23, 1951.

Cast: Fred Astaire, Jane Powell, Peter Lawford, Sarah Churchill, Keenan Wynn

Songs: Ev'ry Night at Seven; Open Your Eyes; The Happiest Day of My Life; How Could You Believe Me When I Said I Love You When You Know I've Been a Liar All My Life?; Too Late Now; You're All the World to Me; I Left My Hat in Haiti; What a Lovely Day for a Wedding; (*Not used*: I Got Me a Baby)

An American in Paris

Music: George Gershwin

Lyrics: Ira Gershwin

Story and screenplay: Alan Jay Lerner

Directed by Vincente Minnelli; choreography by Gene Kelly, assisted by Carol Haney. Musical direction by Johnny Green and Saul Chaplin. Produced by Arthur Freed for Metro-Goldwyn-Mayer; released Nov. 9, 1951.

Cast: Gene Kelly, Leslie Caron, Oscar Levant, Georges Guetary, Nina Foch

1956

My Fair Lady

Music: Frederick Loewe

Book: Alan Jay Lerner, adapted from George Bernard Shaw's play *Pygmalion*

Production staged by Moss Hart; choreography and musical numbers by Hanya Holm. Produced by Herman Levin at the Mark Hellinger Theatre, Mar. 15, 1956; 2,717 performances.

Cast: Rex Harrison, Julie Andrews, Stanley Holloway, Cathleen Nesbitt, Robert Coote, John Michael King, Christopher Hewitt, etc.

Songs: Why Can't the English?; Wouldn't It Be Loverly?; With a Little Bit of Luck; I'm an Ordinary Man; Just You Wait; The Rain in Spain; I Could Have Danced All Night; Ascot Gavotte; On the Street Where You Live; The Embassy Waltz (*instrumental*); You Did It; Show Me; Get Me to the Church on Time; A Hymn to Him (Why Can't a Woman Be More Like a Man?); Without You; I've Grown Accustomed to Her Face; Servants' Chorus; (*Not used*: Say a Prayer for Me Tonight; Come to the Ball; Please Don't Marry Me; Lady Liza)

My Fair Lady (Film Version)

Screenplay: Alan Jay Lerner

Directed by George Cukor; choreography by Hermes Pan. Produced by Jack L. Warner for Warner Bros.; released Oct. 21, 1964.

Cast: Audrey Hepburn (vocals by Marni Nixon), Rex Harrison, Stanley Holloway, Wilfred Hyde-White, Gladys Cooper, Jeremy Brett (vocals by Bill Shirley), Theodore Bikel, Mona Washington, Isobel Elsom, etc.

(*All original songs retained*)

1958

Gigi (Film)

Music: Frederick Loewe

Screenplay: Alan Jay Lerner, based on the novel by Colette

Directed by Vincente Minnelli and Charles Walters. Musical direction by André Previn. Produced by Arthur Freed for Metro-Goldwyn-Mayer; released May 16, 1958.

Cast: Leslie Caron (vocals by Betty Wand), Maurice Chevalier, Louis Jourdan, Hermione Gingold, Eva Gabor, Jacques Bergerac, etc.

Songs: Thank Heaven for Little Girls; It's a Bore!; The Parisians; Gossip; A Toujours (*instrumental*); She's Not Thinking of Me (*dir.*: *Walters*); The Night They Invented Champagne (*dir.*: *Walters*); I Remember It Well; Gaston's Soliloquy: Gigi; Say a Prayer for Me Tonight; I'm Glad I'm Not Young Any More

1960

Camelot

Music: Frederick Loewe

Book: Alan Jay Lerner, based on T. H. White's novel *The Once and Future King*.

Staged by Moss Hart; choreography and musical numbers by Hanya Holm. Produced by Lerner, Loewe, and Hart at the Majestic Theatre, Dec. 3, 1960; 873 performances.

Cast: Richard Burton, Julie Andrews, Roddy McDowall, Robert Coote, Robert Goulet, M'el Dowd, John Cullum, Bruce Yarnell, etc.

Songs: I Wonder What the King Is Doing Tonight; The Simple Joys of Maidenhood; Camelot; Follow Me; C'est Moi; The Lusty Month of May; Then You May Take Me to the Fair; How to Handle a Woman; The Jousts; Before I Gaze at You Again; If Ever I Would Leave You; The Seven Deadly Virtues; What Do the Simple Folk Do?; The Persuasion; Fie on Goodness!; I Loved You Once in Silence; Guenevere; Face to Face

Camelot (Film Version)

Screenplay: Alan Jay Lerner

Directed by Joshua Logan. Produced by Jack L. Warner for Warner Bros.; released Oct. 25, 1967.

Cast: Richard Harris, Vanessa Redgrave, Franco Nero, David Hemmings, Laurence Naismith, Pierre Olaf, Estelle Winwood, etc.

Songs retained from the original: I Wonder What the King Is Doing Tonight; The Simple Joys of Maidenhood; Camelot; C'est Moi; The Lusty Month of May; Then You May Take Me to the Fair; How to Handle a Woman; The Jousts; If Ever I Would Leave You; What Do the Simple Folk Do?; Follow Me; I Loved You Once in Silence; Guenevere

1965
On a Clear Day You Can See Forever

Music: Burton Lane

Book: Alan Jay Lerner

Directed by Robert Lewis; dances and musical numbers staged by Herbert Ross. Produced by Alan Jay Lerner in association with Rogo Productions at the Mark Hellinger Theatre, Oct. 17, 1965; 280 performances.

Cast: Barbara Harris, John Cullum, Titos Vandis, William Daniels, Clifford David, Rae Allen, Michael Lewis, Gerry Matthews, Byron Webster, etc.

Songs: Hurry! It's Lovely Up Here; Ring Out the Bells; Tosy and Cosh; On a Clear Day You Can See Forever; On the S.S. *Bernard Cohn*; At the Hellrakers'; Don't Tamper with My Sister; She Wasn't You; Melinda; When I'm Being Born Again; What Did I Have That I Don't Have?; Wait 'Til You're Sixty-five; Come Back to Me; (*Not used*: I'll Not Marry)

On a Clear Day You Can See Forever (Film Version)

Screenplay: Alan Jay Lerner

Directed by Vincente Minnelli; choreography by Howard Jeffrey. Produced by Howard W. Koch for Paramount Pictures; released June 17, 1970.

Cast: Barbra Streisand, Yves Montand, Bob Newhart, Larry Blyden, Simon Oakland, Jack Nicholson, Pamela Brown, Irene Handl, Roy Kinnear, John Richardson, etc.

Songs retained from the original: Hurry! It's Lovely Up Here; Melinda; He Isn't You; What Did I Have That I Don't Have?; On a Clear Day You Can See Forever; Come Back to Me

Added songs: Love With All the Trimmings; Go to Sleep; (*Not used*: Who Is There Among Us?)

1969

Coco

Music: André Previn

Book: Alan Jay Lerner, based on the story of designer Coco Chanel

Directed by Michael Benthall; musical numbers and fashion sequences staged by Michael Bennett. Produced by Frederick Brisson at the Mark Hellinger Theatre, Dec. 18, 1969; 332 performances.

Cast: Katharine Hepburn, George Rose, Gale Dixon, David Holliday, René Auberjonois, Jeanne Arnold, Jon Cypher, Will B. Able, Jack Dabdoub, etc.

Songs: That's the Way You Are; The World Belongs to the Young; Let's Go Home; Mademoiselle Cliché de Paris; The Money Rings Out Like Freedom; A Brand-New Dream; A Woman Is How She Loves; Gabrielle; Coco; Fiasco; When Your Lover Says Goodbye; Orbach's, Bloomingdale's, Best and Saks; Always Mademoiselle

1971

Lolita, My Love

Music: John Barry

Book: Alan Jay Lerner, based on Vladimir Nabokov's novel *Lolita*

Directed by Tito Capobianco; musical numbers staged by Danny Daniels. Produced by Norman Twain at the Shubert Theatre, Philadelphia, Feb. 16, 1971; at the Shubert Theatre, Boston, Mar. 23, 1971. Closed Mar. 27.

Cast: John Neville, Dorothy Loudon, Leonard Frey, Annette Ferra, (Denise Nickerson in Boston), Gretel Cummings, Dan Siretta, Josh Wheeler, Valerie Camille, etc.

(*Note*: In Boston, Noel Willman was credited with direction and Dan Siretta with choreography.)

Songs: Going, Going, Gone; In the Broken-Promise Land of Fifteen; The Same Old Song; Mother Needs a Boyfriend; Dante, Petrarch and Poe; Sur les Quais; Charlotte's Letter; Farewell, Little Dream; Have You Got What You Came With?; At the Bed-D-By Motel; Tell Me, Tell Me; Buckin' for Beardsley; Beardsley School for Girls; It's a Bad, Bad World; Lolita; All You Can Do Is Tell Me You Love Me; Saturday; Conversation; How Far Is It to the Next Town?; March out of My Life

1973

Gigi (Stage Version)

Book: Alan Jay Lerner, based on the film based on the novel by Colette

Directed by Joseph Hardy; dances and musical numbers staged by Onna White. Produced by Arnold Saint-Subber and Edwin Lester for the Los Angeles and San Francisco Light Opera Companies, at the Uris Theatre, Nov. 13, 1973; 103 performances.

Cast: Alfred Drake, Agnes Moorehead, Maria Karnilova, Daniel Massey, Karin Wolfe, George Gaynes, Joe Ross, Truman Gaige, Sandahl Bergman, Howard Chitjian.

Songs retained from the film: Thank Heaven for Little Girls; It's a Bore; She's Not Thinking of Me; I Remember It Well; The Night They Invented Champagne; Gigi; I'm Glad I'm Not Young Any More.

Added songs: The Earth and Other Minor Things; Paris Is Paris Again; The Telephone; The Contract (A Toujours, *from film*); In This Wide, Wide World; I Never Want to Go Home Again

1974

The Little Prince

Music: Frederick Loewe

Screenplay: Alan Jay Lerner, based on the story by Antoine de Saint-Exupéry

Directed by Stanley Donen. Produced by Donen, assisted by A. Joseph Tandet, for Paramount Pictures; released Nov. 7, 1974.

Cast: Richard Kiley, Steven Warner, Bob Fosse, Gene Wilder, Donna McKechnie, Joss Ackland, Clive Revill, Graham Crowden

Songs: It's a Hat; I Need Air; I'm on Your Side; Be Happy; You're a Child; I Never Met a Rose; Why Is the Desert?; A Snake in the Grass; Closer and Closer; Little Prince; (*Not used*: Matters of Consequence)

1976

1600 Pennsylvania Avenue

Music: Leonard Bernstein

Book: Alan Jay Lerner

Directed by Gilbert Moses; choreography by George Faison (replacing Frank Corsaro and Donald McKayle, respectively). Produced by Roger L. Stevens and Robert Whitehead in association with the Coca-Cola Co. (the company's name is omitted in the New York program) at the Mark Hellinger Theatre, May 4, 1976; 7 performances.

Cast: Ken Howard, Patricia Routledge, Gilbert Price, Emily Yancy, Edwin Steffe, Reid Shelton, Ralph Farnsworth, Hector Jaime Mercado, etc.

(*Note*: Songs indicated by an asterisk were used in the New York production.)

Songs: *Ten Square Miles of the Potomac; *If I Was a Dove; *Welcome Home, Miz Adams; *Take Care of This House; *The President Jefferson March; *Seena; *Sonatina (The British): 1. Allegro con Brio, 2. Tempo di Menuetto [*Program note*: "This movement includes an authentic harmonization (1780) of 'The Anacreontick Song' which is better known as 'The Star-Spangled Banner.'"], 3. Rondo; The Nation That Wasn't There; *Lud's Wedding: I Love My Wife; *Auctions; *The Little White Lie; The Mark of the Man; This Time; *We Must Have a Ball; *The Ball; *Bright and Black; Duet for One (The First Lady of the Land); After-Dinner Entertainment: *1. The Money Lovin' Minstrel Parade (*retitled*: The Robber-Baron Minstrel Parade), *2. Pity the Poor, 3. The Grand Old Part, *4. The Red, White and Blues; American Dreaming; Middle C; To Make Us Proud; Rehearse!; *Forty Acres and a Mule; *I Love This Land; (*Not used*: Monroviad; Lonely Men of Harvard)

1979
Carmelina
Music: Burton Lane
Book: Alan Jay Lerner and Joseph Stein, based on the film *Buona Sera, Mrs. Campbell*
Directed by José Ferrer; choreography by Peter Gennaro. Produced by Roger L. Stevens, J. W. Fisher, Joan Cullman and Jujamcyn Productions at the St. James Theatre, Apr. 8, 1979; 17 performances.
Cast: Georgia Brown, Cesare Siepi, John Michael King, Virginia Martin, Josie de Guzman, Grace Keagy, Gordon Ramsey, Howard Rose
Songs: Mayor's Prologue; Prayer; It's Time for a Love Song; Why Him?; I Must Have Her; Someone in April; Signora Campbell; Love Before Breakfast; Yankee Doodles Are Coming; I Wonder How She Looks; One More Walk around the Garden; All That He Wants Me to Be; Carmelina; The Image of Me; I'm a Woman

1983
Dance a Little Closer
Music: Charles Strouse
Book: Alan Jay Lerner, based on Robert Sherwood's play *Idiot's Delight*
Directed by Lerner; choreography by Billy Wilson. Produced by Frederick Brisson, Jerome Minskoff, James Nederlander and the Kennedy Center at the Minskoff Theatre, May 11, 1983; 1 performance.
Cast: Len Cariou, Liz Robertson, George Rose, Brett Barrett, Jeff Keller, Diane Pennington, Cherl Howard, Alyson Reed, I. M. Hobson, Joyce Worsley, etc.
Songs: It Never Would've Worked; Happy, Happy New Year; No Man's Worth It; What Are You Gonna Do about It?; A Woman Who Thinks I'm Wonderful; Pas de Deux (*instrumental*); There's Never Been Anything like Us; Another Life;

Why Can't the World Go and Leave Us Alone?; He Always Comes Home to Me; I Got a New Girl; Dance a Little Closer; There's Always One You Can't Forget; Homesick; Mad; I Don't Know (Anyone Who Loves); Auf Wiedersehen; I Never Want to See You Again; On Top of the World

1984

Secret Places (*Music: Michel Legrand; film title song*)

1985

Brocades and Coronets (*Music: Gerard Kenny*)

My Man Godfrey (Not Completed)
Music: Gerard Kenny
Book: Alan Jay Lerner, based on the 1936 film
Songs: Garbage Isn't What It Used to Be (*reprised* as Garbage Is Where I'd Rather Be); Dancin' My Blues Away; Some People; Miss Hilary Bacon of Beacon Hill; Don't Do That; Happy Thanksgiving; It Was You Again; I've Been Married; Try Love; I'm Somebody's Girl (*title only*)

LIBRETTOS (TEXT AND LYRICS ONLY)

Brigadoon (with Loewe). In *Great Musicals of the American Theatre* 1. Edited by Stanley Richards. Radnor, Pa.: Chilton, 1973.
Camelot (with Loewe). New York: Random House, 1961.
My Fair Lady (with Loewe). New York: Coward McCann & Geoghen, 1956.
On a Clear Day You Can See Forever (with Lane). New York: Random House, 1966.
Paint Your Wagon (with Loewe). New York: Coward-McCann, 1952.

VOCAL SCORES (LYRICS AND MUSIC)

Brigadoon (with Loewe)
Paint Your Wagon (with Loewe)
My Fair Lady (with Loewe)
Camelot (with Loewe)
On a Clear Day You Can See Forever (with Lane)

BOOKS

The Street Where I Live. New York: Norton, 1978.
The Musical Theatre. New York: McGraw-Hill, 1986.
A Hymn to Him: The Lyrics of Alan Jay Lerner. Introduction and annotations by Benny
  Green. New York: Limelight Editions, 1987.

DISCOGRAPHY

Only compact discs are listed here, except in a few cases where a show or film score exists only in long-playing record format. The latter may be difficult to find and could prove unreasonably expensive—and in any case, it is possible that they may be reissued on CD. The quality of sound on CDs is generally an improvement over that on LPs.

ORIGINAL CAST ALBUMS/FILM VERSION SOUNDTRACKS

Brigadoon (Loewe)
Original Cast: RCA 1001-2-RG
Studio re-creation with Rebecca Luker, Brent Barnet and Judy Kaye; the London Sinfonietta conducted by John McGlinn: Angel CDC 7-54481-2
Soundtrack: MCA 5947 (Coupled with Kern's *Lovely to Look At*)

Paint Your Wagon (Loewe)
Original Cast: RCA 60243-2-RG
Soundtrack: MCA AD 37099

My Fair Lady (Loewe)
Original Cast: Columbia SK 66128
Columbia
Soundtrack:/SK 66711 (Marni Nixon sings for Audrey Hepburn)

Camelot (Loewe)
Original Cast: Columbia CK 32602
Soundtrack Warner Brothers 3102-2

On a Clear Day You Can See Forever (Lane)
Original Cast: RCA 09026-60820-2
Soundtrack: Columbia SK 57377

Coco (**Previn**)
Original Cast: Paramount PMS-8019 (LP only)

Carmelina (**Lane**)
Original Cast: Original Cast Records T4T-CD 9224 (for the recording Paul Sorvino replaced Cesare Siepi)

Dance a Little Closer (**Strouse**)
Original Cast: ibr Classics CDIBR9011

SOUNDTRACK RECORDINGS OF ORIGINAL FILMS

Royal Wedding (Lane)
Columbia 47828

Gigi (**Loewe**)
RCA 68070

The Little Prince (**Loewe**)
ABC Records ABDG-854 (LP only)

COLLECTIONS

An Evening with Alan Jay Lerner. A tribute to Lerner with, among others, Burton
Lane, Liz Robertson, Len Cariou, Patricia Routledge, Placido Domingo. First
Night Records (two-CD set)
Alan Jay Lerner Revisited. Sung by Blossom Dearie, Dorothy Loudon, Roddy Mc-
Dowall, Jerry Orbach, Nancy Walker. Notable for the songs from *The Day Before
Spring* and *Love Life*. Painted Smiles PS 1337 (LP)
Leonard Bernstein Revisited. Sung by John Reardon, Arthur Siegel, Jo Sullivan, et al.
Contains "Bright and Black," "The President Jefferson March," "Take Care of
This House" from *1600 Pennsylvania Avenue*. Painted *Smiles* PSCD-107
Kurt Weill Revisited. Sung by Chita Rivera, Jo Sullivan, John Reardon, Ann Miller,
Arthur Siegel, et al. Contains "You Understand Me So," "I Remember It Well,"
"Is It Him or Is It Me?," and "Locker Room" from *Love Life*. Painted Smiles
PSCD-108

A NOTE ON VIDEOS

Filmed performances of all of Lerner's major musicals have been transferred to video cassettes, with mixed results: *Brigadoon* (pallid, but entertaining with fine moments); *Paint Your Wagon* (brawlingly distorted); *My Fair Lady* (excellent); *Camelot* (ponderous and inept). All the films come off well: *Royal Wedding* (thanks to Astaire and Jane Powell); *Gigi* (outstanding) and *The Little Prince* (strange but a better film than Lerner believed it was). *An American in Paris*, with Gershwin music, is an example of Lerner's screenwriting skills.

APPENDIX II

Bibliography

BIOGRAPHY

Lees, Gene. *Inventing Champagne: The Worlds of Lerner and Loewe.* New York: St. Martin's, 1990.
Shapiro, Doris. *We Danced All Night.* New York: William Morrow, 1990.

GENERAL HISTORIES

Caute, David. *The Great Fear.* New York: Simon and Schuster, 1978.
Daniel, Clifton. *Chronicle of the 20th Century.* Mt. Kisco, N.Y.: Chronicle Publications, 1987.

OTHER BIOGRAPHIES

Crawford, Cheryl. *One Naked Individual.* Indianapolis: Bobbs-Merrill, 1977.
Minnelli, Vincente. *I Remember It Well.* Garden City, N.Y.: Doubleday, 1974.
Rodgers, Richard. *Musical Stages.* New York: Random House, 1975.
Sanders, Ronald. *The Days Grow Short: The Life and Music of Kurt Weill.* New York: Holt, Rinehart and Winston, 1980.
Von Hoffman, Nicholas. *Citizen Cohn.* Garden City, N.Y.: Doubleday, 1988.

HISTORIES OF THE MUSICAL THEATER AND FILM

Engle, Lehman. *Their Words Are Music*. New York: Crown, 1975.

Fordin, Hugh. *The World of Entertainment*. Garden City, N.Y.: Doubleday, 1975.

Green, Stanley. *Encyclopedia of the Musical Theatre*. New York: Dodd, Mead, 1976.

————. *The World of Musical Comedy*, 4th ed. New York: A. S. Barnes, 1980.

————. *Encyclopedia of the Musical Film*. New York: Oxford University Press, 1981.

————. *Broadway Musicals: Show by Show*. Milwaukee: Hal Leonard, 1985.

————. *Hollywood Musicals: Year by Year*. Milwaukee: Hal Leonard, 1990.

Knox, Donald: *The Magic Factory*. New York: Praeger, 1973.

Mueller, John. *Astaire Dancing: The Musical Films*. New York: Knopf, 1985.

Suskin, Steven. *Show Tunes, 1905–1985*. New York: Dodd, Mead, 1986.

————. *Opening Night on Broadway, 1943–1964*. New York: Schirmer Books, 1990.

ACKNOWLEDGMENTS

My thanks are owed to the many who contributed to this work, often over and above what might have been expected in their professional capacity: librarians, archivists, publishers, et al. For their unselfish, generous help and suggestions I am grateful to Emily and Richard Ahlberg, of Audubon, Pennsylvania, for the Philadelphia research and the documentary tape; Elizabeth H. Auman, Music Division, Library of Congress; Bobbie Baird, of New York, for her insights and her interpretations of Lerner lyrics, which he himself frequently acknowledged; Peter Bartok, of Homosassa, Florida, for aid throughout; David Bickman, of New York, for musical materials, rare recordings, and so on; Mary Birdsall, of Saginaw, Michigan, for the Lerner book, discussions, etc.; Dr. Janet Birkett, of the Theatre Museum, London; Carol Convissor, of the Juilliard School of Music, New York; Edward M. Cramer, New York; Kendall L. Crilly, of the Music Library, Yale University, New Haven, Connecticut; Ronny Daniel, of ASCAP, New York; David Farnath, of the Kurt Weill Foundation, New York; Adrian Fisher, of the Harvard Club Library, New York; Kate Gellert, of the Hasty Pudding Theatricals, Harvard University, Cambridge, Massachusetts; David Grossberg, of Cohen and Grossberg, New York; Mark Horowitz, of the Music Divison at the Library of Congress, Washington, D.C.; Carla Jablonski (Cantrell) for insights into the songs, plays, and films; Susan Kidwell and David Jablonski, University of Chicago, for suggestions and insights; Catherine J. Johnson, of the Harvard Theatre Collection, and Susan N. Keliher, Harvard Alumni Association, Cambridge, Massachusetts; William Kenly, of Paramount Pictures, New York; Gerard Kenny, of Sea Cliff, New York; Michael Kerker, of ASCAP, New York; Chester Kopaz, of Bayonne, New Jersey, extraordinary researcher and MGM authority; Susan Laity, of the Yale University Library, New Haven, Connecticut; Bob Landau, of New York, for suggestions and his theater expertise; Lynn and Burton Lane, New York; Maurice Levine, New York, not least for Lyrics and Lyricists; Kathleen A. Markees, of the Harvard University Archives, Cambridge, Massachusetts; Frank Military, Warner-Chappell Music, New York; Richard Miller, of Brooklyn College, New York, for a good lead; Danelle McCafferty of New York, who started it; Janet Raglan of London; Walter Rapperport, of New York, writer, musical and musicals authority and creator of the "eponymous"; Liz Robertson of London; Robin Rupli, of Washington, D.C., musical-theater authority, who has been a joy from the very beginning, often pointing out something I missed; Harold E. Samuel, Music Librarian of Yale University, New Haven, Connecticut; Dan Singer, of Broadcast Music Inc., New York, for a very generous boost; Lawrence D. Stewart, of Beverly Hills, California, for drawing upon his years of working with Ira Gershwin and his recollections of Alan Jay Lerner, and providing other generous aid; Charles Strouse, of New York; Steven Suskin, not only for his valuable books but for suggestions; William Thompson, my cousin from Bay City, Michigan, who found important information that eluded me here; Craig Urquhart, Amberson Enterprises, New York; Joseph Weiss, of MPL Communications, New York, for his wide knowledge of the works of Lerner and other things; Dan W. Williamson, of the Harvard Club, New York; Raymond Wilson, a composer-pianist with invaluable musical insights; Sara Ziff, of Columbia Grammar and Preparatory School, New York; Alicia Zizzo, of Old Brookville, New York, a pianist and encourager as well as interested interrogator with perceptions of Lerner's mysticism.

Last though not least, I owe special thanks to my editor, Ray Roberts, and to Dorothy Straight for her graceful and, I must say, gracious copyediting.

E.J.

INDEX

All song lyrics are by Lerner. Titles are in quotes with composer's name in parentheses.

Lerner, Alan Jay *(cont'd)*
alumni, 270–71; collaboration with Lane,
xii, 105; collaboration with Loewe, xiii–xiv;
collaboration with Loewe begun, 17,
20–22, 24–26; collaboration with Rodgers
(*I Picked a Daisy*) attempted, xii–xiii,
201–7; collaboration with Schwartz, 105;
contribution of, xiv–xv; credo as lyricist,
16; and critics, 33–35, 82; death of,
310–11; and death of father, xi, 106; and
death of Lorenz Hart, 22–24; and death of
Moss Hart, 199; and death of Pascal,
105–6; and death of Weill, 50; decision to
write songs, 8; divorces Karen, 269, 275; divorces Marion, 63, 65; divorces Micheline,
210–15, 225; divorces Nancy, xi, 160,
162–63; divorces Nina, 290–91; divorces
Ruth, 34; Drama Critics Award for
Brigadoon, 35, 105; early education, 4–7;
early interest in music, 5–7; early love of
theatre, xiii, 3–4, 8; education at Harvard,
8–13; epitaph proposed, xi; expelled from
Choate, 6–7; and failure of *Dance a Little
Closer*, 303–5; and failure of *Lolita*, 258,
259; family background, xiii; and father,
xii, 1, 3–4; film script for *Green Mansions*
rejected, 98–99; film work for Freed at
MGM, 51–57; finances, and *Brigadoon*, 49;
finances, and divorce from Micheline,
211–13, 215, 285, 286, 289–90, 291; finances, and gold mine stock, 5, 114; finances, and inheritance from father, 106,
114; finances, and *My Fair Lady*, 145; first
job for advertising agency, 13; first review,
11; first shows written with Loewe, 20–22;
first songs published, 12; fondness for fantasy, 24; freelance radio writing, 13, 17,
24; Harvard diploma withheld, 12–13;
haunted by success of *My Fair Lady*, 236;
and haunted Rockland County house,
117–18; and idea for *Brigadoon*, 26–27; in-
fluences on, 8, 14–17; and interviews, xi,
178–80; Johnny Mercer Award, 309; Kennedy Center Award, 310; leaves ASCAP for
BMI, 304–6; on Loewe, 28–29, 78; Loewe
and, friction during *Camelot*, 193; Loewe
quits partnership, 199–200, 245; and
Loewe's heart attack, 169–70; on Lorenz
Hart, 24; love of writing, 8–9; marriages,

xi–xii; marriage to Karen Gundersen, 229,
236, 238, 239, 243, 248, 269; marriage to
Liz Robertson, 292–93, 295, 308–11; marriage to Marion Bell, 34, 35, 37; marriage
to Micheline Muselli Pozzo di Borgo, 159,
163, 179, 180–82, 199, 208–10, 220, 225;
marriage to Nancy Olson, 63, 65, 66, 70,
92, 159; marriage to Nina Bushkin,
286–87, 289; marriage to Ruth Boyd, 12,
13–14, 34; marriage to Sandra Payne, 269,
275, 283; Mary Martin and, 40, 110–11,
112, 119, 124; meets Loewe, 17; meets
Mayer, 49; methedrine addiction, 208–9,
211, 213, 221–23, 231; MGM contract, 70;
Moss Hart helps finish book for *My Fair
Lady*, 128–29; and mother, 1, 2–3, 225;
moves to Algonquin Hotel, 13, 14, 34, 126;
moves to Lambs Club, 14; moves to New
City, 39; and *My Fair Lady* opening and reception, 141–44; and *My Fair Lady* tryouts,
138–41; and *My Fair Lady* rehearsals,
130–36; nailbiting, 31–32, 248; name, 3;
"no message" musical style of, xiv; perfectionism of, xii–xiii; plans for book of lyrics,
273–74; political views, 177–78, 259,
271–72, 273, 276, 290, 298, 304, 307, 309;
politics, and Stevenson, 103–4; and psychic phenomenon, 4–5; psycholanalysis,
37, 118–19, 182; and Rex Harrison,
132–35, 137, 144; rhymes, xv; and rock
music, 249–50, 259–60; romance with Jean
Kennedy Smith, 224–25, 228, 232; romanticism of, 16–17; Rose contract turned
down by, 31; spending habits, 161; spinal
meningitis, 105; tax problems, 211, 307–8,
311; travels to Europe in youth, 5, 12; travels to London to meet with Harrison, 126;
travels to London to secure rights to *Pygmalion*, 114–17; travels to London to stage
My Fair Lady, 170–71; travels to Paris to
work on *Gigi*, 150–51; tribute to, 289; ulcer
during *Camelot*, 186, 199; and work compulsion, 146–47; working style, 203–5;
writes *American in Paris* screenplay, 64–69;
writes *Brigadoon* screenplay, 92–96; writes
Brigadoon with Loewe, 26–36; writes
Camelot screenplay, 239; writes *Camelot*
with Loewe and Hart, 171–99; writes
Carmelina with reunited Lane, 283–89;